THE POLITICS OF
TERRORISM

A SURVEY

THE POLITICS OF
TERRORISM

A SURVEY

FIRST EDITION

Edited by Andrew T H Tan

LONDON AND NEW YORK

First Edition 2006
Routledge
Haines House, 21 John Street, London WC1N 2BP, United Kingdom
(A member of the Taylor & Francis Group)

© Routledge 2006

All rights reserved. No part of this publication may be photocopied, recorded, or otherwise reproduced, stored in a retrieval system or transmitted in any form or by any electronic or mechanical means without the prior permission of the copyright owner.

ISBN 1 85743 347 5

Development Editor: Cathy Hartley
Copy Editor and Proof-reader: Simon Chapman

Typeset in Times New Roman 10.5/12

The publishers make no representation, express or implied, with regard to the accuracy of the information contained in this book and cannot accept any legal responsibility for any errors or omissions that may take place.

Typeset by AJS Solutions, Huddersfield – Dundee
Printed and bound in Great Britain by MPG Books, Bodmin, Cornwall

Introduction

This ***The Politics of Terrorism: A Survey*** reference volume explores the contemporary political context of terrorism. In particular, it focuses attention on the nexus between politics and terrorism. This volume is not a counter-terrorism text but aims to examine terrorism as a contemporary social phenomenon. While the 11 September 2001 terrorist attacks in the USA are seminal in being the first true mass-casualty terrorist attack in contemporary times and, indeed, signalled the emergence of a deadly form of religion-inspired terror, terrorism has been a significant historical social phenomenon, often also motivated by ethno-nationalism and political ideology. While the attention of the world after those events now known as 9/11 has focused on radical Islam and its associated civilizational conflict with the West, terrorism inspired by religion has also resulted in deadly attacks by a broad swathe of non-Islamist groups, such as Sikh extremists, Japanese religious cults and radical Christian fundamentalist groups in the USA. Even as the West is engrossed in counter-terrorism to eliminate the 9/11 terrorists in the 'global war on terrorism', there remains a vast and motley array of terrorist groups engaged in terrorism in various locales throughout the world, often motivated by political conflict over land, resources, social position or identity. A more complete understanding of the terrorism phenomenon thus requires us to examine terrorism from a more holistic and even historical perspective, in order to arrive at a more in-depth understanding of the complexities of this historical phenomenon, particularly the fundamental grievances that underlie terrorism.

To organize our understanding of contemporary terrorism in its breadth and complexity, this volume is divided into four parts. The first part consists of chapters examining the key facets of terrorism. It begins with a chapter by David Rapoport which examines the contested definition of terrorism and also suggests a classification of groups. The second chapter, by Adam Dolnik and Rohan Gunaratna, focuses on the tactics, weapons and targets of contemporary terrorists. This is then followed by chapter articles on the various types of contemporary terrorism, with Denis Pluchinsky writing on ethno-nationalist terrorism, David Brannan on political terrorism, and Mark Juergensmeyer, Adam Dolnik and Rohan Gunaratna on religious terrorism. No text on terrorism, however, will be complete without a chapter on the state's use of terrorism as a means of political violence. This is examined in a chapter by James and Brenda Lutz. Finally, there is a concluding chapter which examines counter-terrorism strategies and the future of terrorism. Written by Thomas Mockaitis, a professor of history, the chapter presents a historically rigorous perspective of how terrorism has been countered; this is usually through a broad-based multi-dimensional strategy that includes addressing often valid and complex fundamental political, economic

INTRODUCTION

and social grievances, one that goes beyond strictly military-oriented, uni-dimensional approaches.

The second part of the volume consists of an extensive A–Z glossary written by Andrew T H Tan that provides key factual and analytical entries focusing on terrorist groups and major contemporary terrorist incidents. The selection of entries has been guided by their contemporary relevance. Whilst Islamist groups (the term here refers only to groups subscribing to radical, violent interpretations of Islam and is not a general reference to Muslims or Islam) are featured, it will be clear that the majority of terrorist groups are in fact non-Islamist and have varied ethno-nationalist, political and religious agendas. The dictionary section also does not make normative judgements through the use of the often-contested term 'terrorism', recognizing that many such terrorisms, or insurgencies, arise from fundamental conflicts over political, economic or social arrangements in specific local settings. The label of terrorist therefore should not be seen to carry with it the normative and pejorative connotation that privileges the state, since terrorism is often a tool of the weak. (It should be noted that, as mentioned above, this volume has also included a chapter on state terrorism in the first section, recognizing the fact that terrorism as a tool is also used by states to achieve political objectives.)

The third part of the volume consists of a series of maps, which, along with charts and tables, will give the reader the spatial sense, and extent of, contemporary terrorism.

Finally, the fourth part of this volume contains a select bibliography divided into titles that examine terrorism in general, and those that examine it in a more specific regional or national political context.

This volume is meant for training, reference and education. It will be useful to students of security studies and political science, academics studying the terrorist phenomenon, security professionals, those engaged in assessing business risk, government officials and policy-makers, those working in international multi-national organizations, and, finally, to those who generally wish to further their understanding of contemporary terrorism.

Andrew T H Tan
King's College London
November 2005

Contents

Acknowledgements	ix
The Contributors	x
Note on the Transcription of Arabic Names	xiii

PART 1 – ESSAYS

Modern Terror: History and Special Features by DAVID C. RAPOPORT	3
Dagger and Sarin: The Evolution of Terrorist Weapons and Tactics by ADAM DOLNIK AND ROHAN GUNARATNA	25
Ethnic Terrorism: Themes and Variations by DENNIS PLUCHINSKY	40
Left- and Right-wing Political Terrorism by DAVID W. BRANNAN	55
Religion and the New Terrorism by MARK JUERGENSMEYER	73
On the Nature of Religious Terrorism by ADAM DOLNIK AND ROHAN GUNARATNA	80
State Uses of Terrorism by JAMES LUTZ AND BRENDA LUTZ	89
Counter-terrorism by THOMAS MOCKAITIS	103

PART 2 – A–Z GLOSSARY

Glossary of Major Terrorist Groups and Incidents by ANDREW T H TAN	115

PART 3 – MAPS AND STATISTICS

Maps

Map 1: Burma/Myanmar	231
Map 2: Central Africa	232
Map 3: Central Asia	233
Map 4: Ethiopia	234
Map 5: India	235
Map 6: Iraq	236
Map 7: Israel/Palestine	237
Map 8: The Malay Archipelago	238
Map 9: North-West Indian Sub-Continent	239
Map 10: Saudi Arabia	240

Charts and Statistics

Terrorist incidents by region *(chart)*	241
Terrorist injuries by region	242
Terrorism deaths by region	243
Terrorist incidents by region *(statistical table)*	244
Terrorism incidents by target	245
Terrorism incidents by tactic	246

CONTENTS

PART 4 – SELECT BIBLIOGRAPHY

General	249
Middle East	254
Africa	257
Americas	259
Europe	262
Asia	264

Acknowledgements

The editor gratefully acknowledges the support of Routledge for this project. The contributions received here from David Rapoport, Rohan Gunaratna, Adam Dolnik, James and Brenda Lutz, David Brannan, Dennis Pluchinsky, Mark Juergensmeyer and Thomas Mockaitis are gratefully acknowledged. The editor also wishes to record a special word of thanks to Dr Rohan Gunaratna for his invaluable support for the volume. The maps drawn by the University of Southampton are simple but excellent and are much appreciated. The editor is also indebted to the MIPT (National Memorial Institute for the Prevention of Terrorism) Terrorism Knowledge Base for permission to reproduce their data in the Charts and Statistics section of this volume. Last but not least, many thanks indeed to Cathy Hartley of Routledge and to Simon Chapman for their encouragement, guidance and support, without which this volume would not have been possible.

This volume is dedicated to those involved in the global war on terrorism, whose commitment, motivation, and ability to learn and understand the nature of contemporary terrorism is pivotal to preserving our freedom.

The Contributors

David Brannan is associate political scientist for the RAND corporation specializing in terrorism and insurgency issues and is a lecturer at the Naval Postgraduate School, Monterey, California, USA, on Asymmetrical Threats and Homeland Security issues. He served as the Director of Security Policy for the Coalition Provisional Authority within the Ministry of Interior, Iraq. He has contributed to many edited volumes related to terrorism and insurgency. Recently he co-authored *Preparing for Suicide Terrorism: A Primer for American Law Enforcement Agencies and Officers* (Santa Monica, RAND, 2004), which has been very well received. David Brannan is a former law enforcement officer with a Joint Honours MA in Theology and International Relations from the University of St Andrews, United Kingdom. His doctoral research is a delineation of Repentant and Rebellious Identity theology.

Adam Dolnik is a Research Fellow at the Institute of Defence and Strategic Studies, Nanyang Technological University, Singapore, and a Visiting Fellow at the Centre for Transnational Crime Prevention at the University of Wollongong in Australia. Previously, he has worked as a researcher at the WMD Terrorism Project at the Monterey Institute of International Studies in California, USA, and at the United Nations Terrorism Prevention Branch in Vienna, Austria. Adam Dolnik regularly lectures for various governmental and non-governmental organizations and agencies around the world, and his research has been published in a number of books and a variety of international journals, including *Terrorism and Political Violence, Studies in Conflict and Terrorism, International Negotiation: Journal of Theory and Practice, Perspectives: Central European Review of International Affairs* and *Yaderny Kontrol*.

Rohan Gunaratna is Head of the International Center for Political Violence and Terrorism Research at the Institute of Defence and Strategic Studies, Nanyang Technological University, Singapore. He is consultant on terrorism to United Kingdom and US law enforcement agencies, consultant to the *World Terrorism Encyclopedia*, and author of eight books, including the international bestseller *Inside Al Qaeda: Global Network of Terror* (New York, Columbia University Press, 2002). Rohan Gunaratna holds a master's degree in international peace studies from Notre Dame University, USA, and a doctorate in international relations from the University of St Andrews, United Kingdom.

Mark Juergensmeyer is Director of Global and International Studies and Professor of Sociology and Religious Studies at the University of California, Santa Barbara, USA. He is an expert on religious violence, conflict resolution

THE CONTRIBUTORS

and South Asian religion and politics. He has published more than 200 articles and a dozen books. He is the author of *Terror in the Mind of God: The Global Rise of Religious Violence* (University of California Press, 2003), which is based on interviews with violent religious activists around the world, including interviews with individuals convicted of the 1993 World Trade Center bombing, leaders of Hamas and abortion clinic bombers in the USA. Mark Juergensmeyer earned his PhD in Political Science from the University of California, Berkeley.

James and Brenda Lutz. James M. Lutz is Professor and Chair of Political Science at Indiana University-Purdue University at Fort Wayne, Indiana, USA. He co-authored with his wife, Brenda, *Global Terrorism* (London, Routledge, 2004), a well-respected textbook on terrorism. Brenda J. Lutz is a graduate student in sociology at Indiana University-Purdue University at Fort Wayne, focusing on peace and conflict studies.

Thomas R. Mockaitis is Professor of European History at DePaul University, USA. He has written three books and numerous articles on insurgency, peace operations and terrorism. He is author of *Peace Operations and Interstate Conflicts: the Sword or the Olive Branch* (Praeger, 1999), which examines the challenges of intervention in civil wars, and is co-editor of *Grand Strategy in the War Against Terrorism* (London, Frank Cass, 2003). Thomas R. Mockaitis is a frequent commentator on terrorism for television and radio, and is the book review editor of *Small Wars and Insurgencies*.

Dennis Pluchinsky is the senior threat analyst for TranSecur, Inc.—a global security information firm based in Potomac, Maryland, USA. He is on the adjunct faculty at George Mason University, the University of Mary Washington, and George Washington University, where he teaches a course on terrorism which was featured on CNN and in the *Washington Post* newspaper. He retired in 2005 from the US Department of State after 28 years of analysing terrorism for the Office of Intelligence and Threat Analysis. He is a contributing editor to the international journal, *Studies in Conflict and Terrorism*, and has co-edited two books on terrorism.

David Rapoport is Professor Emeritus, University of California, Los Angeles (UCLA), USA. He obtained his PhD in political theory from the University of California, Berkeley, in 1960, and is the editor of the *Journal of Terrorism and Political Violence*. He is also author of some 50 articles. *Assassination and Terrorism* (1971) was his first book, followed by six other edited and co-edited volumes, the most recent being *Democratic Experience and Political Violence* (2001) with Leonard Weinberg. He is the founder and first director of the Center for the Study of Religion, UCLA. Professor Rapoport is working on a project to assemble in four volumes coverage of terrorism by *The New York Times* over the last 135 years.

THE CONTRIBUTORS

Andrew T H Tan is Senior Lecturer (Defence Services), King's College London, and teaches at the Joint Services Command and Staff College, United Kingdom. He holds a PhD from the University of Sydney, Australia, and a master's degree from the University of Cambridge, United Kingdom. A well-known commentator and analyst on South-East Asia, his articles and book reviews have appeared in many academic journals, including *Studies in Conflict and Terrorism* and *Terrorism and Political Violence*. He has written or co-edited six books since 2000. His recent sole-authored books are: *Security Perspectives of the Malay Archipelago: Security Linkages in the Second Front in the War on Terrorism* (Cheltenham, Edward Elgar, 2004) and *A Political and Economic Dictionary of South-East Asia* (London, Europa/Taylor & Francis, 2004). He is editing *A Handbook of Terrorism and Insurgency in Southeast Asia* (Edward Elgar, United Kingdom), with contributions by more than 20 leading and emerging scholars on South-East Asia. His collected conference papers are forthcoming in the volume *Southeast Asia: Threats in the Security Environment*.

Note on the Transcription of Arabic Names

Arabic names occurring in this book have been rendered in the system most commonly used by British and American Orientalists, but with the omission of the diacritical signs. The system used is a transliteration—i.e. it is based on the writing, which is standard throughout the Arab world, and not on the pronunciation, which varies from place to place. In a few cases consistency has been sacrificed in order to avoid replacing a familiar and accepted form by another which, although more accurate, would be unrecognizable.

Sun- and Moon-Letters

In Arabic pronunciation, when the word to which the definite article, *al*, is attached begins with one of certain letters called 'Sun-letters', the *l* of the article changes to the initial letter in question, e.g. *al-shamsu* (the sun) is pronounced *ash-shamsu*; *al-rajulu* (the man) is pronounced *ar-rajulu*. Accordingly, in this book, where the article is attached to a word beginning with a Sun-letter, it has been rendered phonetically.

There are 14 Sun-letters in the Arabic alphabet, which are transcribed as: d, dh, n, r, s, sh, t, th, z, zh (d, s, t and z and their emphatic forms are not differentiated in this book). The remaining 15 letters in the Arabic alphabet are known as 'Moon-letters'.

Essays

Modern Terror: History and Special Features

DAVID C. RAPOPORT

CONCEPT AND DEFINITIONAL PROBLEMS

Government activities in the French Revolution produced the concept and vocabulary of terror, though terrorism itself long preceded that event. The Russian Narodnaya Volya (The People's Will) was the first rebel group to *describe itself* as terrorist in 1879, and the term referred to non-state groups for the next 50 years. In the 1930s terrorism referred again to state activities, as Nazi Germany and the Soviet Union became significant world powers. During the 1960s, when many non-state groups used violence for political ends, terrorism was associated with rebels again, a link that grew firmer over time and which is our subject here.

When Robespierre proclaimed 'Either virtue or the terror' during the French Reign of Terror, he meant that only terror could produce true 'democratic character', the 'Revolutionary Tribunals' special task. Normal courts assess actions; but the Tribunals were concerned with those *inclined* to be lawbreakers. Because guilt or innocence was irrelevant, standard rules of evidence were dispensed with. The fate of prisoners was meant to be didactic lessons for the public. The Tribunals identified appropriate and inappropriate dispositions!

In the spirit of its French predecessors, Narodnaya Volya also understood terrorism as a temporary measure to 'transform the consciousness of the masses'. Victims were chosen for didactic purposes, i.e. as symbols or political effects. Assailants concealed their weapons and signs identifying them as combatants. While the French discarded existing rules of punishment, the Russian terrorists declared the laws of war irrelevant.

Not surprisingly, in time the term accumulated so many abusive connotations that terrorists stopped calling themselves terrorists. The last group to designate itself as terrorist was Lehi (Fighters for the Freedom of Israel, referred to as the 'Stern Gang' by the British) a splinter group of the Irgun (Organization for the Defence of the People). Earlier, Menachem Begin, leader of the Irgun, focusing on purpose not means, described his followers as 'freedom fighters' who were only struggling against government terror (Begin, 1997). Groups everywhere adopted his language, and the claims that they were fighting government terror sometimes resonated internationally, because combatants tend to use similar tactics.

Many viewed struggles against colonial rule as legitimate, and the public discourse during the 1960s made the terms terrorist and freedom fighter mutually exclusive, which meant that those using violence against a Western power were always 'freedom fighters'. By the 1970s the media, presumably to protect its reputation for 'impartiality', had corrupted the language further. American newspapers often described identical persons in the same account alternatively as terrorists, guerrillas, militants and soldiers! Similar inconsistencies plague academic accounts. The unspoken assumption was that if one sympathized with its cause, one could not describe a group as terrorist. The linguistic confusions impeded international counter-terror efforts.

The confusion intensified when some terrorists became legitimate political leaders—in Ireland, Israel, Kenya, Algeria, etc. Four former terrorists even received Nobel Peace Prizes. Menachem Begin and Anwar Sadat shared one (1978) for the Camp David Accords. Nelson Mandela (1994) was indispensable in reconciling fiercely hostile South African elements. After signing the Oslo Accords, Yasser Arafat received one (1995), but he was the only recipient unable to make the appropriate final commitment.

Most scholars understand terror as a means not an end. But some do not discriminate between terror and other forms of political violence, making it difficult to distinguish rebel soldiers like George Washington and Robert E. Lee from their terrorist contemporaries in the Sons of Liberty and the Ku Klux Klan (KKK). The original definition, moreover, makes it easier to understand the special problem terrorism creates for the perpetrators and the assaulted, problems discussed in the counter-terror section below.

MODERN TERROR: THE WAVE PHENOMENA

Pre-modern secular terror had a different form, as the examples of the American Sons of Liberty and the KKK demonstrate. Both used mobs that vastly outnumbered victims. When Alfred Nobel invented dynamite, modern terror began. Tiny groups (even individuals) with the advantage of surprise could frighten large masses. Simultaneously, crucial developments in communication and transportation facilities occurred. The telegraph, mass-circulation daily newspapers and railroads flourished; subsequent innovations continued to shrink time and space. Events in one country were known elsewhere within days. Prominent terrorists travelled extensively inspiring sympathies and groups, often spending more time abroad than at home. Mass transportation enabled mass migrations, creating diaspora communities that became political elements in both their 'new' and 'old' countries.

Modern terrorism develops in the form of waves. A wave contains many groups existing in the same time period in various lands, groups with similar purposes, tactics, and geography. Activity expands and diminishes in a cyclical fashion.

The modern world has experienced four distinct waves. The first three lasted approximately 40 years each; the fourth has lasted 26 years so far. The 'Anarchist' wave ended in the 1920s when the 'Anti-Colonial' one began. The second wave concluded in 1962, and the 'New Left' began soon after. The third wave had virtually disappeared by the first decade of the 21st century; but halfway through its cycle, in 1979, the 'Religious' wave began. No one knows when, how, or whether the current wave will end.

The name of a wave reflects a major feature. Anarchists developed the first wave's doctrine. All second-wave groups sought independence from Western colonial empires. 'New Left' refers to the tumultuous Neo-Marxist era in the 1960s. Religious doctrines inspired fourth-wave groups.

Bombs or explosives were the principal weapon, and in each wave they produced incidents with many casualties. But each wave had its own signature tactics. First-wave terrorists assassinated prominent government officials. Those in the second wave rejected assassination to organize a more complicated undertaking, i.e. that of eliminating the police because their military replacements would not be able to function without committing atrocities that would undermine support for the colonial power. New Left terrorists utilized airline hijacking and hostage-taking on a grand scale. Fourth-wave participants introduced 'self-martyrdom' or 'suicide bombing' and rejected the New Left's inclination to kill from a distance.

Discontent is a necessary but not a sufficient ingredient for terrorism; revolts do not occur if everybody believes that they will make their situation worse. The origin of a wave is associated with confidence or a new hope created by unexpected great political events. When the hope exhausts its force, a wave dissipates.

Groups and waves have very different life cycles. Groups generally have shorter lives; New Left-wave organizations, for example, averaged two years only. But sometimes organizations transcend a wave, and in the process those organizations change. The Irish Republican Army (IRA) has existed in various forms since 1920. When it transcended the second wave to become active in the third, New Left features were added. In the third wave, the Palestine Liberation Organization (PLO) included secular Christians and no Islamic element; today, the Christian element is absent from its successor, the Palestine Authority, and the Islamic dimension is crucial.

In the ancient world, sacred precedents limited the tactics of terror groups, and each religion had its own precedents and peculiar tactics (Rapoport, 1984). Subsequently, the Sons of Liberty and the KKK did 'their dirty work in secret and kept their mouths shut afterwards'. But the Russians followed a very different route, explaining the logic of terror, identifying vulnerable societies, and taking 'credit' for their acts.

Modern groups, unlike ancient ones, normally determine ends and means, altering them as circumstances dictate, and the concept of terror as distinguished from the methods employed has remained unchanged for some 125 years. A 'culture of terror' has been created in which participants feel free to take their lessons from anyone, a 'tradition' without binding precedents, one that caricatures the modern tendency to subject all activities to standards of utility and efficiency. This 'culture' encourages the expansion of the range of means and ends.

Each wave has produced major technical works, reflecting the wave's special properties and contributing to a common effort to formulate a 'science' of terror. The first wave *inter alia* produced Nechaev's *Revolutionary Catechism*, and the second, third and fourth *inter alia* yielded Georges Grivas's *Guerrilla War*, Carlos Marighella's *Mini-Manual of the Urban Guerrilla* and Osama bin Laden's *Military Studies in the Jihad Against The Tyrants*.

We will now look briefly at the distinctive features and precipitating hope of each wave, emphasizing the international interaction of various protagonists, i.e. terrorist groups, states, international organizations, and diasporas. International organizations (League of Nations and the UN) appeared in the second wave; otherwise the actors are the same, but their relationships change.

1. The 'Anarchist' Wave: Creation of a Doctrine

Tsar Alexander II's astonishing efforts to transform Russia virtually overnight excited enormous expectations. In the wake of inevitable disappointments, assassination strikes against prominent officials began, and Alexander himself was murdered in 1882.

The aim was to produce a revolution when the traditional method, spontaneous mass uprisings, either failed or were too costly. Mass uprisings required class hostilities, but modern tensions were latent and diffused. Terror was viewed as a tool to make those tensions public and clearly focused on appropriate objects, which is why terror became known as 'propaganda of the deed'. Bold, dramatic and heroic action demonstrating unconditional commitment would give revolutionaries confidence, attract attention, draw followers, and above all infuse potential supporters with hope, the essential lubricant of revolution. Provoked officials would retaliate indiscriminately against those they could not find, making the oppression of the masses so visible that revolutionary insurrection would be inevitable (Nechaev, 1971). Governments would be 'compelled for many years running, to neglect everything and to do nothing, but struggle with ... [terrorists who] will render its position untenable' (Stepniak, 1982). Terrorism is a 'politics of atrocity', where atrocities are deliberately calculated to produce counter-atrocities redounding to the original assailant's advantage (Rapoport, 1977).

Russian terrorists encouraged and trained other groups, some with nationalist aims. Armenian and Polish separatist groups were the first to emerge. Then the Balkans exploded, as the boundaries of new states torn out of the Ottoman Empire proved unsatisfactory. At the same time groups appeared in Western Europe, the Americas, and India.

Russian anarchists found refuge in the West, where efforts to apprehend them were frustrated because 19th-century states expanded rights for political asylum; Britain, for example, refused Russian requests to return Russian terrorists, while Switzerland even allowed them to operate openly. Various diaspora populations provided essential financial, political and recruiting support. The Irish Americans, for example, were the most active, supplying most of the weapons and personnel for the Fenian uprising in the 1880s. Armenian, Jewish, and Italian diasporas played notable roles too.

The wave's high point occurred in the 1890s, known as the 'Golden Age of Assassination', when assassins crossing international borders struck down monarchs, Prime Ministers and Presidents one after another. Governments clamoured for international police co-operation and better border control, an opportunity seized by President Theodore Roosevelt after his predecessor was assassinated in 1901 to launch the first international effort to eliminate terrorism, a commitment that lasted three years only. Fearing extensive involvement in European politics, the USA spurned a German/Russian invitation to develop effective co-operation mechanisms (St Petersburg Protocol 1904). Democratic states resisted the co-operation efforts most. Italy had a very special concern. If anarchists were returned to their home countries, Italy's domestic troubles might be worse than its international ones!

St Petersburg showed how conflicting interests drove states in different directions, and new expressions of those tensions occurred as the wave developed. Bulgaria became the first notorious state sponsor of terror, giving Macedonian separatists sanctuaries and training grounds for operations in the Ottoman Empire. In 1905 the Russian Terrorist Brigade had its headquarters in Switzerland, launched strikes from Finland, an autonomous part of the Russian Empire, obtained arms from an Armenian terrorist group, and was offered funds by the Japanese to be laundered through American millionaires! The mistaken suspicion that Serbia had assisted the assassin of Austria's Archduke Franz Ferdinand precipitated the First World War. The first wave ended shortly afterwards.

2. The 'Anti-Colonial' Wave: the First Successes

The Versailles Peace Treaty ending the First World War precipitated the second wave when the victors applied the principle of national self-determination to dissolve the defeated states' empires, mainly in Europe, where new European states were created. The League of Nations, a new international actor, established 'mandates' to prepare non-European territories for independence. Willy-nilly, the victors undermined the legitimacy of their own empires. IRA efforts created an Irish state (1922); and after the Second World War, terrorist groups helped establish Israel, Cyprus, Yemen, Algeria, etc. As Western empires dissolved, the wave receded.

Terrorists rarely have successes, and most occurred in this wave largely after Second World War peace arrangements reinforced and enlarged the implications of Versailles. Again, the defeated had to abandon empires. The mandate system was abandoned; instead, colonial territories became states (Korea, Ethiopia, Libya, etc.) or were fully incorporated into other states, i.e. Manchuria. The victors began liquidating their own empires too, as a result of decisions that were generally not related to terrorism, i.e. India, Pakistan, Burma, Ceylon, Tunisia,

Egypt, Morocco, the Philippines, Ghana, Nigeria, etc. One reason for the pattern was that the USA, the West's major power, was determined to eliminate empires.

The terror campaigns appeared in territories where colonial powers feared that they could not relinquish control without creating serious international problems. Jews and Arabs in Palestine, for example, had dramatically conflicting versions of what the end of British rule was supposed to mean. A considerable European population in Algeria did not want France to abandon them, the majority in Northern Ireland considered itself British, and Turkish Cypriots feared that making Cyprus part of Greece would be disastrous.

These problems shaped the way in which struggles were 'settled'. The Irgun fought to gain the entire Palestine mandate but accepted partition, rather than risk civil war between Jews. IRA elements may never stop struggling to gain control of Northern Ireland. The National Organization of Cypriot Struggle for Union with Greece (EOKA), 'accepted' an independent state, which it then tried to subvert, leading to the present division of the island. Algerian rebels seemed to gain everything they sought. But the initial manifesto of the Front de libération nationale (FLN) promised both a home for the European population and a democratic state; neither objective was achieved.

Second-wave terrorists thought that assassinating prominent political figures (the first wave's signature tactic) was ineffective. Outside the Balkans, only Lehi remained committed to an assassination strategy, and as it was much less effective than the Irgun, its Zionist competitor, every subsequent second-wave group absorbed the lesson. The new strategy was more complicated than the old; there were more targets and each was designed to be struck in proper sequence. Eliminate the police first, a government's eyes and ears, through systematic assassinations of officers and/or their families. The military replacements proved too clumsy to cope without producing counter-atrocities, increasing terrorist social support. A well-executed process of atrocities and counter-atrocities favoured those perceived to be weak or without alternatives. Second-wave terrorists achieved a better public image than first-wave terrorists did and enlisted much more public support.

Much energy was expended on guerrilla-like actions against troops, attacks still beyond the rules of war because weapons and identities were concealed. The Irgun introduced warnings to limit civilian casualties, a pattern embraced by other groups. Algerian terror was one aspect of a more comprehensive guerrilla rebellion. In most cases successful terrorists did not attack the homelands of imperial powers; the assumption was that such strikes would harden resolve to hold the territories. Only a divided Algerian FLN leadership (prompted by a notorious French torture campaign) authorized strikes in France, but quickly abandoned that counter-productive effort.

Second-wave terrorists used international contexts more productively. Different groups acknowledged an international revolutionary heritage, but did not co-operate with each other, realizing that ties with foreign terrorists made other international assets less useful. Diaspora groups remained deeply concerned with developments in their original homes. Irish Americans induced the US government to pressure Britain to accept an Irish state. When the Holocaust horror was finally revealed, American Jews were a factor in the decision of the USA to recognize Israel. As in the first wave, states sharing ethnic bonds with terrorist groups actively supported them. Greece encouraged EOKA to subvert the new state of Cyprus, but that made Turkish Cypriots seek Turkish aid. Turkey invaded Cyprus in 1974, and a partitioned island remains an international problem. Arab states gave the Algerian FLN crucial political aid and sanctuaries to stage attacks, and French efforts to eliminate that aid aroused much international opposition.

When Alexander I of Yugoslavia and the French foreign minister Barthou were assassinated in Marseilles in 1934, the League of Nations drafted two anti-terrorist conventions. But League members implicated in aiding terrorists blocked ratification efforts. After the Second World War, the UN inherited the League's authority over mandate territories, now scenes of extensive terrorist activity. When Britain decided to leave Palestine, the UN legitimized a partition; subsequently, all anti-colonial terrorists sought to involve the UN in their struggles. As new states (former colonial territories) joined the UN, anti-colonial sentiments developed more structure, focus, and opportunities.

3. The 'New Left' Wave: Excessive Internationalism?

The effectiveness of Viet Cong terror stimulated hopes that audacious action could overwhelm modern technology. The Viet Nam struggle, combining anti-colonial sentiments with the Cold War, seriously affected the USA's earlier moral credibility as the predominant anti-colonial Western power. Now terrorists spoke of American 'imperialism' as the source of their grievances. Exploiting those views, the Soviet bloc supplied groups with weapons and training. A revolutionary ethos reminiscent of the first wave appeared among Marxist-Anarchist groups which viewed themselves as vanguards for Third World masses; for instance, Weather Underground (USA), Red Army Faction (West Germany), the Red Brigades (Italy), Tupamaro (National Liberation Movement, Uruguay), Montoneros (Movimiento Peronista Montonero, Argentina) and Action Directe (France).

After the extraordinary collapse of Arab armies in the 1967 Six-Day War, the PLO replaced the Viet Cong as the heroic model. Strong support from the Arab states and the Soviet bloc enhanced the PLO's centrality. It had an 'anti-colonial' grievance, and its home in Lebanon enabled it to be the first terrorist organization to develop significant bases for training other groups.

The first-wave practice of linking radicalism and separatism abandoned in the second wave reappeared, i.e. the Palestinians, Armenians, Irish, Corsicans, Basques, Kurds, etc. Nationalism made them the most durable groups, but none succeeded. The last three still struggle against states (Spain, France, and Turkey) that neither view themselves nor are viewed by others as colonial powers. Those states, therefore, lack the 'necessary' ambivalence for terrorists to succeed and since the terrorists involved do not occupy overseas territories, geography makes it virtually impossible to follow the course of second-wave terrorists and avoid home strikes.

The Palestinian case, however, was viewed differently. Much international opinion regarded Israel's occupation of mandate portions intended for the Palestinians as colonial domination; consequently, the PLO received a UN 'Observer Status' (1981), and since then 117 states have recognized it as an 'equal'. However, the West rejected the PLO's claim to the *entire* League of Nations Mandate, and attacks on Western citizens vitiated potential Western sympathies.

Theatrical targets producing much publicity without many casualties became common. Hijacking is one example. Foreign landing fields were accessible, and some 700 hijackings occurred in the wave's first three decades. Ironically, most early hijackers fled Cuba to the USA where they became heroes. But after the PLO simultaneously hijacked three planes to Jordan in 1970 for hostages, the West perceived hijackers differently.

Hostages were gained in other ways too. The Italian Red Brigades kidnapped former Prime Minister Aldo Moro in 1978. The Sandinistas (FSLN) took Nicaragua's Congress hostage in the same year, an act so audacious that it sparked the popular insurrection that overthrew the regime one year later. The Colombian M-19 (April 19 Movement) tried to duplicate the feat when it seized the Supreme Court in 1985; but the government refused to yield, and more than 100 people, including 11 justices, died.

Initially, hostages provided political leverage. When companies insured their executives, negotiations were easier to consummate and money became the object. From 1968–82, 409 international assaults yielded 951 hostages.

The practice of assassinating prominent figures revived. Irish elements assassinated Christopher Ewart-Biggs, Jr, British Ambassador to Ireland (1976), Lord Mountbatten (1979), and attempted to kill Prime Ministers Thatcher (1984) and Major (1991). The Palestinian Black September assassinated Jordan's Prime Minister in 1971 and attempted to kill King Hussein in 1974. It killed the American Ambassador when capturing the Saudi Arabian Embassy, in Khartoum, Sudan, in 1973, the year in which the Basque group Euskadi Ta Askatasuna (ETA) killed Spanish Prime Minister Carrero Blanco.

First-wave victims were assassinated because they held public offices; now assassinations were generally matters of revenge or punishment. Jordan's leaders had forced the PLO out of their country in a savage battle. British Prime Minister Thatcher was 'responsible' for the death of hunger strikers, and the Italian government refused to negotiate for the release of former Prime Minister Aldo Moro.

The term 'international terrorism' disappeared in the second wave, but was revived in the third. A new revolutionary ethos created significant bonds between separate national groups, bonds that strengthened when Cuban and PLO training facilities became available. International targets became commonplace. Some groups conducted more assaults abroad than at home; the PLO, for example, was active in Europe but not on the West Bank, and sometimes more active in Europe than many European groups themselves were! Different national groups co-operated in attacks, i.e. the Munich Olympics massacre (1972), the OPEC ministers' kidnapping (1975) and hijackings to Uganda (1976) and Somalia (1977). Strikes on foreign embassies to secure hostages began when the PLO attacked the Saudi Arabian Embassy in Khartoum in 1973. The Peruvian group Tupac Amaru (MRTA) held 72 hostages in the Japanese Embassy for four months in 1996–97, until a rescue operation killed every terrorist there.

The international targets were normally Western, and Americans were the most common victims with the Israelis, French, and British far behind. The pattern reflected several facts; the reversal of America's credibility in Viet Nam, US aid for many unpopular governments, and the easy availability of American targets. Half of the 350 annual international victims were government officials while a third represented business interests. Cold War concerns made the USA sometimes forgo its distaste for terror by supporting organizations using it in Nicaragua, Angola, etc.

Terrorist groups paid extraordinary prices for their international activity. Alliances with foreign terrorists produced unexpected disastrous consequences. The German 2 June terrorist group, in order to show sympathies with the Palestinians, attacked a Jewish synagogue in Germany on the anniversary of *Kristallnacht*, which marks the beginning of the Holocaust. This 'stupidity', a leader said, alienated domestic sympathizers (Baumann, 1977). When the power of co-operating terrorist entities was very unequal, the weaker suffered. The German Revolutionary Cells, hijacking partners of the Popular Front for the Liberation of Palestine (PFLP), could not obtain PFLP help to release German prisoners. 'Our agenda was very different than theirs after all' (Bourguereau, 1981). The Revolutionary Cells terminated the relationship and soon collapsed itself.

The PLO, always a loose confederation, found that international ties complicated serious internal divisions. So important was the Palestinian cause in their domestic politics that Syria and Iraq felt it necessary to capture organizations within the PLO for their own purposes, making it more difficult to settle for a limited goal, as the Irgun and EOKA had earlier done.

Diaspora support generally was *less* significant than it was earlier, partly because commitments to an international revolutionary ethos alienated potential supporters. When the IRA, for example, tilted left, diaspora support in the USA weakened and no American government made moves to resolve the Irish conflict until the Cold War ended. The Armenian diaspora was active, but Armenian terrorists were ineffective. The Basques in North and South America gave important financial aid to ETA in Spain. Clearly, the Palestinians organized the most effective diaspora. Indeed, there was little rebel activity in the Occupied Territories, and the PLO itself was wholly a diaspora group until the Oslo Accords in 1995.

The origin of the First World War dramatically displayed how international terrorist activity can exacerbate existing tensions or create new antagonisms between states. Second-wave strategy diminished the problem except in Algeria, but the third wave moved back in the direction of the first. Palestinian raids from

Egyptian-occupied Gaza precipitated war with Israel in 1956, and Egypt made sure that none were ever launched from Gaza again. A Palestinian raid from Syrian territory brought Syria into the 1967 War; subsequently Syria kept a tight control on operations from its territories. When a PLO faction hijacked British and American planes to Jordan in 1970 (the first effort to target Westerners), Jordan, fearing international consequences, devastated the PLO, driving it from its second home. The PLO lost its third home when Israel invaded Lebanon in 1982. Eight states led by Tunisia gave PLO elements homes afterwards, but the PLO's inability to train foreigners or use bases to launch strikes eliminated it as an effective terrorist organization. Ironically, the PLO's new weakness led Israel to accept the Oslo Accords allowing the PLO to come home and by virtue of its geography revitalize its significance.

States imposed limited sanctions to counter state-sponsored terror. Britain severed diplomatic relations with Syria and Libya in 1984 for sponsoring terror on British soil, and for the first time joint efforts to implement limited sanctions materialized. The Americans, with British aid, bombed Libya in 1986; simultaneously, the European Community imposed an arms embargo. European governments expelled Libyan diplomats and immigrants. Evidence that Libya was involved in the Pan-Am Lockerbie crash in 1988 produced an unprecedented unanimous UN Security Council demand (1992) that Libya extradite suspects. Economic sanctions were imposed, and ultimately Libya complied. Allied forces bombed Iraqi intelligence headquarters for organizing an assassination attempt against former US President George Bush in 1998. By 2000, in the third wave's last decade, a number of states, i.e. Cuba, Libya, and North Korea, had abandoned state sponsorship of terror. The potential cost of state-sponsored international terror is indicated too by an event that did not happen. Saddam Hussain did not use terror during the first Gulf War (1991), despite widespread predictions that he would carry out his threats to do so. Trying him for war crimes would otherwise have been a war objective, hence his uncharacteristic restraint.

As in the first wave, terrorism created frictions between friendly states. France refused to extradite PLO, Red Brigade and ETA suspects to West Germany, Italy and Spain respectively. The USA and Ireland found technical reasons to refuse British requests to extradite IRA suspects. Italy would not honour Turkey's effort to extradite a Kurdish suspect because Turkey retained capital punishment. The most dramatic clashes between friendly states occurred when Palestinians seized the ship *Achille Lauro* in 1985. The question was which country had legal jurisdiction. US fighters forced an Egyptian plane with the perpetrators to land in Italy, a deed the Egyptian President called an 'act of piracy'. A violent clash between Italian police and US forces almost materialized, and was ultimately a factor in the collapse of Italy's government.

None the less, the international co-operation of national police forces sought in the 1904 St Petersburg Protocol began to materialize. INTERPOL, the body responsible for international control of crime, was established in 1956, but excluded crimes involving political or religious questions. Some states also continued to provide asylum for those committing political acts that others considered terrorist activity. But step by step, attitudes changed, and in 2002 the European Union developed a 'Framework Decision on Combating Terrorism'.

UN views changed dramatically too. Now new states, former colonial territories, found that terrorists, particularly separatists, threatened their interests. In 1960–99, 40 violent rebellions occurred to dismember those new states; but only Bangladesh was successful, so great was the hostility to separation efforts. Major UN conventions in 1970–99 specified new international crimes—hijacking, hostage-taking, attacks on senior government officials, bombing facilities of a foreign state and the financing of international activities. The term 'freedom fighter' became rare in UN debates, and the word terrorist was actually used in the title of a document—'International Convention for the Suppression of Terrorist Bombing' (1997).

The third wave began to ebb in the 1980s. Terrorists were defeated in one country after another. Israel's invasion of Lebanon eliminated PLO facilities to train terrorist groups, and in 1991 the Soviet Union disintegrated. Only a few third-wave groups still function.

4. The 'Religious' Wave: A Different Kind of Internationalism

Religious elements appear frequently in each wave because religious and ethnic/national identities generally overlap, i.e. Armenian, Macedonian, Cypriot, Israeli, Algerian, Palestinian, and Irish cases. Secular purposes justified earlier campaigns; but fourth-wave groups' aim is to create religious states. Secular terrorists sometimes emerged out of this religious strife, i.e. efforts to make Sri Lanka a Buddhist state provoked Tamil terror.

Three dramatic unexpected events in 1979—the Iranian Revolution, Camp David Accords, and the Soviet invasion of Afghanistan—created the requisite new hope. Iran demonstrated that religion was a powerful political force again. The Camp David peace treaty between Egypt and Israel suggested to many that Arab radical nationalism was bankrupt because the strongest Arab state had abandoned Palestine for its own interests. The Soviet Union invaded Afghanistan, inspiring volunteers from the huge Sunni population of the Muslim world armed with the Jihadist-Salafist version of Islam Saudi Arabia had generated. Critical American military and political support was supplied.

Events in the Muslim world preceded similar events in other religions and perhaps influenced them. Sikhs sought a religious state in the Punjab in India. Jewish terrorists tried to destroy Islam's most sacred shrine in Jerusalem and waged an assassination campaign against Palestinian mayors. An American 'Christian Identity' movement materialized, claiming that the Bible, correctly understood, provided the faithful with a racist doctrine. Aum Shinrikyo, combining Buddhist, Hindu, and Christian themes, released nerve gas on Tokyo subways, creating a world-wide anxiety that other groups would soon use similar weapons to produce massive casualties.

Although terrorist activity in other religions peaked early and virtually disappeared, Islam's experience was very different. In the first two decades many states with primarily Muslim populations experienced terror, i.e. Egypt, Lebanon, Tunisia, Libya, Algeria, etc. When the Soviet Union collapsed in 1991, Muslim-populated areas (i.e. Uzbekistan, Tajikistan, Chechnya, and Bosnia) were affected too. In Chechnya and Bosnia, the struggle was against non-Muslims also, as it was in India, Thailand, and the Philippines.

The wave's signature tactic, 'suicide bombing' ('self-martyrdom'), is a very simple, inexpensive, and effective tool, one delivered without warning thus abandoning a common practice developed in the two previous waves. Hezbollah (Party of God) introduced it with attacks on a UN peace-keeping force in Lebanon in 1983, killing 241 US marines, the most American casualties since Viet Nam, and 58 French soldiers, the most French casualties since Algeria in the second wave. Both states withdrew their forces, producing the first strategic terrorist international success since the anti-colonial wave, and one amplified by the Israeli withdrawal in 2000. The tactic inspired other Islamic groups. A few secular groups followed; in 1983–2000 the Tamil Tigers made more suicide attacks than all Islamic groups combined and Kurds used the tactic in Turkey. It is now used most often in Iraq, where in 2005 two out of three attacks employed it. In 2005 it was also used in London to attack the public transport system.

Bombs delivered by human carriers are more likely to be at the correct location at the appropriate time, producing maximum casualties. No escape plan, always a difficult undertaking, is necessary; perpetrators cannot be interrogated afterwards to extract crucial information, and the bomb is likely to destroy all forensic elements. It is extraordinarily difficult to eliminate potential perpetrators without exploding the bomb. The attack focuses public attention on the assailant's zeal. Oddly, despite its immense advantages, groups from other religions did not use the weapon.

Al-Qa'ida, which emerged from the war in Afghanistan, demonstrated that suicide attacks could be used in the sea and the air. It made the first ever terrorist strike on a warship, USS *Cole*, in 2000. The 9/11 air attacks killed some 3,000 people, on the most destructive day by far in the long history of terrorism. (Fewer than 1,000 Americans had been killed in the 30 previous years.) 'In insurance terms, [it was] the costliest single event in history, surpassing the losses inflicted by hurricanes and other natural disasters. [It] also affected the world economy with trillions of dollars in losses and many millions ... unemployed or underemployed.' The attackers lost 19 men and spent perhaps US $250,000 (Gunaratna, 2002).

The most brutal attacks were launched against non-Muslims. When similar strikes were launched against Muslims, they were usually counter-productive and therefore occurred less often. The Algerian Islamic insurrection beginning in 1992, was the most indiscriminate struggle Muslims had ever waged against Muslims, costing more than 100,000 lives. The atrocities were denounced by clerics, alienated potential rebel constituencies and divided rebel forces, compelling some to quit (Miller, 2000). Brutal attacks against non-Muslims in Islamic countries were also counter-productive. When the Egyptian Gama'a Islamiyya massacred 58 European tourists in Luxor in 1997, the effect on the crucial tourist trade ignited public fury and the attacks ceased. More attacks were carried out in Egypt in the Sinai Dessert (Taba in 2004 and Sharm esh-Sheikh in 2005), ostensibly against tourists, but most of the victims were Egyptians and the political consequences are still unknown. Sunni terrorists in Iraq (2004–05) have committed similar atrocities against the Shi'a, but so far clerics in the Arab Sunni world have been largely silent.

With regard to the international scene, Islamic terror has had two phases, initiated by Iran and al-Qa'ida respectively. Iran struck 'outside influences' first. Iranian students held 52 American Embassy staff hostage from 1979 for 444 days, humiliating President Carter and wrecking his re-election bid. Hezbollah's great success against the USA and France followed; and Iran's agents in Western Europe murdered Iranian opposition elements, provoking states to terminate diplomatic relations. Hezbollah took many Western hostages in Lebanon and then joined with Iran in 1992 and 1994 to attack Israeli and Jewish targets in Latin America. Hezbollah also participated in destroying a US military facility in Saudi Arabia in 1996. More recently, it helped train Palestinian groups in the second *intifada*.

Iran's new Constitution prescribed a second international purpose, that of 'bringing political unity to the Islamic world', which meant supporting *mujahidin* ('fighters for God') elsewhere. Ironically, these efforts undermined the enormous prestige Iran had achieved among Muslims for striking 'outsiders' because now Iran, a Shi'a state, ignited Shi'a against Sunnis everywhere, intensifying traditional religious divisions. Saudi Arabia also encouraged its clerics to develop the Jihadist-Salafist movement. Iranian efforts to inspire Shi'a support in Iraq was a factor leading to war in 1980, an eight-year brutal deadlock devastating both participants.

Religious terror among Sunnis followed a different course because radical groups did not capture a state early. Al-Qa'ida, the principal force, emerged from the long Afghan War (1989). It embraced the same two international tasks but focused on that of Islamic unity first. Its recruits came from a very large and widely dispersed population—most came from Arab states but many were from Sunni states in Asia and Africa and from diasporas in five continents. Many left countries where terrorist activity was dissipating, and in some cases recruits were even sent to Afghanistan by anxious governments (those of Saudi Arabia, Egypt and Algeria) in order to remove them from the local scene!

Initially, al-Qa'ida trained individuals from many Sunni states mostly to aid the Taliban struggle against other Afghan elements. Many were integrated into al-Qa'ida's organization in the process. Hardened veterans could choose to continue to stay in Afghanistan or participate in al-Qa'ida's other enterprises. They could return home, and with al-Qa'ida's help, strengthen ongoing terrorist struggles. Another possibility was to join one of the many opportunities the collapse of the Soviet Union made possible. Finally, they could go to a country where there was no activity yet and wait for al-Qa'ida's instructions.

But al-Qa'ida's decision to 'unify Islam first' failed because Muslim states co-ordinated their defence efforts. Algeria's neighbours provide a good example.

Morocco arrested Algerian terrorists, while Tunisia and Egypt gave Algeria material aid and intelligence. In the second wave the same states gave Algerian terrorists sanctuaries and support. Libya (the major state sponsor of third-wave groups), beleaguered by a native group associated with al-Qa'ida, was the first state to label Osama bin Laden an 'international criminal', calling for an international anti-terrorist effort to capture him (1995).

Al-Qa'ida focused on outside influences later, and the USA was the principal target. US troops were forced to abandon humanitarian missions in Somalia (1993) and al-Qa'ida 'declared war' in 1996, ostensibly to compel US troops to withdraw from the region, particularly Saudi Arabia, the location of Islam's holiest shrines. Attacks on military posts in Yemen and Saudi Arabia went unanswered, but attacks on American embassies in Kenya and Tanzania in 1998 triggered cruise missile responses against al-Qa'ida targets, responses so futile that they strengthened the perception of the USA as a 'paper tiger'.

Meanwhile, the struggle against the *status quo* in the Muslim world continued to escalate. 9/11 seems to have been a desperate attempt to rejuvenate a failing cause, by triggering indiscriminate American reactions. This may explain why 15 of the 19 suicide bombers came from Saudi Arabia, a key American ally (Kepel, 2005; Rapoport, 2001).

When President Bush declared the second American 'war' against terrorism, he promised that it 'would not end until *every terrorist group of global reach has been ... defeated*'. In contrast to Theodore Roosevelt's 'war', this time the international community, especially the democratic states that had earlier been the principal opponents, co-operated initially. The UN demanded that Afghanistan expel al-Qa'ida and authorized the first international effort, involving more than 100 members, to invade a sovereign state to destroy a terrorist organization. Even states that had supported religious terrorists before, i.e. Pakistan, whose help was particularly crucial, Iran and Sudan, participated.

No one anticipated how quick and decisive the operation would be. Normally, on their own terrain, terrorists are capable of an enduring resistance, i.e. Cyprus, Algeria, Northern Ireland and Sri Lanka. But to operate extensive training operations, al-Qa'ida made itself visible; and visible terrorist groups are very vulnerable, as Israel demonstrated with the PLO in Lebanon. Al-Qa'ida also failed to plan for the possibility of invasion; did its leaders think that the previous inadequate US responses meant that the USA would avoid 'hard' targets like Afghanistan?

The permanent loss of a secure base, and inroads into leadership and communications may seriously affect al-Qa'ida's capacities, but it is too early to understand what that means, especially since the conflict has been complicated by the US-led invasion of Iraq. Other attacks elsewhere associated with the group both in Islamic states—Indonesia, Turkey, Morocco (2003)—and Western ones—Spain in 2004 and the United Kingdom in 2005—are comparable to conventional terrorist assaults, although the casualties have been much higher and more indiscriminate.

THE PRE-EMPTION ISSUE AND COUNTER-TERROR

States need force to cope with crime and war. Modern terror contains elements of both threats and additional features. Crime and war require deterrence policies; but pre-emption is crucial for counter-terror, and effective pre-emption requires good intelligence facilities. A brief comment on developments and issues follows.

Police forces in the first wave developed new organizational modes and tactics. To reduce surprise, the terrorists' principal advantage, counter-terror elements took their uniforms off. The British Special Branch, the US Federal Bureau of Investigation, the Russian *Okhrana*, etc., were created for this purpose, and plain-clothes police elements remain a permanent fixture.

Obtaining appropriate information required participation in suspicious groups. To gain credibility, infiltrators sometimes encouraged suspected proclivities or became double agents and *agents provocateurs*. Russian police organized assassinations of state officials, fomented strikes, printed stirring calls to 'bloody revolution', and a police agent, Yevno Azev, even became the leader of the 1905 Russian Terrorist Brigade! Because there were many Jews in the Russian terrorist groups, the police fabricated *The Protocols of Zion* as a justification for pogroms. That work still helps inspire Islamic terror groups.

The harsh Russian reactions reflected the country's autocratic tradition. But questionable practices are a normal feature of the history of counter-terrorism. Unlike those engaged in fighting wars and crime, counter-terror forces have no clear accepted guide-lines, and the public's anger and revulsion demands quick results even if those results give rise to abuses. Significantly, no democratic government has been overturned because its anti-terrorist policies were too harsh; but when Uruguay could not cope with Tupamaro attacks, the 'Switzerland of Latin America' experienced a military coup in 1974.

Abuses are often regretted later. Thus, after the third-wave American groups were decimated, severe restrictions were placed on police activities, but those restrictions were removed after 9/11. Congressional outrage against Central Intelligence Agency informants in Central America made the organization use electronic intelligence alone, a less valuable intelligence source and one reason, perhaps, why 9/11 was not detected.

Immigrants committed most terrorist acts in the first wave. One US reaction was the 'Palmer Raids' to send 248 anarchists back to their original countries, even if they had committed no crimes. The Wall Street Bombing in 1922 followed, the most deadly attack on US soil until 1995, creating a 'Red Scare' and new laws restricting immigration from Southern and Eastern Europe, the original homes of most anarchists.

All of the 9/11 bombers were foreigners. While the government made special efforts to curb the public's vigilante passions against Muslims, the Immigration and Naturalization Service reconsidered its monitoring practices, producing significant protests about 'abuses', straining relations between states, and occasioning potentially serious economic costs. A practice of detentions, including secret ones, a common reaction to serious terrorist activities, has been implemented. Supreme Court Justice Sandra O'Connor stated two weeks after 9/11: 'We are likely to experience more restrictions on our personal freedom than has ever been the case in our history.' European states also pay much more attention to immigrant monitoring, complicating tense relationships between immigrant communities and local police.

The military has performed an important role in counter-terrorist activity since the second wave, but their situation is very different from that of the police. Take, for example, the crucial issue of interrogation. Terrorists commit crimes and the police can interrogate them under rules laid down for criminal behaviour. Military prisoners can refuse to be interrogated; they only need state their name, rank and serial number. But terrorists are not military prisoners, which means that when they are held in military as opposed to civilian custody, the only rules applicable are those that the military chooses to use. It is no accident that torture first became conspicuous in the second wave. The most notorious experience occurred in the 'Battle of Algiers'. French paratroopers obtained the information needed to win the battle; but they also generated profound revulsion everywhere, a key element in the FLN's success.

The military is Israel's major counter-terror force; the country operates under a pattern inherited from the British mandate system of emergency legislation. In the Occupied Territories of the West Bank, international law allows military commanders to take 'necessary measures'. They include 'censorship, ... curfews, closing off areas, demolition of houses, closing educational institutions, mass detentions, deportations, restrictions on travelling abroad, cutting off telephone lines, electricity, and water supplies, restricting the marketing of agricultural produce'. Israeli pre-emptive strikes often aim to assassinate suspects not arrest them. The Israeli High Court outlawed torture, but some practices may still occur (Lelyveld, 2005).

In Northern Ireland the British utilized emergency military legislation to intern large numbers of suspected IRA members and supporters, as the third wave materialized there. When the European Court of Human Rights condemned British interrogation procedures in 1971, the UK government abolished them and eventually abandoned internment too. But only in 2000 did the British develop a single police jurisdiction over terrorism no matter where in the United Kingdom it occurred.

Torture had been abolished throughout the West by the beginning of the 19th century, and the UN Convention on Torture and Other Inhuman and Degrading Acts (1984) prohibits torture in the strongest possible manner. Article 2 reads (emphasis added) *'No exceptional circumstances whatsoever*, whether a state of war or a threat of war, internal political instability, or any other public emergency may be invoked as a justification of torture.' Still, in 1995, 100 states used torture and those with the worst records were fighting terrorism (Schmid and Jongman, 1997). One reason for the grim contemporary situation is that military jurisdiction is often preferred. In the American case, Afghan 'prisoners of war' were taken to Guantánamo Bay, Cuba, and refused Geneva Convention rights, which meant they could be subject to dubious interrogations, denied trials, and held for as long as their captors thought appropriate. The invasion of Iraq soon produced serious abuses, most notably at Abu Ghraib, abuses that provoked allies, potential supporters and the American public. The military then developed new interrogation rules, but the issue will not disappear. In the late summer of 2005 a hunger strike by Guantánamo prisoners was initiated.

Counter-terror requirements normally reshape judicial procedures. Intelligence sources must remain anonymous. Judges, juries, lawyers and witnesses all are in serious jeopardy, which is why in the second wave military courts, where secret proceedings without juries prevail, were used, a practice Israel continued in the third and fourth waves. Some European countries during the third wave developed special civilian courts instead, excluding juries, relaxing evidence rules, and using unidentified witnesses.

Appropriate sanctions for terrorist prisoners are unclear. Italian experience suggests that if terrorists repent publicly, a possibility enhanced by pardons or reduced penalties, their comrades may be demoralized (Ferracuti, 1990). Capital punishment creates martyrs for terrorist movements, but can states committed to capital punishment exempt terrorists alone? Put another way, can any state have stiffer penalties for 'ordinary' criminals than for terrorists?

The 9/11 surprise attack led to the most extensive change in internal security arrangements in US history. A Department of Homeland Security with 170,000 employees was created in 2002 to improve intelligence facilities by demolishing barriers against sharing intelligence information generated by some 40 bureaus and offices in 20 separate agencies. Earlier, other countries with serious prolonged terrorist problems (Italy, France, the United Kingdom, Israel, etc.) had made similar decisions.

When the revulsion terrorist acts create combines with inappropriate intelligence, international catastrophes may materialize. The First World War occurred partly because the Austro-Hungarians could not wait for the Serbian government to prove that it was uninvolved in the assassination. 9/11 produced the emotions for the Iraq invasion. The assumption was that Iraq would provide terrorists with weapons of mass destruction (WMD), and Iraq was struck while the information was still incomplete. The Israeli invasion of Lebanon to destroy the PLO was sparked by an attempt to assassinate a diplomat in Britain in 1982. But 'Abu Nidal', who claimed 'credit' for the attempt, was under a PLO death sentence for two previous efforts to murder PLO chairman Yasser Arafat. Israel refused to distinguish between the PLO and its various offshoots and used the assassination attempt as a pretext for invading Lebanon, where the PLO was based, an invasion that was ultimately disastrous. The temptation to use events as a 'justification' that did not previously exist was probably an element in the Serbian and Iraqi cases too.

ORGANIZATIONS: FORMS, STRUCTURE AND MEMBERS

All of the organizations mentioned above had revolutionary aspirations. But other groups existed too. The most common supplemented government responses and were often more indiscriminate than the radical organizations were, except in the fourth wave. Russian police encouraged groups to organize Jewish pogroms, ostensibly because the terrorists had a Jewish component. The second-wave Secret Army Organization (OAS) of European settlers first struck Algerian Muslims and then France itself. The third wave produced the largest number of such groups, i.e. Protestant paramilitaries in Northern Ireland (Ulster Defence Association and Ulster Volunteer Force), Neo-Fascists in Italy (New Order and National Vanguard), Latin American 'death squads' in Argentina, Brazil, and Guatemala, the Turkish Grey Wolves and the Spanish Apostolic Anti-Communist Army. In the fourth wave Algerian 'death squads' and similar groups elsewhere appeared.

Western anarchists often acted alone; the pattern disappeared in the second wave but lone actors re-emerged in the fourth. Baruch Goldstein murdered 29 Muslims at Abraham's tomb in 1994. The Oklahoma City Bombing in 1995 was largely one person's work, and Christian racist elements even developed a 'Leaderless Resistance' doctrine.

The third wave produced many 'single issue' groups, concerned with abortion, animal rights, environmentalism, 'guest workers', etc. Often a lone individual was involved, i.e. the 'Unabomber' (Ted Kaczynski), a 1990s environmentalist.

Group sizes vary. Narodnaya Volya's underground striking force had 22 members and some 500 in supporting roles, a ratio roughly comparable to that of other formal underground organizations. In the second wave, the Irgun had 40 full-time members and more than 2,000 providing organizational support, and EOKA 100 terrorists and 3,000 supporters. Third-wave nationalist groups such as the IRA and ETA numbered between 200 and 400. Special circumstances account for groups that were too large to operate clandestinely. The Argentine chaos in 1974 enabled 1,500 Montoneros (MPM) to operate openly. The PLO in Lebanon numbered some 25,000; but no earlier organization could operate so freely or aimed to create a regular army. Al-Qa'ida trained perhaps 100,000, and more than 90% served as soldiers in various Taliban wars.

Russia was the origin of the organizational model for urban operations, where terrorists flourish best. It resembled a pyramid, containing cells with only four or five persons living together; larger numbers draw unwanted attention. Cells were sealed to limit police penetration. The central cell recruited all of the organization's members and selected targets. But these efforts to control cells made police penetration easier, which is why second- and third-wave organizations modified the pyramid to allow cells to recruit members and choose targets. One cell member had contact with a single individual in a cell above and below. But autonomous cells often made disastrous decisions. On their own initiative two Quebec Liberation Front cells kidnapped and murdered minister Pierre La Porte, creating a backlash that destroyed the organization in 1970.

The Irgun's organizational form was unusual. Most members lived with their families, assembling only after organizational leaders determined a target. The advantages were clear; greater numbers were available for strikes, and as weapons distributed at the assembly point were returned afterwards, members found it easier to live 'normal lives'.

Western anarchists rejected hierarchy and formal organization. Loose arrangements or networks enabled individuals to participate informally in associations. Afterwards they often struck alone, frequently overseas. Personal relationships sustained international bonds.

Al-Qa'ida's network is extraordinary. In its original form, the group was connected to some 30 autonomous entities dispersed over great distances, linked largely by electronic communications, sharing common purposes and training facilities. Afghan-trained members went abroad to perhaps 60 countries, prepared to wait for years in 'sleeper cells' for instructions. Because individuals did not live together, cells could have as many as 15 or 20 members. A cell was forbidden to contact other cells without instructions from the leadership. Major operations, planned by the leadership, were rehearsed several times in protected sanctuaries. Earlier organizations required less time between attacks.

Financing terrorist activity occurs in many ways. Bank robbing, though less significant in the second and fourth waves, has been the most common method. The third wave contributed forced donations, ransoms, protection rackets and drug rings, while the fourth added counterfeiting and fraudulent credit cards. Diaspora sources make crucial contributions, especially for self-determination causes. Foreign states always helped finance groups, but the practice became public only in the third wave, when in 1978 the Arab League pledged US $250m. annually to the PLO, funds used partly to establish the predominance of Arafat's Fatah in the Organization. Arab oil-producing states, particularly Libya, made separate contributions to the PLO and various other organizations, including the IRA. Islamic groups in Lebanon, Israel and Afghanistan received money from various states (Adams, 1986).

Investments combined with state and diaspora support made the PLO virtually self-sufficient in the early 1980s, but al-Qa'ida's financial resources were unmatched. Bin Laden's great personal wealth was a factor, but skilful management of investments and extensive diaspora involvement were more crucial. Never before had a terrorist group helped subsidize a state (Afghanistan) or so freely distributed money for projects to other terrorist groups. Money often transformed groups into ordinary criminal gangs, especially in the third wave (Baumann, 1977). The drugs trade gave Colombian groups a new identity.

Terrorist groups fragment frequently. When leaders leave, groups often split and may dissolve. Secrecy creates obstacles to assessing existing policies. Group unity is primarily negative; participants are clearer about what they are against than what they are for, a weakness that becomes exceptionally divisive when peace negotiations occur. Some elements continue fighting, thus hardening the negotiating group's willingness to compromise for fear of generating new splits; Israeli Prime Minister Rabin called peace-making a terror-producing process *par excellence*. Decisions on tactics also induce splits. Organizations fighting for the 'same' cause usually distinguish themselves from the other groups by special tactics.

No systematic study of the sociological character of members over time exists. Youth is the only common social trait. Few reach the age of 30. Attrition rates are very high. Persons attracted are at the peak of their physical strength, individuals with enormous enthusiasm, great hopes, little patience, and a willingness to take great risks.

Russian terrorist groups attracted members of the nobility and were largely middle-class university students, often involved in scientific and engineering studies. Over time their social composition diversified to approximate Russian society more as a whole, although some ethnic minorities, especially Jews and Poles, had disproportionate influence. Similar patterns appear in later groups, but the data is insufficient. The social profiles of leaders and followers in the Italian revolutionary and right-wing terrorist groups resemble those of left- and right-wing parliamentary parties (Weinberg and Eubank, 1989), but separatists (i.e. the Irish and Basques) normally are more deeply rooted in poorer classes.

The fourth wave in Islam represents all classes too. Some al-Qa'ida leaders, i.e. bin Laden and al-Zawahiri, come from the upper classes. Middle-class Egyptian university students with technological interests are highly represented, but when the ethnic dimension is important (as in Lebanon and Chechnya) the poor are more visible. Many al-Qa'ida recruits came directly from religious institutions, particularly mosques and *madrassas* (religious schools). Afghan training camps gave additional instruction in Islamic law, history, politics, and methods for preserving one's faith in the face of unbelievers.

DEMOCRATIC CONTEXT

Many believe that democratic contexts militate against terrorism, but history reveals something else. Rebel terrorism emerged as a new way to reach the ambiguous goals of the French Revolution after mass European insurrections collapsed in 1820, 1830, 1848 and 1871. A radically egalitarian reform programme inspired the first terrorist wave. The main theme in the next wave was national self-determination, a theme in every wave. The third-wave theme was that existing systems were not truly egalitarian. The religious wave seeks self-determination in a form an earlier time experienced.

Efficient oppressive states destroy the hope terrorists require. An anarchist attempt to assassinate Lenin in 1918 provoked savage repression, eliminating rebel terror for more than 75 years, and it returned only after non-violent resistance brought about the collapse of the Soviet Union and the beginning of its democratic experiments.

Terrorists must make their cause visible. Democracies maximize that opportunity; the public finds terrorist activity interesting and the media seeks to satisfy and even intensify that interest. For 16 days in July 1985, 65% of all American television news coverage concerned the TWA Flight 847 hijacking. In 1981–86 terrorism received more national television attention than poverty, unemployment and crime combined (Martin and Walcott, 1988)!

Terrorists' tactical success often depends upon turning the moral strength of their antagonists into political weakness. The special concern democracies show for the lives of their citizens, for example, makes them vulnerable to hostage-takers. After Iraq found that, unlike the USA, Iran would never negotiate for hostages no more were taken.

Particular issues that the French Revolution bequeathed are crucial for understanding modern terrorism. In separating the concept of the sovereign, 'the people' from the institutions designed to embody it, rebel claims to represent 'the people' are always conceivable and sometimes credible. The Revolution dreamed that refashioned social institutions could make a perfect world possible, a first- and third-wave theme. These themes sometimes create serious ambivalence, to the advantage of terrorists.

THE FUTURE

9/11 has stimulated deep anxieties about a 'new terrorism', anxieties that are unlikely to disappear soon even if no comparable event occurs and al-Qa'ida is destroyed. Apprehensions focus mostly on the potential use of WMD, particularly chemical and biological weapons. It is impossible to prove the negative, and al-Qa'ida has explicitly indicated its interest in such weapons. Deterrence, the chief restraint against states possessing WMD, has little value against invisible enemies. Still, Aum Shinrikyo has inspired no new effort yet, a fact that conflicts with the pronounced proclivities of terrorist groups to copy each other's new devices quickly. Aum failed despite enormous resources. Moreover, when chemical and biological weapons have been employed in wars, they have been ineffective. Finally, the weapons have been costly and difficult to use, factors that discourage terrorists (Simon, 1989; Rapoport, 2000). Extraordinary counter-terror budget increases materialized from 1994, doubling to a cumulative total of US $11,000m. before 9/11. Ironically, most of that money was meant to prepare for a WMD attack even though government and academic sources warned that the airlines were more vulnerable than they had been since the 1980s (Rapoport, 2001). When the 9/11 attack occurred, existing regulations permitted the hijackers to carry the weapons they used (knives).

An extraordinary coalition was organized to launch a 'war against every terrorist group of global reach'. But wars normally end with victories or negotiated settlements and neither seems possible here. A major problem is that the enemy has not been defined yet. Beyond al-Qa'ida and several intimately associated groups, who is the war being waged against?

This struggle requires international coalitions because so many terrorist groups exist in so many different countries. But different terrorist groups divide coalition members in different ways; can one coalition deal with the situations of the Kashmiri, Palestinian and Chechen terrorists? How will the coalition fare, if important, unexpected political events work again to produce a fifth wave of terror?

'Any nation', President Bush stated, 'that continues to harbor or support terrorism will be regarded as a hostile regime'. In the Afghan context that meant one thing. Subsequently, it meant something more troubling. An 'axis of evil' (comprising Iraq, North Korea and Iran) was identified, governments with WMD that they 'might' supply to terrorists, and therefore should be struck before they do. But not many in the original Afghan coalition supported the invasion of Iraq and their opposition seemed justified when the alleged weapons were not found; similar confusions will diminish subsequent coalitions. Beyond that, the divisions that have developed in Iraq since the invasion are generating serious domestic problems with implications that are not yet fully understood.

Dagger and Sarin: The Evolution of Terrorist Weapons and Tactics

ADAM DOLNIK AND ROHAN GUNARATNA

INTRODUCTION

As a violent activity by definition, terrorism involves the use of force through various types of violent means to pursue an ideological agenda. This essay will discuss the scope of terrorist tactics and the technologies as they have been used throughout history. Each tactic profile will provide a brief overview of the history and evolution of the particular terrorist tactic, the technology involved, as well as the identification of terrorist organizations among which the given tactic has been strikingly popular. Each section will also analyse the advantages that make a certain tactic or weapon attractive to the given organization.

PRIMITIVE ASSAULTS

For hundreds of years terrorists have used essentially very crude weaponry, with weapons such as the dagger, the noose or the torch being the terrorist instruments of choice. Historical examples include the Jewish *Sicarii* (Zealots) and the highly mythologized Shi'a Ismaili sect *Hashishin* (Assassins), both of which principally relied on a short dagger, or the Indian cult of Kali worshippers *Thuggees* (Thugs), who preferred to choke their victims to death with a noose. In these historical cases, the weapon selection had much to do with the fact that no other weapons were available. However, even in today's age of nuclear weapons and satellite technology, certain terror organizations still deliberately prefer very primitive modes of attack—this time not out of a lack of better options but mainly because of the distinct strategic advantages such methods offer. First, crude weaponry can help the given group in terms of emphasizing the disproportionate and desperate nature of the respective struggle, which aids the organization in reiterating and politically exploiting the image of an underdog. Second, crude tactics such as throat slashing or hacking the victim to death with a machete have the power of augmenting the horror value associated with the attack. While several centuries ago edged weapons did not have this characteristic since they were the norm, in the age of modern and remotely operated weapons, getting one's 'hands dirty' by killing someone from close proximity carries a curious stigma of extreme and unnecessary brutality. So, while modern technologies have made killing psychologically easier due to the ability of the perpetrator to kill his or her victims from a distance and thus decreased the danger of a last-moment change of mind due to 'looking into the eye' of the victim, some terrorist groups have intentionally killed from close quarters with edged weapons in order to manifest their superior resolve and desensitization to the suffering of their victims. Al-Qa'ida in Iraq, as well as a number of groups in Algeria, Tajikistan, Abkhazia, Chechnya, Pakistan, Iraq and Central Africa, has relied on such tactics, with some groups resorting to recording ritualistic beheadings and sending the tapes to the media.

Another primitive terrorist tactic has been arson attacks, which are often overlooked despite the fact that they account for roughly a quarter of all terrorist violence. While relatively sophisticated incendiary devices have on occasion been used, most arson attacks have employed only a very crude methodology. And yet, such attacks have sometimes been extraordinarily destructive. For instance, the third deadliest terrorist attack prior to 9/11 was the burning of a cinema in Iran in 1978 which killed 442 people. Similarly, the most destructive attack on American soil in terms of property damage other than the World Trade Center bombing, the Oklahoma City bombing and 9/11 was the series of fires lit by the Earth Liberation Front at the busiest US ski resort in Vail, Colorado. Just like knifings, arsons have also been a traditional terrorist tactic for centuries. The advantages that they bring to today's terror groups include the deniability element associated with the fact that fires can occur naturally, allowing the perpetrators to forgo credit if they wish to do so. In addition, the natural characteristic of fires makes arson attacks specifically attractive to ecoterrorist groups, to whom fire represents a natural way for the 'Mother Earth' to fight back against 'inconsiderate civilization'. This type of symbolism is not, of course, unique to ecoterrorists. The origin of the beheading practice mentioned earlier can also be traced to the literal interpretation of Allah's statement: 'When you encounter those [infidels] who deny [the Truth = Islam] then strike [their] necks.' While this quote is certainly taken out of context when used to support the contemporary practice of beheading, for groups like Zarqawi's Jama'at at-Tawhid wal-Jihad, whose logo depicts a *mujaheed* holding a blood-soaked sword, it certainly represents a strict observance of the Koran in the purest sense. Interestingly, the slitting of throats has also been practised by non-Islamist groups, such as Sendero Luminoso (Shining Path), for punishment purposes. Here again a symbolic element was present, this time, however, rooted in Andean mysticism, where a person who is killed in this way cannot be saved because his or her soul cannot escape from the mouth.

Overall, while primitive tactics and weaponry have in the past been largely a product of necessity or lack of a better option, today's terrorist organizations often use such methods deliberately as a strategic choice or for the symbolic or expressive value they carry. The key lesson here is that a group's reliance on primitive weaponry does not necessarily translate into a lack of operational capability to use more modern means.

FIREARMS

The dominance of primitive weapons as the principal terror tool remained unchallenged until the assassination in 1584 of William of Nassau, the Prince of Orange, who became the first ever political figure to be assassinated by a firearm. Fascinatingly, not until the assassination in 1792 of Gustav III Adolf, the King of Sweden, was a firearm successfully used again as an assassination weapon. This more than 200-year gap has yet to be adequately explained, but it is likely that the unreliability and the unfavourable physical characteristics of 16th-century firearms played a significant role. The firearms of today have of course become more efficient, with increased rate of fire, accuracy, range, and reliability, and significantly reduced size and weight. Due to the proliferation of state-sponsored terrorism following the Second World War, many conventional infantry weapons became part of terrorist arsenals. The Soviet-made AK-47 rifle in particular has been a popular terrorist weapon, as have the American-made M-16 rifle, the VZ-58 rifle that was employed by the Japanese Red Army (JRA) during their attack at the Israeli Lod Airport in 1972, and the VZ-61 automatic pistol (Skorpion) that was used by the Red Brigades to murder former Italian Prime Minister Aldo Moro in 1978.

Other assault weapons that have been exploited for terrorist purposes are sub-machine guns, with popular models including the Heckler & Koch MP-5, favoured by the Red Army Faction (RAF), and the M1 Thompson sub-machine gun, which was cherished by the Irish Republican Army (IRA) even after it had become obsolete. But while relying on obsolete weapons in some instances, the IRA has also been able to obtain high-performance firearms, such as the highly regarded Barrett Light .50-calibre sniper rifle with which the South Armagh Brigade killed at least 10 soldiers and members of the Royal Ulster Constabulary in 1992–97 by using one-shot snipers firing from a mobile platform. And even though the IRA never exploited this gun to its full potential, firing the 2,000-m-range weapon from a maximum of 150 m, the fact that a terrorist organization possessed a rifle that has the ability to attack aircraft or penetrate concrete or armoured vehicles, was highly disturbing. In addition to innovations pertaining to firearms design, terrorists have also kept abreast of advances in accessories, such as better sighting systems or silencers, which were used for the first time in 1979 in the attempted assassination of two Palestine Liberation Organization (PLO) officials in Cyprus. Another example is terrorists' acquisition of Teflon-coated bullets capable of penetrating body armour, several of which were recovered from a Weather Underground hide-out as long ago as 1984.

With regard to the tactical use of small arms, shootings account for roughly 13% of all terrorist violence. These have included highly focused assassinations of individuals and sniper attacks against soldiers and civilians, such as the incident in 2002 in which a highly trained Tanzim sniper methodically killed 10 Israel Defence Force (IDF) soldiers and civilians at a West Bank checkpoint, afterwards holding the police down for more than an hour before escaping. Other firearms attacks have included small- to medium-scale roadside ambushes and suicidal shooting sprees in which the objective is to kill as many people as possible before the attackers' own elimination. Examples of such operations include attacks on airports, beaches, synagogues and Jewish settlements by groups associated with the Palestinian cause, occasional attacks on Muslim places of worship by Jewish terrorists, typically dressed in reservist uniform and using IDF-issued M-16s, and numerous *fedayeen* operations carried out in India by Lashkar-e-Taiba (LeT) and Jaish-e-Mohammed (JeM). Another variation of high-fatality shooting attacks have been summary executions—popular especially among Sikh and Tamil terrorists in the 1980s. Such operations usually involved the stopping of a bus and the separation of passengers, after which individuals associated with the enemy nationality, ethnicity or religion were killed. Overall, shooting attacks have enjoyed a more-or-less constant rate of popularity over the last 40 years, a trend that appears to correspond with the limited advances in firearms development that have occurred in that period.

STAND-OFF WEAPONRY

In the category of stand-off weaponry, terrorists have used a wide array of home-made rockets, anti-tank weapons, mortars, and even surface-to-air missiles. One of the first instances in which a stand-off weapon was used for terrorist purposes was the firing in 1964 of a bazooka-type rocket shell triggered by an automatic timing device across the East River in New York by anti-Castro Cubans, who claimed to have deliberately missed their target by about 200 yards in order to divert public attention from the address by Ernesto 'Che' Guevara at the UN General Assembly. Since then, the most significant development in improvised rocket attacks has been the introduction of new safety features and, above all, the increased range of the devices. For instance, while the Chukaku-ha surprised observers in the mid-1980s by constructing home-made rockets with a range of 3.2 km, the latest generation of HAMAS' *al-Qassam* rockets has already reached an estimated range of up to 12 km. For HAMAS in particular this advance is crucial, as a 12-km range gives the group the capability to attack Israeli territory from way beyond the Green Line, thus providing sufficient time for the perpetrators to escape undetected. As this example shows, rockets and mortars have been attractive to terrorists mainly because of the safety factor associated with the fact that they can be fired from afar by timing and solar devices or by remote control. However, rockets and mortars have not been very successful in inflicting large numbers of casualties due mainly to their limited ability to carry large warheads and their generally low level of accuracy. Nevertheless, some attacks in this category have resulted in spectacular operations, such as the mortar attack carried out in 1991 by the Provisional Irish Republican Army (PIRA) on 10 Downing St in London, which came within 5 m of killing the members of the Tory War Cabinet. A similar assessment of advantages and disadvantages can be made for rocket-propelled grenades (RPGs), the traditional unguided anti-tank weapon which has been used extensively by terrorists to attack foreign embassies in countries such as El Salvador, Honduras, Lebanon, Sri Lanka and Afghanistan. In addition to guerrilla struggles, RPGs have been used in urban campaigns for assassination purposes, as in the assassination by the RAF in 1981 of Gen. Kroesen. Another occasional use of RPGs has been associated with unsuccessful efforts to bring down civilian airliners during take-off or landing, such as the attempt in 1975 by the Popular Front for the Liberation of Palestine

(PFLP) to bring down an El Al 707 at France's Orly airport. Much more dangerous for civilian aircraft, however, have been surface-to-air missiles (SAMs), such as the American *Stinger*, the British *Blowpipe* or the Russian SA-7 *'Grail'*. These shoulder-fired weapons are equipped with a chemically cooled seeker that hunts heat sources, independently guiding the missile to its target after it has been fired. The first recorded instance of a terrorist plan to use SAMs against civil aviation was revealed via the arrest in 1973 of an Arab terrorist in possession of two SA-7 missiles in Italy. Since then, SAMs have been used on dozens of occasions by groups in Afghanistan, Sudan, Georgia, Angola, Sri Lanka, Saudi Arabia, Chechnya, Rhodesia and Kenya. Attractive features of the SAM, in addition to its 'fire-and-forget' guidance capability, include its portability and ease of operation by a single person. On the other hand, SAMs are expensive to train with and not so easy to use effectively against civil aviation as is commonly believed.

HOSTAGE INCIDENTS

Terrorists have historically utilized three types of hostage-taking: barricade hostage attacks, kidnappings, and air/land/sea hijackings. The major difference between them is that in barricade incidents the hostage-takers are surrounded in an enclosed area, while in kidnappings the location of the hostages and their captors is unknown. Hijackings combine the first two scenarios, in the sense that the capture of a vehicle—especially an airplane—provides the terrorists with a mobile platform. In all of these scenarios, the key objective of the incident is the creation of an exchangeable 'good', by taking and threatening the lives of hostages, that can be traded for the attainment of terrorist demands. These demands have most frequently involved the release of imprisoned comrades, alteration of government policies, the guarantee of free passage, and money. In some cases, however, terrorists have also demanded specific concessions, such as the increase of hourly wages in a particular factory or investment in an impoverished region.

With the first recorded incident dating back to biblical times, kidnapping is by far the most frequently used type of hostage-taking. This has become especially true since the end of the Cold War, when many organizations with a political agenda were forced to adapt to self-financing, and kidnapping for ransom became a major source of income. As a result, reported kidnappings world-wide have risen by 70% over the last 15 years, even though most of these incidents are attributable to purely criminal elements without a political agenda. Generally speaking, most kidnappings occur in areas where a given group has a large presence, making the task of transporting the victim to an unknown location less challenging. This has been the case especially in Lebanon, Yemen, Colombia, Kashmir, Angola and Chechnya. In some cases (in, for example, Israel, Québec (Canada) and Italy), however, terrorists have succeeded in kidnapping and detaining high-profile victims in urban environments. A disturbing trend, besides the rising overall number of international kidnappings, has been their increased sophistication. Kidnappers often use disguise and research the financial capabilities of the victims by studying their bank information and tax returns. The Revolutionary Armed Forces of Colombia (FARC) even have a database of Colombian millionaires against which they check all of the victims captured at roadblocks. In some cases the kidnappers have even resorted to state-of-the-art technology such as global positioning systems (GPS) and equipment to check the authenticity of ransom money.

Kidnappings are an attractive option to terrorist groups as they are a comparatively low-risk operation—resuce operations are impossible until the location of the victims and the terrorists has been established, and even then they are enormously challenging if the hostages are held in a terrorist stronghold. However, a small number of cases excepted, kidnappings are comparatively low-profile operations, owing to the absence of television cameras where hostages are being held and a consequent lack of media appeal. In contrast to kidnappings, terrorist barricade hostage-taking and hijacking incidents have been much less frequent, but considerably more spectacular. Live broadcasts, minute-by-minute updates, dramatic scenes featuring hostage pleas and terrorist threats, and the possibility of the immediate forceful resolution of the incident maintain viewers' interest. Moreover, close-up coverage, the opportunity for terrorists to fully explain their motives, and the possible imminence of a rescue operation, are factors that usually succeed in generating wide public debate about the moral pros and cons of options available to governments. Further, barricade hostage-taking and hijacking incidents do not usually last long enough for the public to become unreceptive to the message that is being conveyed to them by the terrorists. From this perspective, barricade hostage-taking incidents probably provide better advertisement and propaganda benefits than any other terror tactic, which is the main reason why the majority of historically ground-breaking terrorist events have involved this component. However, barricade hostage-taking and hijacking are high-risk operations in which the outcome is never certain and the safety of the hostage-takers is under constant threat—only the reluctance to risk the lives of the hostages prevents security forces from storming the location and killing the terrorists.

The third type of hostage incident which deserves attention is skyjacking. The first recorded incident occurred in Peru in 1931, when an American airplane was hijacked with the aim of forcing the pilot to fly over Lima to distribute propaganda leaflets. Since this incident, skyjackings have gained considerable prominence as a terrorist tactic. Contrary to popular perception, however, the absolute majority of hijackings throughout history have been carried out by refugees and mentally disturbed individuals, as opposed to terrorists. Skyjacking as a tactic carries many of the advantages of barricade hostage-taking, with several additional benefits. First, the ability of hijackers to relocate from the site where they are surrounded by security forces to a friendly territory due to occupying a mobile platform. Second, the hijacking of an airplane was until recently achievable with a minimum amount of force—successful hijack weapons have included items such as razor blades, coloured water, sharpened toothbrushes, colon bottles, ropes, dining knives and cigarette lighters. Since an airplane at a high altitude can easily be crashed killing everyone on board, gaining control of it gives terrorists' threats considerable credibility. Furthermore, the fact that the aircraft is at a height of several thousand metres eliminates the need for concern regarding hostage escapes or the threat of a rescue mission. However, the flying aircraft needs periodical refuelling, which can effectively be refused by denying landing rights via the blockage of runways. This is why skyjacking requires a greater determination to kill and die during the incident then any other type of hostage event.

Overall, hostage-taking events have evidenced several concurring trends, among them a continual decrease in skyjackings and barricade hostage-taking incidents, and a rapidly increasing number of international kidnappings. A further decline in the number of successful skyjacking attempts can be expected in light of the 9/11 hijackings, which have rapidly altered the way passengers think about their safety during such incidents. Unlike in the past, when official guide-lines insisted that hostages should remain calm, comply with the terrorists' instructions, and wait for their freedom to be negotiated, prospective hostages on hijacked flights post-9/11 are likely to perceive their chances of survival as slim, and are thus more likely to attempt to overpower hijackers than in the past.

SABOTAGE

Another tactic occasionally used by terrorists is sabotage, which constitutes mainly a minor supplement to larger guerrilla campaigns. An exception to this rule seems to be single-issue groups in North America, specifically anti-abortion, animal rights and environmentalist groups, which rely on sabotage as their main means of attack. While anti-abortion organizations such as the Army of God have occasionally killed doctors, their preferred mode of attack has been to release butyric acid—a chemical producing a long-lasting noxious smell—into abortion clinics and Planned Parenthood offices in order to cause a temporary shutdown; or to send letters containing a white powder and the word 'anthrax' to such institutions in order to cause panic and denial of services. Similarly, environmentalist groups such as the Earth Liberation Front have also used the destruction of property as their main tactic, one example being the Colorado arson attack mentioned above, or the contamination of the products of companies such as Nestlé or Mars. Likewise, members of radical groups such as Earth First! or Hardesty Avengers have used the sabotage method of 'monkey wrenching', which involves driving long metal spikes into trees scheduled for harvesting with the intention of deterring lumberjacks from doing their job. After timber companies attempted to counter this tactic by using metal detectors to locate the spikes, certain groups responded by using ceramic or stone nails instead.

The benefits of using sabotage for single-issue groups are clear. Sabotaging companies or facilities not only brings the issue in question to the attention of the uninformed public, but, above all, also damages the interests of the adversary. Sabotage also provides a discriminate way for single-issue groups to target the guilty party, without necessarily alienating the public, as with killing. Sabotage has also been popular with separatist or left-wing guerrilla groups such as the Liberation Tigers of Tamil Eelam (LTTE), the early PLO, the Chechen groups, the FARC, Shining Path, and the Partiya Karkeran Kurdistan (PKK—Kurdish Workers' Party), among others. For such organizations, sabotage serves as an excellent way of weakening the opposing government in the eyes of the general public. Despite the fact that the inconvenience caused by the given attack was perpetrated by the terrorists, the general population usually blames the government for its inability to maintain order. To such a frustrated populace, terrorist propaganda, which is typically based on a negative portrayal of the authorities, gains in credibility and prominence. The end result in many cases has been increased popular support for the insurgency.

Guerrilla sabotage tactics can be divided into three main categories. The first category is mechanical sabotage, such as blackouts caused by blowing up electrical pylons and cutting wires, or blowing up oil pipelines in order to damage foreign investments. Further examples of mechanical sabotage include the derailment of trains, as carried out by groups such as LTTE and Babbar Khalsa, or the contamination of products for export—Israeli fruit was poisoned three times by PLO terrorists in 1977–79, causing a decline of 40% in Israeli fruit exports and substantial economic losses. Similar albeit less successful campaigns were waged in the subsequent two decades in countries such as South Africa, Chile and the United Kingdom. The final type of sabotage is so-called cyberterrorism, which despite the chilling scenarios depicted in the media over the last decade, remains a tool more frequently used by criminals and over-enthusiastic hackers than by groups with a political agenda. And even though many terrorist groups have shown that their operatives are competent in using information technology for communication purposes and operational planning, instances of cybersabotage carried out by terrorist groups have been extremely rare, possibly due to the reduced level of gratification associated with an indirect form of attack. One of the first (alleged) instances of cyberterrorism was the dissemination in 1988 of a data-destroying computer virus at the Hebrew University in Jerusalem. The most significant case was the 'suicide e-mail bombings' carried out by the Internet Black Tigers, a faction of the LTTE, which consisted of inundating the e-mail accounts of Sri Lanka's embassies in Seoul (South Korea), Washington, DC, and Ottawa (Canada) with junk e-mail.

BOMBINGS

Since bombings account for roughly one-half of all terrorist violence, explosives have been by far the most important type of weapon in the arsenals of terrorist groups. The first recorded attempt to use explosives in an act of political violence perpetrated by a non-state actor was the Guy Fawkes Gunpowder Plot of 1605 that targeted the British Parliament. The next bomb plot—an attempt by French royalists to kill Napoléon Bonaparte—did not occur until 1800, again leaving a curious gap of 195 years, similar to that in the use of firearms. The low frequency of the use of explosives for terrorist purposes changed rapidly with the invention of dynamite in 1867. The Irish Fenian Brotherhood and Clan na Gael were the first terrorist organizations to use dynamite, quickly followed by the Russian Narodnaya Volya and by the transnational anarchists. Later, the increased manufacture of TNT during and after the First World War, together with increased attention to the development of plastic explosives, such as PETN, RDX, C4 and Semtex, significantly increased the size and potency of terrorist arsenals. Semtex in particular became a favourite plastic explosive of terrorists after Libya made huge quantities of it available to various revolutionary movements world-wide. The incident that made Semtex infamous was the mid-air bombing, in 1988, of Pan Am Flight 103 over Lockerbie, Scotland, in which less than one-half pound of the explosive hidden in a tape-recorder destroyed the aircraft, killing all 259 passengers on board and 11 people on the ground. Besides obtaining explosives from state sponsors or through theft, terrorists have also repeatedly demonstrated their ability to manufacture their own explosive devices from readily available materials. For instance, only legitimate precursors are needed to make triacetone triperoxide (TATP), a volatile explosive that has frequently been used by HAMAS in the Israeli Occupied Territories of the West Bank and the Gaza Strip. TATP was also used in bombings carried out on the London Underground in July 2005. Similarly, ammonium nitrate—commonly used in fertilizers—and fuel oil (ANFO) mixture has been used in a number of highly destructive terrorist incidents, including the 1995 Oklahoma City bombing which killed 169 people. Overall, the Improvised Explosive Devices (IEDs) most commonly employed by terrorists have been quite simple, using standard commercial or military explosives, or, alternatively, improvised blasting agents made from legally obtainable precursors by following widely available traditional recipes.

Tactically, terrorist bombings can be divided into several categories. By far the most common has been land-based bombings. These have ranged from the detonation of simple devices such as the Molotov cocktails and improvised hand grenades popular with various revolutionary movements to the limpet mines frequently used by the African National Congress (ANC); the letter bombs of Black September, the IRA, the PFLP—General Command and various individual serial bombers; the pressure cooker and propane gas canister bombs of the FARC and the Groupe islamique armé (GIA—Armed Islamic Group); the suicide body suits popular with LTTE, HAMAS and Palestinian Islamic Jihad (PIJ); and to car bombs preferred by groups such as the IRA and Euzkadi Ta Askatasuna (ETA—Basque Fatherland and Liberty). The most destructive land bombing attacks, however, have utilized large explosive charges loaded onto trucks and detonated by remote control or by a suicide bomber, such as those frequently used by virtually all the warring factions in the Lebanese civil war, or the LTTE and al-Qa'ida's associate and affiliate groups today. Trucks are an attractive method of delivering the explosive to the site of the attack, not only because they can carry large quantities of it, but also because they can easily be converted into a shaped charge in order to concentrate the blast effect in a particular area.

Air-based bombings—the next category—have most frequently involved mid-air explosions on commercial airliners, attractive for their especially favourable cost-per-casualty ratio. To date, at least 70 such attacks have taken place, in most cases involving explosive devices brought on board the aircraft by passengers who disembarked at a transfer stop leaving the explosive behind to be detonated by a timer. Alternatively, devices have been smuggled on board using mules, in most cases young women transporting items of luggage for their Middle Eastern boyfriends who had promised to join them later. A less frequent means of attack has included suicide bombers, although there are only three examples of such attacks having been carried out by terrorists. Another alternative has been the posting of explosive devices via air mail in order to circumvent screening procedures, using a barometric pressure activator for detonation at a given altitude. Another form of air-based bombing has involved the dropping of explosive devices from small aircraft onto a given target. The first of three such incidents occurred in 1963, in Cuba, where the Cuban Freedom Fighters unsuccessfully attempted to bomb oil refineries in the vicinity of Havana by dropping a 100 pound bomb and several smaller ones from a small plane. Two similarly unsuccessful attempts were carried out by the IRA in 1974. Finally, aircraft have been flown into buildings in order to cause destruction. This tactic, of course, achieved notoriety only after 9/11, but it must be emphasized that while the planning and execution of that attack were impeccable, the idea itself is far from new. Between 1973 and 2001, the plan of flying airplanes into buildings was a part of at least 22 different plots, two of which were carried out. The first incident took place in 1976 when a Japanese pornographic film actor crashed his Piper Cherokee aircraft into the home of Yoshio Kodama, a right-wing political figure accused of accepting 'pay-offs' from the Lockheed Aircraft Corporation. The pilot wore a kamikaze pilot's headband and shouted a ritual cry over the radio prior to crashing into his target. The second occurred in the USA in 1994, when a heavily intoxicated and suicidal individual crashed a stolen Cessna 150 aircraft onto the South Lawn at the rear of the west wing of the White House.

The last bombing category consists of maritime bombings. The idea dates back as far as the 1870s, when the Fenian Brotherhood invested more than US $20,000 in the construction of the 'Fenian Ram', a submarine designed to attack British ships in harbours. Other sea-based schemes have included the planting of explosives on board ships, such as the incident in 1975 in which the Montoneros sank a $70m.-Argentine naval destroyer under construction in Buenos Aires by planting a powerful bomb in the engine room. An alternative approach has been the attachment of explosives beneath the ship's water-line by frogmen, as in the bombing of a Spanish Navy destroyer by ETA in 1981 and the bombing in 1980 of a Libyan gunboat anchored in Genoa, Italy, by the Maltese Liberation Front. The final and most destructive form of maritime bombing has been sea suicide bombings. Pioneered and perfected by the LTTE in Sri Lanka, this tactic gained notoriety after the bombing in 2000 of the USS *Cole* off the coast of Yemen, in which two al-Qa'ida-linked terrorists rammed a customized fibreglass boat packed with lightweight C4 explosive into the side of the ship, killing 17 soldiers and causing more than $240m.-worth of damage. Two years later PIJ became the third organization to use the tactic when two suicide bombers detonated explosives in their fishing boat after pulling alongside an Israeli patrol boat in Gaza, injuring four soldiers.

Bombing has several distinct advantages. First, whether detonated by a long fuse, a timer or remote control, explosives enable terrorists to carry out attacks without being present at the point of detonation. This makes bombing a relatively safe tactic with regard to the threat of capture, but it also makes it psychologically easier to kill, because the perpetrator does not need to witness the potentially traumatizing death of the victims. Second, explosives instil great fear, not only by the level of destruction they cause, but also by the imposing sound effect associated with a blast. In this sense, an explosion can also be viewed as an act that symbolizes the channelling of the bombers' internal rage. Probably for this reason, some psychologists have equated the preceding tension followed by a dramatic release of energy in the explosion to the physical and psychological processes accompanying a sexual act. The final advantage of bombing is its cost-effectiveness and the fact that many powerful explosive mixtures can be assembled with very little previous knowledge out of ordinary household products.

SUICIDE BOMBINGS

Suicide bombings have been separated into a distinct category, mainly because they have in recent years become the ultimate terrorist tactic. Since its commencement some 25 years ago, the phenomenon has spread around the world at an unprecedented pace—at the time of writing, in 2005, there have been more than 600 suicide bombings carried out by 26 organizations in 28 different countries. Another reason why suicide bombings deserve special attention is the fact that they represent one of the deadliest terror tactics: more than 70% of the 30 most lethal attacks carried out since 1990 have involved suicide delivery. The first modern suicide bombing by a terrorist group occurred in 1951, when a young communist suicide volunteer assassinated French Brig.-Gen. Charles Marie Chanson in Sadec, French Indochina (now Viet Nam), by detonating a grenade in his pocket. The current wave, however, was triggered only after the suicide truck bombing in 1981 of the Iraqi Embassy in Beirut, Lebanon, by a member of al-Dawa, which killed 61 people and injured more than 100 others. Over the next 10 years suicide bombings gained notoriety, mainly through high-profile operations carried out by the Lebanese Hezbollah, such as the synchronized bombings in 1983 of the US Marine camp and the French troops' barracks in Beirut, and two attacks on the American embassies in the same city. The striking effectiveness of the tactic resulted in its spread throughout Lebanon, where it was employed by a number of secular, pro-Syrian groups. Furthermore, Hezbollah also facilitated the introduction of suicide bombings into Israel in 1993 by training HAMAS bomb-makers. A similar role can be ascribed to al-Qa'ida, which used suicide bombers for the first time in 1998 in attacks on the US embassies in Kenya and Tanzania. Since then, suicide bombing has not only become the principal al-Qa'ida tactic, but the group has also been instrumental in facilitating its adoption by groups in Pakistan, Afghanistan, Yemen, the Philippines, Saudi Arabia, Turkey, Indonesia, Morocco, Tunisia, Chechnya, Qatar, Iraq and the United Kingdom. This list is likely to expand in the future. Of all the groups that have used suicide bombings, however, the often overlooked LTTE has been the true master of the tactic. Not only did the LTTE carry out more suicide bombings than any other organization, but it also pioneered many innovations in its use, such as sea-based and air-based suicide attacks, and suicide truck convoys. Moreover, the LTTE demonstrated an unparalleled level of organizational sophistication and patience, illustrated by the assassination of President Premadasa of Sri Lanka, whose assassin first infiltrated the President's household and became acquainted with a valet before carrying out the act. Similarly, the bomber who blew up the Independence Memorial Hall building in 1995 with a bomb placed on a coconut cart had been selling coconuts in Colombo for three years prior to the attack.

Suicide bombings have become the fastest spreading terrorist tactic for several reasons. The first obvious benefit of a suicide operation is its tactical advantage over other forms of attack. A suicide bomber can target places that would be difficult to attack successfully by someone hoping to stay alive. The fact that the bomber also has the capability of selecting the location, time, and exact circumstances of the attack explains the remarkable effectiveness of suicide operations in terms of delivering a high number of casualties. Suicide attacks are also attractive to terrorist organizations because they eliminate the need to plan an escape route, and they remove the danger of capture and subsequent interrogation of the terrorist. Possibly even more important than the tactical advantage, however, is the threefold message suicide operations convey. First, the fact that the bomber is willing to sacrifice him- or herself sends a strong message to the enemy population that the group cannot be deterred, as it values victory more than life. The general population perceives that neither military nor police measures, but only acquiescence in the group's demands, can stop further attacks. Second, the apparent irrationality and incomprehensible nature of the attack can have a legitimizing effect on the terrorists' cause for some segments of the international community. As people around the world try fruitlessly to comprehend the motivations of such an act, they are left wondering about the systemic foundations of the enormous dedication and hatred demonstrated by the bomber. The image of the group becomes that of committed believers who will do anything to reach their goals, also implying that the present circumstances are so humiliating that death is preferable to life. And, finally, the message conveyed by suicide operations is also directed inwards. An act of self-sacrifice in the name of an organization's cause is a uniting factor. Overt praise of the martyr's accomplishment by prominent members of the group can also increase the self-sense of group prestige and inspire future volunteers. The willingness to die for a cause is sometimes also used as evidence of the superiority of a group's members over its adversaries, who are portrayed as pleasure-seekers who, in spite of their military dominance, are essentially weak. The resulting perception among the group is that, owing to superior determination, their final victory is inevitable.

From a tactical perspective, suicide bombings have recently evidenced a number of important trends. First, the increasing internationalization of the phenomenon, not just in the sense that it has spread to other countries, but also that terrorist organizations have demonstrated an increasing ability to mount suicide operations outside of their common theatres of operation. Another trend has been the increasing synchronization of suicide bombings, with the clear intention of causing as many casualties as possible. In some instances, suicide bombings have involved secondary and even tertiary devices, the delayed detonation of which has been calculated to target first-responders and crowds of onlookers. Another recent innovation has been the addition of chemical, biological, radiological and nuclear materials into explosive devices used in Israel, where traces of pesticide and even cyanide have been detected on the remains of at least six bombs used in HAMAS suicide attacks. In addition, attacks against hard targets such as embassies have recently employed suicide truck convoys and suicide gunmen or bombers whose role is to clear the way for the suicide truck. Another trend has been the incorporation of insurance detonation mechanisms for bombs carried by suicide bombers on foot by the inclusion of a remote detonation option, and the global spread of female suicide terrorism. Overall, suicide bombings world-wide have displayed an increasing level of organization, planning, patience, synchronized execution, and lethality.

CHEMICAL, BIOLOGICAL, RADIOLOGICAL AND NUCLEAR AGENTS (CBRN)

Another tactic that has been employed to a limited extent by terrorist groups has been the use of chemical, biological and radiological agents. However, regardless of the grim scenarios that have been forecast in recent years, terrorists have not utilized such technology to the extent predicted. One of the first incidents of chemical terrorism after the Second World War was the poisoning, in 1946, of bread consigned to the US prisoner-of-war camp near Nuremburg by a group of Jewish terrorists called Avenging Israel's Blood (DIN). The attacks, in which arsenic mixed with glue was smeared on the bottom of 2,500–3,000 loaves of bread, succeeded in hospitalizing 207 former German Schutzstaffel (SS) officers, but failed to kill a single person. Another noteworthy attempt was the unsuccessful plot in 1986 by the apocalyptic white Christian supremacist group calling itself the Covenant, Sword and Arm of the Lord (CSA) to poison the water supply of several large American cities with only 30 gallons of cyanide. The next form of CBRN terrorism includes biological agents. The first notable incident in this category was the unsuccessful plot in 1972 by a small environmentalist cult calling itself R.I.S.E. to culture large quantities of *salmonella typhi* in order to contaminate the water supply of several large cities. The first successful bio-terrorist attack occurred in 1984 in Oregon, USA, when members of the

Rajneeshee cult infected the salad bars of several restaurants with *salmonella enterica* with the aim of influencing participation in a local election. All of the incidents described above fall into the category of crudely delivered, low-level attacks that have utilized primitive agents, such as potassium cyanide, arsenic, salmonella, various pesticides, rat poisons and other dual-use items. These attacks have been comparatively ineffective in causing large numbers of casualties, but have had a disproportionate psychological impact. Nevertheless, more potent unconventional agents have only rarely been used by terrorists. In fact, only two groups—Aum Shinrikyo in Japan and unknown anthrax letter mailer(s)—have ever killed anyone by resorting to a chemical warfare agent, and even then the number of fatalities was limited. The most significant example was the activities of Aum Shinrikyo, the apocalyptic Japanese cult that shocked the world in 1995 with its sarin attack on the Tokyo subway system, in which 12 people died and 1,039 were injured. But, even though the group possessed an estimated US $1,000m. in assets, had at its disposal 26 university-trained chemists and microbiologists working in leading research facilities, and had the freedom to conduct virtually unlimited experiments, its chemical and biological activities essentially failed. After investing some $30m. in obtaining the highly toxic nerve agent *sarin*, Aum Shinrikyo killed only 12 people in its most successful attack—a number that pales when compared with the 192 persons who died in the 2003 suicide attack on the Seoul subway, which was executed by a mentally disturbed individual who used technology requiring investment of only about $3 in a paper milk container filled with gasoline and a cigarette lighter. This example shows that the cost-benefit ratio in terms of killing potential does not necessarily lie on the side of CBRN agents, as is commonly believed.

Still, CBRN agents can be attractive to terrorist groups for several reasons. First, the acquisition of biological, chemical and radiological materials is relatively unchallenging due to the dual-use nature of many precursor chemicals and agents. Biological materials, in particular, can be very advantageous due to the ease of their procurement, which allows a potential perpetrator to start with only a small amount of the agent in order to obtain large quantities. The next possible advantage is the prestige element involved in using exotic weaponry, which would gain for the perpetrator disproportionately high public attention. Finally, possibly the greatest advantage of using CBRN agents is their psychological impact on the population. The fact that virtually any toxic agent discovered in the possession of terrorists is publicly mislabelled as a 'weapon of mass destruction' (WMD) often leads to an unparalleled level of largely unwarranted panic among the public. However, the use of CBRN materials as a terror tool also has many significant disadvantages. First, the almost universal perception of WMD as supremely immoral and inhumane makes this option unattractive for the majority of politically ambitious terror groups for reasons of image. Second, procuring and handling toxic substances is highly dangerous and requires a comparatively high level of expertise to be conducted safely. Third, while the acquisition of many agents is simple and relatively inexpensive, the same cannot be said with regard to their mass-casualty-capable weaponization. As the example of Aum Shinrikyo demonstrates, even an organization with unparalleled resources was unable to develop delivery systems that were effective enough to produce mass casualties in any of more than a dozen attacks with chemical and biological agents, despite an unquestionable intent to do so.

CONCLUSION

One of the most striking trends in terrorism has been its increasing lethality. Some of the commonly cited explanations of this include terrorists' constant quest for attention, the increased prevalence of state sponsorship, the proliferation of terrorist groups motivated by a religious imperative, and also developments in terrorist weaponry and the increasing sophistication of professional terrorism. However, as we have seen throughout this essay, the scope of terrorist tactics and technologies is relatively limited and remarkably unchanging. In fact, surveying the last 50 years of terrorist operations case by case reveals very few incidents that strike the observer as creative in any way. The main advances have included incremental innovation, in the sense that terrorists have arguably improved their use of the traditional tactics and technologies already available to them. Additional points of incremental innovation have included the increased range of home-made artillery, miniaturization and improvements in remote detonation systems for explosive devices, and the greater incorporation of dual-use technologies, such as the internet, mobile phones, computers, radar detectors, encryption software and GPS into terrorist operations at the planning and execution phases. Another important trend has involved the synchronization of attacks and the incorporation of various tactics into a single operation. A somewhat surprising emerging trend may be the increased emphasis of modern terrorism on technologically crude modes of attack, suicide bombings and beheadings, for example, both of which are technologically unsophisticated. Overall, the global trend is moving towards the multiplication and synchronization of traditional tactics, rather than the use of new tactics or weaponry.

Ethnic Terrorism: Themes and Variations

Dennis Pluchinsky

INTRODUCTION

Over the past 15 years, the variety of terrorism strains confronting the world has declined. In the 1980s, left-wing, right-wing, state-sponsored, single-issue, religious, anarchist, and ethnic terrorism infected the international arena. Each strain was different in terms of objectives, strategy, targeting patterns, tactical tendencies, operational area, and operational code. The common element which bound all of these strains together was their selection of violence as a method to redress a particular grievance, caused in most cases by a state, but sometimes by another group or issue. In the 1990s, several of these terrorism strains weakened significantly. Left-wing terrorism declined after the disintegration of the USSR and the East European communist states. State-sponsored terrorism declined as a result of the disintegration of the USSR and the 1991 Gulf War. Anarchist and right-wing terrorism strains were never powerful and prevalent in the 1980s and did not become so in the 1990s. The ethnic and religious terrorism strains, however, proliferated in the 1990s, fuelled primarily by the numerous ethnic conflicts that surfaced after the disintegration of the USSR and Yugoslavia, and by a militant tendency with an Islamic orientation that spilled out of Afghanistan.

At present (November 2005), the ethnic and religious terrorism strains continue to cause the international community the most concern and to create the most international 'headaches' and crises. In January 2005, the author identified 99 groups that used political terrorism: 45 had a religious agenda, 30 an ethnic agenda, 10 were left-wing groups, five were right-wing, and four were single-issue militant movements. More than 70% of militant groups in the world today have either an ethnic or a religious agenda. In about 5% of these cases, the two agendas merge; that is, a group would have an Islamic revolutionary orientation with a separatist agenda. Separatism is one of the characteristics of ethnic terrorist or insurgent groups. The fact is that from 1968, the generally accepted beginning of the modern phase of terrorism, until the present, the most prevalent agenda for terrorist or insurgent groups has been an ethnic one. Ethnicity has been a primary generator of political violence over the past two decades. The main by-product of such ethnic conflict has been the emergence of either ethnic insurgent or ethnic terrorist groups, whose objectives have been independence, autonomy, or the reunification of a splintered homeland.

Since the end of the Cold War, ethnic militancy has become a major security and political 'headache' for the international community. Palestine, Northern

Ireland, the Basque region, Chechnya, East Timor, Kurdistan, Burundi, Rwanda, Sri Lanka, Kashmir, Punjab, Mindinao, Tibet, Kosovo, Bosnia, Abkhazia, Sudan, Cyprus, Nagorno-Karabakh and Aceh are some of the ethnic battlefields that have caused consternation and concern for the international community over the past 15 years. In time, Iraq, and possibly Afghanistan, may be added to this list. Potentially explosive ethnic issues exist in both countries. The international public has also become familiar with these battlefields primarily because violence was used by one or more parties to these conflicts. The more violence the conflict produced, the more familiar it became to the international public. Violence, especially at the sub-state level, has always attracted attention and publicity. While the evolution of these ethnic conflicts, the actors involved, the motivations for their involvement, and the international community's response to them is often complicated, their basic cause is relatively simple: the existence of a grievance on the part of a discontented ethnic community.

THE EVOLUTION OF AN ETHNIC INSURGENT OR TERRORIST GROUP

The two primary manifestations of ethnic militancy are ethnic terrorist and ethnic insurgent groups. The major difference between the two is their numerical strength. Any ethnic militant group with 500 or fewer members can be classified as a terrorist group, while a group with 1,000 members or more is a candidate for classification as an insurgent group. The key factor that determines whether or not

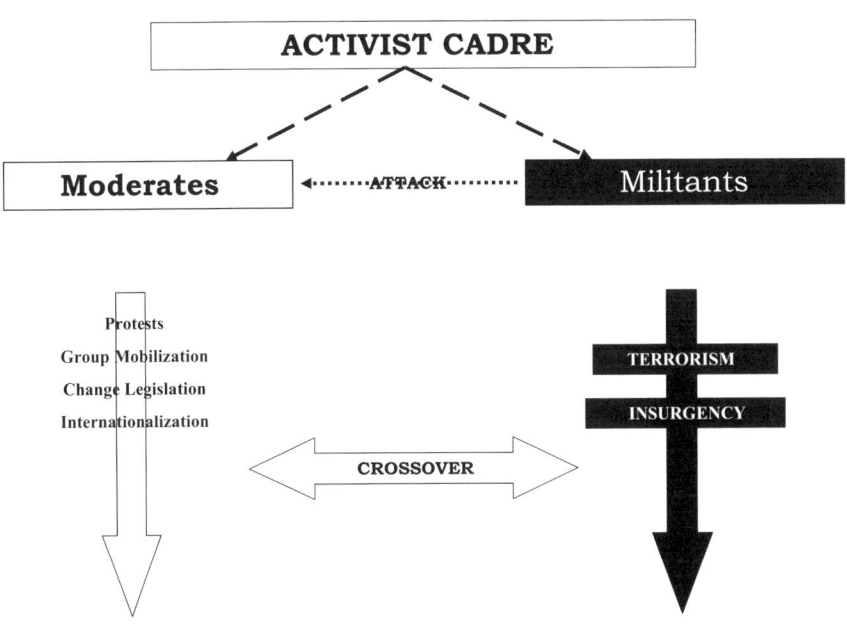

a group is an insurgent group is whether or not it directly controls or has significant influence over a particular piece of territory. Terrorist groups do not control territory. These two types of militant groups are created by a process that begins when a discontented ethnic group desires to redress a particular grievance, real or imagined. This grievance may comprise one or more social, political, economic, security, educational or linguistic components. Ethnic insurgent and terrorist groups do not simply appear for no reason. They surface from grievances. A grievance is an issue, problem, or situation that causes discontent in a large segment of an ethnic population. The existence of an ethnic grievance is potentially dangerous only if an activist cadre emerges from the discontented ethnic group to take steps to correct it. In some situations, no activist cadre emerges. In others, an activist cadre will emerge from future generations. It is this activist cadre that translates the grievance into action.

An activist cadre generally comprises a small, core group of activists who believe that something must be done to redress this grievance in order to mitigate or eliminate it. This activist cadre engages in a political mobilization of the discontented ethnic group. This mobilization usually has two outcomes. The first is the production of a political group or organization that believes in following a non-violent path in order to redress the grievance. This means organizing protests, demonstrations, working against discriminatory legislation, forming a political party, negotiating with the state, or appealing to the international community. The underlying assumption of this approach is that the actor responsible for the grievance is a rational actor that can be influenced by reason, public opinion, and international pressure, and is willing to compromise. An ethnic grievance is either anti-state or anti-group. For most discontented ethnic groups, the cause of their grievance is the state.

The second and most disruptive outcome of ethnic mobilization is the emergence of a group of activists who apply a militant analysis of their ethnic group's grievance and conclude that the state will not negotiate or compromise, will not willingly make concessions, and only understands and responds to violence. The militants believe that it is necessary to engage in an armed struggle against the state to force it to make concessions. This militant analysis almost always results in the founding of an ethnic insurgent or terrorist group. In either case, ethnic terrorism surfaces to pollute the security environment. It is important to understand that the moderate and militant factions are essentially competing with each other for the hearts, minds, and money of their discontented constituency. This translates into political power within the ethnic group, increased manpower, and more resources. In some instances, the militant faction may target moderates in order to reduce or eliminate their influence within the discontented ethnic group. Each faction is promoting a different solution to their ethnic group's problem or grievance. The moderates are asking their ethnic group to engage in non-violent tactics, while the militants are asking their ethnic group to take risks, to endanger themselves, and to possibly kill other people. Given these two choices, it is not surprising that militant factions usually represent a minority viewpoint within the discontented ethnic group.

What causes one element within a discontented ethnic group to select a non-violent approach while another chooses armed struggle? It is most likely the individual mindset and experiences of the activist cadre who initially form one of the two competing groups. What determines whether a militant ethnic faction will evolve into a terrorist or insurgent group? Some contributing factors would be: geography, the size of the ethnic population, whether there is a mother country link or not, the level and history of violence by the state against the discontented ethnic group, the dispersal pattern of the ethnic population in the targeted state, and topography.

A militant faction can form independently or emerge from the moderate faction. In the latter situation, activists within the moderate faction become disillusioned over time when the moderate approach fails to produce progress on their grievance. They leave the moderate group and establish a militant one. For example, the ethnic Albanian 'Kosovo Liberation Army', or KLA, was created by dissidents from the 'Democratic League of Kosovo', or LDK, a moderate ethnic Albanian political party.

The militant ethnic groups may over time be confronted with schisms or factions. There may be disagreements over policy or the continued use of violence, or there may be personality clashes. The Irish, Basque, Kashmiri, Sikh, Corsican, Tamil, Croatian, Armenian and Palestinian nationalist movements furnish multiple examples of splits within militant groups. Some instances follow:

1. The Nationalist Socialist Council of Nagaland (NSCN) AND the Nationalist Socialist Council of Nagaland—Issac Muivah faction.
2. The Corsican National Liberation Front (CNLF) AND the Corsican National Liberation Front—Historic.
3. The Armenian Secret Liberation Army (ASALA) AND the Justice Commandos of the Armenian Genocide (JCAG).
4. The Provisional Irish Republican Army (PIRA) AND the Official Irish Republican Army (OIRA). And more recently, the Real IRA and the Continuity IRA.
5. The Front for the Liberation of Cabinda Enclave (FLCE) AND the Front for the Liberation of Cabinda Enclave—Renewed faction.
6. The Basque Homeland and Liberty—Military wing (ETA—M) AND the Basque Homeland and Liberty—Political/Military wing (ETA—PM). There were even splits within ETA—PM that produced factions such as ETA—PM VII Assembly and ETA—PM VIII Assembly.
7. Consider the Palestinian nationalist movement. There is the Popular Front for the Liberation of Palestine (PFLP) AND there was also the PFLP—Special Operations Group, the PFLP—Special Command, and the PFLP—General Command.

These splits within the militant ethnic groups can sometimes lead to 'intra-ethnic terrorism'. One group may target the other as each is perceived by the other as a competitor. The Tamil Tigers of Tamil Eelam (LTTE) and the Kurdistan Workers Party (PKK) are salient examples of groups that have assassinated and kidnapped representatives of rival groups. In the 1990s, in northern Iraq, the PKK, the Patriotic Union of Kurdistan (PUK), the Kurdish Democratic Party of Iran (KDPI) and the Kurdish Democratic Party (KDP) all feuded with each other. The current situation in Iraq and the opportunities for the Kurdish people have caused these feuds to be curtailed for now. In 1996–98, factions within the Corsican National Liberation Front conducted an intra-ethnic feud that caused more than 50 deaths. Intra-ethnic feuds have also taken place within Kashmiri, Bodo and Chechen militant groups. Probably the most extensive and bloody intra-ethnic feud involved the Palestinian nationalist movement in the 1970s and 1980s, when competing Palestinian militant terrorist groups carried out assassinations against each other in the refugee camps of Lebanon and in some Western European capitals (Pluchinsky and Alexander, 1992).

There are also instances when militant groups ended their armed struggle against the state. Over time, their operational capability may become severely damaged, their support from their ethnic constituency may decline significantly, or political conditions may change. Whatever the reason, the militant group concludes that a militant analysis is no longer applicable or effective under the current circumstances. The most prominent recent example of such a development would be the Irish Republican Army's (IRA) evolution during the period 1998–2005 through cease-fire, abandonment of armed struggle and disarmament. In their historic statement of 28 July 2005, the IRA stated:

> 'Notwithstanding these difficulties our decisions have been taken to advance our republican and democratic objectives, including our goal of a united Ireland. We believe there is now an alternative way to achieve this and to end British rule in our country. It is the responsibility of all Volunteers to show leadership, determination and courage. We are very mindful of the sacrifices of our patriot dead, those who went to jail, Volunteers, their families and the wider republican base. We reiterate our view that the armed struggle was entirely legitimate.' (*Republican News*, 2005)

Of special note is that the IRA did not admit that its application of a militant analysis in Northern Ireland had been wrong. The group considered it legitimate and has only shifted to a more moderate path because it has now discovered an 'alternative way' to accomplish its goal.

STRATEGY OF ATTRITION

In most cases, due primarily to wars and treaties, discontented ethnic groups have found themselves politically subsumed in a state that is ethnically dissimilar. These ethnic groups are usually concentrated in a particular region, which they regard as their homeland. This homeland can be intact or partitioned, with a portion often situated in a neighbouring state. Such ethnic groups are usually highly organized politically. An objective examination of the ethnic group's history will generally uncover a specific period when the group operated an independent or autonomous political entity. In short, the discontented ethnic group believes that it has all the credentials to be an independent state. However, the moderate elements in the ethnic nationalist movement have accepted the international community's reluctance to recognize violent separatist movements in established states and understand that autonomy, in various forms and to various degrees, may be a more reachable goal.

Militant elements in the ethnic nationalist movement, however, believe that only violence will pressure the state into acquiescing to their demands. These demands are either for complete independence or greater autonomy. The militants have analysed the situation of their ethnic group, the history of their group's relations with the targeted state, and the history of the targeted state. They have deduced that the targeted state only understands violence and that armed struggle is the most viable and appropriate option to attain their goals. The KLA stated in their communiqué No. 35, dated August 1997:

> 'Because we are dealing with an enemy that understands nothing but the language of force, we are compelled, albeit against our will, to talk down the barrel of a gun, not as 'terrorists,' but as a liberation organization that has set itself the task of fighting mercilessly against the invader and his collaborators until the Albanian lands are totally liberated.'

Or, as a militant Irish republican stated in an article in the Sinn Fein newspaper, *Republican News*, in June 1992:

> 'Any organization, movement, or nation with a grievance has, of course, a moral obligation to explore all non-violent methods before considering a resort to violence. Thus, if someone can credibly demonstrate to me as a republican that prayer, or appeal to reason, or engaging in British constitutional politics, will lead to a realization of the Irish people's wish for a united Ireland, then count me in. However, all experience and history points to the opposite conclusion.'

The ethnic insurgent and terrorist groups apply a strategy of attrition to their armed struggle with the central government of the state that contains their ethnic homeland, which they usually refer to as the 'centre'. The intent of the ethnic insurgent or terrorist groups is to create social, economic, and political instability in their homeland by engaging in bombings, kidnappings, assassinations, and other forms of physical and psychological intimidation. They believe that the successful application of this strategy will over time cause the centre to perceive the discontented ethnic region as ungovernable and/or too costly, that is, not worth the financial drain, casualty toll, or loss of international prestige necessary to retain it. At the minimum, the state could then agree to some degree of autonomy for the discontented ethnic region.

When political instability in the discontented ethnic region reaches a certain level and scope, the centre may retract local rule and assert direct rule, from the centre. This plays into the hands of the militants, since the centre will most likely deploy more security forces to re-establish control over the ethnic region. The militants then depict these security forces as 'forces of occupation' and the centre's administrators as 'proconsuls'. The insertion of security forces into the ethnic region can lead to human rights abuses against the local population, which further plays into the hands of the militants. In some cases, the militants may target family members of the security forces in order to provoke them into heavy-handed retaliation against the local population. Even without the direct targeting of their family members, security forces stationed for an extended period in high-risk and inhospitable areas are vulnerable to extra-judicial action. It is crucial for the militants to create the perception that their ethnic homeland is ungovernable. To this end, they will often attempt to sabotage local elections or oppose local participation. The successful staging by the centre of local elections in which the ethnic population participates undermines the militants' efforts to destabilize the region.

In general, there is little popular support for the militant ethnic factions among the discontented ethnic community. Violence begets violence and the people are the ones who generally suffer, as they become the innocent victims of both sides. The strategy of attrition that the militants follow can have negative consequences. The more violence they engage in, the more the state responds. This cycle of violence can eventually cause a gradual erosion of popular support for the militant group until it falls below a minimally accepted level within the ethnic community. In spite of legitimate and acute grievance, ethnic communities can tire of the militants' violence.

OPERATIONAL LEVELS AND TACTICS

Ethnic insurgent and terrorist groups operate at three different levels. At the first level, these groups operate in their respective ethnic homelands. Most of their operations take place here. This is logical, since this is where their support is located, they are familiar with the terrain, and this is the area that they must destabilize. Most militant ethnic groups will try to employ somewhat more discriminate tactics in their ethnic region in order to avoid causing casualties to their own ethnie. Many militant ethnic groups will also operate at a second level, where attacks are launched outside of their homeland but within the targeted state. In most cases, these attacks take place in the capital of the targeted state, or in what ethnic militants refer to as the 'centre'. These attacks in the 'centre' are a necessary component of the militants' strategy of attrition and have multiple objectives: (1) they demonstrate the threat projection of the group; (2) they embarrass the security forces; (3) they attract more national publicity; and (4) they bring the conflict and its consequences directly to the general population.

Attacks in the centre by militant ethnic groups are generally more indiscriminate than operations in their own ethnic region. The most common tactical operations at the second level are car bombs, shrapnel bombs, mortar attacks, rocket attacks, etc., that are designed to cause casualties among innocent civilians. Most of the targets at the second level are public transportation facilities, major streets and public areas. Other targets are security forces and politicians. The attacks in the centre also contribute to the 'internationalization' of the conflict in that the targets and tactics used can cause casualties to innocent

Militant Ethnic Groups: Operational Levels

Level	Operational Area	Conflict's Dimension	Publicity Spotlight	Tactics	Threat Projection
1	Ethnic Homeland	Regional	Low	Discriminate	Low
2	Targeted State	National	Moderate	Indiscriminate	Moderate
3	Outside State	International	High	Discriminate	High

foreigners—such as tourists or businesspeople. In some cases, the objective of the attacks in the centre may be to damage the tourism industry of the state. Although the majority of ethnic terrorist and insurgent operations are considered to be domestic terrorism, any attack that injures a foreigner is considered to be an international terrorist incident. A sustained campaign of terrorism in the capital by a militant ethnic group could compel other countries to issue travel warnings or travel advice for their citizens who intend to visit that city. This in turn impacts on tourism revenue and the state's international image.

The third operational level for some militant ethnic groups is attacks outside of the targeted country. Such third-level operations have the following benefits: (1) they amplify the group's threat projection; (2) they attract international publicity; (3) they frame the conflict as an international problem; and (4) they take place in an environment where targets are generally 'softer', that is, security awareness is lower and protective security measures are less stringent. However, few militant ethnic groups operate at the third level. The group that has carried out the most attacks at this level was the IRA. It has carried out more than two dozen terrorist attacks against British targets on the European continent. Other groups, such as the Basque Homeland and Liberty (ETA), the LTTE, Sikh extremists and Kashmiri extremists, have periodically operated at the third level, but in a limited way. Supporters of the old PKK in Germany, as opposed to the core PKK cadre, were also responsible for several hundred incidents of political terrorism during 1994–96 against Turkish targets in Western Europe—primarily in Germany.

Logistical considerations prevent many militant ethnic groups from operating at the third level. Those that do must be careful not to cause casualties to citizens of the state where the attack is carried out. Killing or injuring citizens of this state can turn public opinion against the militant ethnic group's cause, or reduce any sympathy for it that may exist. There may be circumstances, however, in which the militant ethnic group's strategic situation in the targeted state or a change in the general political conditions may lead it to decide that publicity, even if negative, is more important than public sympathy. This assessment is more likely to take place during the initial stage of a militant ethnic group's armed struggle when it is attempting to alert and sensitize the international community to its cause.

The IRA spoke for many militant ethnic groups that operate or would like to operate at the third level when it made the following statement concerning its attacks on British overseas targets:

> 'Overseas attacks also have a prestige value and internationalize the war in Ireland. The British government has been successful in suppressing news about the struggle in the North. With its huge propaganda machine administered by ambassadors and officials, one example being Peter Jay when he was in America, it can spread a rosy picture which does much to undermine the people's sacrifices and completely ignores the people's suffering. But we have kept Ireland in the world headlines, our struggle is kept in the news, and sooner or later an expression of discontentment probably from the English people rather than from the army, will snowball and the British government's ability and will to stay, which we are sapping, will completely snap.'

Since most militant ethnic groups operate at the first level, the decision to advance to level two or three is an important one that is dictated by the group's perception of its current strength, strategic progress, and the attitude of the centre. To effectively implement a strategy of attrition against the centre, a group must operate at the second level. The advancement from level one to level two is more crucial than progressing from level two to level three. The escalation from one level to another brings attendant benefits and risks that must be evaluated. Attacks in the centre have been an operational 'leitmotif' for militant ethnic groups. Consider IRA strikes in London, ETA attacks in Madrid, LTTE suicide bombings in Colombo, PKK attacks in Ankara, Chechen rebel terrorist attacks in Moscow, Muslim Uighur attacks in Beijing, and Kashmiri and Sikh separatist attacks in Bombay and New Delhi. It is clear that most militant ethnic groups realize that, for their armed struggle to be effective, at some point they must strike at the centre. The IRA has carried out the most attacks at the second level in the centre, having been responsible, over a 25-year period, for more than 300 terrorist incidents in London (BBC, 2005).

ETHNIC TERRORIST GROUPS: THE GLOBAL GROUPS

Ethnic terrorism has also had a global dimension, and the groups involved may be referred to as global ethnic terrorist groups. The primary manifestations of global ethnic terrorism were the Palestinian, Croatian, and Armenian ethnic terrorist groups. For various reasons, these groups made the decision to operate primarily outside of their ethnic homelands in the international arena (the third level). For instance, militant Palestinian groups concluded in the late 1960s that there was insufficient international attention to their situation. Moreover, effective Israeli security measures inside the state and along its borders made it difficult for Palestinian guerrillas to infiltrate Israel to establish guerrilla bases. Given the objectives of these groups and the security and political conditions at the time, it is not surprising that the decision was made to strike at Israeli and Jewish targets in the international arena, with a clear preference for Western Europe. It is estimated that more than 15 militant Palestinian ethnic terrorist groups carried out over 600 terrorist attacks outside of Israel from 1968–97. These attacks took place in more than 50 countries (Pluchinsky, 1997).

Militant Croatian ethnic groups also operated primarily in the international arena in the 1970s and early 1980s. Their targets were official Yugoslav personnel and facilities and their objective was a free and independent Croatian state. All of these Croatian groups were émigré organizations with tenuous and limited links to militant elements in Croatia. Given the autocratic nature of the communist regimes in Belgrade and Zagreb, it was difficult for militant Croatian ethnic groups to emerge and operate inside Croatia. It was easier for these groups outside of Croatia to strike at Yugoslav targets. Moreover, such attacks attracted international publicity. The most notorious were the seizure, in 1971, of the Yugoslav consulate in Göteborg, Sweden; the mid-air bombing of a Yugoslav airliner in 1972 that killed 27 people; the hijacking, again in 1972, of a Swedish airliner to force Sweden to release several imprisoned Croatian militants; the hijacking, in 1976, of a TWA airliner in New York; and the seizure, in 1980, of the Yugoslav consulate in Chicago, Illinois. In 1962–82, militant Croatian ethnic terrorist groups carried out 128 anti-Yugoslav terrorist attacks world-wide. This campaign also triggered 'pro-state terrorism' by the Yugoslav intelligence services, which, it has been estimated, carried out some 46 attacks against Croatian émigrés world-wide during this period (Pluchinsky, 1992).

Militant Armenian ethnic groups were also active in the international arena, from 1975–86. Their primary objective was to avenge the alleged genocide by Turkey in 1915 of 1.5m. Armenians who were reportedly forced to march into western Syria. They also demanded that the Turkish government officially acknowledge this genocide. The standard ethnic militant objective of an independent homeland was mentioned by these Armenian groups, but it was not the focus of their campaign. Demographic realities in south-eastern Turkey, overlapping territorial claims with Kurdish ethnic groups, and the existence of an Armenian republic in the USSR undermined their desire for an independent Armenian entity in Turkey. Militant Armenian ethnic groups carried out 30 assassinations, 16 attempted assassinations, 129 bombings, 19 attempted bombings, one airport attack, and three embassy seizures from 1975–86. The majority of these attacks were directed at Turkish targets. However, 38 non-Turkish persons were killed and 357 were injured as a result of them. The attacks were carried out in 22 countries, including Turkey (Corsun, 1981, 1988). Armenian terrorist groups were second only to the Palestinian terrorist groups in the level and scope of their international terrorist activity.

Global ethnic terrorist groups within the Palestinian, Croatian, and Armenian nationalist movements had to concentrate their militant activities in the international arena because it was difficult to carry them out in their respective ethnic homelands. They are exceptions. Most militant ethnic groups are able to operate in their homeland and consequently focus their operations there. However, the Palestinian, Croatian, and Armenian cases could serve as a strategic and operational template for a discontented ethnic group contained in a repressive state and which has a significant émigré community or diaspora.

DIASPORAS: UMBILICAL CORDS FOR MILITANT ETHNIC GROUPS

Ethnic diasporas play a major role in fuelling ethnic insurgent and terrorist groups. They are umbilical cords that provide manpower and moral, logistical, financial and political support. It is well known that Irish-Americans provided such support to Irish Republican groups. Other examples would be the Kurdish diaspora, especially in Western Europe, and its aid to the PKK; the Sikh diaspora and its support for Sikh militants, especially in the aftermath of the Indian army's attack on the Golden Temple in Amritsar in 1984; and the Tamil diaspora's support for the LTTE. Global militant ethnic groups in particular rely on the support of their diasporas. Since these groups operate principally in the international arena, they need connections to their diasporas in various countries in order to establish logistical infrastructures to support their attacks. The Palestinian diaspora, especially in Western Europe, provided crucial support to militant Palestinian groups in the 1960s, 1970s and 1980s. The Armenian diaspora's aid to militant Armenian groups, such as ASALA and JCAG, was essential to enable these groups to operate in more than 22 countries. Many of the members of these two groups were recruited from the Armenian diaspora, especially in Lebanon, France, and the USA. Croatian militant ethnic groups also benefited significantly from the Croatian diaspora, especially in Western Europe.

An interesting example of the importance of a diaspora to a militant ethnic group was the birth and growth of the KLA. While most militant ethnic groups are formed in their ethnic homelands without significant external support, it appears that the KLA is the first example of a militant ethnic group being established outside of its ethnic homeland (i.e. Kosovo). The idea and initial impetus for the KLA reportedly came from the Albanian diaspora in Switzerland (*Christian Science Monitor*, 1998). The KLA could not have developed to the extent it did without the manpower and financial and logistical support from the Albanian diaspora in Western Europe and the USA. Richard Holbrooke, the leading US diplomat overseeing the Kosovo problem, stated in July 1998: 'I realized during my trip how important countries like Germany, Switzerland, and Denmark are, in which the KLA funds are organized and men are recruited.'

(Reuters, 2001). The KLA acknowledged its reliance on the Albanian diaspora when it admitted that it 'has reference points in every city in Europe where there are Albanians who collect money for the Kosovo cause' (*Corriere Della Sera*, 1998).

It is clear that the evolution of the KLA from an ethnic terrorist group into a victorious insurgent group was due to a set of factors that most militant ethnic groups do not generally encounter. First, it received significant support from its diaspora. This support was a determining, not just a contributing, factor to the KLA's metamorphosis. Second, it had the advantage of a 'mother-country' link in that various elements in Albania provided it with official and unofficial support. Third, it faced an enemy (the Milošević regime) that attracted little international sympathy or support. In fact, the regime was ostracized by the international community and non-government organizations who labelled its members as war criminals. And, last, it benefited from NATO military intervention. The confluence of these four factors contributed to the KLA's success in restoring significant autonomy to Kosovo.

The KLA's success inspired other Albanian ethnic militant groups in southern Serbia and Macedonia. In November 2000, an Albanian insurgent group—the 'Liberation Army of Presevo, Medjedja, and Bujanovac', or UCPMB—surfaced in the Presevo valley area of southern Serbia. Its initial stated aim was to protect from Serbian forces some 100,000 ethnic Albanians living in this area—the south-western tip of Serbia. This seven-month insurgency ended in May 2001 when the UCPMB signed a NATO-sponsored agreement to disarm and disband in exchange for amnesty and increased rights for ethnic Albanians in the region. A more serious Albanian insurgency surfaced in neighbouring Macedonia in February 2001. It was triggered by a group calling itself the 'National Liberation Army', or NLA. Its objective was to gain equal rights for Albanians in Macedonia. From February to June 2001, the NLA, whose strength was estimated at about 1,500–2,000, had limited success against Macedonian military forces. They were more successful in causing alarm to the Macedonian government, NATO, the USA and the European Union (EU). As with the KLA, the NLA appears to have established connections with the Albanian diaspora for support (*The New York Times*, 2001). In early July 2001, a cease-fire took effect in northern Macedonia while representatives of the Macedonian government and ethnic Albanian politicians in Macedonia discussed, under the auspices of the USA and the EU, ways to end the conflict. In August 2001, the NLA and the Macedonian government signed a Western-backed peace agreement that called for more Albanian rights in Macedonia. By October 2001, the NLA had officially disbanded.

While the level of violence in all three of these Albanian enclaves has significantly declined over the past five years, periodic incidents of violence underline the fact that many issues remain unresolved in these areas. Reducing violence does not necessarily mean that the cause of that violence has been eradicated. In some cases, the current militant ethnic group simply leaves the unfinished agenda for another generation to address. The potential for a reignition of conflict will always exist if the basic underlying causes of the conflict are not properly and effectively addressed. It is clear that a militant ethnic group with access to a large and active diaspora has a better chance of internationalizing their conflict and keeping their armed struggle active than those groups which have no diaspora. Internet sites of both moderate and militant ethnic groups are designed to appeal to the diaspora first and then to the general public. Websites play an important role in keeping diasporas informed and engaged in the armed struggles in their respective homelands (Weimann, 2004).

MILITANT ETHNIC CONFLICTS: CURRENT STATUS

In the 1990s, ethnicity, in its more secular form, was the primary generator of political violence in the world. At the beginning of the 21st century, religion has replaced ethnicity as the primary generator. It is clear that the primary terrorist and insurgent threat confronting the world today is driven by Islamic revolutionary terrorists, in particular those who adhere to the mindset and programme of the global jihadists. Since the terrorist attacks in New York and Washington, DC, on 11 September 2001, there have been two noticeable macroterrorism-related trends. The first is that these attacks launched a global jihad movement consisting of lone terrorists; small, home-grown jihadist cells; sympathetic domestic jihadist groups; and remnants of the al-Qa'ida organization. The major jihadist terrorist attacks that have taken place in 2002–05 have been diverse with regard to their perpetrators, location, tactics and targets. The centralized, bureaucratic, powerful, pre-9/11 al-Qa'ida has been replaced by a diverse, leaderless, less powerful, jihadist movement. The second major terrorist-related trend has been the decline in active ethnic insurgent and terrorist groups. It would appear that the 9/11 attacks were a catalyst that caused many militant ethnic groups to initiate or accelerate pursuit of a resolution to their conflicts. The 9/11 attacks gave terrorism a 'bad name'. The number of civilian casualties in those attacks, the largest in the history of the modern phrase of terrorism, compelled some militant ethnic groups to re-evaluate their armed struggles.

An example would be the conflict in Northern Ireland. While the reduction of this conflict began in 1998 with the signing of the Easter Peace Accords, the IRA did not abandon armed struggle and disarm until 2005. The 9/11 attacks probably accelerated the decision-making process of the leadership of the IRA and of Sinn Fein on these two final concessions. Another example would be the conflict in Sri Lanka. Although the LTTE has initiated many cease-fires over the past 15 years, the one that has lasted the longest and has produced forward momentum in mitigating this conflict is that of December 2001—after the LTTE was able to gauge the world's reaction to the 9/11 attacks. The LTTE also abandoned its demand for an independent Tamil state and will now settle for greater autonomy. It is important to note that the LTTE, like the IRA, has a history of mass-casualty, indiscriminate attacks against civilians. In April 2002, the PKK changed its name to the more politically-correct 'Kurdish Freedom and Democracy Congress' (KADEK). In the summer of 2002, the Bodoland Liberation Tigers Force in

India's north-eastern state of Assam abandoned its demands for an independent state. In December 2002, the Free Aceh Movement in Indonesia signed a Cessation of Hostilities Agreement with the government. On 15 August 2005, both sides signed a formal peace treaty ending 30 years of conflict in which more than 15,000 people were killed. In September 2005, the United Liberation Front of Assam responded positively to overtures from the Indian government to participate in conflict-resolution discussions.

Since the 9/11 attacks, the Basque group ETA has sent numerous signals to the Spanish government that it is willing to negotiate an end to their conflict. There also appears to be growing sentiment inside the Basque nationalist movement and even inside ETA itself for negotiation. There is a nascent realization within the militant Basque nationalist movement that ETA is out of touch with the Basque people and is becoming antiquated. Since the 9/11 attacks, ETA has adopted a policy of informing the police of the general locations where it has planted car bombs in Madrid, in order to give them enough time to find and defuse the devices. This is an attempt by ETA to minimize civilian casualties. The ETA of the 1970s, 1980s and 1990s would not have adopted this 'advance notice' approach. The attacks on commuter trains in Madrid on 11 March 2004, for which ETA was initially blamed, also contributed to a modification of ETA's tactics. In the Philippines, the Moro Islamic Liberation Front initiated serious negotiations with the government in October 2001. While these negotiations have, like most ethnic-conflict negotiations, encountered periods of backward, stagnant, and forward movements, the government believes that a formal peace agreement can be signed by early 2006.

One other by-product of the 9/11 attacks has been the way governments have used this seminal terrorist event as an excuse to suppress opposition elements by designating them as terrorists and, in some cases, if they are Muslims, linking them to al-Qa'ida. Al-Qa'ida is an international 'bogeyman' that governments can use to their advantage. The Chinese government has certainly taken advantage of the 9/11 attacks to suppress Uighur Muslims in Western Xinjiang province. The Chinese government claims that more than 260 terrorist attacks were carried out in Xinjiang by Uighur 'splitists', or separatists (BBC, 2005). It has also claimed that the Uighur terrorists are linked to al-Qa'ida. The global war on terrorism has provided some countries with the opportunity to place their own opposition elements in the same category as al-Qa'ida. Due to the nature of ethnic conflicts, ethnic insurgent and terrorist groups tend to carry out more attacks that cause casualties to innocent civilians than other types of terrorist groups. Religious terrorist groups show the same tendency. The 9/11 attacks stand out as the most devastating on a civilian population in the post-Second World War era. It is this mass-casualty, indiscriminate tactical link between the 9/11 attacks and the ethnic insurgent and terrorist groups that compelled some militant ethnic groups to reassess their armed struggles against the state.

The militant option for discontented ethnic groups has become less viable and attractive since the 9/11 attacks. The number of active ethnic terrorist and insurgent groups has declined over the past four years. All this does not signal the end of this particular terrorist strain, but it does reduce its prevalence. The high watermark for ethnic terrorist and insurgent group activity was the 1990s. It is doubtful that the level of militant ethnic activity in that decade will ever be matched again.

Left- and Right-wing Political Terrorism

DAVID W. BRANNAN

This essay discusses terrorism motivated by the politics of the extreme Right and Left. While they are examined together here, their ideological foundations and sometimes targets, if not their tactics, are very different. Despite this polar distinction, the two ideological motivations for political terrorism are appropriately dealt with in this manner, as the contrast between the two motivations is illustrative at a number of points. Traditionally, left-wing terrorists have attacked with the intent of changing the controlling political structures of a country and the assumption is that right-wing terrorists are similar. While, historically, Leftist groups may have made propaganda statements to that effect, there were often more discrete goals being advanced than those which the propaganda suggested. On the Right, the propaganda has rarely equalled the actual goals, which are generally far less nationally directed than the propaganda would suggest. The exception to this is found when some theologically based groups take on the right-wing agenda and regard themselves as engaged in an ultimate and eschatological struggle. Where an ethno-nationalist organization might actually hope to achieve its asserted goal of a homeland, neither left- nor right-wing terrorists are ever likely to succeed in altering the political climate to the extent that they would wish.

It is certainly true of terrorist groups, as of many types of extremism, that ideological motivations and political agendas do not always follow an unbroken chain of logical or rational thought. Rather, what may be found is a group, belief structure or movement that is identified broadly with a particular political persuasion but has ongoing and perhaps important interaction or cross-fertilization with groups or ideological beliefs that might be argued to be counter to the group's basic political foundation, be it either the Left or the Right. There have been some examples of this dichotomy recently within US right-wing organizations, such as the neo-Nazi/Christian Identity group, The Aryan Nations, whose leader, August Kries, recently called for a link with the Salafist Islamic organization al-Qa'ida (Schuster, 2005).

Defining terrorist organizations as simply politically Left or Right in their motivation for terrorist action can be problematic. For example, an organization such as the Kurdistan Workers Party (PKK) is fundamentally left-leaning in its political foundations, but is at the same time an ethno-nationalist movement attempting to establish a homeland for a particular ethnicity of people—not a people based on socialist principles. Similarly, the Basque Fatherland and Liberty

Group (ETA), founded in 1959 on left-wing ideologies, is socialist in its political foundations but is apparently driven to terrorist acts because of ethnic rather than purely socialist motivations.

This essay outlines the fundamental ideological underpinnings for both left- and right-wing terrorist organizations. It discusses the tactics and targeting of groups from both the Right and Left and how they were influenced by their ideological positions. The essay cites examples from throughout the modern terror period (Hoffman, 1998), showing the rise and decline of various segments of the extreme political Left and Right. Additionally, the essay touches on groups on the extreme Right that utilize other forms of motivation—such as religion—to organize and recruit membership while remaining an extreme right-wing rather than merely a religious group. Similarly, the essay discusses some manifestations of politically-focused extremist groups, which are sometimes still categorized as the 'New Left' or, more recently, the 'New-New Left.' These have perhaps been most appropriately identified in this volume by David Rapoport as the 'fourth wave'.

LEFT-WING MOTIVATIONS

Violent Leftist activism can be generally understood as striving to bring about political and social change from a Capitalist *status quo* to a Marxist, Leninist, Maoist, Communist or other socialist style of government. The Leftist groups that have used terror while attempting to advance these aims have generally tried to portray their organizations as 'vanguards of the oppressed proletariat'. Because these groups have held society and the general public to be oppressed by capitalists in control of government, they have tended to adjust their tactics to avoid targeting the workers they hope to co-opt to their cause. Rather than targeting 'workers', many of these groups have chosen to target government and business structures, leaders and symbolic targets that are counter to their ideology.

Left-wing terrorist groups often incorporate several Leftist schools of thought rather than one particular one. Marxism, Leninism, Maoism and Trotskyite writing continue to form the foundational ideology of what is generally regarded as the extreme political Left. Occasionally groups do identify with a specific vein of left-wing ideology, as in the case of the Communist Party of Nepal—Maoists (CPN—M), whose foundations are Maoist rather than simply Leftist in nature. Although the CPN—M is also considered an insurgent group, it has used terrorist tactics to target Nepalese parliamentarians—in pursuit of its broader (insurgent) goal of replacing the democratic leadership with Maoist communism.

In 1968 Andreas Baader and his girlfriend Gudrun Ensslin bombed a department store in Frankfurt, Germany, and shortly thereafter the Red Army Faction (RAF) was formed. Sometimes referred to as the Baader-Meinhof Gang by journalists and the authorities, the RAF hated the misnomer because the designation 'gang' lent a tone of criminality to the organization (Aust, 1987), which regarded its political and violent actions as necessarily revolutionary, but not criminal.

The RAF drew ideological foundations from several Leftist schools of thought. Historian and terrorism commentator, Walter Laqueur, has written of the West German terrorist motivations that:

> ... they were not really an ideological movement but eclecticists borrowing certain concepts from various doctrines, including the Leninist theory of imperialism. Above all they believed in the 'primacy of action.' As the RAF put it, only the practice of terror would show whether an armed opposition could be built up. This voluntarist concept had been borrowed from Mao and Castro, even though in other respects the life-style of the New Left terrorist was the negation of everything the Chinese stood for. (Laqueur, 1987)

The various Leftist theorists differed in their understanding of the need for and use of violence during revolution. Most left-wing extremists have viewed their attacks as part of a legitimate revolution to wrest control of the government away from the bourgeois leadership and 'restore' it to the proletariat. Marx, though he did not eschew violence in revolutionary struggle, also allowed for peaceful transition (where possible) within his political framework. He suggested during a speech in Amsterdam in 1872 that the USA and England might be two of those places where the revolution he envisioned could take place without violence:

> ... there are countries like America [and] England ... where the workers can achieve their aims by peaceful means. However true that may be, we ought also to recognise that, in most of the countries of the continent, it is force that must be the lever of our revolutions. (McLellan, 1980)

Unfortunately, terrorist groups 'advancing' Marxist thought in the USA and England blended their Marxist theory with other Leftist ideology and did bring terrorist violence to those countries. For instance, the Weathermen, or Weather Underground, was a Leftist terrorist organization that emerged from the Students for a Democratic Society (SDS) in the late 1960s and mixed Marxism with anarchism. The Weather Underground believed their organization to be the beginning of what would grow to be nation-wide socialist revolution in the USA. Their attacks against police stations and Reserve Officer Training Corps (ROTC) centres on various university campuses underscored their anti-war stand from an extreme Leftist position.

THE ROLE OF ANARCHIST THOUGHT

The link and influence of the ideology of the anarchist-communists in the age of modern terrorism is significant. As terrorism specialist Bruce Hoffman suggests:

> To the nascent anarchist movement, 'the propaganda by the deed' strategy championed by Narodnaya Volya provided a model to be emulated. Within four months of the Tsar's murder, a group of radicals in London convened an 'anarchist conference' which publicly applauded the assassination

and extolled tyrannicide as a means to achieve revolutionary change. (Hoffman, 1998)

Though understood in diverse ways by modern terrorist groups, the idea of 'propaganda by the deed' became an important influence on the way terrorist organizations understood their use of violence within the various Leftist (and other) ideological strains. Terrorist groups sought to make their arguments known to the masses through the method and target they chose for their attacks. Targeting capitalist businesses, 'bourgeois' government leadership and other symbols counter to Socialism was the preferred course of Leftist groups for such dissemination. Long, written explanations still accompanied the violence on occasion, but the 'deed' was expected to explain the grievance as much as any document that might accompany it.

By the 1980s, leaders of Western governments had begun to wonder if Leftist terrorism might be a plot by Soviet agents to target Western/capitalist countries. The election of Republican Ronald Reagan in November 1980 to the presidency of the USA complemented the election of Conservative Margaret Thatcher in May 1979 as British Prime Minister. The two leaders had been outspokenly anti-communist figures throughout their careers and the rise in Leftist terrorism during the 1970s strengthened the suspicions of some conservatives that the USSR was orchestrating a clandestine campaign against the West using terrorists as agents. This view of international terrorism was bolstered in 1981 when Claire Sterling's influential book, *The Terror Network*, was published. Sterling's thesis asserted that it was 'well known' by the intelligence community that international terrorism was being orchestrated by the KGB. Sterling's quote from West German anti-terrorist specialist Dr Hans Josef Horchem reflected the book's general thesis:

> The KGB is engineering international terrorism. The facts can be proven, documented, and are well known to the international Western intelligence community. (Sterling, 1981)

Horchem's assertion matched the views of the US and British leadership, and their efforts to counter international terrorism in general during this period took account of a supposed 'evil empire'. With the collapse of the USSR, the casual observer might then have believed that international terrorism—and certainly terrorism from the extreme Left—would disappear completely without the Soviet state structures to support, train and direct it. This was not the case, however; international terrorism continued, increasing in political significance and effectiveness even into the new millennium. Left-wing terrorism continued too, although it became less frequent and less effective following the collapse of the USSR.

LEFTIST TARGETS AND TACTICS

RAND Corporation analyst Brian Jenkins described terrorist attacks in 1974 as 'theater' (Jenkins, 1974). Jenkins regarded the terrorist actions of that time as being instrumental, by narrowly focusing the violence on a small section of the population, in an effort to force the group's views into the public eye rather than simply to attempt to kill large numbers of innocent civilians (Hoffman, 1998). Jenkins made the now often quoted statement about terrorists of the period, that, 'Terrorists want a lot of people watching and a lot of people listening and not a lot of people dead.' While the higher body counts resulting from modern attacks of Salafist Islamist and self-styled leaderless resistance (Beam, 1992) terrorists such as Timothy McVeigh may lead modern terrorism observers to adjust their framework for understanding some modern attacks, the adage was certainly accurate during the late 1960s, 1970s, and, indeed, throughout most of the 1980s. Left-wing terrorists helped prove the general accuracy of Jenkins's statement by repeatedly attacking a very specific type of target that fitted neatly with their ideological motivations. Attacks against diplomats, government officials, police and businesses all convey the message of the extreme Left, namely that the bourgeois capitalist forces are to be revolted against by the oppressed proletariat. An exception to this trend in the 1980s would be the car and truck bomb attacks against the US and European embassies and military facilities in Lebanon and elsewhere in the Middle East that resulted in very high body counts. For instance, on 23 October 1984 241 US Marines and 58 French soldiers were killed in attacks on their barracks.

Leftist terrorists have attacked a number of diverse targets that fitted with the above description of their violence as metered or instrumental. The Mexican communist/anarchist organization Liga Comunista 23 de Septiembre (LC-23S— September 23 Communist League), for instance, sought to overthrow the Mexican government and proposed a communist structure to take its place. Its attacks reflected the socialist ideology and primarily targeted businesses and high-profile government officials. The violence used was metered and specifically directed to highlight the group's socialist beliefs. Similarly, French terrorists of the Action Directe (Direct Action) acted out their ideological violence on targets that represented their ideological opposition in the form of capitalist businesses and government officials, in the hope of initiating a groundswell of socialist support.

This relationship between targeting and ideological underpinnings has not changed in more recent attacks by Leftist terrorists. The Ecuadorian Marxist-Leninist organization Grupos de Combatientes Populares (GCP—Group of Popular Combatants) has been active since 2000, carrying out attacks on diplomats and leaving pamphlets with their bombs explaining their political objectives. While not relying on the target to the same extent to explain its aims, its use of explosives has been instrumental and metered, in much the same way as earlier left-wing groups. For instance, a bomb attack carried out on 1 May 2000 was accompanied by pamphlets that stated:

> A social expansion is nearing and the armed struggle will emerge in the midst of this. In this struggle, the exploited ones will form their own army to subdue the oligarchs, traitors and thus defend and guarantee the constitution of the anti-imperialist people's government. (MIPT, 2005)

The bomb did not kill or injure anyone in the above attack, but the socialist/communist ideology transmitted by the accompanying pamphlets conveyed the message of the group. While many, if not most, today assume that terrorist attacks necessarily equate with high body counts, they may also be carried out by weak or politically powerless groups, to gain attention and a political voice, with little or no loss of life. In some cases this remains true of the extreme Left today. Indiscriminate violence towards the public has never been a common tool of Leftist terrorists because it does not fit with the Left's idea of socialist ideology being the protector of the worker. Leftist terrorists do not want to target the very proletariat from which they hope to gain support.

Like most terrorists throughout modern history, the weapons of choice for the extreme Left have been the gun and the bomb—as frequently noted by Dr Bruce Hoffman. Despite the media's focus on exotic or unusual (e.g. biological, chemical, radiological or nuclear) terrorist weapons, guns and bombs remain the preferred weapons. Early anarchist terrorists, such as the Narodnaya Volya, attacked the Russian Tsar Alexander II by throwing hand-held bombs at his passing sleigh. The weapons of choice had not changed by the 1970s and 1980s as Leftist terrorist organizations continued to bomb targets with improvised explosives. The bombs were potentially more potent—but they were still bombs. Similarly, the gun remains a favourite choice. Among many examples from Leftist terrorism, the Red Brigades used automatic weapons to assassinate retired US diplomat Leamon Hunt in Italy in 1984. The armoured vehicle in which he was travelling was stopped and the terrorists used AK-47 rifles to kill only their target, Hunt.

Leftist terrorists have been particularly successful in using kidnapping as a tactic in combination with the shooting of their victims. For instance, in the late 1970s and early 1980s the Red Brigades kidnapped two high-profile and symbolic targets, whom they later shot dead. These events were probably in emulation of the RAF's kidnapping of Hans-Martin Schleyer in September 1977.

In 1978 former Italian Prime Minister Aldo Moro was kidnapped and held captive for 55 days. The kidnapping received extensive coverage in the Italian media. The leader of the cell which carried out the attack was eventually captured and stated during the investigation and trial that followed that Moro had been kidnapped and killed for his 'intrinsic value' as a symbol of that which the Red Brigades opposed, rather than because of his individual actions or beliefs (Hoffman, 1998).

Following their success in gaining publicity through the kidnapping and assassination of Aldo Moro, the Red Brigades struck again in 1981, this time abducting US Brig.-Gen. James Dozier, the ranking officer in the Southern NATO command. The terrorists abducted the general from his apartment in Verona, Italy, while posing as plumbers, leaving his wife bound but unhurt. The kidnapping was supposedly carried out to demonstrate the group's identification with the efforts of the Palestine Liberation Organization (PLO) (Anderson and Sloan, 2002). The Red Brigades used the subsequent media attention to put forward an anti-NATO manifesto that reflected their socialist/communist ideology. The special forces of

Italy, which also arrested five of the general's captors, rescued the general alive in January 1982 (Thompson, 1998).

The Symbionese Liberation Army (SLA) also used firearms and bombing, but did not kill their well-known captive once she was kidnapped. Rather, the SLA held Patricia Hearst, daughter of newspaper publisher William Randolph Hearst, and used her to gain notoriety and media coverage without killing her. Patricia Hearst eventually joined the group, taking part in several bank robberies and bombings. She was eventually arrested, tried and imprisoned for her part in the SLA's crimes. In addition to the tried and tested use of guns and bombs, the group used also non-violent tactics in an attempt to gain popularity among the poor in California's Bay Area, forcing William Randolph Hearst to provide free food to low-income neighbourhoods. In the end, however, the poor were not supportive and no groundswell of socialist support emerged for the SLA's Leftist cause.

COUNTER-EFFORTS CONSIDERED

While left-wing terrorists have claimed to be the 'vanguard' of the proletariat, they have received very little support from the masses they claim to represent. This, together with operational security issues, has meant that many Leftist terrorist groups have been small and this has made them particularly susceptible to the efforts of governments seeking to eradicate them from their jurisdictions. Certainly these successes have not been achieved overnight: the 17 November (17N) group operated for almost 30 years without being intercepted. Nor have the counter-terrorism measures been absolutely successful. But there have been a number of efforts by the police and the military which have significantly reduced particular Leftist organizations, leaving them virtually ineffective.

Paul Davis and Brian Jenkins have suggested that government efforts to deter terrorist attacks can be understood in an escalating ladder of influence that begins with co-option of those elements of the group that can be deterred (for instance, support from the general public) up to the crushing of the group to avoid future attacks (killing terrorist leaders). Davis and Jenkins break down their understanding of deterrence and counter-efforts further by suggesting two terrorist types that are readily seen in Leftist groups. The first they designate as 'Type A' terrorists, who, they suggest, must be captured or killed to be stopped. The second, 'Type B' terrorists or support personnel, they suggest, may be deterred by other methods (Davis and Jenkins, 2002).

Left-wing terrorists were and remain ideologically driven, and they are often considered to be more intellectually competent than their right-wing counterparts. Many, if not most, of the European Leftists in the 1970s and 1980s were middle- or upper-class college students who were none the less very committed to their extremist causes. The German, Italian and other left-wing terrorists assumed the proletariat, for which they were 'fighting', would come to their aid—but proletarian support rarely emerged to lend viable support to these groups. The workers whom they sought to defend were instead mainly deterred by the policies and actions of the governments the terrorist groups attacked. The hardcore 'Type A' followers became increasingly isolated and in several cases—for example the Greek organization, 17N or the SLA (discussed above)—were almost entirely captured or killed by the authorities, leaving no significant body of terrorist personnel to carry on the fight. In the Western Hemisphere, Cuba remains a refuge for those left-wing terrorists who fled the USA in the 1970s and 1980s. While Leftist terrorism has continued, in the context of Maoist insurgency in Asia and in isolated pockets in South and Central America, the collapse of the USSR in 1989–91 has led to a significant reduction in European left-wing terrorism.

THE NEW-NEW LEFT AND ECO-TERRORISTS

Despite the apparent abandonment of the international stage by ideologically driven Marxist/Leninist/Trotskyite terrorists, several groups often identified as 'single-issue activists' have emerged as what some have called the New Left or, in some cases, the New-New Left (von Sternberg, 2000). This loosely confederated cadre of radical environmentalists, anarchists and anti-globalist factions have taken violent actions against their respective foes in very different ways from the more traditional socialist and communist groups of the recent past.

Extremists of this type are rarely 'full-time' terrorists, hiding underground as the historic Leftist terrorists of the 1970s and 1980s did. Today, anti-globalists and anarchists alike come together in a virtual environment, utilizing the internet to organize rallies and protests that are only loosely Marxist in their world view and are rarely explicit in their understanding of the ideological motivations of the past. Traditional Marxist thought has been replaced with a 'left-leaning' hatred and distrust of big business in general and of international corporations in particular. The traditional socialist understanding of protecting the working 'proletariat' has been replaced with a general disgust at the perceived abuse of the Third World by big business. The internet has almost made obsolete the need to gain media attention in order to publicize the group's manifesto. Almost any organization that wishes to be heard can post its beliefs on the web. This access makes demands less necessary and the nature of the contemporary Leftist conflict quite different from its predecessors.

Targets as diverse as World Trade Organization (WTO) meetings and Colorado ski areas have replaced the kidnappings and shootings carried out by Leftist organizations in the past. The targets of the New Left reflect the changed organizational structures of these groups. Whereas in the past Leftist groups were led by charismatic individuals extolling Marxist ideology in a traditional hierarchical manner, today's groups are independent and act according to diverse ideologies without specific leadership by a central command. The Earth Liberation Front (ELF) website is illustrative of this transition:

> The ELF is an underground movement with no leadership, membership or official spokesperson. The intention of this web site is to inform and chronicle issues related to E.L.F. This web site's management, webmasters, affiliates, or other participants are not to be considered spokespersons, members, or affiliates of The Earth Liberation Front.

Because the ELF structure is non-hierarchical, there is no centralized organization or leadership. There is also no "membership" in the Earth Liberation Front. In the past, individuals have committed arson and other illegal acts under the ELF name. Individuals who choose to do actions under the banner of E.L.F. do so only driven by their personal conscience. These have been individual choices, and are not endorsed, encouraged, or approved of by the management, contributors, or readers. (ELF, 2005)

While the unions between the various contemporary left-oriented extremists are loose and only rarely explicitly linked to the traditional ideologies of the historic Left, recruiting power and group-sustaining capacity is strong. The attraction for young adults—primarily college-educated—remains similar to the attraction of earlier Leftist organizations. In addition though, the groups—especially those focused on environmental issues—find more support with adults who are now middle-aged but perhaps recollect the activism of the 1960s and 1970s with some sympathy. Where these groups have moved from activism to violence, the Federal Bureau of Investigation (FBI) has identified them as a primary terrorist threat to the USA; and as they are found throughout Europe, they are a threat there as well (Jarboe, 2002).

RIGHT-WING MOTIVATIONS

To understand the motivations behind extreme right-wing political views can be more difficult than many assume. The issues and ideological drives that underpin the Right are not laid out efficiently as they are on the extreme Left. Marx, Mao and even Che Guevara each tried, through their writings, to give the world their plan for what they believed would be a better society. They set out their particular understanding of socialism in relation to violence in terms that were, essentially, intellectually coherent. Leftist terrorists built their organizations in many cases directly on what those writings suggested, thereby giving the group a direct link to a particular ideology. While there have obviously been influential writings that have had a similar impact on the radical Right—for instance Hitler's *Mein Kampf*—few have accused most of the modern right-wing terrorists of widespread intellectual coherence.

Presuppositions about extreme Right politics generally assume a racist, xenophobic, anti-Semitic foundation, which looks forward to the rule of an oppressive and dictatorial—in a word, Fascist—government. The extreme Right is assumed to be conservative and against change; yet the literature coming from the various movements that constitute the radical Right is full of calls for change to the current government order, which they generally view as immoral or biased against them. In that respect the radical Right is anything but conservative. For instance, the neo-Nazi National Alliance views its political platform in direct opposition to those on the radical Left:

Whether one prefers the Marxist goal of the greatest happiness for the greatest number or the National Alliance goal of stronger, wiser, and more

> beautiful men and women is a matter of one's values. It was not on its choice of values that Marxism foundered, however, but on its refusal to recognize the fact of human inequality and the nature of human motivation...Rather than following the Marxist path of robbing the successful in order to reward the unsuccessful, we must take measures to ensure that society's lowest elements do not multiply and become more numerous in later generations. (National Alliance, 1996)

Kaplan and Weinberg make the following observation about the movement in general:

> The Euro-American radical right movement is one whose followers are in the process of developing a common identity based upon a shared sense of racial solidarity, that is, as self-defined whites, "Aryans" or "Teutons," besieged by the threatening masses from the third world and of the prospect of multiracial societies. Or, if racialism is not the sole basis for the establishment of such an identity, cultural affinity and a sense of common historical experience and a shared ultimate destiny form yet other pillars of this shared identity. (Kaplan and Weinberg, 1998)

While the classic assumptions apply to many of the groups associated with right-wing terrorism, not all of these suppositions fit universally. Some hybrid ideologies will be discussed below. Perhaps the most stereotypical are the neo-Nazi groups found both in Europe and the USA, but even with these, relationships with other ideologies may alter the base upon which they have been built. For instance, the neo-Nazi organization known as Aryan Nations simultaneously worships a construction of God derived from their particular exegesis of text through an idiosyncratic hermeneutic while at the same time revering Adolf Hitler as their political hero. The message from their website can be confusing to the uninitiated, as it calls for an alliance with Islamic terrorists, whom they extol, while simultaneously making calls for a pure white nation. Take for instance this statement by Aryan Nations' national leader, August Kreis:

> This passion of True Islamic Believers is something that we have envisioned establishing within our own Aryan Nations promotion of National Socialism and the "Aryan Way of Life" while presenting a spirit of Aryan jihad. Although, because of long-term jewish (sic) control, this may not be a viable possibility with adherence to any presently available belief system(s) generally referred to as, "religion(s)." Due to this we shall be delving into hitherto uncharted waters constructing an underlying faith needed to establish and perpetuate an honourable (sic) way of life for the Aryan. (Aryan Nations, 2005)

While there is apparent ideological inconsistency in much of the writing on the extreme Right, other, more trivial issues—such as the poor quality of the textual construction— make understanding the groups problematic. Adding to the difficulty of understanding the ideology of the extreme Right is the fact that few genuine right-wing terrorist organizations have ever existed. Individual terrorists have emerged from the various movements and associations on the extreme Right, but few terrorist organizations have supported them.

Different from their left-wing counterparts, the Right has tended to spawn individuals who have acted alone or in small groups on a mixture of rightist ideology put forward by larger and generally non-criminal movements and organizations. While the Aryan Nations, National Alliance, various militias and recent manifestations of the Ku Klux Klan (KKK) are all generally written about as terrorist organizations, the reality is that these organizations operate legally and openly in the USA and are only somewhat deterred in Europe. For instance, Germany has stricter controls on Nazi elements than the US and British laws governing 'hate speech', allowing the government to suppress some extremist material. But only when individual members of the groups take violent action against their perceived enemy are the groups then singled out—generally only to disavow any complicity with the individual—and they are subsequently allowed to return to disseminating their extreme, yet legal, views. For instance, the following public statement by Aryan Nations on the internet appears designed to incite individuals to violence motivated by the extremist ideology:

> Say NO to funding the rebuilding of New Orleans with your tax dollars! Why pump billions into an area infested by all sort of evils? New Orleans = queers, transvestites, all forms of satanic religions, stick-waving, shit-flinging negroid aberrations such as Voudon and Santeria, rampant race-mixing, gambling, etc., etc.. Instead of wasting funds rebuilding send in a few fighters and strafe the city with some napalm! Once what remained of Katrina and Rita burns to the ground bury the rest! These storms are the wrath of Yahweh! Rejoice, for the cleansing is just beginning! (Aryan Nations, 2005)

In the USA a familiar motivating belief on the extreme Right is that Jews are controlling the government and, indeed, international politics. In recent years this perception of ZOG, or Zionist Occupational Government, has also spread to parts of Europe. Most right-wing extremists identify Jewish conspiracy behind almost everything, including, recently, the devastation wrought by nature. For instance, Hurricane Katrina that devastated the Gulf region of the USA in September 2005 was viewed as a Jewish attempt to subvert white neighbourhoods on an online Aryan Nations website:

> BLUFFDALE, Utah, Sept. 9 – Carrying the scraps of their lives in plastic trash bags, citizens of the drowned city of New Orleans landed in a strange new place a week ago and wondered where they were. The land was brown, and nearly everyone they saw was white. (Here is the jews (sic) plan! To darken the White areas of our nation with wetbacks and now Negros (sic). It's not enough that they leave the floodwater gates open from Mexico, now they are behind yet another scheme to spread filth throughout White communities.) (Aryan Nations, 2005)

Those from within the extreme Right view the Jewish conspiracy as so thoroughly in place as to allow the aligned forces to use any natural calamity to immediately subvert the established white order in an effort to further ingrain Jewish control. It makes no difference if the facts of the case reveal something different—there is an assumption by many of these groups that a secret cabal of Jewish people is quietly controlling the world in an effort to destroy a pure white race. As we shall see later in this essay, this assumption vacillates between secular and religiously motivated ideological strains on the extreme Right.

Right-wing extremism differs slightly between the USA and Europe and differs yet again between countries within Europe. For instance, as noted, the US reference to government as ZOG has been adopted in Sweden and Norway while it has not taken hold in Germany. The religious undertones found in the USA are much less apparent in Europe. Another substantial difference is the manner in which the radical Right is promoted in these two areas. In the USA small groups surround a charismatic leader, holding rallies, selling literature in support of their ideology and occasionally engaging in some violent action to 'support' the cause. In Europe, where hate laws are more stringent than in the USA, radical Right extremism is much more likely to find expression in fringe political parties (Kaplan and Weinberg, 1998).

Bruce Hoffman called Identity theology a 'thin veneer' of religion used on the extreme Right to cover an ideology of hate. In many cases this description is accurate, as a wide variety of right-wing extremist groups have used the language and organizational capabilities of Identity theology to recruit and retain their membership. Militias, the KKK, tax protesters and neo-Nazis alike have used portions of the theology in their language and propaganda.

Identity theology has been incorrectly characterized as a unified belief system by much of the academic and popular literature under the doctrines espoused by 'seed-line' Identity theology. In reality, there are two major theological divides within the diverse Identity community—both of which have been used by right-wing extremist groups. The first and best-known strain of Identity theology is called 'seed-line' Identity theology. This form suggests that Jews are the literal offspring of a sexual union between Eve and the Devil. Furthermore, 'seed-line' adherents believe that all non-white people are actually referred to in Genesis 1:24 as 'beasts of the field'.

Though abhorrent, 'seed-line' theology has been a powerful tool on the extreme Right, providing a religious justification for dehumanizing the enemy. When an Identity adherent kills a Jewish person, they no longer need to regard themselves as killing another human. The perspective that the theology provides is that the 'true believer' has killed one of the literally half-devil enemies. Similarly, in light of the text from Genesis cited above, 'seed-line' adherents advocate slavery, removal from a particular country or even death for all non-whites, regarding them as mere cattle. When overlaid in a social milieu of general distrust of the ruling government and presupposing an overarching Jewish conspiracy, it is immediately apparent that 'seed-line' theology contributes to and feeds off other types of right-wing ideology in a continuous loop of hate.

Perhaps less theologically virulent is the British-Israel style of Identity theology. While not so well known as 'seed-line' theology, such right-wing extremist icons as Pete Peters, author of *Death Penalty for Homosexuals* (Peters, 1992), follow the non-'seed-line' variant of Identity theology. The primary theological issue of the British-Israel form of Identity theology is that the 'identity' of true Israel is actually to be found in the British, Anglo-Saxon, Germanic and Scandinavian peoples rather than in Ashkenazi or Semitic Judaism, thus making Aryans rather than Jews the 'chosen people'.

RIGHT-WING TARGETS AND TACTICS

Right-wing ideology and theology play a significant role in determining where and how a terrorist organization will strike. The assumption by the radical Right that there is a vast Jewish conspiracy against white Europeans, white Americans and Christians makes Jews, or those suspected of being Jewish, obvious targets. Bill Roper, the Deputy Membership Co-ordinator for the National Alliance, illustrated the importance of the Jewish people as targets for right-wing extremists shortly after 9/11. Roper wrote on a public e-mail list:

> ... the enemy of our enemy is, for now at least, our friends ... We may not want them marrying our daughters ... but anyone who is willing to drive a plane into a building to kill Jews is alright (sic) by me. I wish our members had half as much testicular fortitude. (ADL, 2005)

Other targets of terror by the Right may include any people of colour, immigrants, homosexuals or even whites who are believed to have 'sold out their race' by their conduct. That conduct could include anything that the group perceives as counter to their ideology. Thus, a white, Christian, male might be regarded as the enemy by a right-wing group if he was believed to be in collusion with a government the group viewed as illegitimate. This was the case in a 1983 shooting of a white male killed by Covenant, Sword and Arm of the Lord (CSA) Identity theology adherent Richard Wayne Snell. Snell mistakenly believed the pawn storeowner to be Jewish and therefore a 'legitimate' target according to Snell's extremist right-wing belief system. Snell was later executed for the 1983 shooting of the pawn storeowner as well as the killing of a black Arkansas State Trooper in 1984 (ADL, 2005). The execution took place on 19 April 1995—an important date in the world of right-wing terrorism.

An interesting tactic of the extreme Right—not actually terrorism, yet used to support the ideologically motivated groups on both sides of the Atlantic from which right-wing terrorists emerge—is the White Power music scene that has found acceptance in the skinhead and other neo-Nazi-style groups throughout Europe and the USA. The National Alliance record label, Resistance Records, is an important source of funds for the group. Likewise in Europe, bands such as the now defunct Skrewdriver and Blood and Honour produce similarly racist and anti-Semitic music that is aimed at younger adherents of the extreme Right.

The single most violent right-wing terrorist act in modern history was the bombing of the Alfred P. Murrah building in Oklahoma City on 19 April 1995. The truck bomb planted by Timothy McVeigh, with the support of Terry Nichols and Michael Fortier, killed 168 people and left many Americans wondering how a white veteran of the US military could attack his fellow countrymen. McVeigh, who was arrested shortly after the explosion occurred, had used traditional terrorist methods and his target selection explained much of his ideology.

For McVeigh, like many on the radical fringes of the American Right at the time, two events during the 1990s served as motivational and recruitment tools for terrorism from the extreme Right in the USA. The first catalyst was a stand-off between law enforcement officers and a family of Identity theology adherents at Ruby Ridge, northern Idaho, in August 1992. The second was the 51-day Waco, Texas stand-off between Branch Davidians and the FBI.

Randy Weaver's failure to appear in court on weapons charges led to his arrest and the eventual 10-day stand-off at Ruby Ridge with the FBI. During the incident Weaver's wife, Vicky, and his 13-year-old son were killed. Particularly disturbing to many on the radical Right was the fact that Vicky Weaver was shot while holding her infant daughter. The Ruby Ridge incident was perceived by the radical Right to be confirmation of the Federal government's intention to oppress and even kill white Christians. Weaver was eventually acquitted of all charges except his original failure to appear in court and the federal government paid the Weavers US $3.1m. in compensation. The cash settlement added to the extremists' perception of an immoral government trying to buy its way out of wrongdoing. The Weavers' own account of what happened is chronicled in a book written by Randy Weaver and his eldest daughter, Sara (Weaver and Weaver, 1998). McVeigh, like many on the fringe, was outraged and further convinced that the federal government was out of control and intent on depriving white Americans of their rights and forming a 'one world government'.

On 19 April 1993 the Waco stand-off concluded violently when a raid by the FBI on the Branch Davidian compound resulted in the death of 74 people. The siege was used by the radical Right to bolster their argument that the federal government was out of control and ready to kill Christians whom it regarded as dangerous. McVeigh was again outraged, but this time from a front-row seat. He drove as near as he could to the site of the siege in order to protest and distribute anti-government literature, witnessing at first hand what he believed was an attack on private citizens' rights.

To McVeigh and many on the Right, the government was simply seeking a pretext to subvert Americans and deprive them of their rights. McVeigh was a staunch advocate of American citizens' right to own firearms—a right protected by the Second Amendment of the US Constitution; and feared that the government would eventually outlaw and seize privately owned firearms. McVeigh was an avid reader of *The Turner Diaries*, a right-wing cult classic that recounts how a fictional group of US citizens tries to take back America from a government that has usurped gun rights and the rights of white citizens in general (Macdonald, 1978). The book was written by William Pierce of the National Alliance, but was widely read, and regarded as prophetic by many on the extreme Right.

McVeigh's attack on the Murrah building was his attempt to stop the federal government from making further (perceived) encroachments on the rights of private American citizens. The target housed many federal offices and the date of the attack commemorated many events important to the Right. The nineteenth of April 1775 is the date celebrated as the beginning of the American Revolution at Lexington and Concord; on 19 April 1985 the federal stand-off with the CSA began; on 19 April 1993 the Branch Davidian compound was burned to the ground; on 19 April 1995 Richard Wayne Snell was executed, and on the same day the Alfred P. Murrah federal building was attacked. Few dates have acquired so much importance for terrorists.

The tactics and targets of the radical Right are not dissimilar to terrorists motivated for other reasons. Guns and bombs continue to be the weapons of choice. Their targets of attack hold ideological significance and, at least in relation to the Oklahoma attack, the symbolic nature of the event was captured in the date chosen to carry out the bombing. The Oklahoma bombing encapsulates the dangerous mixture of beliefs that influence the radical Right.

COUNTER-EFFORTS CONSIDERED

Sections of the radical Right have been particularly susceptible to undercover law enforcement incursions. Well-known right-wing extremist leader Louis Beam complained, after leaving the KKK, that the organization was thoroughly infiltrated by federal, state and local law enforcement officers. This has made the use of terrorist cells on the extreme Right more difficult and has given rise to a new strategy, explained by Beam in an article in *The Seditionist*, called Leaderless Resistance (Beam, 1992). The strategy called on individuals and very small groups to carry out attacks based on Ideology rather than organizational structures in order to spark a broader revolution that would eventually allow the extreme Right to break away or take over the government. Many have suggested that McVeigh was operating in accordance with this strategy when he carried out the Oklahoma bombing. The strategy continues to find favour on the Right today, as is evident from this Aryan Nations web posting:

> 'Centralization' is a thing of the past – 'decentralization' is the key to the manifestation of certain forces including 'the Lone Wolf' which represents a portion of the future-wave of activism. In this sense, our proclaimed opponents may find it pragmatic to fear the unknown. Regardless, the Aryan Nations will work in a direction that involves ruthless, intentional and cold-blooded use of forms inimical not only to the infrastructure of ZOG but to the infrastructure of society itself as it is known today. (Aryan Nations, 2005)

A weakness of the leaderless resistance strategy is that if groups or individuals are arrested, then the effectiveness of the group is completely destroyed. The organizations have to operate with so few personnel that almost any disruption is catastrophic to the group. On 18 June 1984 one of the few, but dangerous, terrorist organizations to emerge from the right-wing, The Order, assassinated Denver Colorado radio host Alan Berg in the driveway of his apartment (Flynn and Gerhardt, 1990). Berg was an outspoken opponent of the radical Right, often using his radio show as a mouthpiece to denigrate the icons of right-wing extremism. The Order—led by Robert 'Bob' Matthews—went on to rob armoured cars and worked to distribute the money they stole to various high-profile extremist groups operating in the USA. The group's robberies and counterfeiting activities raised several million dollars in funds for the broader movement. The Order was brought down and their leader killed in a shoot-out with the FBI on Washington's Whidbey Island. When compared with terrorist organizations, such as the Provisional Irish Republican Army, which maintain hundreds of active members with developed leadership capacity, the organizational weakness of right-wing terrorists is apparent. The Order comprised mainly members from the religious milieu on the Right. Most of the members emerged from Christian Identity theology backgrounds. For instance, Richard Scutari was influenced by his association with the CSA and Matthews himself followed the Identity teachings of Richard Butler. Although the group has now effectively been destroyed, surviving former members continue to have an influence on the radical Right. Finding the motivation of Identity somewhat lacking, David Lane and Richard Scutari have continued to publish on the internet from prison, but from a modern Odinist religious standpoint rather than strictly Identity theology.

The future for right-wing terrorist organizations should probably be considered as limited. Operational security issues, vulnerability to law enforcement infiltration and the lack of broad-based support from any national populations suggest that large-to-moderate terrorist groups are not the primary threat in the near future. Rather, as suggested by Louis Beam in his essay on leaderless resistance, countries will probably continue to be attacked by individuals or very small groups acting on an idiosyncratic mixture of various strains of right-wing extremist ideology.

RIGHT-WING SINGLE-ISSUE TERRORISM

Just as there are single-issue groups associated with the extreme Left, so there are single-issue groups that are naturally grouped with the radical Right. The violent wing of the pro-life movement would be appropriately categorized in this way. Pro-life followers are not typically anti-Semitic, racist or particularly anti-immigrant in their outlook. They lack the common traits associated with Fascist groups and movements. Nevertheless, they are commonly viewed as right-orientated. The Army of God is a group commonly associated with violence in the name of pro-life. The group initially achieved prominence through publishing a 'how to' book—the Army of God Manual. Not unlike the leaderless resistance strategy promoted by former KKK and Aryan Nations leader Louis Beam, violence from the pro-life movement has tended to be committed by individuals in accordance with their understanding of biblical theology.

Pastor Michael Bray is the author of *A Time to Kill* (Bray, 1994), an exegetically based apologetic for why Christians should take up arms against abortion providers in an effort to save the lives of the unborn, using traditional Christian hermeneutics. The book gives no tactical suggestions as the Army of God Manual did. Rather, it appeals to the spiritual understanding of potential followers. The theology upon which the defence of what Bray and his friends describe as justifiable homicide actions is based is not related to Identity theology, the more common doctrine associated with the radical Right.

Several notable terrorists convicted of killing abortion clinic providers are currently in custody, and in 2003 the State of Florida executed Rev. Paul Hill for killing Dr John Britton and his escort outside the doctor's abortion clinic. Perhaps the most famous terrorist related to the movement is Eric Rudolph, who was recently convicted of the Atlanta Olympics bombing in 1996, the bombing of an Atlanta gay nightclub in 1997 and the bombing of a Birmingham, Alabama abortion clinic. While the motivations for the attacks were similar, the methods employed were different from those of anti-abortion activists. Michael Bray, Paul Hill and those commonly associated with the now defunct Army of God have not generally applauded the use of indiscriminate bombings, such as those carried out by Rudolph. They have instead used more precise attacks not dissimilar to those by the early Leftist organizations discussed above.

FUTURE PROSPECTS

Throughout this essay historical evidence has been arrayed that suggests that ideological motivations, be they left- or right-wing in nature, have a significant impact on the actions of groups engaged in terrorism. While the historical examples are instructive, it would be a mistake to assume from this that the groups of today or the future will maintain the same interpretation of past motivations and ideologies. Rapoport's illustration of the various waves of terrorism in this volume shows how those ideological motivations are manifested differently during progressive periods of history. While Communism and Socialism have failed in recent years as predominant political ideologies, the current understanding of what it means to be radically left-wing still provides a framework for violent Leftist activism in some parts of the world.

Currently more vibrant than the radical Left is the violent right-wing ideology serving to motivate sub-national political violence in both the USA and Europe. There appears to be little chance that this will diminish in the near future. Neo-Nazi, anti-Semitic, racist, xenophobic and often religiously understood variations of the extreme Right continue to inspire today. Modern versions of the extreme right-wing ideology breed hate groups—allowed, to varying degrees according to their national location, to openly disseminate their views in the name of free speech and occasionally responsible for acts of violence and terrorism carried out under the strategic framework known as leaderless resistance.

Both left- and right-wing groups consider globalization a motivation for violence, but for different reasons. On the Right, cheap transportation and porous borders have fuelled a resentment of incoming migrants to many nations, such as the USA, Britain, Sweden and Norway, which has led to terrorism against the alien populations. On the other hand, fourth wave or 'New-New Leftist' groups and individuals take issue with the impact of globalization too. Thus, modern anarchist activists have attacked WTO meetings with the aim of bringing their issues to the public's attention. It would appear unlikely that either of these ideological polar opposites will stop motivating terrorism in the immediate future. But while these ideologies continue to motivate terrorism, the targets, if not the tactics, have changed slightly. Guns and bombs continue to serve both sides as the primary means by which they attack. Yet these are used in novel and innovative ways, which force police and the military to constantly hone their counter-terrorism skills in an effort to meet the latest, and hopefully next, terrorist attack from the Left or Right.

Notes:

All citations are located in the bibliography, except the following:

Aryan Nations Website: http://www.aryan-nations.org

Bobvon Sternberg, 'Call it Anarchism or New New Left, it has a Big Voice', *Star Tribune* (Minneapolis), 21 May 2000.

Earth Liberation Front Website: http://www.earthliberationfront.com

Henry Schuster, *CNN*, An Unholy Alliance Aryan Nations Leader Reaches Out to al-Qaeda, Tuesday March 29, 2005, http://www.cnn.com/2005/US/03/29/schuster.column/index.html, 8-22-05

James F. Jarboe, Congressional Testimony, February 12, 2002

Louis Beam, 'Leaderless Resistance', *The Seditionist*, Issue 12, February 1992

National Memorial Institute for the Prevention of Terrorism – MIPT Website: http://www.tkb.org

Peters, Peter J., *Death Penalty for Homosexuals is Prescribed in the Bible* (LaPorte, CO: Scriptures for America, self-published 1992).

What is the National Alliance? Ideology and program of the National Alliance (National Vanguard Books, 1996). Unsigned pamphlet distributed to the author by NA members in California, 1998.

Religion and the New Terrorism

MARK JUERGENSMEYER

INTRODUCTION

What does religion have to do with the virtually global rise of religious violence? In one sense, very little. Osama bin Laden's al-Qa'ida network, for example, is a small group at the extreme end of a subculture of dissatisfied Muslims who are in turn a small minority within the world of Islam. Osama bin Laden is no more representative of Islam than Timothy McVeigh is of Christianity, or Japan's Shoko Asahara is of Buddhism.

Still, it cannot be denied that the ideals and ideas of these activists are permeated by religion. The authority of religion has granted bin Laden's cadres moral legitimacy in their use of violence to assault the symbol of global economic power. It has also provided the metaphor of cosmic war, an image of spiritual struggle that every religion has within its repository of symbols—the conflict between good and evil, truth and falsehood. In was in this sense, then, that the attack on the World Trade Center was religious. It was meant to be catastrophic, an act of scriptural proportions.

What is striking about the World Trade Center assault and many other recent acts of religious terrorism is that they had no obvious military goal. These are acts meant for television. They are a kind of perverse performance of power meant to ennoble the perpetrators' view of the world and to draw us in to their notion of cosmic war.

The attacks in New York and Washington, DC, although unusual in scale, are remarkably similar to many other acts of religious terrorism around the world. In all of these cases, concepts of cosmic war are accompanied by strong claims of moral justification and an enduring absolutism that transforms worldly struggles into sacred battles. It is not so much that religion has become politicized: rather, politics have become 'religionized'. Worldly struggles have been lifted into the high proscenium of sacred battle.

This is what makes religious terrorism so difficult to combat. Its enemies have become 'satanized' and cannot easily be negotiated or compromised with. The rewards for those who fight for the cause are transtemporal, and the time lines of their struggles are vast. Most social and political struggles seek conclusions within the lifetimes of their participants, but religious struggles can take generations to succeed. It was once put to Dr Abdul-Aziz Rantisi, the political head and successor to Sheikh Ahmed Yassin as leader of the Hamas movement in Palestine, that Israel's military force was such that a Palestinian military effort could never succeed. 'Palestine was occupied before, for two hundred years', Rantisi replied. He went on to explain that he and his Palestinian comrades could 'wait again—at least that long', for the struggles of God can endure for eons. Ultimately, however, they knew that they would succeed.

In such battles, waged in divine time and with heaven's rewards, there is no need to compromise one's goals. No need, either, to contend with society's laws and limitations when one is obeying a higher authority. In spiritualizing violence, therefore, religion gives terrorism a remarkable power.

Ironically, the reverse is also true: terrorism can give religion power as well. Although sporadic acts of terrorism do not lead to the establishment of new religious states, they make the political potency of religious ideology impossible to ignore. Terrorism not only gives individuals the illusion of empowerment, it also gives religious organizations and ideas a public attention and importance that they have not enjoyed for many years. In modern America and Europe, it has given religion a prominence in public life that it has not held since before the Enlightenment more than two centuries ago.

EMPOWERING RELIGION

Radical religious movements that have emerged from cultures of violence around the world have three things in common. First, they reject the compromises with liberal values and secular institutions that, for the most part, mainstream religion, whether Christianity, Islam, Judaism, Hinduism, Sikhism or Buddhism, has made. Second, radical religious movements refuse to observe the boundaries that secular society has placed around religion—keeping it private rather than allowing it to intrude into public spaces. And third, these radical movements try to create a new form of religiosity that rejects what they regard as weak modern subsitutes for the more vibrant and demanding forms of religion that they imagine to be essential to their religion's origins.

One of the men accused of bombing the World Trade Center in 1993 explained that the critical moment in his religious life came when he realized that he could not compromise his Islamic integrity with the easy vices offered by modern society. The convicted terrorist, Mahmud Abouhalima, claimed that the early part of his life was spent running away from himself. Although involved in radical Egyptian Islamic movements since his college years in Alexandria, he felt there was no place where he could settle down. He stated that the low point came when he was in Germany, trying to live in the way that he imagined Europeans and Americans lived: a lifestyle in which the superficial comforts of sex and inebriants masked an internal emptiness and despair. Abouhalima described how his return to Islam as the centre of his life carried with it a renewed sense of obligation to make Islamic society truly Islamic, to 'struggle against oppression and injustice' wherever it existed. What was constant, according to Abouhalima, was his family and his faith. Islam was both 'a rock and a pillar of mercy'. But it was not the Islam of liberal, modern Muslims: they, he felt, had compromised the tough and disciplined life the faith demanded. Abouhalima wanted his religion to be 'hard', not 'soft' like the humiliating, mind-numbing comforts of secular modernity.

Activists such as Abouhalima—and, for that matter, Osama bin Laden—imagine themselves to be defenders of ancient faiths. But in fact they have created new forms of religiosity. Like many present-day religious leaders, they have used the language of traditional religion in order to build bulwarks around aspects of modernity that have threatened them, and to suggest ways out of the mindless humiliation of modern life. It was vital to their image of religion, however, that it be perceived as ancient.

The need for religion—a 'hard' religion as Abouhalima called it—was a response to the 'soft' treachery they had observed in the new societies around them. The modern secular world that Abouhalima and other activists inhabited was a dangerous, chaotic and violent sea in which religion was an anchor in a harbour of calm. At some deep and almost transcendent level of their consciousnesses they sensed their lives to be slipping out of control, and they felt both responsible for the disarray and victims of it. To be abandoned by religion in such a world would mean losing their own individual locations and identities. In fashioning a 'traditional religion' of their own making, they exposed their concerns not so much with their religious, ethnic, or national communities, but with their own personal, perilous selves.

ASSAULTS ON SECULARISM

These intimate concerns have been prompted by the perceived failures of public institutions. As Pierre Bourdieu has observed, social structures never have a disembodied reality; they are always negotiated by individuals in their own strategies for maintaining self-identity and success in life. Such institutions are legitimized by the 'symbolic capital' they accrue through the collective trust of many individuals. When that symbolic capital is devalued, when political and religious institutions undergo what Jürgen Habermas has called a 'crisis of legitimacy', this devaluation of authority is experienced not only as a political problem but also as an intensely personal one, as a loss of agency.

It is this sense of a personal loss of power in the face of chaotic political and religious authorities that is common to Osama bin Laden's al-Qa'ida group and most other movements for Christian, Muslim, Jewish, Sikh, Buddhist, and Hindu nationalism around the world. The syndrome begins with the perception that the public world has gone awry, and the suspicion that behind this social confusion lies a great spiritual and moral conflict, a cosmic battle between the forces of order and chaos, good and evil. Such a conflict is understandably violent, a violence that is often felt by the victimized activist as powerlessness, either individually or in association with others of his/her gender, race or ethnicity. The government—already delegitimized—is perceived to be in league with the forces of chaos and evil.

One of the reasons why secular government is easily labelled as the enemy of religion is that, to some degree, it is. By its nature, the secular state is opposed to the idea that religion should have a role in public life. From the time that modern secular nationalism emerged in the 18th century as a product of the European

Enlightenment's political values, it did so with a distinctly anti-religious, or at least anti-clerical, posture. The ideas of John Locke about the origins of a civil community and the 'social contract' theories of Jean-Jacques Rousseau required very little commitment to religious belief. Although they allowed for a divine order that made the rights of humans possible, their ideas had the effect of removing religion—at least Church religion—out of public life. At the time, religious 'enemies of the Enlightenment'—as the historian, Darrin McMahon, describes them—protested against religion's public demise. But their views were submerged in a wave of approval for a new view of social order in which secular nationalism was thought to be virtually a natural law, universally applicable and morally right.

Post-Enlightenment modernity proclaimed the death of religion. Modernity signalled not only the demise of the Church's institutional authority and clerical control, but also the loosening of religion's ideological and intellectual grip on society. Scientific reasoning and the moral claims of the secular social contract replaced theology and the Church as the bases for truth and social identity. The result of religion's devaluation has been 'a general crisis of religious belief', as Bourdieu has put it.

In countering this disintegration, resurgent religious activists have proclaimed the death of secularism. They have dismissed the efforts of secular culture and its forms of nationalism to replace religion. They have challenged the notion that secular society and the modern nation-state are able to provide the moral fibre that unites national communities, or give it the ideological strength to sustain states buffeted by ethical, economic and military failures. Their message has been easy to believe and has been widely received because the failures of the secular state have been so real.

ANTI-GLOBALISM

The moral leadership of the secular state was increasingly challenged in the last decade of the 20th century and the first decade of the 21st by the rise of a global economy. The Cold War had provided contesting models of moral politics—communism and democracy—that were replaced by a global market that weakened national sovereignty and was conspicuously devoid of political ideals. The global economy became controlled by transnational businesses accountable to no single governmental authority and with no clear ideological or moral standards of behaviour. But while both Christian and Enlightenment values were left behind, transnational commerce transported aspects of Westernized popular culture to the rest of the world. American and European music, videos and films were transmitted across national boundaries, where they threatened to obliterate local and traditional forms of artistic expression. Added to this social confusion were convulsive shifts in political power that followed the break-up of the USSR and the collapse of Asian economies at the end of the 20th century.

The public sense of insecurity that came in the wake of these cataclysmic global changes was felt not only in the societies of those nations that were economically devastated by them—especially countries in the former USSR—but also in economically stronger industrialized societies. In the USA, for example, there was a remarkable degree of disaffection with political leaders and right-wing religious movements that fed on the public's perception of the inherent immorality of government.

The rise of religious terrorism may well have been related to these global changes. Many of the groups associated with violence in industrialized societies have had an anti-modernist political agenda. At the extreme end of this religious rejection in the USA were members of the American anti-abortion group, Defensive Action; the Christian militia and Christian Identity movement; and isolated groups such as the Branch Davidian sect in Waco, Texas. Similar attitudes towards secular government emerged in Israel—the religious nationalist ideology of the Kach party was an extreme example—and, as the Aum Shinrikyo movement has demonstrated, in Japan. As in the USA, contentious groups within these countries were disillusioned with the ability of secular leaders to guide their countries' destinies. They identified government as the enemy.

The global shifts that have given rise to anti-modernist movements have also affected less-developed nations. India's Jawaharlal Nehru, Egypt's Gamal Abdel Nasser, and Iran's Reza Shah Pahlavi were once committed to creating versions of the USA—or a kind of cross between the USA and the USSR—in their own countries. But new generations of leaders no longer believed in the Westernized visions of Nehru, Nasser or the Shah. Rather, they were eager to complete the process of decolonization and build new, indigenous nationalisms.

When activists in Algeria who demonstrated against the suppression of the Islamic Salvation Front in 1991 proclaimed that they were continuing the war of liberation against French colonialism, they had the ideological rather than the political reach of European influence in mind. Religious activists such as the Algerian leaders, Ayatollah Khomeini in Iran, Sheikh Ahmed Yassin in Palestine, Maulana Abu al-Ala Mawdudi in Pakistan, Sayyid Qutb and his disciple, Sheikh Omar Abdul Rahman in Egypt, L. K. Advani in India, and Sant Jarnail Singh Bhindranwale in India's Punjab have asserted the legitimacy of a post-colonial national identity based on traditional culture.

The result of this disaffection with the values of the modern West has been a loss of faith in secular nationalism. Although a few years ago it would have been a startling notion, the idea has now become virtually commonplace that secular nationalism—the idea that the nation is rooted in a secular compact rather than religious or ethnic identity—is in crisis. In many parts of the world it is viewed as an alien cultural construction, one closely linked with what has been called 'the project of modernity'. In such cases, religious alternatives to secular ideologies have had extraordinary appeal.

This uncertainty about what constitutes a valid basis for national identity is a political form of post-modernism. In Iran it has resulted in the rejection of a modern Western political regime and the creation of a successful religious state. Increasingly, even secular scholars in the West have recognized that religious ideologies might offer an alternative to modernity in the political sphere. Yet, what lies beyond modernity is not necessarily a new form of political order, religious or not. In nations formerly under Soviet control, for example, the spectre of the future beyond the socialist form of modernity has been one of cultural anarchism. The fear that there will be a spiritual as well as a political collapse at modernity's centre has, in many parts of the world, led to terror.

The al-Qa'ida network associated with Osama bin Laden takes religious violence to yet another level. The implicit attack on global economic and political systems that is levelled by religious nationalists from Algeria to Indonesia is made explicit: America is the enemy. Moreover, it is a war waged not on a national plane but on a transnational one. Their agenda is not for any specific form of religious nation-state but an inchoate vision of the global rule of religious law. Rather than religious nationalists, transnational activists like bin Laden are guerrilla anti-globalists.

POST-MODERN TERROR

Thus bin Laden and his acts of violence have a credibility in some quarters of the world because of the uncertainties of this moment of global history. Both violence and religion have appeared at times in history when authority is in question, since they are both ways of challenging and replacing authority. One gains its power from force and the other from its claims to ultimate order. The combination of the two in acts of religious terrorism has been a potent assertion indeed. Whether or not the perpetrators of these acts consciously intended them to be political acts, any public act of violence has political consequences. Insofar as they have been attempts to reshape the public order, they have been examples of what José Casanova has called the increasing 'deprivatization' of religion. In various parts of the world where attempts have been made by defenders of religion to reclaim the centre of public attention and authority, religious terrorism is often the violent face of these attempts.

The post-modern religious rebels, such as those who rally to the cause of Osama bin Laden, have therefore been neither anomalies nor anachronisms. From Algeria to Idaho, their small but potent groups of violent activists have represented masses of supporters, and they have exemplified currents of thinking and cultures of commitment that have risen to counter the prevailing modernism—the ideology of individualism and scepticism—that in the past three centuries emerged from the European Enlightenment and spread throughout the world. They have come to hate secular governments with an almost transcendent passion. They have dreamed of revolutionary changes that would establish a godly social order in the rubble of what the citizens of most secular societies have regarded as modern, egalitarian democracies. Their enemies have seemed to most people to be both benign and banal: such symbols of prosperity and authority as the World Trade Center. The logic of this kind of militant religiosity has therefore been difficult for many people to comprehend. Yet its challenge has been profound, for it has contained a fundamental critique of the world's post-Enlightenment secular culture and politics.

For this reason, acts of religious terrorism have been attempts to purchase public recognition of the legitimacy of religious world views with the currency of violence. Since religious authority can provide a ready-made replacement for secular leadership, it is no surprise that when secular authority has been deemed to be morally insufficient, the challenges to its legitimacy and the attempts to gain support for its rivals have been based on religion. When the proponents of religion have asserted their claims to be the moral force undergirding public order, they sometimes have done so with the kind of power that a confused society can graphically recognize: the force of terror.

On the Nature of Religious Terrorism

ADAM DOLNIK AND ROHAN GUNARATNA

INTRODUCTION

Terrorist violence differs from ordinary crime principally by the presence of an altruistic motive and an ideological justification. In terrorism, ideology is all-important, as an organization's ideological foundation frames the world-view of its members and thus provides a sense of collective identity. Moreover, ideology is instrumental in identifying the enemy, while also providing the necessary explanation and justification for its targeting. In addition, it is again the ideology of a group which determines its core objectives and the strategy for how and by what means these objectives are to be achieved. And finally, ideology is also a critical component in determining a group's ambitions, as well as the overall perception of urgency for armed action in order to fulfil these aspirations. At the operational level, then, the group's core strategy translates into the frequency and intensity of its military operations, in that different ideologies provide different levels of acceptability of mass-casualty and indiscriminate targeting. Consequently, the tactics and targeting preferences of a group are also very much influenced by the given group's belief system. Overall, the understanding of a group's ideology is one of the most important aspects of predictive threat-assessment of terrorist violence.

Over the last 20 years, there have been alarming developments in the trends in international terrorism: a continual decrease in terrorist incidents, which has, however, been accompanied by an increasing number of overall casualties in those fewer incidents. In other words, terrorist attacks are becoming increasingly lethal. Besides the rising average casualty rate, qualitative analysis of all terrorist attacks seems to provide additional support for this claim: while the deadliest incidents prior to the 1980s involved 'only' dozens of fatalities, in the 1980s and 1990s, in the most lethal attacks, they numbered hundreds, and in the new millennium the plateau has reached into the thousands for the first time in history. Similarly, until 9/11, there had been only 76 terrorist bombings in which more than 25 people had been killed. Over the course of the next four years, this number has more than tripled.

One of the most common explanations for this trend of increasing lethality has been the proliferation of terrorist campaigns inspired by religion. According to Bruce Hoffman, who was one of the first scholars to identify this causal link:

'The fact that for the religious terrorist violence inevitably assumes a transcendent purpose and therefore becomes a sacramental and divine duty arguably results in a significant loosening of the constraints on the commission of mass murder. Religion, moreover, functions as a legitimizing force, sanctioning if not encouraging wide scale violence against an almost open-ended category of opponents. Thus religious terrorist violence becomes almost an end in itself – a morally justified, divinely instigated expedient toward the attainment of the terrorists' ultimate ends. This is a direct reflection of the fact that the terrorists motivated by a religious imperative do not seek to appeal to any constituency but themselves and the changes they seek are not for any utilitarian purpose, but are only to benefit themselves. The religious terrorist, moreover, sees himself as an outsider from the society that he both abhors and rejects and this sense of alienation enables him to contemplate – and undertake – far more destructive and bloodier types of terrorist operations than his secular counterpart.' (Hoffman, 1993: 12)

As can be seen from the previous quote, an integral part of the argument concerns the core characteristics of religious terrorists, which allegedly set them aside from their secular counterparts. This important hypothesis has contributed to the wide perception that religious terrorists are by default more lethal and more dangerous than secular terrorists, a finding that has a profound impact on the methods of predictive threat-assessment. However, in practice there has been considerable disagreement about the uniformity of categorization of groups as 'religious', as opposed to 'ethnic' or 'nationalist'. This essay will attempt to shed more light on this issue by providing an alternative perspective on the characteristics of mass-casualty terrorism.

GENESIS AND SCOPE OF RELIGIOUS TERRORISM

The turn to religion as the main ideological support basis for terrorism over the last 20 years did not take place in a vacuum. It has been motivated by a number of factors, among them lack of progress with regard to the widening gap between the West and the rest of the world and the inability of secular organizations to resolve core communal problems, as well as larger issues such as the Israeli–Palestinian conflict, and the overall breakdown of secular ideologies such as Marxism and purely secular nationalism (Laqueur, 1999: 128). One of the most important events in this regard has been the Iranian Revolution in 1979, in the sense that it provided evidence of the feasibility of establishing an Islamic state, and also served as a strong support base for violent Shi'a groups such as Amal and Hezbollah in Lebanon or al-Dawa in Iraq. Another pivotal event in the same year was the Soviet invasion of Afghanistan, the resistance to which quickly became the unifying issue for *mujahidin* from all over the world. This was important in providing personal contacts and battleground experience for many radicals, and, even more importantly, the addictive taste of victory. These elements would later form the foundation for the phenomenon we now know as al-Qa'ida. But radical Islam was certainly not the only religion that became used as a terrorist ideology during the early 1980s. Christianity was represented by the rise of the Christian Identity and anti-abortion movements in the USA, represented by groups such as The Order, The Covenant the Sword and Arm of the Lord, Aryan Nations, and the Army of God; just as radical Judaism became the main ideological foundation for the Gush Emunim terrorist campaign in Israel. Similarly, the Sikh campaign represented by groups such as Babbar Khalsa International (BKI), Dal Khalsa or the Khalistan Commando Force in India became increasingly religious, following 'Operation Blue Star' in which Indian troops violently raided the holiest Sikh temple in Amritsar. The Palestinian and Kashmiri conflicts have also continually transformed from primarily nationalist to dominantly religious ones from about the end of the 1980s, and the same trajectory could be observed during the 1990s in other conflicts in, for example, the Balkans or the Caucasus. In the 1990s new-age cults based on eclectic religious ideologies also arose, such as the Japanese Aum Shinrikyo, whose apocalyptic mix of prophetic cultic practices derived from a wide array of writings, such as those of Nostradamus, the Book of Revelation in the Bible and imagery from Hindu and Buddhist texts, as well as science fiction elements from the novels written in the 1940s by Isaac Asimov. Other influences were Japanese nationalism, anti-American and anti-Jewish sentiments, the Hindu God Shiva, the Old and New Testaments of the Bible, Jesus, nuclear holocaust and the Tibetan Book of the Dead. As we can see from these examples, no major religion has been excluded from being exploited as a divine justification for terrorist violence.

The single most important factor for the observed rise of religion as a dominant characteristic of modern terrorism has been the end of the Cold War, which signified the utter historical failure of communist ideologies, as well as the end of the bipolar world order. These events not only diminished the attractiveness of ideological compliance with one of the two world power centres in order to attract state assistance, but they also triggered immense fear of 'one-worldism', symbolized by the emergence of the unipolar world order, which was perceived by radical members of various cultures as a threat to their identity and survival (Ranstorp, 1996:18). In the absence of alternatives among secular ideologies, many extremists shifted to religion as the main ideological foundation of their activities. This shift in ideological support mechanisms, however, does not necessarily mean that the nature of core terrorist motivations and beliefs has changed, or that religion became the primary *motivating* factor for acts of violence. As previously noted by Walter Laqueur, terrorist belief systems may differ significantly based on history, culture or the influence of charismatic leaders. But the ideological content is only secondary to 'burning passion', which serves as the primary driving force behind terrorist activity (Laqueur, 1999: 230). In other words, while religion has in the last 20 years become a more prominent factor as the supporting philosophical basis for many terrorist organizations, the underlying *motives* in the belief systems of the majority of today's terrorists have *not* changed. Even the religious fanatic views his violent activity as an essentially altruistic act of self-defence. It is still the perception of humiliation, victimization and injustice that drives the so-called 'religious terrorist', rather than a perceived universal command from God. The use of holy rhetoric by most groups commonly labelled as 'religious' serves much more as a uniting and morale-boosting tool than as a universal justification for acts of unrestrained violence. That is not to say that for many terrorists religion does not represent a tremendous legitimizing force, and that it does not inspire the perception of enormous gratification and empowerment. But the terrorists are still primarily motivated by a grievance that is very real—even though, just like most ordinary people, they also look for the support of their arguments wherever they can. Religion, then, represents only one of the possible sources of support. The key point to emphasize here is that terrorist *ideology* is fundamentally different from *motivation* for terrorist violence. Motivation in essence refers to an individual's decision to join a violent group, and its sources typically differ even among members of the same terrorist organization. This element is sometimes referred to as the 'root causes' of terrorism, in the sense that it forms the preconditions that make an individual susceptible to joining a terror movement. Ideology then, has the role of an umbrella which enables the unification of frustrated individuals by linking their grievances by an all-encompassing explanation that blames the system, which is so corrupt and unjust that it must be destroyed. In this way a terror group provides its members with a single mind-set and objective, together with the firm prescription of violence as the only possible chance for remedy. In addition, ideology provides terrorists with mechanisms for enemy-dehumanization and for the diffusion of responsibility in order to facilitate their ability to kill non-combatants for a higher purpose. The important implication here is that the common perception of religious terrorists as less rational because their motivational drive is a divine call is ultimately incorrect, since religion in the context of terrorism essentially constitutes an ideology and not a motive.

How does one then distinguish between religious and secular groups for the purposes of typologization? Most authors confirm that drawing the line between religious and secular terrorists is challenging, as many secular organizations also have a strong religious component, and many religious terrorists in addition possess goals that are of a political nature. This distinction becomes even more blurred in the case of Islamic fundamentalism, as Islam does not differentiate between religion and politics. Further, in trying to make the distinction we should be careful to not fall into the trap of rhetorical nuances. In many cultures the word 'God' figures very strongly in the language and in cultural and political traditions, which can sometimes be misleading. For instance, to an outsider phrases such as 'In God We Trust', printed on American currency, or the use of the popular slogan 'God Bless America' by the American President could easily create the false impression that the USA is essentially a theocratic state. Another factor besides language that has the capacity to mislead us in terms of labelling a terrorist organization as religious is government propaganda. Virtually all states that are victims of a terrorist campaign insist on projecting their opponents as religious fanatics. This is quite understandable, as such labelling can have a delegitimizing effect on the terrorists' cause—someone who views himself as fighting on God's orders is popularly perceived as an irrational zealot, with whom no compromise is deemed possible. Rather, this 'worshipper of evil' is regarded as an exceptionally dangerous creature who uses claims of a just grievance only as a misleading cover, and who can only be stopped by merciless elimination. Israel and, to a lesser extent, Russia and India are examples of countries that have used such a strategy with some success. But while this strategy of promoting an image of the opponent as an irrational religious fanatic may in some cases be politically successful, it entails the danger of failing to address the actual real-life grievances, which in turn can eventually result in increased support for the terrorists. In sum, while the religious dimension is present in the language of many terrorist organizations, when categorizing terrorist groups for the purposes of threat-assessment we must read between the lines of rhetoric.

CHARACTERISTICS OF RELIGIOUS TERRORISTS

Some terrorism scholars have attempted to define the core characteristics of religious terrorists, pointing mainly to the radically different value systems, mechanisms of legitimization and justification, concepts of morality, mechanisms of victim dehumanization and an overall world-view. The difficulty, however, is that most of the defined characteristics fail to pinpoint a clear dividing line between religious and secular terrorists.

For instance, Mark Juergensmeyer characterizes religiously motivated struggles primarily as those involving images of divine warfare (Juergensmeyer, 2000: 146). Such images represent what Juergensmeyer calls a 'cosmic struggle' which is played out in history as a war between good and evil, order and chaos. Religious terrorists identify with such a struggle and project its images onto the present situation, which they seek to address. Such heavily mythologized conflict between the believers and their enemies then becomes absolute. Juergensmeyer also describes in great detail the creation of martyrs as a distinct characteristic of religious terrorists in their dominant reliance on the concept of martyrdom. In the context of a 'cosmic war', he argues, martyrdom is not only regarded as a testimony of one's commitment, it is also a performance of the most fundamental religious act found in virtually every religious tradition in the world: the act of sacrifice. The images of sacrifice thus transform destruction performed within the religious context into something positive, making killing not only permissible but even mandatory. Juergensmeyer also contends that by giving up their lives, martyrs not only demonstrate their commitment, but they also engage in sacrifice—the most fundamental form of religiosity. But the key to emphasize here is that *all* violent campaigns find it useful to create and glorify martyrs, as documented by the fact that the majority of suicide bombings have been carried out by secular as opposed to religious terrorist groups. An act of self-sacrifice in the name of the organization's cause, whether religious or secular, is a uniting factor. Overt praise of the martyr's accomplishment by prominent members of the group can also increase the self-sense of group prestige and can inspire future volunteers. The willingness to die for a cause is sometimes also used as evidence of the superiority of the group's members over their adversaries, who are portrayed as pleasure-seekers and who in spite of their military dominance are essentially weak. The resulting perception among the group is that due to superior determination, their final victory is inevitable.

Another allegedly distinct characteristic of religiously motivated struggles is the aforementioned images of divine warfare, which are equated to the present struggle and are consistently used to create a sense of historical purpose and urgency (Juergensmeyer, 2000: 146). This, however, is again a characteristic that is psychologically natural to all ethnic, cultural, or national communities, and is consistently used by all violent movements. Juergensmeyer's 'cosmic struggles' are in essence what psychiatrist Vamik Volkan calls 'chosen traumas': 'heavily mythologized historical sufferings that bring with them powerful experiences of loss and feelings of humiliation, vengeance and hatred that trigger a variety of unconscious defense mechanisms that attempt to reverse these experiences and feelings' (Volkan, 1997: 82). Such defence mechanisms serve as a powerful dehumanization tool for killing, regardless of ideological context—the new enemies of current conflicts are psychologically transformed into extensions of the old enemy from a historical event. Whether they are the Crusades for the Muslims, the Holocaust for the Jews, Black September for the Palestinians, the Battle of Karbala for the Shi'as, Bloody Sunday for Irish Catholics, the battles of Mahabharata and Ramayana for the Hindus, Operation Blue Star for the Sikhs, the Viet Nam War or 9/11 for the Americans, the Wounded Knee Massacre for the Lakota Indians, deportation from Turkey for the Armenians, or the Battle of Stalingrad for the Russians, all of these events can become mythological 'chosen traumas' or 'images of cosmic warfare', which will help to dehumanize the enemy in future conflicts. Religious groups are in this respect no different from secular entities.

As these examples show, religious terrorists are essentially very similar to their secular counterparts: they are narrow-minded individuals who fail to see alternative perspectives on the issues on behalf of which they fight. This is not only a natural, but also an absolutely necessary characteristic for any terrorist—one has to believe in the absolute nature of the cause in order to kill in its name. And while it is true that some organizations are more discriminate and restrained in their violent actions than others, *any* ideology used to support a terrorist campaign becomes in essence a religion—a comprehensive world-view which constitutes an unquestionable higher truth of an absolute nature. Any terrorist is motivated by feelings of frustration and humiliation, any terrorist regards his or her use of violence as a defensive war, any terrorist fights in the name of the absolute good. In addition, any perpetrator of a terrorist act empathizes with his or her own victimization and protests against cruelty towards his or her own people, but at the same time demonstrates minimum empathy for those whom he or she kills. Any perpetrator of such an act feels empowered by the execution of 'just' violence in the name of a great cause. For all of the reasons stated above, Juergensmeyer's characterizations are excellent descriptions of the characteristics of terrorists in general, but fail to provide a useful tool for identifying religious terrorists.

In contrast, Hoffman's analysis of the distinct features of religious terrorists is much more specific, but in the end suffers from a different weakness—virtually none of the terrorist organizations that exist today fit Hoffman's description. For instance, the number of groups that execute their terrorist acts for 'no audience but themselves or God' is rather limited. In fact, most of the existing religious terrorist organizations complement their violence with realistic alternatives to secular rule, by backing their 'military' activities with social, medical, and other communal services. As a result, many religious terrorist organizations have over time developed impressive constituencies. Thus, Hoffman's argument that 'the restraints on violence that are imposed on secular terrorists by the desire to appeal to a tacitly supportive or uncommitted constituency are not relevant to the religious terrorists' is hardly valid. Furthermore, religious organizations that 'unlike secular terrorists who see violence as a means to an end, tend to view violence as an end in its self' are also quite scarce. Even though many terrorist groups today carry out acts of violence that are motivated by revenge, the altruistic component of such violence even when accompanied by religious rhetoric cannot be over-emphasized. And while it is true that the goals of some religious terrorists tend to be less clearly defined and seem much less tangible, most organizations commonly labelled as religious nevertheless have a clear strategic calculation behind them and seek to benefit a specific group of people. Even Hoffman more or less confirms this claim by stating that the aims of 'religious political' terrorists are defined as 'the attainment of the greatest possible benefits for themselves and for their co-religionists only, as opposed to the indiscriminately utilitarian goals of secular terrorists'. This observation again shows the complexity of defining the distinct features of religious terrorists. Are not all ethnically or nationalistically based secular organizations also restricted in their violent actions to the attainment of the greatest possible benefits to members of their own ethnic or national community only? And does not, on the other hand, the religiously motivated Algerian Groupe islamique armé (GIA—Armed Islamic Group) indiscriminately kill its co-religionists in some of the most brutal ways imaginable?

CONCLUSION

As this essay has hopefully demonstrated, the commonly defined characteristics of the 'religious terrorists' as irrational fanatics who do not seek to benefit a constituency and whose violent actions are not a means to an end but rather a self-serving end in themselves, and who are therefore unrestrained in their violence and thus more likely to perpetrate acts of mass destruction, do not apply to the absolute majority of today's terrorists. At the same time, it is true that the religiously ideologized terrorist groups have demonstrated a different world-view and strategy, which is more immune to indiscriminate mass-casualty violence than in the case of nationalist separatist groups. But given the difficulties in making a clear distinction between religious and non-religious terrorists, it may be a more productive approach to focus on more specific elements of a group's belief system than the general dichotomy of 'religious' versus 'non-religious'. This is especially true in view of the absence of any religious element whatsoever in genocides such as those that occurred in Nazi Germany, Stalinist Russia, Rwanda and Cambodia. Clearly, the presence of religion in a group's ideology by itself does not provide a reliable indicator of a group's willingness to progress to causing indiscriminate mass casualties.

A possibly more useful method of threat-assessment may be to focus on the specific ideological characteristics that are responsible for the shifting of the threshold of violence, such as the presence of an apocalyptic justification that could be described by the objective of 'destroying the world to save it'. Religious and other cult-like organizations that share the world-view that the planet requires a radical makeover are not in short supply. Fortunately, most such organizations have yet to resort to outward violence. If that were to occur, however, the potential ability of apocalyptic organizations to justify killing people as actually benefiting them by sending them to a better place than this world makes such groups particularly dangerous. As in most terrorist attacks, the use of violence in this scenario would again be perceived by the terrorists as altruistic, with the critical difference that the constituency in this case would be the victims themselves. In such cases, the victims would not necessarily be regarded as an enemy whom one kills in hate or for symbolic value, but rather as poor human beings who will be saved by being killed. Under such circumstances, killing thousands of people indiscriminately would be psychologically much easier than to do so as part of a political strategy or in revenge.

The most lethal terrorist groups in history have incorporated such an apocalyptic element into their ideology. For instance, Kozo Okamoto, the leader of the Japanese Red Army squad which carried out one of the most lethal and indiscriminate terror acts *of its era* by killing 26 people at Lod Airport, Israel, in 1972, believed that his victims would 'become stars in the sky'. This element was also present in the ideology of Aum Shinrikyo, which adopted a twisted version of the Tibetan Buddhist Tantric concept of '*poa*'—the act of merciful killing which would provide the victims with the opportunity for a more favourable rebirth on a higher spiritual plane in their next life. Under such circumstances, the cult's attempt to kill indiscriminately thousands of people was psychologically much easier, especially given the presence of a self-sacrificial element in the sense that the one who killed took the victim's bad karma onto himself. In this way, for Aum members killing people became an act of self-sacrifice for the sake of the victim. The 'benefiting the victim' facet can also be found among the most lethal Islamist terrorist groups, such as the Algerian GIA, whose leader had argued that it is justifiable to kill innocent civilians since they would be considered 'martyrs' for the cause. Similarly, Osama Bin Laden was also not troubled by the issue of collateral damage or the fact that Muslims also died in the 9/11 attack, arguing that if those killed were good Muslims, they would benefit by becoming martyrs and by being granted special treatment in paradise. A final important point to emphasize is that a terrorist group does not necessarily have to be religious in nature in order to reach an apocalyptic stage. Fundamentalist environmental or animal rights groups, as well as ethnic-based violent movements might under certain circumstances also reach this phase. Consider for instance the RISE, an environmentalist group which attempted to culture large quantities of *salmonella typhi* as part of a ludicrous plan to contaminate the water supply of several large cities and indiscriminately kill thousands of people. The logic behind the plot was to kill every human except the group's members, who would later reproduce among themselves in order to repopulate the earth with a more environmentally friendly population. Similarly, Sendero Luminoso (Shining Path), a Peruvian group, has killed more than 6,000 people in the absence of a religious ideology, but in the presence of apocalyptic elements in its interpretation of Maoist doctrine. Under the slogan 'In the end, we all must mix our warm blood with the cold blood of our death brothers', Sendero Luminoso not only carried out numerous massacres of civilians, but also implemented a quota for casualties *for its own side* in order to monitor its revolutionary progress.

In conclusion, it will be the presence of this type of apocalyptic element in the ideology of a group rather than the generic typologization of the ideology itself, that will provide us with critical insight into a group's potential to commit mass-casualty acts of violence.

State Uses of Terrorism

JAMES LUTZ AND BRENDA LUTZ

INTRODUCTION

Governments have been directly connected with supporting terrorism as a part of their policies in two general contexts. The two contexts are quite different since in the first case the targets for the terrorist attacks are foreign, while in the second case they are domestic. In the first case, they have used personnel from their own intelligence services as well as dissident groups abroad as tools to achieve foreign policy objectives. Spies, agents, and saboteurs have initiated actions against enemy states in both 'hot' and 'cold' wars. When governments have had the opportunity in the context of these hot and cold wars, they have also provided direct support to dissident organizations already using terrorist and guerrilla violence against the regimes in enemy or competing states. The groups receiving this support have not usually been directly controlled by the foreign state even if this aid by foreign governments has given the outside supporters some important leverage with the dissidents. If the potential enemy state has been having difficulties with dissidents, foreign governments have often been quite willing to 'stir the pot', hoping to bring it to the boil to create difficulties for the other state. In the best of all possible worlds, there is a chance that an allied government will be established to replace an antagonistic one. At the very least, the potential enemy state can be weakened with the provision of such aid to its dissident groups. A more passive way in which states may assist terrorist groups in other countries is by ignoring their organizational activities or fund-raising on their own soil. The second case of government aid for terrorism is when they become involved in providing active or passive support to groups in their own country to deal with political, economic, or social groups that the government fears. Paramilitary organizations, party activists or militias, or death squads may launch the attacks, but the government is able to avoid direct responsibility for the attacks and to retain at least a pretence of 'plausible deniability'.

STATE ACTIONS AS FOREIGN POLICY

Operatives of state intelligence agencies frequently are active in attempts to gain information from enemies (and friends), and they also undertake more violent actions. The CIA (the US Central Intelligence Agency), the former Soviet KGB (Komitet Gosudarstvennoi Bezopaznosti), MI6 (Military Intelligence 6) in the United Kingdom, Mossad in Israel, and many other intelligence and counter-intelligence agencies have been involved in violent activities. Some of these actions have been designed to generate terror in target audiences, including the general public in foreign countries. When this kind of activity is undertaken by one state against an enemy nation in the international political system, it is an adjunct of foreign policy. In wartime such actions are part of a broader strategy for victory. In peacetime or during a cold war the actions are more covert, but they are still part of state-to-state interactions.

Governments, however, engage in other kinds of activities abroad where the targets are not foreign states or their populations. A number of governments have frequently been willing to target dissidents from their own land who are residing abroad and offering criticism or organizing opposition groups. One objective of this type of targeting is the reduction or elimination of the effectiveness of these expatriates who are attempting to publicize the problems in their homelands. If a number of them can be eliminated, through assassination or other violent attacks, then it is possible that the remainder of the refugee or expatriate community can be cowed into silence, thus removing a thorn in the side of the government. Bulgarian security agents, undoubtedly working in collaboration with the KGB, attempted to kill a number of persons who worked for Western-operated radio stations broadcasting information at odds with government releases to their homelands. The intent was not only to remove the specific dissidents, but also to silence the expatriate Eastern European communities in general. Middle Eastern governments have also targeted prominent exiles or refugees. Iranian agents have tracked down former supporters of the Shah and killed them, and the Iraqi intelligence services in the past eliminated some critics of Saddam Hussain who were in exile abroad. The Israeli intelligence and covert operations agencies have also tracked down specific Palestinian operatives or officials abroad and eliminated them in efforts to dissuade further attacks on Israel or Israeli interests abroad. While the Israeli attacks may have provided some psychological satisfaction since they were often performed in retaliation for earlier attacks, the primary objective was either to discourage attacks in general or attacks on specific kinds of targets (e.g. civilians, diplomatic agents). In all of these cases governments seek to intimidate the exiles and to persuade their dissident citizens residing abroad to abandon their involvement in plans—violent or otherwise—that challenge the regime in the home state.

Governments frequently are willing to support the dissident groups that already exist in other countries. These groups create difficulties for governments of unfriendly countries and may become acceptable clients for aid. Assistance can take the form of funds, arms, training, and safe havens where dissidents can be secure from attack. A wide variety of countries have run training camps, sometimes for a bewildering array of dissident groups. The USA trained guerrillas for action in Tibet, Cuba and the former Communist countries of Eastern Europe. The USA also supported the Contras in their guerrilla and terrorist actions in Nicaragua. The USSR and its allies provided some support for the Red Brigades in Italy, the Red Army Faction (RAF, sometimes referred to as the Baader-Meinhof Gang) in Germany, and a variety of other groups. Cuba was active for a period in supporting leftist groups in Latin America. Some of the dissidents were local nationalists who lacked Marxist-Leninist credentials, but if their activities weakened the Western countries or their allies in the developing world, there could be more opportunities for Soviet gains. The conservative 'oil monarchies' in the Middle East have supported the Palestine Liberation Organization (PLO) and other groups for a number of years even though they did not necessarily agree with the more modern and secular ideas of the PLO or comparable groups. Libya supplied arms to the Irish Republican Army (IRA) not so much because of Col al-Qaddafi's interest in Irish reunification, but rather to create difficulties for the United Kingdom, which stood by the USA in its confrontations with Libya. India and Pakistan have seemed quite willing to aid each other's dissident groups as part of efforts to weaken a potential enemy.

It is even possible that the foreign support for violent dissident groups willing to use terrorism as a tactic reflects virtually no compatibility of goals or ideology, as was the case when Libya provided aid to the IRA. In fact, the foreign government might even be in a worse position internationally if it were facing a government dominated by the dissidents or their allies who had come to power. The real goal of the foreign government may simply be to weaken the potential enemy, to leave it more vulnerable to actions in the future, or perhaps to prevent it from interfering with other foreign policy objectives in the area by keeping the government occupied with the threat of the internal dissidents. Similarly, if the country is forced to deal with internal dissidents, it may be less likely to undertake foreign activities contrary to the interests of the first state. Iraq has supported middle-class and leftist forces using terrorism that were opposed to the Islamic Republic of Iran in the past, not out of ideological conviction but as a means of weakening a potentially threatening neighbour. The USA had virtually no common ground with the *mujahidin* in Afghanistan, but it supported them in their guerrilla and terrorist campaign against the USSR and the communist regime in Afghanistan. The Israeli government initially supported Hamas when it first appeared because it was possible that the presence of an avowedly religious organization opposed to the more secular PLO would split the Palestinian community, and a divided Palestinian movement would be less dangerous to Israel. It should be noted, however, that this Israeli policy was not pursued for very long. In general, the support that is provided can be very weak in terms of principle and very strong in terms of pragmatism. Similarly strong *vis-à-vis* pragmatism and weak *vis-à-vis* principle is the possibility that the dissidents can be abandoned with relatively little cost when foreign policy needs change. If the terrorists become unruly or an embarrassment or otherwise a liability, support can be discontinued with few if any negative ramifications.

The final kind of potential state support for dissidents from foreign countries that can be present is more passive or subtle. A government may tolerate operatives of terrorist organizations on its soil as long as they do not launch local attacks or otherwise target the interests of the host country. In these cases the government does not actively seek to support the terrorist organization, but it conveniently chooses not to arrest its members or make any attempt to disrupt the organization. This toleration may reflect some general agreement with the goals of the terrorists, but it could also reflect the fear that the group might launch attacks on the soil of the sheltering country or otherwise create problems if the government were to suppress it. A government with limited security forces or a desire to avoid taking sides in another country's domestic problems may simply attempt to follow a policy of neutrality as far as is possible. Ultimately the hope in these cases is that the neutral soil is too valuable an asset for terrorist groups to risk losing that advantage. France at one time had such a policy towards foreign terrorist groups. As long as they did not attack French interests, they were relatively free to operate on French soil. Italy had a similar practice towards Palestinian groups. In other cases inaction results from different considerations. The USA never placed the IRA on its official list of terrorist organizations because of the political influence of Catholic Irish-Americans, who have often been anti-British and at some level identified with the hopes of the IRA for a unified Ireland. Elected politicians in at least some locations and states could not afford to alienate this group of voters. Presidents have had to be wary as well. While this type of passive response may not be as important as money, arms, or training for terrorist groups, it can be important for providing locations for fund-raising activities and a place where dissidents can rest, safe from capture, between operations.

It was thought by some that the end of the Cold War would lead to a decline in the above kinds of state support for violent dissident groups. It was assumed that the ongoing conflict between the superpowers explained much of the terrorist violence in the world and that the external support was essential to the groups involved. In fact, the dissident groups existed because they disagreed with some significant aspect of the policies of their government or even with being citizens of the state where they were located, not because of external support. It is, of course, difficult to indicate exactly how many terrorist attacks occurred in the past because of foreign assistance since these kinds of statistics are not officially kept by government bureaucracies, but the expected peace dividend *vis-à-vis* terrorism really did fail to appear. While there may have been some decline in state support for terrorism, it has not been on a major scale, in part because the end of the Cold War occurred after the heyday of the terrorism of leftist groups in Europe and Latin America that had received at least some support from the USSR and its allies. The end of communism in Europe sounded the death knell of these movements, but most of them were already in serious decline. The fact that terrorism failed to decline resulted from a number of factors. The most important, of course, is that the vast majority of groups have domestic origins, domestic agendas, and operate domestically. In many cases they have had no external support from governments, and in other cases the support has been minimal. Even when the support was important in helping the group to operate and to even become more deadly, the organizations could survive without that assistance. For example, Libyan aid for attacks launched in Europe made them more deadly, especially in the case of Pan American Flight 103 that was destroyed over Lockerbie, Scotland, but some attacks would have taken place without any Libyan role. Further, religious and ethnic conflicts have remained important and have generated continuing violence, and some ideological conflicts are even still present in some countries. A final reason why the decline has not been as great as anticipated is that not all foreign support that existed in the past (and thus is likely to exist in the future) was related to the Cold War. India and Pakistan are still at odds. Arab governments and Iran are still willing to assist Palestinian groups, even if somewhat more circumspectly than in the past. The government of Serbia was willing to intervene in Bosnia, raising the cost of ethnic cleansing in that country. Similar instances of overt or covert state support in the future remain likely even if it is not going to be at the same level as during the half-century after the end of the Second World War.

One final point about foreign involvement and assistance for domestic terrorist groups needs to be made. The importance of outside backers has no doubt always been exaggerated. Governments have found it easier to blame meddling neighbours or superpower conflict for their own domestic problems. Foreign intervention becomes a convenient scapegoat for domestic policy failures or reactions to repression. If the terrorists are foreign-controlled, the local political élite is not forced to take responsibility for their policies that created the dissidents. Further, it is easy to argue that the inability to deal with terrorists is a consequence of the foreign support. The claim of external assistance for the terrorists may serve as a useful lever to gain foreign economic or military assistance from an ally. Thus, even when foreign intervention is present it is convenient to exaggerate its effects or its importance. France could believe in 1956 that its problems in Algeria would end if Egypt stopped sending aid to the dissidents. Israel could claim that there would be no serious Palestinian problem if it had not been for the foreign assistance given to the PLO. The Sandinista government in Nicaragua could claim that there would have been no internal dissent had it not been for the support the USA gave to the Contras, just as the government of El Salvador blamed its problems on the external support that Nicaragua was giving to the rebels in that country. India would have no problem in Kashmir if Pakistan would cease providing aid to the dissidents. This exaggeration of the importance of foreign assistance to domestic terrorists also helps to explain why the end of the Cold War did not lead to the expected decline in terrorism.

STATE SUPPORT FOR TERRORISM AGAINST DOMESTIC GROUPS

The second way in which governments make concrete choices to become involved in supporting terrorism centres on providing aid for attacks by domestic groups against fellow citizens. Sometimes governments choose to support the groups engaged in terrorism because the targets are viewed as part of a broader audience that is considered disloyal—either to the country, the political system, or the élite in power. In other cases governments make the conscious decision not to interfere with the terrorists—they willingly decide to do nothing. In these circumstances, it is assumed that governments could actually make a difference if they chose to do so. Some very weak governments have been incapable of stopping terrorism. For example, what remained of the central government in Lebanon during that country's long civil war could not effectively contain terrorism, armed attacks, and civil war—as well as assaults launched from Lebanese soil against Israel or other targets in other countries. In most cases, however, governments have real options and choices that they can make. It is important to note that support for domestic terrorism is quite different from repression and other control mechanisms that governments may use. Many autocratic governments, past and present, have used force against their own citizens to maintain the system and to stifle dissent. Such repression, however, is selective—members of unions are harassed; opposition political leaders are arrested and then imprisoned or executed or die while in custody; rallies are banned; jobs or import licences are denied to those who have not adequately demonstrated their loyalty, etc. In these cases, however, the actions are taken against individuals identified as dissidents, and they are prosecuted or persecuted for their specific actions. Terrorist attacks choose members of groups as targets with the intention of intimidating and terrorizing the remainder of the disloyal population. Government repression, of course, also aims to intimidate, and again individuals are selected as targets, but not as random members of a larger population. The purges in the USSR when Stalin was in power, however, demonstrate a grey border area. The purges went well beyond repression and included many people as representatives of the groups that were being terrorized. The disloyalty of the group being terrorized by the domestic terrorists may be defined by the political beliefs or ideology of the members, by their religious affiliation, which is assumed to threaten the state or the leadership, by language or ethnicity, or by some combination of factors. The violence against members of the targeted population also has to be pervasive to genuinely qualify as a campaign of terrorism. There are probably many countries where there are isolated occurrences of attacks, but the action has to be organized to qualify as terrorism.

Government support for terrorism against its own citizens can take a variety of forms. Political leaders may choose to turn a blind eye to the violent activities of pro-government organizations in their societies. The groups that are being attacked are considered suspect by the government, and thus the political leaders view the terrorism as supporting the government in some way. Perhaps the attacks target dissidents that the government would like to eliminate, but whose criminal activity or treason it lacks the ability to prove by trial in open court. The unofficial attacks may also successfully intimidate others into passivity and silence. The government could also doubt its ability to use repression and the state security forces effectively; consequently, it is willing to let private groups operate. Party militias or paramilitary groups or other organizations may be allowed to attack opponents of the regime with impunity. The Ku Klux Klan (KKK) operated in many parts of the USA in both the 1920s and 1950s with relative freedom. Local officials ignored attacks on blacks, Jews, Catholics, immigrants, and others. If members of the KKK were ever brought to trial, acquittals were highly likely. The locally elected officials, including many involved in law enforcement, reflected the community standards and were unwilling to intervene to protect members of the minority groups that did not fit in with the local culture. It took legislation and intervention at the national level to remedy the problem, in part because national officials and the Federal Bureau of Investigation (FBI) could withstand local public opinion and pressure. There have been instances in Germany unified after the demise of Communism when local police officials have been slow to respond to harassment and attacks on refugees or asylum-seekers from Eastern Europe or Asia or Africa. In India local authorities have clearly tolerated attacks by Hindu activists on individual Muslims, mosques, or Muslim neighbourhoods. In the street brawls between the left and the right in many parts of Europe in the 1920s and 1930s, the police and courts frequently treated right-wing defendants leniently while being more severe with the leftists who were charged with criminal violations. Adolf Hitler's short prison term for attempting to ignite an uprising to overthrow the government of Germany is probably the most famous example, but hardly the only one. Governments may also tolerate attacks on unpopular domestic groups (defined by ethnic, religious, political, cultural, or sexual identity). If the attacks occur often enough, they can fulfil the same purposes as an organized terrorist campaign. Attacks against racial minorities or unusual religious groups or homosexuals may be prosecuted so rarely that it appears that the government is encouraging such attacks. Throughout Eastern Europe in recent years there have been attacks on Gypsies that have often not been prosecuted by the authorities given the negative cultural view that the majority populations hold of this minority. Under such circumstances the minority group is sufficiently terrorized to consider relocation or other members of the group are dissuaded from migrating to the country or region in question (thus meeting the implicit objective of both the general population and the authorities).

Government support can be more active. The groups launching the attacks may receive clandestine support in the form of funds, arms, or training from the regime in power. The support may be forthcoming because the domestic terrorist groups are able to target a population that the government cannot. The groups may be too strong for outright attack by the governments. In other cases the target group may be suspected of harbouring terrorists or guerrillas who are attacking the government, but it is difficult to use conventional legal or military means to deal with the problem. The unofficial groups can strike where the government might be constrained. In other cases governments will also be concerned about public opinion in other countries. Blatant disregard for political rights or civil liberties might endanger economic or military support from abroad. The plausible deniability that may exist with the actions of irregular forces permits the government to appease foreign opinion while still trying to strike at the dissidents and their supporting groups. Government aid to the irregulars weakens opposition groups while still providing the government with the desired element of deniability.

Examples of indirect government support for terrorism against domestic groups abound. During the French Revolution the radicals in the government supported street demonstrations and other actions against their opponents. This non-state activity reinforced the actions of the government itself when the Reign of Terror began. In the USA before the Civil War, the Mormons in Missouri and Illinois faced attacks and discrimination. The state authorities ignored the attacks against the Mormons in both cases, and even supported the non-Mormons in their confrontations with the religious minority. In both states the local authorities eventually sided with the majority and supplied them with critical support in the confrontations (and made it obvious that the Mormons would receive little if any protection). The Mormons, of course, decided to migrate to Utah. The Boxer Rebellion in China represents a progression of government support for a terrorist group. The Boxers were opposed to Western influences—political, cultural, and economic—in China. They attacked Western symbols, Chinese Christians—as a symbol of Western influence rather than directly for their religious beliefs—and eventually Westerners themselves. Initially the Manchu (Ching) government tolerated the attacks, given the court's own opposition to Western intrusions. The government later supplied clandestine support to the Boxers in their anti-Western attacks. In the final stage of involvement the government openly sided with the Boxers, and government troops fought alongside them in an unsuccessful attempt to expel the foreigners. Especially in Nazi Germany, but elsewhere in Europe after the First World War, members of a number of political parties and others undertook attacks against Jews or national minorities. In Nazi Germany, the attacks were not only tolerated but encouraged. In some other countries the government chose to tolerate the attacks even if it did not encourage them. Local authorities and military officers in Indonesia in recent years have aided Muslim militants when they have intervened in areas of Christian–Muslim confrontations to help their local co-religionists in violent activities. In the Philippines, Christian groups opposed to the Muslim separatists in the southern areas of that country have received intermittent assistance from government sources.

A variety of governments around the world have employed death squads to deal with dissidents in their own countries. These kinds of operations clearly receive support from the state and generally go far beyond state toleration or even clandestine support of private activity. Governments actively become involved with the groups in question. These death squads have become in some cases a preferred form of counter-terrorism as governments seek to deal with terrorist groups threatening the stability of the state. Such death squads often include members of the police, security forces, and the military, but they are still not official groups operating openly under government direction. In some cases these death squads target groups that the government fears, even if the individuals in question have neither taken up arms against it nor are in open defiance of its authority. The death squads frequently operate at night when they abduct their victims, whose bodies are subsequently left in public places (town squares, outskirts of towns, steps of public buildings, etc.). The display of the bodies is intended to intimidate other potential opponents of the regime in power. If the death squads, however, are eliminating large numbers of people, the sheer number of disappearances is often sufficient to inspire the fear that is the government's aim. The death squads have the advantage of government support, and they are immune from prosecution, at least until there is a change in government. They also have access to government records and information, which makes them more effective in terms of targeting individuals that the political élite would like to have removed.

Examples of the use of death squads, unfortunately, abound. A succession of authoritarian governments in Guatemala used such groups against the Indian population of the country. They feared that villages or different Indian groups would join rebel groups, and the attacks were often intended to be pre-emptive in order to prevent recruits from joining local guerrillas. South Africa under the white minority government used death squads against its opponents. The activities of the squads supplemented the stock of repressive tactics available to the government, but disappearances and assassinations were effective in removing individuals who were too much in the public eye to arrest or prosecute on flimsy or false charges. In Haiti under François Duvalier ('Papa Doc') the local security forces (the Ton-Ton-Macoutes) terrorized the population and prevented any opposition from appearing. No one was immune to the activities of this group, and villages or family members would be punished for the transgressions of specific individuals. This terror was sufficient to maintain Duvalier securely in power and to prevent the appearance of any effective opposition. The government of Burundi dominated by the minority Tutsi group has periodically acquiesced in attacks against the majority Hutu population of the country. Frequently the attacks result in purges that eliminate educated Hutus who might eventually form a leadership core for the majority population. To date these tactics have permitted the minority group to remain in power.

Death squads have been used by governments to deal with both guerrilla and terrorist groups. Argentina had witnessed terrorist violence prior to the return of Juan Perón from exile in Spain and his election as President. Once in power he began to move against some of the leftist groups that had supported him. Perón's death led to only a temporary respite as the government of his wife, Isabel, used death squads in an effort to defeat increasing terrorist violence. The failure of this campaign led to a military coup and the launch of a massive campaign against suspected leftists, members of their families, and presumed supporters. When the campaign was over tens of thousands of Argentinians had 'disappeared', and the leftist groups had been destroyed. Indonesia took over East Timor when Portugal relinquished its colony in 1974, ignoring a local declaration of independence. Faced with a national liberation struggle by the East Timorese, the Indonesian government resorted to the use of death squads in an effort to maintain control of the new province. The government also supported militias and other loyal paramilitary groups that sought to defeat the national liberation movement. India has also utilized death squads in dealing with some of its internal problems. In the 1980s, India faced a campaign of guerrilla activity and terrorist attacks by a variety of Sikh groups seeking either greater autonomy or independence for the Punjab. The government used conventional security tactics and military attacks to deal with the dissidents, but eventually death squads were employed as well. Suspected dissidents were apprehended, and many were eventually killed. Their deaths would be announced as due to causes such as a failed escape or rescue attempt and as casualties of battles between the rebels and the military or security forces. There was, of course, little doubt that the deaths were a direct consequence of the government's suspicion of their involvement on the rebel side. Similar tactics later came to be used in Kashmir against the local guerrilla and terrorist groups that were seeking either an independent Kashmir or incorporation into Pakistan. Persons suspected of anti-government activities have been assassinated or killed after their arrest. There have also been attacks against the local Muslim population. The security forces managed to control the Sikhs in the Punjab, but the situation in Kashmir has remained volatile. Other governments have resorted to death-squad tactics at least some of the time. The Spanish government briefly used assassination against Basque separatists, as has the government in Sri Lanka in dealing with a leftist terrorist campaign to overthrow it. Such groups have been used in other Latin American countries, the Middle East, and the Philippines at various times as governments have been willing or felt compelled to use more extreme measures to deal with the violent dissident groups that threaten their states. Of course, the use of such squads is an open secret, both for the potential victims and for other governments. In this sense the use of death squads has provided the government with either minimal plausible deniability or perhaps implausible deniability in some cases.

Another form of terrorism that has often involved the active participation of governments has been ethnic cleansing. Ethnic cleansing can take place without government sanction or support, as occurs with communal riots or its use by dissident groups when they attempt to drive out elements loyal to the government. With ethnic cleansing, attacks are launched against specific target groups that are usually identified by their religious preference, ethnicity, or language as a means of 'encouraging' the chosen community to leave. The goal is to drive the group from a particular area either because they are different or because they are viewed as potential dissidents. The attacks are designed to cleanse an area, not to eliminate the group as occurs with genocide. In addition to beatings, property attacks, and murders, rape has been introduced as a tactic in more recent examples of ethnic cleansing. The threat of rape increases the terror in the targeted community, and it can be a means of cultural humiliation of the targeted population. It can be an effective psychological mechanism since it threatens the community even should the victims be successful in fighting off some of the attacks.

Ethnic cleansing takes many forms. It can include forced assimilation, which is not deadly even if it eliminates the distinct culture of a group or the group identification. The attempt to use terror to force survivors to leave a region is much harsher. The most extreme form of ethnic cleansing is genocide, where the elimination of a group is sought. Actions such as the Armenian genocide in the Ottoman Empire, the Holocaust, and the genocide in Rwanda against the Tutsi population do not really qualify as terrorism since there is no attempt to spread fear in the group; the goal is its destruction. In fact, one of the distinctive aspects of genocide is the attempt to hide the scope of the attacks from the victims to prevent them from reacting. In the case of the Armenians, the Jews, and the Tutsi, the governments actually sought to avoid publicity so that the victims would be unaware of what was happening. Rather than attempting to spread news to increase the fear of the population, the government sought to reduce the fear and terror in order to further the elimination of the targeted population.

Governments in a number of countries have supported ethnic cleansing. There were two major examples in the former Yugoslavia. In Bosnia the Croat, Muslim, and Serb communities were all perpetrators and victims of ethnic cleansing, although the Bosnian Serbs resorted by far most frequently to it. The attacks were designed to drive those who were not members of the dominant groups out of particular areas by the use of terror and the threat of continued violence. Rape became a conscious tool in efforts to purify regions and to stake claims to larger areas of territory. Serb militias were also responsible for the massacre of Muslim males old enough to bear arms in the struggle for control of the country, both as a practical mechanism for reducing the number of potential soldiers on the other side and as an additional form of terrorism. The groups practising the ethnic cleansing were quasi-governmental militias in some cases since they were commanded by the local leaders in particular areas of the country. The Serbs also received external support from the government of Yugoslavia (Serbia and Montenegro), which helps to explain why the Bosnian Serbs were so well equipped with heavy weapons. After failing in its efforts to claim at least a portion of Bosnia for Serbia, the government of Serbia and Montenegro also attempted to use ethnic cleansing as a means of maintaining control over the province of Kosovo. The government in Belgrade eventually decided to force out significant numbers of the Albanian population in that province by claiming that they were not really legal citizens. This attempt failed due to external intervention by the West. The new Albanian authorities in the autonomous provincial administration of Kosovo, however, have tolerated, and probably aided, ethnic cleansing by Albanian groups directed against the remaining Serb and the Gypsy population of the region. The final result of the initial attempt at ethnic cleansing by the government of Serbia and Montenegro has been the departure of most of the Serbian population from the province except in a few areas that border Serbia.

Ethnic cleansing has occurred elsewhere. The Indonesian government attempted to drive out local inhabitants in its effort to assert control over East Timor. The government brought in Muslim migrants from elsewhere to help populate the province at the same time that residents of East Timor were fleeing to the western parts of the island where they were safe. If the ethnic balance of the province could have been changed, Indonesian control would have become much easier. Although these efforts contributed to the high cost of the conflict, they were no more successful in defeating the national liberation forces than the death squads were. In the early history of the USA the process of Indian relocations was in effect a slow process of ethnic cleansing of most of the territory east of the Mississippi River. Not all of the actions that forced the Indians progressively westward qualify as terrorism, but in many cases terror was used, and was supported by the action or inaction of the national government or the states. Assaults and murders of Indians by settlers were seldom punished by the court systems. If the Indians attempted to defend their rights and their property against settler encroachments, the military was brought in. In the case of the Creeks and Cherokees in Georgia, the state government actively sought to cleanse the land of Indians. Anyone attacking the Indians was almost assured of a sympathetic hearing in a state court if the matter ever progressed that far. The national government at the time basically pursued a hands-off policy that permitted the Indians to be driven out. The original inhabitants of Australia and the Indian populations in some other areas of the Western Hemisphere suffered a similar process of gradual dispossession of land and territory. Most recently, the government of Sudan has practised ethnic cleansing in the southern part of that country and in Darfur in the western part of the country. During the long conflict with the Christian and animist groups in the south, the national government supported Muslim militias in their depredations against the southerners. The government has been using the same tactics against the population in Darfur and seems intent on clearing the province of the indigenous groups. In this case the basis for the attacks is not religious, since the inhabitants of Darfur are Muslims, but rather tribal and regional. The government considered the inhabitants to be untrustworthy, a negative political attitude that has been virtually assured by the attacks against them.

Terrorism that is endorsed or supported by governments against their own citizens, whether it is in the form of failing to prosecute violent groups that are in political agreement with the government, aiding the activities of party groups or militias, using death squads, or supporting ethnic cleansing, has often taken a heavy toll among the target groups. Terrorism in these cases usually leads to more casualties than the attacks by domestic dissident groups using terror because the resources of the government are available to assist in the violence. Even groups that have had strong support from foreign governments do not often inflict as many casualties as government-supported domestic terrorism. The groups launching the attacks, however, will suffer few casualties since they are relatively immune to capture or prosecution, while anti-government groups run the risk of capture, imprisonment, and execution as well as the dangers that are always present due to confrontations with security forces. Government death squads can take a particularly heavy toll of suspected and actual terrorists since extra-judicial executions by death squads do not have to rely on evidence or catching the terrorists in the commission of violent acts. Suspicion is sufficient. Members of the death squads can suffer casualties, of course, but the risk is much lower for them than for dissident terrorist groups. Casualties can be particularly high since the groups with links to the government may also have access to state documents and lists of suspects that the government bureaucracy can provide. The cost of ethnic cleansing can be particularly high. This form of terrorism frequently involves the state apparatus in some fashion unless the group being cleansed is quite small. The combination of unofficial forces with regular forces in some cases, or the advantages that the cleansers have with the effective support of the state, is what usually makes cleansing both possible and deadly. The freedom from likely prosecution for any crimes that are committed is also a factor that can generate more fatalities among the targeted population, since consequences for the attackers may appear to be few. Ethnic-cleansing efforts in Bosnia, East Timor and Sudan have led to massive casualties among the victims on a scale that has not been reached by most dissident groups relying on terror.

CONCLUSION

The involvement of governments in terrorism illustrates that terrorism is a tactic that can be used by many different kinds of organizations. The technique of terrorism is neither limited to anti-government dissidents nor to governments. Support for foreign groups has obviously been one weapon in the arsenal of states that have been competing with each other or for countries engaged in disputes or cold wars. The creation of additional problems for a potential enemy is often too tempting for governments to forgo. In the domestic arena the state can support attacks on its own citizens, and, in fact, violence and terrorism are more deadly when supported by the state. The fact that governments may have to rely on irregular forces or irregular techniques to deal with dissident groups is at some level a sign of weakness in a government. If the government could deal with the dissidents with the regular police and courts or even through massive repression by regular security forces, then it probably would. In many cases, however, these options are not available. The government is constrained in some way, be it by international public opinion, domestic public opinion, lack of military or security resources, the unwillingness of the conventional police or security forces to engage in illegal violence, divisions within the élite, or lack of effective intelligence-gathering to enable the use of these other options. The reliance on terrorism demonstrates a weakness somewhere within the state and this reliance then becomes a substitute for dealing with challenges to the authority of the government.

State support for dissidents in other countries would appear to have declined to some extent in recent years. Terrorism, like any other tactic, will go through changes over time. The end of the Cold War changed the context of international relations significantly. It is now more dangerous for states to openly support dissidents in other countries because it is no longer possible to balance the USA against the USSR or vice versa. State support does exist in cases where a major foreign power is not involved, but it can still be limited by the broader international context. Other kinds of foreign support have emerged to replace some of the prior involvement of states. Criminal organizations seem to be more involved with violent dissident groups than in the past. The link is most obvious with the drug cartels in Colombia and the waves of terrorism that have afflicted that country, but drug groups have been actively involved with terrorist groups in many other parts of the world. It is unclear what the level of involvement of Chechen criminal elements has been in the violence occurring in that part of Russia, but it is clear that there has been some involvement by the Chechen underworld. Criminals and dissidents both frequently seek to weaken government authority so that they can operate more freely to achieve their goals. International terrorist groups such as al-Qa'ida are becoming more active and are providing at least some of the external assistance that was previously provided by governments. The improvements in modern transportation and communications (and opportunities for money-laundering and financial transfers first pioneered by criminal groups) have made such international co-operation easier to arrange and maintain. Terrorist organizations also receive important external support from diaspora populations around the world. Fund-raising among such groups has been important in the past and continues to be so for some groups today. The IRA, the PLO, the Basque separatists in Spain, the Sikhs, the Tamils in Sri Lanka, and the Chechens have all been quite effective in raising funds from among their ethnic communities outside their home countries. These funds can be as useful as foreign assistance and have fewer direct limitations on their use, although the dissident groups receiving the money have to be careful to avoid attacks that appear to be too indiscriminate, since these kinds of attacks could diminish the flow of funds from compatriots abroad. While support from diaspora groups may not be quite as effective as money, arms, and training from foreign governments, such assistance is much harder to disrupt. These alternative forms of support do indicate that the techniques and tactics involved in terrorism are constantly changing and in flux. As one form of foreign support is blocked or limited, new ways of accessing that support emerge.

Government support for terrorist groups targeting its own citizens within a country has undergone fewer changes in recent years. Governments will continue to face problems from opposition and dissidents within their countries, and there will always be a temptation to take a more drastic approach to dealing with these 'enemies'. If repression will not work or if the state lacks the resources for effective repression, support to domestic paramilitary or militia groups and death squads can become very tempting. The temptation increases when the state is dealing with violent attacks and terrorism from the dissident group. Such actions may be particularly tempting for dealing with ethnic separatist movements since they provide a way for the state to attack the presumed support base of the dissident groups. Ethnic cleansing may even become a preferred option since it is a means of removing the support group from national territory. Religious minorities may be targeted for much the same reasons. Groups that represent political opposition without an ethnic or communal base are unlikely targets for ethnic cleansing since they are more difficult to identify, but they can still be targets for death squads or paramilitary actions. What makes states willing to rely on terrorism against their own citizens is the possibility that such action will be effective in some cases. The leftist threat to the military government in Argentina was eliminated. The Punjab is relatively quiet although terrorist and dissident groups still operate in Kashmir. The Serbs gained additional territory to administer in Bosnia. The Mormons left for Utah and the Cherokees were relocated to Oklahoma. The violent right-wing parties reclaimed the streets from the leftists in Germany and Italy for their governments, but at the cost of Hitler and Nazism and Mussolini and Fascism. Since these kinds of actions appear to have been successful for the governments of states in at least some cases, they will continue. The occasional success will be more than enough for political leaders willing enough or desperate enough to try drastic means of dealing with political crises.

Counter-terrorism

THOMAS MOCKAITIS

Counter-terrorism has become such a broad, catch-all category bandied about in government circles and popular parlance that it risks losing any precise meaning. To begin with, a clear distinction must be made between counter-terrorism and counter-insurgency. Insurgency is an organized effort to overthrow the established government through a combination of subversion, guerrilla warfare, and terrorism. Insurgents tend to focus on a particular state or region, and they use terror quite selectively to avoid alienating people whose support they need in order to succeed.

In its broadest sense, the term counter-terrorism requires no definition at all. Simply put, it consists of any and all measures taken to oppose or 'counter' terrorist acts. Historically such measures have fallen to the police and special agencies tasked with addressing espionage and political crime. Today the term has come to signify a comprehensive approach, what in conventional war would be called a 'grand strategy', for opposing terrorism. Both the US military and the North Atlantic Treaty Organization (NATO), however, have a more precise definition for counter-terrorism. However, a truly comprehensive and effective counter-terrorism strategy has yet to be devised.

HISTORIC RESPONSES

Scholars generally agree that modern terrorism dates to the last quarter of the 19th century. Ideological movements such as nationalism, socialism, and anarchism motivated revolutionaries to seek violent remedies to intransigent political problems. Since the perpetrators preferred assassination to more lethal forms of terrorism, dealing with them remained predominantly a police matter. In some cases, however, threatened governments expanded police powers or created specific organizations to deal with the new threat. The British created a Special Branch to deal with political crime, first in Ireland and then later in Britain. In Russia, one of the most threatened states, the Tsars set up a secret police unit known as the Okrana.

The anti-colonial insurgencies that swept across Asia and Africa in the aftermath of the Second World War also made use of terror. To counter this threat the colonial powers made use of existing police, including (in the case of Britain) Special Branch units. Where the police proved inadequate to the threat, military units were tasked with counter-terrorism. The French used Colonial Paratroopers to combat terrorism in the infamous battle of Algiers. The unit compiled a highly accurate intelligence picture of the insurgent order of battle. This 'organogram' enabled the troops to arrest or eliminate the insurgents in the city. However, revelations that much of the intelligence had been acquired through torture produced revulsion in France and internationally. As a result the army won the battle of Algiers but lost the war as France withdrew from its former department of Algeria.

As the experience of the French Colonial Paratroopers illustrates, tasking regular army units with counter-terrorism proved problematic. Conventional forces lacked both the experience and the training that would enable them to use force in a sufficiently selective manner. Special Forces seemed to offer a better alternative. Developed out of the Commandos and Rangers employed during the Second World War, these élite units conducted a broad range of unconventional operations. Their counter-terrorism role consisted largely of hostage rescue missions and occasional clandestine raids. The need for such forces became painfully clear during the 1972 Summer Olympics in Munich, West Germany, when Black September terrorists killed several Israeli athletes.

Perhaps the best known and most successful of these Special Forces is the British Special Air Service (SAS). Although the unit had existed since the Second World War, it achieved notoriety as a counter-terrorism force in the 1980s. In 1981 an SAS hostage rescue team recaptured the Iranian Embassy in Prince's Gate, London. In 1987 the SAS destroyed the South Tipperary Brigade of the Irish Republican Army (IRA) in a shoot-out at Loughal South substation of the Royal Ulster Constabulary. That same year they killed three members of an IRA active service unit preparing to plant a bomb in Gibraltar. Controversy surrounded each of these operations, however, as all but one resulted in the death of every single terrorist, leading many to question whether the unit made any effort to apprehend rather than kill the perpetrators.

Other threatened states considered terrorism little more than a nuisance to be dealt with by the ordinary police, perhaps supported by other instruments of state security. The regime of Francisco Franco in Spain paid little attention to the Basque Fatherland and Liberty (ETA), leaving them to the local police and the infamous *Guardia Civil*. This approach allowed the organization to grow from relative insignificance into a major security concern. ETA achieved its greatest success in 1974 with the assassination of Franco's hand-picked successor, Adm. Louis Carrero Blanco.

Even when states did take terrorism seriously their approach to dealing with it remained limited. Counter-terrorism during this era remained primarily a tactical term, an assignment given to Special Forces or other units designated for such difficult tasks. Rarely did a threatened government mount a concerted campaign against terrorism. One exception to this rule occurred in Italy in the 1970s. The Italians had for some time been plagued by nuisance-level terrorism in the form of the Red Brigades, a small but fanatical Marxist organization committed to social revolution. Although committed to violent revolution, the impact of the Brigades' terrorist activity remained small, far less than that of Italy's perennial Mafia problem. Government apathy toward the threat changed dramatically with the kidnapping and murder of former Prime Minister Aldo Moro. The murder produced public outrage and galvanized the government into action. Italy's paramilitary police, the *Carabinieri*, mounted a concerted effort to destroy the Red Brigades, which they did by the end of the decade.

The nature of the terrorist threat through the 1990s explains the *ad hoc* approach to combating it. With the exception of insurgent terror, which tends to be limited, focused and part of a broad revolutionary strategy, terrorism has tended to be sporadic. Because few states have faced a sustained campaign of violence directed at their civilian populations, few have felt the need to dedicate resources or to develop a concerted counter-terrorist strategy. The 1990s would witness a dramatic change in the pattern of terrorism but little adaptation on the part of threatened states.

Historically, religion has far too often fuelled fanaticism and violence. In the USA anti-abortionists have bombed medical clinics and murdered doctors. In 1995 two right-wing extremists motivated by a mixture of racist ideology and Christian fundamentalism blew up the Morrow Federal Building in Oklahoma City, killing 168 people. These incidents, however, seemed at best loosely connected. The speed with which Oklahoma City bombers Timothy McVeigh and Terry Nichols were apprehended perhaps discouraged any effort to develop a comprehensive approach to counter-terrorism. After all, law-enforcement, supported by the Federal Bureau of Investigation, seemed to be doing a pretty good job. Neither the Republican administration of George H. Bush nor the Democratic administration of Bill Clinton saw any reason to develop a counter-terrorism strategy.

In retrospect the evidence of an emerging Islamist threat was mounting throughout the 1990s, although the USA did not connect the dots until after 9/11. In 1993 an exiled Egyptian cleric masterminded an attempt to bomb the World Trade Center. The attempt failed, and once again the perpetrators were caught almost immediately. At the time no one realized the connection between these terrorists and a largely unknown Saudi named Osama bin Laden. Two years later unknown terrorists bombed the Khobar Towers in Saudi Arabia, killing almost 60 American servicemen. Three years after that al-Qa'ida delivered its first unambiguous calling card, the near simultaneous destruction of the US embassies in Nairobi, Kenya, and Dar es Salam, Tanzania. Other than fire a few largely ineffective cruise missiles into Afghanistan and destroying what was probably just a pharmaceuticals factory in Sudan, the USA did little. Neither did it respond effectively when al-Qa'ida attacked the USS *Cole* in Aden harbour. These attacks, occurring far from America's shores, did little to shake American lethargy.

THE GLOBAL WAR ON TERRORISM

The 9/11 attacks, of course, changed everything. Nine days after they occurred President George W. Bush addressed a joint session of Congress and a frightened nation to declare a Global War on Terrorism. War, however, requires a clear definition of what constitutes victory and a strategy for winning. America had neither and, arguably, still does not. One action that garnered widespread domestic and international support immediately commended itself: removal of Afghanistan's Taliban regime, an undeniable state sponsor of terrorism.

Soon after defeat of the Taliban but long before Afghanistan had been stabilized, Washington turned to Iraq. Whether the administration merely used the Global War on Terrorism as a pretext to settle an old score continues to be hotly debated. Claims that Saddam Hussain possessed weapons of mass destruction and had ties to al-Qa'ida have not been substantiated. The invasion of Iraq does, however, illustrate the American approach to counter-terrorism: a disproportionate emphasis on state sponsors that could be eliminated by conventional military means. Beyond attacking these alleged rogue states, the USA arguably had no coherent strategy for the new war. The one exception was in the area of Homeland Defense where concrete steps are being taken to harden potential terrorist targets, improve co-operation among law enforcement and intelligence organizations, and especially improve airport security. These initiatives led to the creation of the Department of Homeland Security.

NATIONAL STRATEGY FOR COMBATING TERRORISM

In February 2003, the USA adopted a *National Strategy for Combating Terrorism*. The document begins with an improved definition of terrorism as 'premeditated, politically motivated violence against noncombatant targets by sub-national groups or clandestine agents'. Although this definition leaves out some acts that could be considered terrorism and includes some that might not, it at least identifies the enemy America chooses to fight. Ironically, however, the Pentagon uses a different definition, one that eliminates the 'non-combatant' caveat. This change allows attacks on the US barracks at the Khobar Towers in Saudi Arabia and the attack on the USS *Cole* in Aden harbour to be considered terrorism.

The *National Strategy* articulates the ambitious goal of ensuring that 'Americans and other civilized people around the world can lead their lives free of fear from terrorist attacks'. To achieve this end state the document outlines four broad goals each with several objectives. According to the 'four-D' strategy, the USA will *defeat* terrorist organizations, *deny* state sponsorship to any and all terrorist organizations, *diminish* the root causes of terrorism, and *defend* US citizens at home and abroad. Concrete objectives for defeating insurgents include expanding law enforcement, forming international partnerships, and using military force in a focused and decisive way. Denying terrorists sanctuary requires establishing and maintaining international standards of accountability for all nations; strengthening international efforts by working with weak states, persuading reluctant states, and compelling unwilling ones to oppose terrorism; and eliminating terrorist sanctuaries. To diminish root causes of terrorism the USA will partner with weak states to address domestic conditions which foster terrorist support and win the war of ideas. The goal of defending US citizens at home and abroad has the most objectives: implementing the national strategy of Homeland Security (a separate strategic document), promoting domestic awareness of terrorist threats, protecting information-based infrastructure, integrating measures to protect US citizens abroad, and ensuring an integrated incident-management capability.[1]

The *National Strategy* and in particular its implementation have been subject to considerable criticism. Writing for the Strategic Studies Institute of the US Army War College, Jeffrey Record has described the American approach as far too simplistic (Record, 2003). To begin with, the stated goal of eradicating terrorism is impossible. In addition, the American strategy erroneously views the terrorist threat in monolithic and Manichean terms. Not all terrorist organizations target the USA, so it makes little sense to provoke them into doing so. Furthermore, however reprehensible terrorist acts may be, some insurgencies use them in opposition to repressive governments. Finally, the *National Strategy* does not recognize the destructive and destabilizing role state terrorism plays in the international system (Record, 2003).

In implementing the *National Strategy* Washington has placed far too much emphasis on conventional war against state sponsors. While the connection between Afghanistan's Taliban and al-Qa'ida could clearly be demonstrated to the satisfaction of the international community, Saddam Hussain's support for international terrorism has yet to be established. Considerable evidence suggests that in addition to being unnecessary, the US-led invasion of Iraq may be counterproductive in the long run. Many analysts fear that Iraq has become the training ground for a new generation of skilled al-Qa'ida fighters just as Afghanistan was in the 1980s.

A recent analysis of American 'grand strategy' in the aftermath of 9/11 suggests that the USA now stands at a crossroads. It may weigh the cost of short-term gain versus long-term consequences. Using Cold War metaphors, Stephen Biddle maintains that we must choose between containment and rollback. Rolling back terrorism will require a sustained and costly ideologically driven effort spanning years and with no guarantee of success. Containment requires a more pragmatic approach with the goal of reducing the terrorist threat to an acceptable level. Such a strategy requires promoting stability rather than democracy in turbulent regions such as the Middle East (Biddle, 2005).

NATO AND THE EUROPEAN UNION

The USA is not, of course, the only state threatened by al-Qa'ida and its affiliates. Islamist extremists blew up commuter trains in Madrid in March 2004, murdered the controversial film maker Theo van Gogh in Amsterdam in November 2004, and bombed the London Underground in July 2005. With the exception of the United Kingdom, which has more than 30 years' experience fighting the IRA, European states and Europe collectively have been slow to respond to the threat. The European Union (EU) only began to develop a concerted response after the Madrid bombings and has so far confined its efforts to improved police co-operation, a legal framework for European-wide arrest and extradition, and protection of critical infrastructure.

Led by the USA, NATO has adopted strategic doctrine to guide joint operations. NATO divides the campaign against international terrorism into three categories. *Anti-terrorism* consists of those measures taken to protect member states from terrorist attack. Anti-terrorist measures consist of physically hardening potential targets, protecting critical infrastructure (everything from highways and bridges to the electrical grid and the internet) and improved intelligence collection and sharing to pre-empt attacks. *Counter-terrorism* refers to military and other operations to attack terrorist organizations and their supporters. *Crisis management* consists of measures taken to mitigate an actual attack. Primary responsibility for crisis management falls to civilian authorities directing emergency responders (police, fire, and medical personnel) supported by the military if and when necessary. Civil authorities should also take the lead in anti-terrorism with the exception of coastal and air security, which must be shared with the military. Counter-terrorism includes both police and military efforts.

Not surprisingly, most EU and member state effort has gone into anti-terrorism and crisis management. Every state must have some capacity to deal with natural and human disasters. Managing the consequences of floods, earthquakes, fires and industrial accidents requires at least a national effort and often international co-operation. Consensus among alliance members on improving disaster-management capacity is not difficult to achieve. Since mitigating the effects of a terrorist attack does not differ markedly from responding to other disasters, few states will argue over the value of the improved crisis management.

Although in and of itself uncontroversial, anti-terrorism evokes considerable debate based on cost-benefit analysis. Citizens of open and free societies have been understandably reluctant to implement measures that remind them of oppressive regimes in the not-so-distant past. Even passive measures to protect public buildings meet with resistance in most European countries. Augmented police powers face concerted opposition. On both sides of the Atlantic business and industry have been reluctant to bear the cost of protecting the large percentage of critical infrastructure under private control.

Counter-terrorism has been the most problematic. While many NATO members contribute troops to the International Stabilization Force in Afghanistan, few supported the invasion of Iraq. Only Britain has contributed a sizeable contingent to the coalition. Co-operation on police measures and intelligence sharing has been somewhat better, but even here the Euro-Atlantic partnership has been strained by the 'Global War on Terrorism'. Virtually none of the European allies considers the current struggle a war at all. This divergent perception led to the release of terrorist suspects apprehended in Hamburg. The defendants demanded to call witnesses in US custody, the USA refused to supply them arguing that they were prisoners of war, and the German courts had no choice but to release the suspects.

A REALISTIC APPROACH

If counter-terrorism is to evolve beyond a mere collection of tactical responses, a more realistic strategy needs to be crafted. My previous research suggests that counter-insurgency rather than conventional war points the way to such a strategy. In 2003, I argued that what the USA and its allies face is an insurgency on a global scale (Mockaitis and Rich, 2003). Al-Qa'ida is a highly decentralized network of organizations, loosely connected and highly flexible. They embrace both realistic and millenarian goals. They wish to replace the 'apostate' regimes of many pro-Western and/or secular Muslim governments with theocratic ones. Ultimately, they hope to unite all Muslims in a revived Caliphate embracing the entire Islamic *umma* or community. Like any insurgency, Islamist extremism feeds on legitimate grievances that must be understood and addressed.

Countering this threat requires a balanced, long-term strategy that combats terrorist organizations while addressing the root causes of terrorism. While the West cannot be blamed for all of the problems of the Muslim World, it can contribute to their solution. A combination of concerted support and persistent pressure on both Israel and the Palestinians to devise a two-state solution to the current crisis would undermine support for extremists. Relief and development aid such as that delivered following the tsunami in December 2004 can also improve the situation. In Indonesia alone support for al-Qa'ida fell dramatically after US aid arrived. The relief effort undermined Osama bin Laden's central claim that the war against terrorism was really a war against Islam.

A more enlightened foreign policy will not eliminate the need for military measures. Such measures should not, however, be undertaken unilaterally. Counter-terrorism depends heavily on legitimacy. The international system finds unilateral military action unacceptable. Lack of legitimacy has profoundly hindered the American effort in Iraq. With virtually no state sponsors left to target, military operations will increasingly be limited to covert operations. Counter-terrorism will also depend heavily on improved intelligence gathering and dissemination. International law enforcement co-operation is also essential. The London bombings led to one of the first uses of a European arrest warrant to detain a suspect in Italy.

In the area of anti-terrorism, considerable progress has been made, at least in the USA. Here too, however, progress has been hindered by persistent use of 'global war' to condemn dissent as unpatriotic and the manipulation of fear for political purposes. Arguably the President won the last election in part by convincing Americans that he had kept and would continue to keep them safe from a threat less pervasive than most people believe. Black and white thinking in a climate of fear, however, discourages the kind of cost-benefit analysis every driver makes each time he/she gets into a car. Individually and collectively in so many areas of life we constantly ask, 'How much risk am I willing to accept, and at what cost can I reduce that risk?' The same question needs to be applied to discussions of terrorism. Life in contemporary America and Europe is safer than it has ever been, but it is and never will be risk free. Consideration of security measures ranging from identity cards to baggage screening should be made with this realization in mind.

COMPREHENSIVE APPROACH

What, then, would a truly grand strategy for counter-terrorism look like? Such a strategy must begin with a clear working definition of terrorism that a majority of the international community can accept. It should then delineate concrete actions under the three categories of anti-terrorism, counter-terrorism, and consequence management. At the regional and international level these actions will begin as least-common-denominator but may expand from there. Individual states facing focused threats must be empowered to act against them but should do so within a framework of international law and legitimacy.

Achieving international consensus on a definition has proven to be particularly difficult. UN discussions on the matter have stalled over distinguishing between legitimate resistance to oppressive regimes and other forms of violence by non-state actors (Palti, 2004). Whatever disagreements on motives may exist, however, consensus on the illegitimacy of certain acts is emerging. Different groups and nations may dispute the legitimacy of 'resistance organizations', but they should be able to agree that suicide bombing of civilians is always unacceptable as are targeted killings of political leaders and house demolitions to punish families and communities for the actions of individuals. A working definition based on methods, targets and weapons should be achievable. Conventions restricting or banning chemical, nuclear, and biological weapons already exist for conventional war as do rules governing treatment of non-combatants.

Abandoning the 'Global War on Terrorism' would also contribute to consensus-building. In international law, war has a precise definition not readily applicable to a grey-area phenomenon like terrorism. Counter-terrorism may involve conventional operations, but these operations represent but one part of a larger strategy that is not primarily military. Eliciting co-operation from allies will be much easier once the USA abandons the unhelpful metaphor of 'global war'. As already noted, the American view actually impeded co-operation between the USA and Germany in prosecution of alleged terrorists arrested in Hamburg. Insistence upon a state of war coupled with repeated assertion of the right to unilateral and even pre-emptive military action has cost the USA the international support it had in abundance after 9/11. The invasion of Afghanistan fell easily under the self-defence provision of the UN Charter and drew NATO support under Article 5 of the Washington Treaty (the collective defence provision) as well. In the absence of such support, a threatened state should seriously consider whether any gains from pre-emptive war will outweigh the loss of international support and legitimacy that such action entails.

However valuable it may be, agreement upon a definition of terrorism will not automatically produce a viable counter-terrorism strategy. Such a definition must then lead to clearly defined, achievable goals and an approach to attaining them. Eradicating terrorism has as little chance of success as eliminating poverty or drug abuse. Like these other threats to the public welfare, however, terrorism can be reduced to a level at which it no longer produces widespread fear, dominates political discourse, or absorbs an inordinate share of national and international resources. Reaching such a desired end state will require a concerted effort over a protracted period. NATO doctrine provides a useful framework for delineating tasks.

Anti-terrorism has progressed considerably since 9/11, at least in the USA. Passenger-screening at airports has improved dramatically and baggage-screening continues to improve. Federal, state and local authorities have hardened high-profile targets, setting up barriers to impede car bombs and controlling access to buildings. Security along the Canadian and Mexican borders remains a concern as does the even greater threat posed by the millions of containers that enter the USA each year, largely uninspected before reaching their destinations. Even in these areas, however, improvements continue to be made. The USA is spearheading international efforts on maritime security. The 80% of critical infrastructure in private hands, however, needs to be protected. Business and industry will only take such steps when they receive government assistance or tax incentives to do so. Besides these passive measures, co-ordination among local, state, and Federal law enforcement and between these groups and various intelligence agencies has improved. In fostering such co-operation, the Department of Homeland Security has been a mixed blessing. While anti-terrorism requires co-ordination and strategic oversight, it means creating yet another top-heavy bureaucratic agency using resources that might be better spent on local law enforcement. Too much intelligence flowing to the top can also overload intelligence analysts. Finally, subordinating multi-purpose agencies like the Federal Emergency Management Agency to the campaign against terrorism can impede their function, as 'Hurricane Katrina' amply demonstrated.

One measure that could further enhance domestic security remains controversial. Given the impossibility of securing thousands of miles of coastline, border, and airspace, the next best thing may be to have greater accountability of those within those borders. Despite the concerns it raises with civil libertarians, a national identity card has much to commend it. Such a card with a biometric chip would be very hard to forge. Inclusion of medical data such as blood type, medications, and allergies could also improve emergency medical treatment. Privacy advocates might do well to consider that credit agencies already collect and disseminate far more information than such an identity card would carry.

Outside of the USA and its closest ally, the United Kingdom, anti-terrorism has been largely neglected. Most countries simply lack the resources to protect all but a few crucial sites. The prosperous nations of the EU have the resources but have been reluctant to use them for internal security. Economic considerations explain this reluctance in part, but social and psychological factors may be even more important. The totalitarian regimes of the Second World War remain a living memory for many and the Communist dictatorships a recent experience for even more. Europeans even more than Americans resist trading civil liberties for security and find even passive protection of buildings an intrusion on their freedoms. It is difficult, however, to walk through the cathedrals, museums, and historical sites of Europe without believing that they are disasters waiting to happen. One week after Dutch Royal Marine Commandos captured a terrorist cell in The Hague, the parliament building in that city remained relatively unguarded.[2] Sadly, most societies seem unwilling to take preventive measures until after an attack occurs. Americans seem unwilling to accept even low levels of risk and so waste money buying precautions that make them feel safer without actually making them more secure. Europeans often seem unwilling to acknowledge the presence of any threat at all.

Consequence management strategy continues to improve for the simple reason that every state needs the capacity to respond to disasters. Preparations for a terrorist attack can piggy-back on existing disaster-relief plans and agencies. Planners must, however, prepare for contingencies like biological and chemical attack and the possibility of armed terrorists being in the area. Emergency workers must also be trained to treat a terrorist site as a crime scene. Drills and exercises can improve co-operation between primary responders in an emergency. These improvements and refinements of existing arrangements continue to be made in the USA and abroad.

Counter-terrorism continues to be the most problematic strategic task. As has been noted, the USA has focused too much on conventional war against 'state sponsors' of terror. Without rehashing the debate over Iraq, the fact is that no state targets worth attacking remain. Moving against Syria to prevent its covert support for Sunni insurgents in Iraq seems as likely to widen the war as to contain it. The same can be said for using force against Iran to stop its aid to Shi'ites in southern Iraq. In any case, the USA lacks the troops for either operation while it continues to occupy Iraq and Afghanistan. The emphasis in counter-terrorism needs to shift more towards law enforcement and covert operations. Persistent, low-level pressure over time will be more effective than concentrated, massive force.

Counter-terrorism also requires more enlightened domestic and foreign policies. The London bombings in July 2005 and the French riots in November 2005 clearly demonstrate how marginalized youths can be drawn into violent activities. Moving to address social inequities attacks at least one root cause of terrorism. Confronting problems of poverty, hunger, and disease globally could do even more to increase international and domestic security. An enlightened foreign policy is, however, far harder to develop, deploy, and sustain than an armoured division.

NOTES

[1] Preceding discussion and citations from the *National Strategy for Combating Terrorism*, February 2003.

[2] I visited this site a week after the raid. Pedestrians and automobiles had unimpeded access to the courtyard in front of the building.

A–Z Glossary
of Major Terrorist Groups and Incidents

By Andrew T H Tan

17 November Revolutionary Organization – *see* Revolutionary Organization 17 November

Abadan Theatre Attack

Until the **September 11, 2001 terrorist attacks** in the USA, the Abadan theatre attack in 1978 in Iran was infamous as the single deadliest act of contemporary terrorism. On 20 August 1978, the Cinema Rex in the city of Abadan in Iran was locked from the outside and set on fire, killing 430 people. Little verifiable information has emerged regarding the perpetrators of the attack and why it took place. However, there was popular speculation that agents of the then government of the Shah of Iran, Mohammed Reza Pahlavi, had carried it out against several dissidents inside the building. This event caused outrage in Iran and was one of the factors that led to mass demonstrations against the Shah's rule and his overthrow by Muslim fundamentalists six months later.

Abu Nidal Organization

The Abu Nidal Organization is a Palestinian extremist group that split from the **Palestine Liberation Organization (PLO)** led by Yasser Arafat in November 1974. Its official name is Fatah al-Qiyadah al-Thawriyyah or Fatah Revolutionary Council. It was led by Sabri al-Banna, who assumed the *nom de guerre* 'Abu Nidal', or 'Father of the Revolution'. Abu Nidal strongly opposed any compromise with the Jewish enemy and believed that the only solution to the Palestinian problem was the use of armed struggle to achieve total liberation. He also targeted Arab leaders who were prepared to engage with or accommodate Israel and the West. This led to conflict with Yasser Arafat. Indeed, many of Abu Nidal's operations targeted the PLO, which he regarded as having betrayed the Palestinian struggle through its preparedness to negotiate. The Abu Nidal Organization succeeded in recruiting as many as 800 active members, mostly from refugee camps in Lebanon. With the support of President Saddam Hussain in Iraq, where it maintained its headquarters in Baghdad, and with training facilities in Libya and assistance from Syria, the Organization carried out a wave of terrorist attacks from 1974 that killed or injured more than 900 people in the Middle East and Western Europe. It was responsible for a number of widely-reported attacks, such as the Rome, Italy, and Vienna, Austria, airport attacks in 1985, the Pan Am hijacking in Pakistan in 1986 and the 'City of Poros' ship attack in Greece in 1988. It was also believed to have been responsible for the assassination of PLO leaders 'Abu Iyad' and 'Abu Hul' in 1991, and the murder of a Jordanian diplomat in Lebanon in 1994. However, the Organization declined in the late 1980s. In 1989 internal dissension led to a bloody purge that resulted in the deaths of many members. In 1993 its head of special operations, 'Abu Ali Majid', was arrested in Lebanon. Support from state sponsors also evaporated owing to the growing pressure from the West and the USA on states that sponsored terrorist groups. Abu Nidal was also in poor health and sought medical treatment in Baghdad. In August 2002 he was killed by Iraqi security services, most probably on the orders of Saddam Hussain. The Organization is no longer considered to be active.

Abu Sayyaf Group

The Abu Sayyaf (literally 'sword bearer') Group is a violent Islamist group fighting for a separate Muslim state in the southern Philippines. Founded by Amilhussin Jumaani and Abdurajak Abubakar Janjalani in 1991, the Abu Sayyaf is opposed to any religious accommodation with the majority Christians and believes that violent action is the only solution. The Abu Sayyaf has been able to attract the support of a number of former supporters of the separatist **Moro National Liberation Front (MNLF)** who have been disillusioned by the Front's willingness to negotiate with the government. With its expertise and willingness to carry out urban terrorism, and its uncompromising stand, the Abu Sayyaf is considered more violent and dangerous than the main separatist insurgent movement, the **Moro Islamic Liberation Front (MILF)**, which eclipsed the MNLF after the latter signed the Davao peace accord with the government in 1996. The Abu Sayyaf has strong connections with international terrorist groups, particularly with **al-Qa'ida**. Its founder, Janjalani, was a veteran of the Afghan conflict, and had brought back with him enthusiastic fellow veterans who were inspired by pan-Islamic militant ideology. The name Abu Sayyaf is a tribute to Rasool Sayyaf, an ally of Osama bin Laden, with whom Janjalani fought during the Afghan War. Bin Laden himself sent the Pakistani terrorist Ramzi Yousef, who had carried out the **World Trade Center bombing** in 1993, to train the Abu Sayyaf in the use of sophisticated explosives. Bin Laden also helped to finance the activities of the group, mainly through his brother-in-law, Mohammad Jamal Khalifa, who administered a Muslim charity in Manila, Philippines. With this assistance, and through criminal acts such as extortion and kidnapping for ransom, the Abu Sayyaf was able to wreak havoc in the southern Philippines, including a spectacular raid in 1995 in the Christian town of Ipil in Mindanao, where it killed 57 people and razed the town centre. It was, however, through the daring raid on the Malaysian resort of Sipadan Island in April 2000 that the Abu Sayyaf gained world-wide notoriety. The Abu Sayyaf kidnapped 21 people, including 12 Western tourists. The Abu Sayyaf then issued a demand for a separate Islamic state in the southern Philippines and for the release by the US government of three Islamic militants jailed for terrorist activities in the West, including Ramzi Yousef. While the Abu Sayyaf was reported to have become factionalized and to have degenerated into a criminal organization because of its kidnapping operations after the death of Janjalani in 1997, its urban bombing campaigns have continued apace. Philippine intelligence has alleged that the group has maintained links with al-Qa'ida as well as with the regional radical network, the **Jemaah Islamiah (JI)**. In October 2001 fears emerged that Abu Sayyaf might attempt to poison Manila's water supply, resulting in heightened alerts at water supply plants. The Abu Sayyaf has been blamed for the **Superferry bombing** in Manila Bay in February 2004 that resulted in the death of 118 people. Such deadly attacks have led to fears that the Abu Sayyaf may be reverting to its radical religious roots. After the **September 11, 2001 terrorist attacks** in the USA, US forces arrived in the Philippines in 2002 to help train their Philippine counterparts to combat the Abu Sayyaf. The Abu Sayyaf is currently believed to have about 1,000 fighters.

Abu Musab az-Zarqawi (al-Zarqawi) – *see* Jama'at at-Tawhid wal-Jihad.

Aceh Merdeka – *see* Gerakan Aceh Merdeka (GAM)

Achille Lauro Hijack

The luxury Italian cruise liner, *Achille Lauro*, was hijacked in October 1985 by four armed men from the **Palestine Liberation Front (PLF)**, which is part of the **Palestine Liberation Organization (PLO)**. More than 500 passengers and crew were taken hostage. The hijackers demanded the release of 50 Palestinian prisoners held by Israel. When the vessel approached the Syrian port of Tartus, the Syrian authorities refused permission for it to dock. At this point, the hijackers shot dead a wheelchair-bound US citizen of Jewish extraction among the hostages and threw his body overboard. The ship then sailed to the Eygptian port of Port Said, where the hijackers were eventually persuaded by Eygptian officials and PLF leader 'Abu Abbas' to release all of the hostages in return for safe passage to Tunisia. However, the Boeing 737 aircraft that was carrying the hijackers to Tunisia was intercepted *en route* by jet-fighters launched from the US aircraft carrier, the USS *Saratoga*, which forced it to land at a North Atlantic Treaty Organization airbase in Italy. The hijackers, including Abbas, were arrested but the Italian authorities subsequently refused to release them for trial in the USA. Abbas was allowed to leave Italy for Yugoslavia, an action that provoked much US criticism. Although there was only a single fatality in this terrorist attack, the events were reported sensationally in the international media. The PLO publicly condemned the attack. Abbas was finally arrested in 2003 in Iraq after US-led forces intervened in that country. He died controversially in US custody in March 2004.

Action Directe

Action Directe (Direct Action) was a French left-wing terrorist group founded by Jean-Marc Rouillan and Nathalie Menignon in 1979, with the aim of overthrowing by force the French political system. Its *modus operandi* was by assassinations and bombings, while its activities were financed through bank robberies. The group split into two factions in 1982. Its violent activities included the murder of a French general and of the president of the Renault car firm. One faction co-operated with Germany's **Red Army Faction** and Belgium's **Communist Combatant Cells** (Cellules Communistes Combattantes—CCC) to attack US and NATO targets. They succeeded in killing, for instance, two US citizens in a car bomb attack at a US air base in Frankfurt, Germany, in 1985. The French authorities tracked down members of the group, and by 1989 most of its leaders had been arrested and were serving long jail sentences. The group has become inactive and defunct.

Aden Abyan Islamic Army (AAIA)

Also known as the Islamic Army of Aden, the Aden Abyan Islamic Army (AAIA) is a clandestine radical Islamist group that came to attention in 1998 through its public call for the overthrow of the government of Yemen and for attacks on Western and US interests in the country. The group, which is a splinter from the radical **Yemen Islamic Jihad**, has ex-Afghan *mujahidin* members, subscribes to radical *Salafi* teachings and has close ties with **al-Qa'ida**. It advocates the overthrow of the government and its replacement by one that would apply the *Shari'a*, or Islamic law. The group has since carried out kidnappings and bombings, such as the kidnapping of 16 US, British and Australian tourists in south Yemen in December 1998 and the bombing of the British embassy in San'a in October 2000. The group also claimed responsibility for the **USS *Cole* bombing** in October 2000 that killed 17 US sailors. The leader of the AAIA, 'Abu Hasan', was later captured and sentenced to death for his role in the December 1998 kidnappings, which resulted in the death of four of the hostages. The group remains active and has attacked military convoys and other government targets.

Air India Bombing

On 23 June 1985 Air India Flight 182 was destroyed by a bomb while it was flying at a height of some 9,500 m over the Atlantic Ocean, just south of Ireland, killing all 329 passengers and crew on board. One of the deadliest single acts of terrorism in contemporary times, the Air India bombing was also the deadliest act of air sabotage until the **September 11, 2001 terrorist attacks** in the USA that involved four hijacked airliners. The Air India Boeing 747 jetliner had left Montréal in Canada and was *en route* to Bombay (Mumbai), India, via London, United Kingdom, when it disappeared over the Atlantic. Subsequent investigations revealed that a bomb had exploded in the forward cargo hold when the jetliner was in mid-flight. This caused rapid decompression and the break-up of the aircraft. On the same day, an explosion in an item of baggage that arrived at Tokyo's Narita Airport from Canada and was being transferred to an Air India flight to Bangkok, Thailand, killed two baggage handlers. Investigations in Canada suggested that Sikh extremists (*see* **National Council for Khalistan**) fighting for the independence of Punjab in India might have been involved, and that the attack was in retaliation for the assault by Indian security forces on the holiest of Sikh shrines, the Golden Temple of Amritsar, in 1984. While two Sikh militants were arrested in Canada, they were not charged for the bombing and were subsequently released for lack of evidence. In 1991 one of the two men, Inderjit Singh Reyat, was convicted in Britain of constructing the Narita bomb and sentenced to 10 years' imprisonment for manslaughter. After a costly, 15-year investigation, in 2000 two other men were formally charged with the Air India bombing. However, when, after numerous postponements, a lengthy trial was finally held, the British Columbia Supreme Court acquitted the two defendants in March 2005. However, Inderjit Singh Reyat was extradited to Canada from Britain and convicted in February 2003 of constructing the Air India bomb. He was sentenced to five years' imprisonment.

Al-Aqsa Martyrs' Brigades

The al-Aqsa Martyrs' Brigades constitute an armed Palestinian group that emerged with the outbreak of the second *intifada* (or 'uprising') in 2000 in the Israeli-occupied territories of Gaza and the West Bank. The name al-Aqsa is derived from the al-Aqsa mosque in Jerusalem, one of Islam's holiest shrines and a symbol of the Palestinian movement. Despite the use of Islam to mobilize support, the group has the political-nationalist objective of establishing an independent Palestinian state. The group hopes that the use of force will eventually compel Israel to withdraw from the occupied territories. Many of the group's members are also members of **al-Fatah**, a secular political-nationalist movement that is also the largest faction in the **Palestine Liberation Organization (PLO)**. However, the group is not openly recognized by al-Fatah, nor was it acknowledged by the long-time PLO leader, Yasser Arafat, who renounced terrorism after the establishment of the Palestinian Authority. However, some believed that he secretly supported the group in order to put pressure on Israel. Indeed, the alleged leader of the brigades is reportedly Marwan Barghouti, a leader of al-Fatah, who was captured by Israeli security forces in 2002 and later sentenced to life imprisonment. The *modus operandi* of the group includes suicide bombings and shootings, as well as targeting Jewish settlers in the occupied territories, Israeli soldiers, and civilians in Israel itself. In March 2002, after a deadly suicide bombing in Jerusalem that killed 11 Israelis and wounded another 50, the US Department of State designated the brigades as a terrorist organization. In January 2003 two suicide bombings in Tel-Aviv killed 23 people and wounded more than 100. In retaliation, Israel has attacked the group's leaders, either through assassination or arrest. For instance, Raed Karmi, the group's West Bank leader, was assassinated in a bomb explosion that was widely believed to have been carried out by Israeli security forces. After Yasser Arafat's death in November 2004, the group's name was changed to Brigades of Martyr Yasser Arafat. (*See* Map 7.)

Al-Badr Mujahidin

This group first appeared in 1971 when it attacked Bengalis in East Pakistan during Pakistan's civil war. It then became part of the extremist organization in Afghanistan, the **Hizb-i-Islami**, led by Gulbuddin Hekmatyar. In 1989 it was transformed into the **Hizb ul-Mujahidin**, operating in disputed Kashmir. In 1998 al-Badr reappeared as an offshoot, led by Lukmaan, from the Hizb ul-Mujahidin. It refused to recognize the cease-fire declared by the Hizb ul-Mujahidin, and began a campaign of terrorist suicide bombings in Jammu and Kashmir, in India, targeting both the military and government officials. Its objective is to separate these two states from India and merge them with Pakistan. The Indian government has claimed that the group is supported by the government of Pakistan, given its various transformations in the past, allegedly at the behest of Pakistani intelligence. It is doubtful if this is any longer so, however, in view of the group's opposition to the government of President Musharraf, which has taken firm action against extremists. Its strength is estimated to be up to 200. (*See* Map 9.)

Al-Fatah

Al-Fatah is a major component of the **Palestine Liberation Organization (PLO)**. Founded by Yasser Arafat and other activists in 1957, it started as an underground nationalist Palestinian organization that carried out military operations against Israel. The organization was affected by internal dissension from the start, with various leaders differing over the scope and timing of attacks against Israel. Al-Fatah joined the PLO in 1968 and by 1969 dominated it. In late 1967, after Israel's victory over Arab forces in the Six-Day War, al-Fatah attempted a series of attacks in the occupied West Bank but was defeated by Israeli forces. In 1970 it suffered a serious setback when Jordan expelled the PLO from its bases there. A terrorist splinter group that maintained links with al-Fatah, **Black September**, was then established to avenge the PLO defeat by Jordan. Al-Fatah and the PLO relocated to Lebanon. In the 1970s al-Fatah carried out a number of terrorist attacks in Wwestern Europe and the Middle East. It was, however, again evicted when Israeli forces invaded southern Lebanon in 1982. Al-Fatah and the PLO then moved to Tunisia. In 1987 the first Palestinian *intifada*, or uprising, took al-Fatah by surprise as it led to the formation of **Hamas**, which took on an overtly Muslim religious identity and rejected the secular nationalism of al-Fatah and the PLO. The PLO and al-Fatah eventually agreed to the Oslo peace accords in 1993, which led to the transformation of the erstwhile terrorist/guerrilla movement into a governing authority in the form of the Palestinian Authority. However, the renunciation of terrorism and efforts to negotiate a lasting agreement with Israel led to considerable internal dissension. Some al-Fatah members joined the **al-Aqsa Martyrs' Brigades**, led by Marwan Barghouti, to carry out suicide bombings and other attacks on Israeli settlers, soldiers and civilians. (Marwan Barghouti was captured by Israeli security forces in 2002 and later sentenced to life imprisonment.) Others left to join the more extremist Hamas or the **Palestinian Islamic Jihad**. Al-Fatah and the PLO maintained that they had no connection with the al-Aqsa Martyrs' Brigades, but Israel accused Yasser Arafat of covertly supporting and even controlling them. Yasser Arafat's death in 2004 led to the ascension to the leadership of al-Fatah and the PLO of Mahmud Abbas. A moderate, he was Prime Minister for four months in 2003. He clashed with Yasser Arafat, criticized the second *intifada*, which broke out in 2000, and pursued negotiations with Israel. However, the movement is today factionalized with no single leader able to command widespread authority. Mahmud's leadership, for instance, could be challenged by more radical and nationalist elements.

Al-Gama'a al-Islamiyya

This is a radical Islamist group in Eygpt that emerged in the late 1970s, gaining adherents in prisons, universities and among the urban poor. The group is heavily influenced by the radical writings of the Muslim ideologue Sayyid Qutb, who was executed in Eygpt in 1966. The group aims to establish an Islamic caliphate ruled by the *Shari'a*, or Islamic law. However, the group is not a centralized entity and can best be described as a movement united under radical ideology. It has been estimated to have several thousand members, organized in autonomous and self-contained cells. Its spiritual leader, Sheikh Omar Abdel-Rahman, was sentenced to life imprisonment in the USA for his role in the **World Trade Center bombing** of 1993 in New York. The group opposed the peace agreement with Israel signed by President Anwar Sadat of Egypt in 1979, becoming the subject of intense Egyptian government attention after its members were involved in the assassination of President Sadat in 1981. The group has also carried out a number of terrorist acts, including the **Luxor massacre** of tourists in 1997, in which 62 people died. Government officials and ministers, police officers, intellectuals, Christians and tourists have been targeted in its terrorist campaign. However, the indiscriminate nature of the group's attacks, in which ordinary Eygptians died and which damaged the tourism industry on which many Eygptians depended for a living, resulted in widespread condemnation of the group. The government also took harsh measures, executing many of its members after they had been captured. Shortly after the Luxor massacre, the group split into factions led, respectively, by Osama Rushdi and Mustafa Hamza, who supported a cease-fire, and others, such as those led by Refaei Ahmed Taha and Sheikh Omar, who wished to continue violent activities against the state.

Al-Ittihaad al-Islami (AIAI)

Al-Ittihaad al-Islami (AIAI) is a radical Islamist group that was formed to oppose the government in Somalia in the late 1980s. It emerged as a major force following the collapse of the Siad Barre dictatorship in 1991. It has received funding from the Middle East and some of its members also received training in Afghanistan in the 1990s. The AIAI's objective is the establishment of an Islamic state in Somalia and the neighbouring Ogaden region in Ethiopia. The collapse of the state in Somalia after 1991 resulted in a warlord zone in which various political factions battled for power; the AIAI, from its power base in east Somalia, targeted other factions as well as Ethiopian forces, and was responsible for bomb attacks in Addis Ababa, the capital of Ethiopia, in 1996–97. It also established links with **al-Qa'ida** and is believed also to operate in neighbouring Kenya. In 1998 AIAI is believed to have assisted al-Qa'ida in the **East Africa embassy bombings**. Recent developments have reduced the threat from the AIAI. Ethiopian military offensives and the establishment of a self-governing state in eastern Somalia under secular authorities have resulted in a reduction in its strength to an estimated 2,000 members.

Al-Qa'ida

Al-Qa'ida ('The Base') is a radical Islamist organization that is considered as the epitome of the 'new' terrorism that emerged in the 1990s. Unlike many ethnonationalist or politically-motivated insurgent or terrorist groups that drew their membership from a particular ethnic group, al-Qa'ida is regarded as the first truly multinational terrorist organization, with more than 40 nationalities among its ranks, and an unprecedented ability to operate world-wide. It is represented in at least 60 countries and has formed affiliations with local regional terrorist groups motivated by the same radical *Salafi* ideology. Al-Qa'ida is strongly opposed to most Muslim governments, viewing them as corrupt and apostate. Its goal is the establishment of a world-wide caliphate ruled by the *Shari'a*, or Islamic law. Al-Qa'ida is prepared to use extreme violence, including suicide and mass casualty terrorist acts, to achieve its goal. Its leaders have openly expressed interest in acquiring, and using, weapons of mass destruction. Al-Qa'ida regards itself as a secret, élite, revolutionary vanguard organization, being highly selective in its recruitment and paying careful attention to training and motivation. Despite its world-wide presence, it has never had more than 4,000 members at its peak.

The success of al-Qa'ida owes much to the genius of its famous leader, Osama bin Laden, a wealthy Saudi Arabian, and his deputy, Dr Ayman Muhammad Rabi' az-Zawahiri (al-Zawahiri), the leader of the radical Eygptian group, the **Islamic Jihad**, and a surgeon by training. The antecedent of al-Qa'ida was the *Maktab al-Khidamat* (MAK), or Afghan Services Office, which was established by Osama and the leader of the Palestinian Muslim Brotherhood, Abdullah Azzam, to co-ordinate the flow of Muslim volunteers or *mujahidin* from all over the world to fight the Soviet invasion of Afghanistan in 1979. Osama won over many of these veteran fighters through his personal wealth, charisma and obvious leadership qualities. After the withdrawal of Soviet forces from Afghanistan in 1989, Osama returned to Saudi Arabia. The use of Saudi facilities by US and other allied Western forces to attack Iraq in the first Gulf War in 1991 was bitterly opposed by Osama, who, even though he did not support the authoritarian regime of Saddam Hussain in Iraq, regarded their presence in the Arabian peninsula as an affront to Islam. Osama began to target the Saudi regime as well as its US ally. He moved some of his best-trained cadres from al-Qa'ida's original headquarters in

Peshawar, Pakistan, to Sudan, where the regime of Hasan at-Turabi welcomed his presence. However, pressure from the West resulted in him moving the organization back to Afghanistan in 1996, where he forged a close alliance with the fundamentalist Muslim **Taliban** regime then in control in Kabul. In 1998, Osama announced the formation of an umbrella organization called 'The Islamic World Front for the Struggle Against the Jews and the Crusaders'. At training camps in Afghanistan, al-Qa'ida and the Taliban trained many thousands of radical Islamists in urban warfare and terrorism until their eviction by US-led forces in late 2001. These al-Qa'ida trained operatives returned to their home countries where they have established local or regional terrorist organizations—modelled on al-Qa'ida—and have also contributed to improving the efficiency of local insurgent and terrorist groups.

Al-Qa'ida and its affiliates have carried out some of the deadliest terrorist attacks in contemporary times, although al-Qa'ida itself rarely publicly claims credit for them. It has been blamed for the **World Trade Center bombing** in New York in 1993, which killed six people and injured more than 1,000; the **Khobar Towers bombing** in Saudi Arabia in 1996, which killed 19 US servicemen and wounded 370 people; the **East Africa embassy bombings** in Kenya and Tanzania in 1998, which killed 224 people; and the **USS *Cole* bombing** in Yemen in 2000, which killed 17 US servicemen. It was responsible for the **September 11, 2001 terrorist attacks** in the USA. Nineteen al-Qa'ida suicide operatives hijacked four US civilian aircraft and used three of them as missiles to attack the Pentagon in Washington, DC, and the World Trade Center in New York. The fourth, possibly *en route* to the White House or the US Congress, crashed in Pennsylvania after passengers attempted to recapture it from the hijackers. In all, 2,986 people of many nationalities, ethnic and religious backgrounds perished in the unprecedented attack, which is considered the first truly single mass casualty terrorist act in contemporary times. The subsequent US-led 'war' on global terrorism included military action in Afghanistan to evict the Taliban regime there as well as al-Qa'ida. World-wide counter-terrorist action resulted in the decimation of the ranks of al-Qa'ida as its operatives and leaders were killed or arrested in the Middle East, South-East Asia and Western Europe. However, Osama and his deputy, az-Zawahiri, remain at large and al-Qa'ida subsequently carried out several attacks in Saudi Arabia in 2003–04—see **Saudi Bombings (2003)**. Its local and regional affiliates have also succeeded in carrying out numerous deadly attacks in Morocco, in Madrid (Spain), Moscow (Russia), Istanbul (Turkey), and in Jakarta and Bali in Indonesia and other places, indicating that the radical religious terrorist threat that al-Qa'ida originally represented has been transformed into a generalized, ideological threat. The US-led intervention in Iraq in 2003 has also transformed Iraq into what Afghanistan was to the Muslim World in the 1980s: a symbol of Muslim suffering inflicted by the West, resulting in a continued supply of recruits world-wide to the radical Islamist cause, and in the replenishment of the ranks of the Islamists. Ultimately, one of al-Qa'ida's greatest achievements, according to Rohan Gunaratna, author of the seminal *Inside Al Qaeda*, has been to have 'raised the profile of the Islamist threat and increased the likelihood of long-term, more or less continuous, conflict with the West'. Gunaratna concludes that: 'The global fight against Al-Qaeda will be the defining conflict of the early 21st century. Osama bin Laden has built an organization that functions both operationally and ideologically at local, national, regional and global levels. Defeating Al-Qaeda and its associate groups will be the single biggest challenge confronting the international security and intelligence community, law enforcement authorities and national militaries in the foreseeable future.'

Al-Qanoon

Al-Qanoon ('The Law') is an umbrella group that covers a loose coalition of radical Islamist organizations in Pakistan, including the **Lashkar-e-Taiba**, **Lashkar-e-Jhangvi** and **Jaish-e-Mohammed**. It is also believed to have ties with **al-Qa'ida**, elements of which are believed to have regrouped in the border area of Pakistan and Afghanistan with the help of local radical sympathizers after its eviction from its Afghan bases by US-led forces in late 2001. The group came to public knowledge after claiming responsibility for a suicide truck bombing at the US Consulate in Karachi, Pakistan, on 14 June 2002, which killed 10 people and wounded 51 others. It declared that 'the bomb blast is the beginning of Al-Qanoon's *jihadi* activities in Pakistan', and that 'America, its allies and its slave Pakistani rulers should be prepared for more attacks.' The group also called on President Musharraf to resign. The sophistication of the attack raised suspicions of links to al-Qa'ida, given its similarity to an attack in May 2002 on a bus in Karachi, which killed 14 people, including 11 French citizens.

As-Saiqa

There are today several groups using this name. The first as-Saiqa ('thunderbolt') is a Palestinian nationalist group that is part of the **Palestine Liberation Organization (PLO)**. It was established in 1966 by the Ba'athist regime in Syria and is based in that country. As-Saiqa functioned virtually as part of the Syrian army, with a Syrian general becoming its first leader. In 1971, Zuhayr Muhsin was made secretary-general, but he was assassinated in Cannes, France. The organization is now led by Issam al-Qadi. As-Saiqa carried out a number of attacks against Israel and Arab states, such as Lebanon and Eygpt. It has supported the PLO, but has also criticized its efforts to negotiate with Israel. However, it is no longer of any major significance as its strength within the PLO is small compared to the dominant **al-Fatah**. In 2002 another group with the same name appeared in Pakistan. This, however, is a radical Islamist group that has carried out attacks against the Musharraf government in Pakistan, accusing it of being non-Muslim and vowing to attack security personnel. This second group is led by Inayat Shah and is believed to have close ties with **al-Qa'ida**, although little else is known about it. A third group with the same name appeared in 2003 in Morocco, claiming responsibility for the **Casablanca bombings** that killed

45 people, including a number of tourists and the 12 suicide bombers who carried them out. This is a previously unknown group and it remains obscure.

At-Takfir Wal Hijrah

The at-Takfir Wal Hijrah is best described as a radical Islamist movement in the Middle East that was originally founded in Egypt. The literal meaning of the name is 'Redemption and Flight', a reference to the Prophet Muhammad's flight from Mecca to Medina, and the movement aims to establish a pure Muslim society based on Islamic law—the *Shari'a*. At-Takfir Wal Hijrah aims to overthrow all secular Muslim governments and replace them with a pan-Islamic caliphate. The movement is therefore hostile to all Middle Eastern governments and has used violence to pursue its aims. It first emerged in the 1970s, when it kidnapped and killed a cabinet minister in Egypt. The members of this original group were arrested and imprisoned, although some escaped to Jordan and elsewhere. However, the group they had established soon became a movement as other Islamists adopted its approach. It has spread across the Middle East and has also found a following among alienated Muslim migrants in Western Europe. The killer of Dutch film-maker Theo Van Gogh in 2004, who was accused of expressing anti-Muslim sentiments and blasphemy, is alleged to have links with at-Takfir Wal Hijrah. In Kuwait the movement's adherents have been accused of kidnapping Western expatriates and liberal academics as well as arson attacks against newspapers and bookstores selling Western books and videos. The movement has been involved in attacks elsewhere, such as that on a mosque of the Ansar as-Sunna sect linked to the Saudi royal family that killed at least 20 people in Sudan in December 2000.

As-Sunna Wal Jamma

The as-Sunna Wal Jamma ('Followers of the Prophet') is a radical Islamist movement in Nigeria that aims to create a fundamentalist Muslim state ruled strictly by Islamic law—the *Shari'a*. The group admired the **Taliban** regime in Afghanistan, and is believed to have links with **al-Qa'ida**. It has a strong following among university students in Maiduguri, a major city in northern Nigeria. In the context of a fractious state racked by ethnic conflict, deep corruption, poor governance, Christian–Muslim animosities and economic malaise, it is no surprise that radical Islamist teachings have found some support among the millions of Muslims in Nigeria. As-Sunna Wal Jamma has been blamed for inciting religious violence between Muslims and Christians in northern Nigeria in the 1980s. In late 2003 and early 2004 the group resorted to direct violence for the first time when it launched an armed insurrection. About 200 militants seized police stations and arms in Yobe. In the fighting with security forces that ensued, about 20 of the militants were killed. Despite the efforts of the security forces, there remain an estimated 1,000 members of the radical group, organized in an extensive network of cells. There are fears this group will expand its membership and operations given the conditions in Nigeria.

Al-Umar Mujahidin

Al-Umar Mujahidin is a clandestine Kashmiri separatist organization that aims to merge the Indian state of Jammu and Kashmir with Pakistan. The group was formed in 1989 by Mushtaq Ahmad Zargar and is named after Srinagar cleric Maulvi Umar Farooq. It has launched a number of attacks on Indian government and security personnel, particularly in the city of Srinagar. Zargar was captured in 1992, but was released in December 1999 in exchange for the release of the passengers of a hijacked Indian civilian airliner in Afghanistan. Indian security forces killed al-Umar Mujahidin's alleged operational commander, Rafiq Ahmad Lidri, in 2004. The group allegedly had close ties with Pakistani intelligence, as well as links with the radical Islamist organization, the **Jaish-e-Mohammed**. It has an estimated strength of 700 and is based in Pakistan Kashmir. (*See* Map 9.)

Aldo Moro Murder (1978)

The kidnapping and murder of former Italian Prime Minister Aldo Moro in 1978 by the **Red Brigades** was a huge shock as he was a leading political figure in a major industrialized state. Aldo Moro was a leading Italian Christian Democrat and had helped to draft the Italian Constitution after the Second World War. In the 1970s he was instrumental in elaborating a historical compromise with the Italian Communist Party that allowed it to participate in a coalition government, brought it into the mainstream and legitimized its role in national politics. However, the compromise enraged the extreme left-wing radicals in the Red Brigades, which kidnapped Moro in Rome after killing his five bodyguards. The Red Brigades demanded the release of imprisoned terrorists in exchange for his life, but the Italian government refused to negotiate. After 55 days of detention, Moro was killed and his body left in the boot of a car. Moro's murder was condemned by all sectors of society in Italy and led to concerted police action that substantially reduced the terrorist threat from the Red Brigades.

Alex Boncayao Brigade

The Alex Boncayao Brigade is a breakaway faction of the Communist Party of the Philippines (CPP). Formed in the mid-1980s, it broke away in 1994 after the CPP ordered it to disband in response to a public outcry over its urban terror tactics. It is active in Manila and in cities on the islands of Luzon, Negros and Visayas. It has specialized in urban terrorism and has been responsible for a number of high-profile assassinations. In 1997 the Alex Boncayao Brigade formed an alliance with another armed communist group, the Revolutionary Proletarian Army, resulting in a combined strength of about 500. Led by

Carapali Lualhati, it has rejected any negotiation with the Philippine government, is opposed to the CPP, and has vowed to continue attacks on 'abusive state agents and die-hard capitalists'. In March 2000 it attacked the Shell Oil offices in central Philippines as a protest at rising oil prices. The Alex Boncayao Brigade is anti-US in orientation, having murdered a US colonel in the Philippines in 1989. It was designated as a terrorist organization by the USA in December 2001.

All Burma Student Democratic Front (ABSDF)

The democratic ferment in Myanmar (formerly Burma) in 1988 was carried out by student activists. The massacre of some 3,000 demonstrators in August 1988 and the failure of the military regime to recognize the results of the elections held in 1990, which were won overwhelmingly by the National League for Democracy led by Aung San Suu Kyi, resulted in the flight of the student activists. They made their way to safe areas controlled by the rebel ethnic **Karen National Union (KNU)**, where they established the armed All Burma Student Democratic Front (ABSDF) in November 1988. The KNU provided training and some weapons. However, many student activists were unable to cope with the harsh jungle conditions in the face of superior government forces and returned to their homes. The ABSDF remains in existence due to the efforts of committed activists, and is also active in training and lobbying overseas. It advocates democracy for Burma/Myanmar and a federal state system.

Alliance of Eritrean National Force (AENF)

The Alliance of Eritrean National Force (AENF) is an umbrella organization of some 13 Eritrean groups opposed to the government of Issaias Afewerki in Eritrea, which gained independence from Ethiopia in 1993. It was founded in 1999 under the sponsorship of Sudan, probably in retaliation for alleged Eritrean support for the rebel **Sudan People's Liberation Army**. It is led by Abdellah Idris, the leader of one of the constituent groups, the Eritrean Liberation Front-Revolution Council. The AENF is critical of the allegedly authoritarian policies of the Eritrean Government, which it accuses of engaging in a military build-up at the expense of the people. In 1998 Eritrea launched a military offensive along the disputed border with Ethiopia, resulting in some 80,000 casualties. Both Ethiopia and Sudan hoped that the AENF would be able to garner support against the Eritrean government from some Ethiopian military successes, such as the advance into Eritrea in 2000 that created a temporary western enclave for the AENF. However, in 2002 the conflict appeared to have ended when the Permanent Court of Arbitration in The Hague awarded much of the disputed area to Ethiopia, although Eritrea gained some territory in the west. The AENF has made little headway thus far. (*See* Map 4.)

Allied Democratic Forces (ADF)

The Allied Democratic Forces (ADF) is a coalition of opposition groups in Uganda. It is an amalgamation of fundamentalist Muslims of the Tabliq sect and of another rebel group, the National Army for the Liberation of Uganda (NALU). It has been supported by Sudan, apparently in retaliation for Ugandan support for the **Sudan People's Liberation Army** and for Hutu groups in East Africa. It operated in western Uganda, with support bases in the Democratic Republic of the Congo. Beginning as a relatively minor rebel group in the mountainous Rwenzori region in 1996, the ADF expanded in size and attacked villages, refugee camps, markets and other public places, as well as military personnel and installations. It also laid mines and abducted youth. Its use of wanton violence against civilians resulted in a huge internal refugee crisis. In 1998 the group killed 80 students in a technical college by setting fire to locked dormitories. Government counter-insurgency offensives, particularly in 2000, resulted in the capture of a number of ADF camps. By the end of 2001 the number of insurgent attacks had decreased sufficiently for the tens of thousands of displaced persons to return home, even in the Rwenzori region where the fighting had begun. The threat from the ADF has thus been much reduced, although there are remnants of the group in eastern Congo. The ADF is regarded as no more than a nuisance today, especially when compared to the threat to the Ugandan government posed by the **Lord's Resistance Army**. (*See* Map 2.)

Amal

Amal ('Hope') is a radical Shi'ite group in Lebanon. It was founded by a religious cleric, Musa as-Sadr, in 1975 as the military arm of his political party, the Harakat al-Mahrumin. Amal participated in the Lebanese civil war in 1975 and became entangled in the very complicated political circumstances in Lebanon that involved the interests of many different groups and states, including the **Palestine Liberation Organization (PLO)**—which had a presence in Lebanon at that time—and Israel, which invaded southern Lebanon in 1978. Amal was opposed to Israel but also found itself fighting the PLO for control of southern Lebanon. It thus had two formidable adversaries. In addition, the charismatic as-Sadr was murdered in Libya in 1978, dealing the group a major blow. The Iranian Revolution of 1979 also revitalized the Shi'ites in Lebanon, resulting in the establishment of the Iranian-backed radical Shi'ite religious group, **Hezbollah**, in 1982. Amal soon lost support to Hezbollah, which is led by religious clerics and aimed to establish a Muslim state modelled on Iran. In the mid-1980s, however, Syria began to provide support and assistance to Amal, which proceeded to besiege Palestinian refugee camps in Beirut. In 1988–89 Amal and Hezbollah fought each other in a bitter civil war. Amal, under Nabih Berri, a French-trained lawyer, subsequently entered mainstream Lebanese politics, with Berri becoming Speaker of the Lebanese parliament in 1992. From 2000 the withdrawal of Israeli forces from southern Lebanon resulted in tensions between Amal and Hezbollah as both fought for leadership of the Shi'ite community. However, the increasing popularity of Hezbollah and the shift in Syrian support to it has undermined Amal.

American Front

The American Front was founded in 1990 by Bob Heick and is a neo-Nazi, extreme right-wing, white supremacist group. First based in Oregon, USA, it has spread and now has a presence in several parts of the USA. Comprising skinheads with long records of violence, its slogan is 'National Freedom, Social Justice, Racial Identity'. It espouses anti-capitalist ideas, is anti-Jewish, and seeks 'social revolution in a racialist context'. Individual members of the group have been involved in a number of often race-related violent attacks, carried out particularly against blacks, gays and Jews.

Andres Castro United Front (FUAC)

The Andres Castro United Front (Frente Unido Andres Castro—FUAC) is an armed group in Nicaragua that emerged after the civil conflict between the left-wing Sandinista government and the US-backed Contras in the 1980s. The Sandinista National Liberation Front (SNLF) was defeated in elections in 1990 and thus fell from power. The FUAC was formed in 1995 as an armed pressure group that aimed to persuade the new government to take proper care of former SNLF soldiers by, for example, providing them with jobs and land. Operating in the Matagalpa-Jinotega region of Nicaragua, the FUAC was able to cause some disruption to the coffee industry. In 1997 the government and FUAC reached an agreement to end the rebellion in exchange for credit and technical assistance to rural areas under FUAC control. This has not ended the violence, however, as disaffected FUAC members have continued to wage terror attacks in the country.

Animal Liberation Front

The Animal Liberation Front was formed in Britain in 1976 by animal rights activist Ronnie Lee, but is now present in the USA and Europe, particularly in Scandinavia. In Britain it has an estimated 400 members. It has used violent tactics in pursuit of its objective of ending the suffering of animals used in scientific research or in business activity. It also aims to inflict economic damage on those who profit from animals' suffering. The Front, however, is not a centralized organization, but consists of a network of cells which operate in secret, choosing their own targets and modes of operation. It welcomes anyone to join, so long as they are prepared to take 'direct action'. In Britain companies specializing in breeding animals for scientific research, scientists using animals for such research, and individuals involved in the fur trade and fox hunting, have been the Front's principal targets. It has been particularly active in the areas around Oxford and Cambridge owing to the presence of research laboratories there. Since the early 1980s its methods have become increasingly violent. Its *modus operandi* has included raids on laboratories, vandalism, letter bomb campaigns, car bombs and arson. Sympathizers also take part in demonstrations that are intended to intimidate workers at research laboratories and other targeted businesses. In the USA animal rights activists have also carried out hundreds of attacks, particularly at universities. The violence of these activists has been of concern to the British government, but counter-terrorist legislation has not covered their activities.

Ansar al-Islam

Ansar al-Islam ('Supporters of Islam') is a radical Islamist organization in Kurdish Iraq. It was created in 2001 from the merger of disparate radical groups and has links with **al-Qa'ida**, from which it has reportedly received some funding. The group is led by former *mujahidin* of the Afghan war in the 1980s and aims to establish an Islamic state adminstered in accordance with the *Shari'a*, or Islamic law. It has enforced strict decrees reminiscent of the **Taliban** regime in Afghanistan in the areas where it operated. It opposed the regime of Saddam Hussain in Iraq, but has also clashed repeatedly with secular Kurdish nationalists, principally those in the **Patriotic Union of Kurdistan (PUK)**. Ansar al-Islam has succeeded in assassinating a number of PUK leaders and officials through bombings and shootings. In September 2002 it suffered a set-back when its spiritual leader, Mullah Krekar, was arrested in the Netherlands on suspicion of having links with al-Qa'ida. While the PUK sided with the USA when US-led forces attacked and occupied Iraq in 2003, Ansar al-Islam, which at that time had an estimated 700 members, adopted an anti-US position. The USA has accused the group of being in league with al-Qa'ida and the Saddam Hussain regime, and of developing chemical and biological weapons of mass destruction. Whatever the truth of these charges, Ansar al-Islam was dealt a heavy blow by US forces in 2003, when they raided and destroyed Ansar al-Islam bases along the Iran-Iraq border, forcing its members, as well as al-Qa'ida operatives sheltering there after being evicted from Afghanistan by US-led forces in late 2001, to flee to Iran or disperse within Iraq. However, the conflict in Iraq has resulted in many foreign volunteers joining the loose coalition of anti-US groups, including Ansar al-Islam. The group remains a menace to security in Iraq, and has carried out suicide bomb attacks, including a devastating one in February 2004 which killed 109 PUK supporters and officials.

Anti-Imperialist Territorial Nuclei

The Anti-Imperialist Territorial Nuclei (Nuclei Territoriali Antimperialisti—NTA) is an extreme left-wing group that first appeared in Italy in 1995. It is regarded as the successor to the **Red Brigades** of the 1970s and 1980s, and indeed incorporated its logo. It believes in class struggle and opposition to capitalism as well as the government of Italy, the USA and the North Atlantic Treaty Organization alliance, which it regards as imperialist. It is believed to be a small group with no more than 20 members, but reports indicate that it is working to co-operate with other left-wing extremist groups, such as the **Revolutionary Proletarian Initiative Nuclei**. It has been involved in bomb and arson attacks.

Arab Liberation Front

The Arab Liberation Front is a member of the **Palestine Liberation Organization (PLO)**, although it is dwarfed by the PLO's dominant faction, **al-Fatah**. It was founded in 1969 as a left-wing Palestinian nationalist organization on the initiative of the Ba'athist Party in Iraq. It has carried out attacks on Israeli targets. In recent years the Front has financed Palestinian suicide bombings by paying compensation to the families of suicide bombers. It rejected the Oslo peace accords, but remained nevertheless within the PLO. The Front is led by Rakad Salem and has an estimated strength of 500. It was financed by Iraq, but the fall of the Saddam Hussain regime after the US-led attack and occupation of the country in 2003 has marginalized it.

Armata Corsa

Armata Corsa ('Corsican Army') is a group that emerged in 1999 out of the **Front de libération nationale de la Corse (FLNC)**, the main separatist group on the island of Corsica, France. Armata Corsa claims to be a purely nationalist group and has denounced the links of other Corsican resistance groups with organized crime. Despite its small size of about 30 members, it has carried out a series of attacks on foreign businesses, government and security buildings and government personnel. Most of the attacks have taken place in Corsica, although a few have also been carried out on the mainland. The FLNC's leader, Jean-Michel Rossi, was assassinated in 2000, while another key figure, François Santoni, was murdered in 2001, both possibly by rival Corsican or organized criminal groups.

Armed Islamic Group (GIA)

The Armed Islamic Group (Groupe islamique armé—GIA) is a radical Islamist group in Algeria. It emerged after events in 1991–92, when the fundamentalist **Islamic Salvation Front (Front islamique du salut—FIS)**, which had won the first round of legislative elections and was guaranteed a majority in parliament, was prevented from taking office by the ruling National Liberation Front government, which also cancelled the second round of voting in early 1992. FIS was forced to go underground, establishing an armed wing, the Islamic Army of Salvation (Armée islamique du salut—AIS). Some more radical members, many of whom had served as volunteer *mujahidin* in Afghanistan in the 1980s, later split from it to establish a militant faction, the GIA. While the AIS and the GIA initially co-operated, the GIA soon alienated the FIS/AIS through its unrestrained use of terror tactics. Government and security personnel, intellectuals, journalists and foreigners were kidnapped and murdered, and the GIA also carried out car bombings. In rural areas entire villages were attacked and their inhabitants murdered. The GIA even turned on the more moderate FIS, murdering some of its top leaders. The group also hijacked an Air France flight to Algiers in 1994, and in 1995 carried out attacks in France, where it has some support among Algerian migrants. Within Algeria, the combination of terrorist and guerrilla tactics, and the tough government response, turned the country into an arena of battle. More than 100,000 people have died since 1992 in the unrestrained violence. By 2000 many of the original GIA military commanders had been killed. In 2002 its leader, Antar Zouabri, was killed by security forces. The new leaders of the GIA were by this time beginning to have reservations about the strategy of unrestrained terror, which has alienated much of the Algerian population. As a result, the number of attacks has decreased in recent years, as has the level of violence.

Armenian Secret Army for the Liberation of Armenia (ASALA)

The Armenian Secret Army for the Liberation of Armenia (ASALA) was a left-wing Armenian separatist organization that was founded in 1975 and aimed to establish a separate Armenian homeland, an area that includes eastern Turkey, northern Iran and Armenia in the then USSR. Based in Beirut, Lebanon, it had Syrian support and reached out to the world-wide Armenian diaspora. It was strongly opposed to Turkey owing to that country's role in the massacre of more than 1m. Armenians in 1915, and demanded Turkish acknowledgement of the atrocity as well as reparations. Its terrorist activities were thus targeted at Turkish interests in the 1970s and 1980s, most spectacularly at Orly Airport in Paris in 1983, when a bomb attack at the Turkish airline counter killed eight people. The movement then splintered into competing factions. The establishment of an independent Armenia following the collapse of the USSR in the early 1990s appears to have ended the ASALA's terrorist activities.

Army for the Liberation of Rwanda

The Army for the Liberation of Rwanda (Armée pour la libération du Rwanda—ALIR) is the armed guerrilla group of the former Hutu-dominated Rwandan regime that carried out the shocking genocide of some 937,000 people, mostly Tutsis, in 1994. This genocide was carried out by the then Rwandan armed forces and the Hutu civilian militia, the Interahamme. However, Tutsi forces overcame the Rwandan regime and took power in July 1994. Hutu members of the Rwandan armed forces and the Interahamme fled to the Democratic Republic of the Congo (DRC, formerly Zaire), where they formed the ALIR. Operating in eastern Congo, the ALIR's objective is the overthrow of the Tutsi government in Rwanda and the restoration of Hutu domination. The ALIR was supported by the DRC, which fought a war with Rwanda in 1998. It is also anti-Western on account of alleged Western sympathy and support for the Tutsi government in Rwanda. In 1999 eight foreign tourists along the DRC-Uganda border were kidnapped and murdered. However, after the Lusaka peace accord of 2001 that ended the conflict with Rwanda, the DRC government ceased its support for the ALIR. In 2001 the ALIR was supplanted by a Democratic Front for the Liberation of Rwanda (FDLR), which has established ties with anti-government Tutsi groups in Rwanda. Due to the continued guerrilla activities of the ALIR/FDLR and the presence of large numbers of Hutu refugees, however, Rwandan forces remained in eastern Congo. An agreement signed in Pretoria, South Africa, in July 2002 affirmed that Rwanda would withdraw from the DRC, in return for that country's assistance in disarming and demobilizing ALIR combatants. In 2004, however, Rwanda continued to make armed incursions into eastern parts of the DRC in response to attacks by Hutu guerrillas. (*See* Map 2.)

Artibonite Revolutionary Resistance Front

The Artibonite Revolutionary Resistance Front (Front de résistance de l'Artibonite) is the main rebel group in Haiti that succeeded in forcing President Aristide into exile in early 2004. This led to chaos in Haiti and to intervention by a UN peace-keeping force. The Front emerged from the controversial re-election in 2000 of President Aristide, a result that was contested by all of the country's principal opposition groups. His former paramilitary supporters in the so-called Cannibal Army, however, turned against him. Although Aristide had previously been ousted in a coup in 1991 and then reinstated through US intervention, this time the USA did nothing, having lost confidence in Aristide following years of misrule and corruption. Under Guy Philippe and Buteur Métayer, the Front led the armed opposition that started at Gonaives, eventually gaining control of half the country and forcing Aristide into exile. Although the strength of the rebels was only about 500–600, such was the poor condition of the Haitian police that little effective resistance could be offered. The US-dominated multinational peace-keeping force has conducted investigations and arrested members of the former Aristide government on charges of corruption and involvement in the illicit drugs trade.

Aryan Nations

The Aryan Nations is a white supremacist organization in the USA. Founded by Richard Butler in the mid-1970s, it maintained its headquarters, which it called the 'international headquarters of the White race', in Idaho, USA, until it was evicted from them in 2000. The Aryan Nations functions as a nation-wide umbrella of racist groups. Many of its members also belong to the racist Ku Klux Klan. It subscribes to the Christian Identity ideology, which teaches that white Anglo-Saxons are God's chosen people. The ideology advocates the establishment of a white racist state, and teaches adherents to hate blacks, gays and Jews. Adherents believe in a conspiracy theory, according to which Jews control the government, business and the media. The operational and ideological manual of the organization is *The Turner Diaries*, which suggests a revolution in the USA based on a race war. In 1996 the Aryan Nations made a Declaration of Independence for the Aryan race. It has held summer race hate festivals, at which participants receive military training. The organization has also been active in prisons, with a Christian-like outreach programme to recruit prisoners to its cause. Members of the organization have been involved in violent activity in the USA, including involvement in a group known as The Silent Brotherhood, or **The Order**, whose objective was the violent overthrow of the US government. Other splinter groups include **Posse Comitatus** and smaller, neo-nazi groups. Many members of the Aryan Nations and its splinter groups are now serving long jail sentences for criminal and other violent activities. In recent years internal dissension, pressure by anti-race groups, and federal government attention have sapped the strength of the Aryan Nations. It has now split into several factions but remains of concern to the authorities due to its advocacy of hatred and violence.

Aum Shinrikyo

Aum Shinrikyo ('Supreme Truth') is an extreme religious sect in Japan that was founded in 1987 by Shoko Asahara (real name: Chizuo Matsumoto). Aum Shinrikyo is a millenarian, apocalyptic religious cult that aims to overthrow the government of Japan and also take over the world. The sect espouses a monastic lifestyle and predicted a coming apocalypse. However, it also used violence and intimidation tactics to ensure rigid loyalty and to deal with critics. Indeed, critics and opponents of the sect were murdered. Members of Aum Shinrikyo contested elections in 1990 but none were successful. From 1992 the sect expanded into Russia, where it gained a number of adherents, as well as into other countries, such as the USA, Germany, Sri Lanka, Taiwan and Australia. By 1995 it claimed to have as many as 35,000 members world-wide. It had its greatest success in Japan, however, where its utopianism attracted many young, idealistic Japanese searching for meaning in life in the midst of material plenty. Among them were many well-educated professionals such as scientists and surgeons. The deadly objectives of the Aum were already evident when it murdered eight people in Japan through the use of sarin nerve gas in 1994. In March 1995 members of the group carried out an audacious attack with sarin nerve gas on the Tokyo subway, killing 12 people and injuring more than 5,000 (*see* **Tokyo Subway Attack**). Had the attack, the first real attempt at a mass casualty terrorist act in contemporary times, been more successful, thousands would have perished, dealing a massive political and economic shock to Japan that would have reverberated throughout the world. Aum also planned to attack the Japanese parliament and had made serious efforts to acquire weapons of mass destruction. Aum evidently hoped that the subway attack in 1995 would lead to chaos and, in turn, to its ascendancy to power in Japan. The apocalyptic objectives of the cult are best summed up by the title of the book, *The Cult at* *the End of the World*, by David E. Kaplan. In the aftermath of the attack the authorities arrested Asahara and the leaders of the Aum. They were tried in April 1996. Thirteen members of the sect have been sentenced to death, with Asahara receiving the death sentence in February 2004 after a long trial, although none of the sentences has yet been carried out. Despite the evident danger that the sect posed to the public through its stockpiling of chemical weapons and its anti-government stance, the authorities failed to ban it altogether. In recent years fears have been expressed that the sect has made a comeback. It changed its name to Aleph after the Tokyo subway attack and claimed to be committed to correcting its past errors. Some Aum members also left to found separate sects based on the doctrines developed by Asahara. Through its business activities it has been able to raise large amounts of funding to revive itself. Many of its followers in Russia also remain active. While the Moscow office was closed after the Tokyo attack, in 1999 Moscow police uncovered a plot by Russian Aum followers to free Asahara by force. The sect reopened a liaison office in Moscow in 2001. In 2004 the cult was believed to have 1,650 followers in Japan and 300 in Russia. Several key Aum leaders wanted by the authorities also remain at large.

Autodefensas Unidas de Colombia (AUC)

The Autodefensas Unidas de Colombia (AUC) is a loose coalition of paramilitary self-defence organizations in Colombia. Created in 1997, its constituent units are civil defence units organized by the government in the 1960s to provide local security against left-wing insurgents, as well as private security units set up to protect landowners and businesses. It is believed that some of these units also developed links with organized crime, particularly drugs cartels, in the 1980s. The various loose units were brought under the umbrella of the AUC in 1997, providing for the first time some form of central co-ordination. The AUC itself originated as a paramilitary organization set up in the 1980s by two brothers, Fidel and Carlos Castano, to avenge the kidnapping and murder of their father by guerrillas of the left-wing **Revolutionary Armed Forces of Colombia (FARC)**. In 1997 the AUC was established by Carlos Castano as a nation-wide organization. Better funding and co-ordination enabled it to carry out operations against the left-wing insurgents of both the FARC and the **Ejército de Liberación Nacional**. The AUC has engaged in violence, such as summary executions, in its conflict with the FARC. There have also been allegations of collusion and complicity with the Colombian military. It claims to have a strength of 11,000 and has expressed a desire to be recognized as a legitimate political force in the civil war in Colombia between the government and the left-wing FARC. However, the government of Colombia has viewed illegal paramilitaries as a menace and has established a National Co-ordination Center to co-ordinate the war against them, as well as prosecuted military officers accused of collaborating with them.

Autodefensas Unidas de Venezuela (AUV)

This is a Venezuelan counterpart of the Colombian right-wing paramilitary organization, the **Autodefensas Unidas de Colombia (AUC)**. Established in 2002, it targets communist and left-wing groups, and, in particular, the populist left-wing Government of Hugo Chávez in Venezuela, which took power after elections in 1998. The group's objective is the removal from power of President Chávez, who is accused of supporting the left-wing **Revolutionary Armed Forces of Colombia (FARC)** in Colombia. Colombia's AUC has acknowledged that the AUV is a partner in solidarity and that it has provided training to the AUV. The AUC has also alleged that the Venezuelan government has provided sanctuary to guerrillas of its adversary, the FARC. The AUV's strength is unknown although it claims to have 2,000 members. The appearance of the AUV and an unsuccessful military coup against Chávez in April 2002 resulted in the setting up of a rural defence force, the Bolivarian Liberation Forces, which has pledged to defend the Chávez government. The AUV has operated in the commercial centre of San Antonio and the proliferation of armed groups along the Venezuela-Colombia border has made this area dangerous.

Badr Corps

The Badr Corps is a militia force commanded by the Supreme Council for the Islamic Revolution in Iraq (SCIRI), a Shi'ite-dominated organization that fought against the Sunni-dominated regime of Saddam Hussain in Iraq as well as the regime's ally, the **Mujahedin-e-Khalq**, which is made up of Iranians opposed to religious clerical control in Iran. In Iraq the regime of Saddam Hussain began the repression of the Shi'ite religious clergy in the late 1960s, executing some and imprisoning others. The Grand Ayatollah Sayyid Muhsin al-Hakim was placed under house arrest; one of his sons was assassinated in 1988 while in Sudan, and another, Sayyid Mohamad Baqir al-Hakim, the leader of SCIRI, was sentenced to life imprisonment, although he later managed to escape to Iran. In 1980 Grand Ayatollah Sayyid Muhsin al-Hakim's successor, Mohamad Baqir as-Sadr, was executed. This repression resulted in open revolt by SCIRI, which mobilized fugitive Iraqi Shi'ites in Iran into a militia known as the Badr Corps. The Iran–Iraq War in the 1980s also resulted in a number of defections from the Iraqi armed forces to the Badr Corps, whose strength rose, accordingly, to number many thousands. The Badr Corps established resistance cells inside Iraq. In 2003, during the second Gulf War, it mobilized to take advantage of the US-led attack on Iraq, but was warned to keep out of the fighting, the USA choosing to enlist the help of Kurdish militias instead. After the fall of Saddam Hussain's regime, US demands for the Badr Corps to be disbanded were ignored. The leader of SCIRI, Sayyid Mohamad Baqir al-Hakim, was assassinated in a car bomb attack in Najaf in August 2003. While no group claimed responsibility for the assassination, suspicion fell on rival Shi'ite factions as well as on anti-US Iraqi insurgents. The Badr Corps is rivalled by the **Mahdi Army** led by Muqtada as-Sadr. Indeed, there have been deadly clashes between the two in the struggle for power among Shi'ite clerics in Iraq.

Bagramyan Battalion

The full name of this group is 'Marshal Bagramyan Battalion' and it was composed of ethnic Armenians living in Abkhazia in the former USSR who wished to fight for Abkhazia's independence from Georgia. When the Soviet Union began to disintegrate at the end of the 1980s, long-standing ethnic tensions between Abkhazians in the region of Abkhazia in Georgia and the majority Georgians resulted in open conflict after Georgia declared independence in 1991. In 1992 Abkhazia too declared independence, precipitating a war between Abkhazian separatists and the government of Georgia. The Bagramyan Battalion directed its attacks against Georgians living in Abkhazia. Together with other Abkhazian groups, they were able to ethnically cleanse the region of Georgians, forcing some 250,000 to flee. In 1994 a cease-fire was effected and a UN peace-keeping force dominated by Russia has monitored it. The Battalion was reported to have been disbanded in 1996, but in 1998 a high-profile terrorist attack in Georgia was attributed to it. Since then nothing has been heard of the Bagramyan Battalion, indicating that it is probably now inactive. Abkhazian independence, however, has not been recognized by the international community, and its irresolute attempts to join the Russian Federation have, moreover, not been favourably received by Russia. Georgia, on the other hand, has insisted that it would never tolerate an independent Abkhazia. Abkhazia fell in to economic limbo and political chaos, following the inconclusive and disputed results of presidential elections contested in October 2004 by Sergey Bagapsh and a pro-Moscow candidate, Raul Khadzhimba. Fresh elections in January 2005, however, resulted in Bagapsh's victory. He was duly inaugurated as President in 2005.

Bali Attack

On 12 October 2002, 202 people were killed in a terrorist attack on the popular Kuta Beach resort in Bali, Indonesia. The Westerners killed consisted of: 88 Australians, 26 Britons, nine Swedes, seven Americans, six Germans and four Dutch. In all, citizens from 21 countries were killed, including 38 Indonesians. This was the most devastating terrorist attack since the **September 11, 2001 terrorist attacks** in the USA. The Bali attack was carried out by local suicide bombers. One entered a popular drinking and dancing venue and detonated explosives that were strapped to his body. Moments later, a car bomb was detonated, causing further damage and casualties. Shocked by the attack, the Indonesian government abandoned its previous attitude of general denial of any terrorist problem in Indonesia and accepted the assistance of the Australian Federal Police in conducting forensic and other investigations into the incident. Those investigations led to the arrest of more than 30 suspects, mostly activists of the covert radical Islamist network, the **Jemaah Islamiah (JI)**, which has links with **al-Qa'ida**. The mastermind of the Bali Attack, Imam Samudra, a computer expert who also learnt bomb-making techniques in Afghanistan, was sentenced to death in September 2003. The attack devastated the local Bali economy and was a serious set-back to Indonesia's economic recovery effort following the Asian financial crisis of 1997, which had affected the country particularly severely. However, it resulted in a new resolve by the Indonesian government to tackle the problem of radical Islamist terrorism in the country. This led to the arrest and conviction (on a charge of forging identity documents) of Abu Bakar Bashir, the alleged head of the JI, who was sentenced to three years' imprisonment in December 2003. It also resulted in the enactment of the Anti-Terrorism Law in 2003. The Bali attack was followed in August 2003 by the Marriott Hotel bombing in Jakarta, which killed 12 people, and an attack on the Australian Embassy in Jakarta in September 2004, which killed 11 people. These and a second Bali attack in October 2005, which killed 23 people, were also believed to have been carried out by the JI. (*See* Map 8.)

Barisan Revolusi Nasional (BRN)

The Barisan Revolusi Nasional (BRN) is a Muslim Malay separatist group in southern Thailand. Founded in 1960, it is leftist in orientation, developed close links with the Communist Party of Malaya, and actively promoted communist ideology among Thai Malays. However, armed confrontation between Malaysia and Indonesia in the 1960s split the movement between supporters of Indonesia and supporters of Malaysia. One splinter group, the Barisan Nasional Pembebasan Pattani was formed in 1971. BRN itself is said to have splintered into at least four factions and its total strength is currently estimated at less than 100. As some BRN members hold dual Thai-Malay citizenship, neighbouring Malaysia became a safe haven for the organization. Of late, however, the Malaysian government's crackdown on separatists has forced some to go into hiding in southern Thailand. The BRN is a small separatist group compared to the main **Pattani United Liberation Organization**.

Basque Fatherland and Liberty – *see* Euzkadi Ta Askatasuna (ETA)

Beslan School Siege

The Beslan school siege in September 2004, in which 344 people, half of them school-children, died, was one of the most devastating terrorist incidents in contemporary times. On 1 September 2004, 32 armed Islamists, comprising Chechens, Ingush and other ethnic groups from the Caucasus, took 1,300 school-children and adults hostage at a school in Beslan in North Ossetia, Russia. Russian security forces surrounded the school complex and called in special forces trained in counter-terrorism operations. The hostages were assembled by their captors into the school's gymnasium, which was rigged with tripwires and explosives. Some of the female captors also wore suicide bomb belts. Negotiations were begun in which the hostage-takers demanded the withdrawal of Russian troops from Chechnya. However, on the third day of the siege, gunfire and large explosions took place as medical teams were about to remove executed hostages from the school grounds. One account of the confusing events that resulted in the subsequent violence indicates that it was the accidental detonation of an explosive device in the building that led to the ensuing chaos, in which some hostages tried to escape, provoking shooting by their captors, Russian security forces and armed civilians at the scene. Believing themselves to be under attack, the captors detonated the explosives, causing the school gymnasium's roof to collapse and setting fire to the school. At this point, Russian special forces decided to storm the complex to rescue any surviving hostages. In the confusion, some of the captors escaped to nearby buildings, where they were cornered and killed. Ultimately, only one of the 32 hostage-takers survived and was arrested. Shamil Basayev, leader of the Chechen Islamist group, the **Riyadus-Salikhin Reconnaissance and Sabotage Battalion of Shahids**, claimed responsibility for the attack. The Beslan attack resulted in much criticism of the Russian government's handling of the incident, and also prompted the government of President Vladimir Putin to institute stringent counter-terrorism measures, the reintroduction of the death penalty and the reform of the intelligence services.

Black September

Black September was a Palestinian terrorist group that carried out a number of high-profile attacks in the early 1970s. In 1970 the **Palestine Liberation Organization (PLO)** suffered a serious set-back when it was expelled from Jordan, where it had been operating. Several thousand Palestinians were killed in fighting with the Jordanian army at the time of the expulsion. Black September was established by 'Abu Daoud' to avenge this defeat, taking its name from the month in which the PLO had been defeated by Jordanian forces. Although it functioned separately, as a splinter terrorist group, it nevertheless maintained links with **al-Fatah**, the dominant faction of the PLO. It was responsible for many terror attacks, including the assassination of the Jordanian Prime Minister in Cairo, Egypt, in 1971, the hijacking of an airliner at Lod airport in Israel in 1972, the **Munich massacre** of 11 Israeli athletes competing in the Munich Olympic Games in 1972, an attack on the Israeli Embassy in Bangkok, Thailand, in 1972, and an attack at Athens airport in 1973. Israeli security forces mounted intense operations to target and eradicate the Black September group, assassinating its key leaders and operatives. Black September was dissolved in 1974 by al-Fatah after it had begun to assassinate diplomats, including, in 1973, the US envoy to Sudan.

Buenos Aires Bombing (1994)

On 18 July 1994 a Jewish cultural centre, the Argentine-Israeli Mutual Association building in Buenos Aires, Argentina, was the target of a massive car bomb attack. The building, a centre of the Jewish community in Argentina, was destroyed in the attack, which killed 86 people and injured more than 300, making it the worst terrorist attack in Argentina. The attack occurred two years after another, in 1992, on the Israeli Embassy, had killed 29 people and wounded 242. The Government of Israel alleged that **Hezbollah**, with the assistance and backing of Iran, was responsible for the attacks. Indeed, Argentina issued an arrest warrant in 1999 for Imad Mugniyah, a senior Hezbollah commander, who was believed to be responsible for many major terrorist attacks, including the **Marine barracks bombing** in 1983 and other operations against US and Israeli targets. Imad is currently on the US Federal Bureau of Investigation's most wanted terrorist list, with a US $25m. reward offered for his capture. Israel has tried to assassinate him, including by a car bombing in 1994 that instead killed his brother. In 2003 an Iranian diplomat, who was Iran's ambassador to Argentina at the time of the attack, was arrested in Great Britain and charged with having planned and financed the Buenos Aires bombing.

Cambodian Freedom Fighters

The Cambodian Freedom Fighters is a Cambodian resistance organization based in the USA. It emerged in 1998 following a violent coup carried out by the ruling Cambodian People's Party against the other political parties that shared power at the time. Cambodian politicians and others opposed to Prime Minister Hun Sen's regime fled the country. The group is led Chun Yasith, a former member of Cambodia's opposition Sam Rainsy Party, and is based in California, USA. Its objective is the overthrow of the Hun Sen government in Cambodia. It has been able to build a network among the world-wide Cambodian diaspora, although its main source of funding has been from those residing in the USA. In November 2000 it carried out an attack on government facilities in the Cambodian capital, Phnom-Penh, in which eight people were killed, thus indicating that it had begun to take direct, violent action against the government. Forty-five members of the Cambodian Freedom Fighters were arrested for this attack, however. Further arrests of members took place in Cambodia in 1999 and 2003, for their alleged planning of attacks. The group has failed to carry out any other major attack since 2000. The Cambodian Freedom Fighters' activities in the USA have also been curtailed since the **September 11, 2001 terrorist attacks** in New York and Washington, DC.

Caprivi Liberation Front

The Caprivi Liberation Front is a separatist group in Namibia. Founded in 1994, it is led by Mishake Muyonge and aims to establish Itenge as a separate state from

Namibia. Itenge, or the Caprivi Strip, is located in northern Namibia and is mainly populated by the minority Lozi people, who have a history of ethnic conflict with the majority Ovambos. The Lozi of Namibia also identify strongly with their ethnic kin in nearby western Zambia, who are also aiming to establish their own state separate from Zambia. The Caprivi Strip has a population of about 100,000 and is a strategically important area as it borders four countries: Zambia, Angola, Botswana and Zimbabwe. It is also famous for its game parks and as a tourist destination. In 1999 the Caprivi Liberation Front first carried out attacks on Namibian military and government installations, which resulted in the death of several members of the security forces. In 2002 it declared independence for Itenge. In 2003 the government of Namibia placed 120 alleged secessionists on trial for the insurrection in 1999.

Casablanca Bombings (2003)

On 17 May 2003, a series of suicide bomb attacks in Casablanca, Morocco, killed 45 people, including 12 suicide bombers, and wounded more than 100 others. The targets included a Spanish social club, the Belgian consulate, a hotel and a Jewish cultural centre. At least three of the attacks involved car bombs. The attacks took place a few days after the **Saudi bombings** on 12 May 2003 that killed 35 people, wounded more than 200, and were blamed on **al-Qa'ida**. The co-ordinated attacks in Casablanca were carried out by the **Moroccan Islamic Combatant Group**, a radical Islamist group known to have close links with al-Qa'ida. The same group was later responsible for the **Madrid train bombings** in Spain in March 2004 that killed 191 people and injured some 1,800 others. Another group, **as-Saiqa**, also claimed responsibility for the Casablanca bombings. Four members of the Moroccan Islamic Combatant Group were later executed for the attack and 39 sentenced to long terms of imprisonment. More than 600 people were also arrested in an extensive crackdown on Islamic militants by the Moroccan authorities, in which King Muhammad VI vowed that 'the moment of truth' had arrived for those among them seeking to destabilize the country.

Chin National Front

The Chin National Front (CNF) is one of the various ethnic insurgent groups opposed to the authority of the central government in Myanmar (formerly Burma). The Chins reside in Chinland, an area along the Indo-Burma border, and number some 1.5m., the majority of whom are Christian. The Chins have complained bitterly of discrimination, economic exploitation and underdevelopment, political repression, and the suppression of local culture and beliefs. They have opposed the central government for much of the period since Burma gained independence in 1948, forming various resistance groups, such as the Chin National Organization and the Chin Democracy Party. In 1988 the Chin National

Front was formed. It advocates a democratic, federal Burma/Myanmar, under which it feels Chin rights and culture would be best protected. (*See* Map 1.)

Chukakuha

Chukakuha ('Middle Core' or 'Nucleus Faction') is a left-wing group in Japan. Its antecedents emerged from the split in the Japan Communist Party in the 1950s, in which Trotskyites left the party to establish their own group. The Chukakuha emerged in a further split in 1963. With an estimated strength of 3,500, it is implacably opposed to what it considers to be the imperialist governments of Japan and the USA. It has strongly supported farmers whose land was expropriated for the construction of Narita Airport, joining them in violent clashes with the police. The group has also carried out sabotage operations and arson attacks, as well as launched rocket attacks on government and US installations in Japan. Despite its purported violence, it has not, however, engaged in large-scale terrorist acts that have resulted in fatalities.

Communist Combatant Cells

The Communist Combatant Cells (Cellules Communistes Combattantes—CCC) was an extreme left-wing group in Belgium. Founded by Pierre Carette in 1982, it was a small urban terrorist group with about 10 members. Carette was inspired by both the **Red Army Faction** in Germany and by **Action Directe** in France, and hoped to emulate those groups in Belgium. His small group attacked North Atlantic Treaty Organization installations, US firms and Belgian businesses, causing damage to property and some casualties. Carette and several other comrades were arrested in 1985. Carette was imprisoned until 2003. The group ceased to exist after these arrests.

Communist Party of Nepal

The Communist Party of Nepal-Maoist (CPN-M) is a Maoist communist insurgent group battling to overthrow the government in Nepal and establish a communist state. It emerged out of the increasing radicalization of the left-wing groups that have thrived in Nepal since the advent of democracy in 1990. The failure of the Maoists to win the minimum required vote in the 1991 elections led to their exclusion from the 1994 elections. In 1996 the CPN-M split from the mainstream United Marxist-Leninist Communist Party of Nepal which had participated in the political process, and initiated a guerrilla war against the government. Corruption and deep socio-economic disparities have led thousands of poor peasants to join its ranks. Led by Pushpa Kamal Dahal (Chairman Prachanda), the CPN-M has proven itself to be well led, motivated and effective. It subscribes to the Maoist tactic of encircling cities from the countryside and using guerrilla methods to wear down government forces. The death of King Bhirenda and much of the royal family in 2001 as a result of internal fratricide, as well as battlefield reverses in 2001–03, also weakened the government considerably. Today the CPN-M controls large areas of the countryside and has grown into a credible threat to the central government in Kathmandu. In urban areas the governing élite, such as officials and politicians, as well as government installations, have also been the target of attacks. In response, King Gyanendra has resorted to the suspension of parliament and rule by executive decree. Some analysts believe that if the CPN-M ever took power, the consequences could be devastating, as it would probably physically eliminate the current élite, impose autocratic one-party rule and collectivize agriculture, in much the same way as the Maoist Khmer Rouge did in Cambodia in the 1970s.

Communist Party of the Philippines – *see* New People's Army

Congolese Rally for Democracy

The Congolese Rally for Democracy (Rassemblement congolais pour la démocratie—RCD) is a Tutsi-dominated rebel movement in the Democratic Republic of the Congo (DRC). Since gaining independence from Belgium in 1960, the DRC has suffered considerable internal instability. After 1996 war—and genocide—in Rwanda between the Hutus and the Tutsis spread to the DRC, to which Hutu militiamen fled after having been defeated by the Tutsis. In 1997 Laurent-Désiré Kabila overthrew the regime of Mobuto Sese Seko with the support of Rwanda and Uganda. However, he soon quarrelled with his foreign backers, the dispute resulting in the creation of the RCD, backed by Rwanda and Uganda. The RCD accused the government of mismanagement and nepotism. A fierce internal power struggle within the RCD caused it to split after mid-1999 into several factions, of which the RCD-Kisangani (RCD-ML), led by Ernest Wamba dia Wamba and backed by Uganda, and the RCD-Goma, led by Emile Ilunga and backed by Rwanda, are the most prominent. In 1999 Uganda also helped to establish another rebel group, the **Movement for the Liberation of Congo**, which is led by Jean-Pierre Bemba. Tremendous violence since 1996 is estimated to have cost the lives of more than 200,000 people and to have displaced more than 4m. others. In August 1999 the Lusaka peace accord was finally implemented by Joseph Kabila, the son of Laurent-Désiré, who was assassinated in 2001. Under the agreement, a UN peace-keeping force was deployed and all foreign forces were withdrawn. In 2003 a power-sharing agreement was signed in Pretoria, South Africa. Elections are to take place in 2006. However, violence continued in late 2004, raising fresh doubts over the DRC's future stability. (*See* Map 2.)

Covenant, Sword and Arm of the Lord (CSA)

This is a paramilitary survivalist group in the USA that was founded in 1971 by a former fundamentalist Christian minister. Subscribing to Christian Identity ideology, it believed in a coming race war between, on the one hand, white Christians, and other races, including Jews, on the other. The group believed that US society would collapse as a result of the race war, and that it had a mission to build an ark to prepare for the coming tribulation. CSA therefore established a settlement called Zarephath-Horeb along the Arkansas-Missouri border, stockpiling food, survival equipment and weapons. It also set up urban warfare and survival training camps. In 1983 it carried out arson attacks on a church and a synagogue, and attempted to blow up gas pipelines. In 1985 eight members of the group were arrested and convicted, the authorities having recovered a vast arms cache as well as drums containing potassium cyanide that the group had planned to use to poison the water supply of several major US cities. The group apparently believed that mass casualty attacks would hasten the coming collapse and bring about the Messiah's return as well as the inauguration of God's kingdom. CSA had about 100 members at its peak, but is today believed to be inactive.

Delhi Bombings (2005)

On 29 October 2005, three co-ordinated bomb explosions in the Indian city of Delhi killed 62 people and wounded more than 200 others. One bomb was placed in a crowded market near the main railway station in central Delhi. Another two bombs exploded in the south of the city, one on a bus and another in a crowded marketplace. An obscure group, the Islamic Inquilabi Mahaz (Islamic Revolutionary Group), claimed responsibility for the blasts. It is believed this group has strong links with the **Lashkar-e-Taiba**, an Islamist militant organization with ties to **al-Qa'ida** and dominated by Pakistanis, that has fought for Kashmir s independence from India. The attack happened days before Diwali, a major Hindu festival, which would have been followed by the Muslim Eid festival a few days later. It is believed the attack was an attempt to derail the nascent peace process between Pakistan and India.

Democratic Front for the Liberation of Palestine (DFLP)

The Democratic Front for the Liberation of Palestine (DFLP) is a faction of the mainstream **Palestine Liberation Organization (PLO)**. It is Marxist-Leninist in orientation and was supported, before the end of the Cold War, by the former Soviet Union and Cuba. Founded by Nayaf Hawatmeh in 1969, it is a breakaway group of the **Popular Front for the Liberation of Palestine**. In 1991 the DFLP split into two factions, of which the main group, led by Nayaf Hawatmeh, opposed the PLO's peace negotiations with Israel. The DFLP itself was therefore excluded from the Palestinian Authority when it was established to administer parts of the West Bank and Gaza. It has carried out some attacks on Israeli targets in both Israel and in the Israeli-occupied territories, although not on the same scale as **Hamas** and **Islamic Jihad**. The DFLP receives some support from Syria. The two DFLP factions have a combined strength of about 500.

ETA – *see* Euzkadi Ta Askatasuna

Earth Liberation Front

The Earth Liberation Front is a covert environmentalist group that was founded in 1992 in Britain and later established a presence in the USA and Canada. The Front is not a centralized organization but a network of environmental activists prepared to take 'direct action', in accordance with its guide-lines. These guide-lines, available from the Front's website, advocate action against those profiting from the destruction of the natural environment, including the harming of humans or animals. The Front advises its adherents to use sabotage, arson and vandalism to inflict economic damage, but not to resort to murder.

East Africa Embassy Bombings

The East Africa bombings refer to simultaneous terrorist attacks carried out against the US Embassies in Kenya and Tanzania on 7 August 1998. A truck bomb in Nairobi, Kenya, killed 213 people and injured thousands of others, while another truck bomb attack in Dar es Salaam, Tanzania, killed 11 people. The number of injured totalled almost 5,000. Although 12 US citizens died, the vast majority of those killed or injured were local East Africans. More than 300 US government security personnel drawn from the US Federal Bureau of Investigation and other agencies arrived in both countries to help local authorities conduct detailed investigations into the attacks. The US government charged that **al-Qa'ida** had been responsible. Several suspects were later arrested and convicted of the attacks. President Clinton also subsequently ordered cruise-missile attacks on al-Qa'ida bases in Afghanistan and on a pharmaceutical plant in Khartoum, Sudan, that was suspected of having the capacity to manufacture nerve gas for al-Qa'ida. The devastating nature of the East Africa bombings was an early indication of al-Qa'ida's deep hatred of the USA, and of its ability to launch major terrorist attacks in various locations.

Eastern Turkistan Islamic Movement (ETIM)

The Eastern Turkistan Islamic Movement (ETIM) is a terrorist-insurgent network consisting of 13 organizations whose objective is the secession of Eastern Turkistan, or Xinjiang province (officially known as the Xinjiang Uygur Autonomous Region), from the People's Republic of China. There is evidence that elements within ETIM subscribe to radical Islamist ideology. The ETIM draws its support from the 6m. ethnic Muslim Uygurs in Xinjiang. The Uygurs are a Turkic-speaking people in Central Asia, with a long history of conflict with the Chinese. Indeed, the Uygurs have often rebelled against Chinese rule as well as attempts at assimilation. In recent times the world-wide Islamic renewal and China's open-door policy after 1978 led to a greater emphasis on religion among the Uygurs, a number of whom served as volunteer *mujahidin* fighting Soviet forces in Afghanistan in the 1980s. This led to a process of radicalization and the desire on the part of some to establish a separate pan-Islamic state in Central Asia, covering Kazakhstan, Kyrgyzstan, Kazakhstan, Xinjiang, and even parts of Pakistan, Afghanistan and Turkey. Since the early 1990s ETIM has carried out numerous terrorist attacks in China, most of them in Xinjiang province. Some bombings and assassinations have also taken place in neighbouring Central Asian states. In May 2002 two ETIM members were deported to China for planning an attack on the US Embassy in Kyrgyzstan. ETIM is believed to have strong connections with **al-Qa'ida**, having received financial and training assistance from it. Indeed, US-led forces in Afghanistan captured a number of Uygurs during operations there following the **September 11, 2001 terrorist attacks** in the USA. In 2002 the USA designated ETIM as a terrorist organization.

Ejército de Liberación Nacional (ELN)

The Ejército de Liberación Nacional (ELN—National Liberation Army) is a left-wing insurgent group in Colombia that has been influenced by Che Guevara and the Cuban Revolution. It was established in 1960 following the victory of Fidel Castro in Cuba in the previous year. The ELN consisted of left-wing intellectuals, trade unionists and Catholic clergy influenced by liberation theology, as well as poor farmers. The ELN had a socialist agenda and, like Castro, aimed to represent the poor and the dispossessed against foreign capitalism. In 1965 it seized the town of Simocota and then distributed the so-called Simocota Manifesto, in which it called for the overthrow of the government of Colombia and the establishment of a more egalitarian 'popular democracy'. Over the decades it has proven to be a persistent and disciplined group that has been able to thrive on the economic discontent and social inequalities in Colombian society. It has engaged in extortion and kidnapping, and has in particular targeted the foreign oil sector in order to cause maximum economic disruption. In the face of government offensives and repeated set-backs, however, the ELN's centralized structure gave way to a much more decentralized organization in the 1980s. In 1993 one group, the **Guevarist Revolutionary Army**, split from it. Despite this, the ELN has also proven to be less amenable than the other main left-wing rebel group, the **Revolutionary Armed Forces of Colombia**, in negotiating with the government. It has also been more principled in that it refuses to become involved in the lucrative drugs trade, although it does levy taxes on poppy and coca cultivators. The ELN has an estimated strength of about 3,500, and has been actively opposed by the right-wing paramilitary organization, the **Autodefensas Unidas de Colombia**.

Eritrean Islamic Jihad Movement

The Eritrean Islamic Jihad Movement (or Harakat al-Jihad al-Islami) is a radical Islamist group seeking the overthrow of the authoritarian one-party dominant regime of Issaias Afewerki in Eritrea, and its replacement by an Islamic government. The movement itself is an amalgamation formed by the merger of five Muslim groups in 1988. It has charged that Islam has been suppressed under the rule of the Afewerki government after Eritrea achieved independence from Ethiopia in 1993. In 1998 it changed its name to the Islamic Salvation Front (Harakat al-Khalas al-Islami). The group is based in Sudan and received support there from the Islamist Turabi government. Sudan in turn accused the Afewerki government of supporting the rebel **Sudan People's Liberation Army**, a charge it denied. The group is led by Sheikh Khalil Mohamed Amer and is believed by some analysts to have close ties with **al-Qa'ida**. It has carried out attacks on Eritrea from Sudan, including attacks on Westerners living there. (*See* Map 4.)

Ethnic Liberation Organization (Laos)

The Ethnic Liberation Organization is an insurgent group consisting of minority Hmongs in Laos. Established in 1975 as the Chao Fa ('Lords of the Sky'), it was reorganized as the Ethnic Liberation Organization in 1985. It was led, until his assassination in Thailand in October 2002, by veteran Hmong leader, Pa Kao Her. The Hmongs, who live in the mountains of Laos, were recruited by the US Central Intelligence Agency into a clandestine army to fight the communists during the Viet Nam War. After the Paris peace agreement was signed in 1973, however, the Hmongs were abandoned. The communist government that took power after 1975 has had to contend with the small-scale insurgent movement dominated by these disaffected Hmongs. Counter-insurgency operations in the late 1970s resulted in the flight of some 300,000 Hmongs and Laotians from the country. Most of these were eventually resettled in the USA, Australia, France and other countries, where some have supported the resistance with funding. Within Laos itself, the estimated 250,000 Hmong are living in extreme poverty, having been forced to abandon their semi-nomadic lifestyle and to work in collective farms in the lowlands. From 1992 Thailand took steps to close Hmong refugee camps along the Thai-Laotian border and repatriated the remaining Hmong refugees, thus denying the resistance sanctuaries as well as sources of recruitment. By 1994 armed Hmong resistance had been reduced to isolated incidents. However, the resistance continues to exist, and sporadic bombings and other attacks are attributed to this group.

Euzkadi Ta Askatasuna (ETA)

Euzkadi Ta Askatasuna (ETA—Basque Fatherland and Liberty) is a separatist group in Spain and France that advocates the establishment of a separate Basque socialist state covering the Basque region of northern Spain and southwestern France. It originated in the 1950s as an alternative to moderate Basque political parties and actively opposed the dictatorship of the Franco regime in Spain. It adopted Marxism as its guiding ideology in 1965. ETA has carried out assassinations, bombings, kidnappings, armed robberies and extortion, targeting members of the security forces, politicians, government officials, businessmen, journalists and foreign tourists. It has financed its activities by levying a so-called 'revolutionary tax' on Basque and Spanish businesses, and in the past also received assistance from Libya and Cuba. It also developed a close relationship with the **Irish Republican Army**, whose struggle it regarded as similar to its own. ETA suffered a temporary set-back when its top leaders were arrested in France in 1992. In 1998 it declared a cease-fire and entered into negotiations with the government, but it resumed its violent urban guerrilla campaign in 2000 after having accused the government of bad faith. The **September 11, 2001 terrorist attacks** on the USA had repercussions for ETA owing to the subsequent hardening of attitudes towards the activities of terrorist or insurgent groups. Its youth and political wings were outlawed in 2002 and many arrests of ETA activists took place in both Spain and France. In 2003–04 several of ETA's high-ranking leaders, including its military commander, were arrested. While the **Madrid train bombing** of March 2004 was initially blamed on ETA, it soon transpired that radical Islamists had been responsible for the attack. ETA, however, has continued its own bombing campaign. To date, more than 800 deaths have been attributed to ETA. The government of Spain has refused to negotiate with it until it renounces violence and surrenders its weapons.

FARC – *see* Revolutionary Armed Forces of Colombia.

Forces nationales de libération (FNL)

The Forces nationales de libération (FNL) is the armed wing of the Parti pour la libération du peuple hutu (PALIPEHUTU), a Hutu rebel group in Burundi fighting against the Tutsi-dominated government and armed forces. The murder of President Melchior Ndadaye in 1993 sparked ethnic violence between the majority Hutus, who constitute more than 80% of the population, and the minority Tutsis, who have held power in Burundi. The violence has claimed the lives of more than 200,000 people, as well as displaced more than 500,000 refugees. In response to rebel attacks, the government carried out the forced relocation of large numbers of people to massive, squalid camps. In 2000 mediation led by Nelson Mandela resulted in the Arusha peace accords, which were accepted by the main Hutu and Tutsi political parties but not the two main Hutu rebel groups, the FNL and the Forces for the Defence of Democracy. In November 2003, however, an agreement was signed in Tanzania under which the Forces for the Defence of Democracy would participate in government and its fighters would be integrated into the national Burundi armed forces. However, the FNL, led by Agathon Rwasa, continued fighting. The murder, in 2003, of the Vatican's representative, Monsignor Michael Courtney, has been attributed to the FNL. In April 2004 a cease-fire between the government and the FNL was announced. In May 2005 both sides finally agreed to end hostilities.

Forces nouvelles

Forces nouvelles ('New Forces') is a rebel movement in Côte d'Ivoire that is opposed to the government. Elections were held in 1999 following the overthrow of the regime of Henri Konan Bédié. However, these were marred by nationality laws which prevented the Muslim candidate as well as the two main opposition parties from participating. This, together with a failed military coup in September 2002, led to a descent into chaos as the Muslim north and parts of western Côte d'Ivoire rebelled against the central government in Abidjan led by Laurent Gbagbo. Three separate rebel groups appeared, namely the Ivory Coast Patriotic Movement (MPCI), the Movement for Justice and Peace (MJP) and the Ivorian Popular Movement of the Far West (MPIGO). The three groups joined together in 2003 to form the Forces nouvelles. Although subsequent peace talks resulted in Forces nouvelles' participation in the government in January 2004, ethnic tensions and violence resulted in its withdrawal soon after. Fresh violence broke out and the Forces nouvelles contemplated secession. In November 2004 the United Nations imposed an arms embargo on Côte d'Ivoire owing to the continuing instability and violence.

Front de libération nationale de la Corse (FLNC)

The Front de libération nationale de la Corse (FLNC) is a Corsican separatist group that aims to achieve independence from France. It is left-wing, nationalist and also anti-immigrant in orientation, and stresses the preservation of Corsican language and culture. It was established in 1976 following the merger of two previous groups. Since then the FLNC has been responsible for a large number of bombings that have targeted government facilities and personnel, mostly on Corsica itself. In 1998 it succeeded in assassinating the French prefect, or governor, of Corsica. It has also been accused of fomenting racist attacks and of discrimination against African migrants. The FLNC has been affected by considerable infighting, resulting in many splits. It also has links with organized crime, and has financed itself from extortion, bank robberies and other forms of criminal activity. This resulted in the establishment of the breakaway **Armata Corsa** ('Corsican Army') in 1999, which denounced the links of other Corsican resistance groups with organized crime. Infighting has claimed the lives of as many as 200 Corsican separatists over the years. In 1999 the FLNC declared a cease-fire after negotiations with the Jospin government in Paris. This broke down in 2000, however, and bomb attacks resumed. In 2003 the French government held a referendum on greater autonomy for Corsica, which was narrowly rejected by Corsican voters.

Front for the Liberation of the Cabinda Enclave

The Front for the Liberation of the Cabinda Enclave (FLEC) is a separatist group that aims to establish a separate state of Cabinda in Angola. Cabinda is a territory of 7,283 sq. km in northern Angola, with a population of some 300,000. (*See* Map 2.) The FLEC has a long history, having been founded in 1963. However, the group subsequently split into a number of competing factions. Supporters of independence for Cabinda want the region's rich natural resources to be used to benefit Cabinda itself. Indeed, Cabinda is an important oil-producing region, with offshore oil deposits that have been described as some of the world's richest. Cabinda produces 700,000 barrels of oil per day, accounting for more than 60% of Angola's total oil production. The various factions of the Front have battled the central government since Angola's independence in 1975. In addition to guerrilla warfare, it has resorted to violence, intimidation and the kidnapping of workers and executives of the oil industry to cause major economic disruption and to further its agenda. The Angolan government's military offensive in Cabinda in 2002 has resulted in some success due to the capture of rebel bases belonging to the main factions, the FLEC Armed Forces of Cabinda (FLEC-FAC) and the FLEC-Renewed. In 2004 tentative negotiations to resolve the Cabinda issue began. However, they quickly broke down, resulting in renewed fighting in 2005. (*See* Map 2)

Gerakan Aceh Merdeka (GAM)

Aceh, located in northern Sumatra, Indonesia, has historically been an independent kingdom. There exists strong local pride and traditions, and Islam is a strong unifying factor and a focal point for nationalist sentiments. There has been much resentment over what the local Acehnese regard as Javanese domination, corruption and rapaciousness. There has also been much anger over the repressive and heavy-handed tactics of the military in the past, which have allegedly included torture and summary executions. The poverty, unemployment and backwardness of the province contrast with the presence of huge gas deposits, which has benefited mostly non-Acehnese, the bulk of the revenues having accrued to the central government in Jakarta. In addition the transmigration programme has resulted in Javanese settlers establishing themselves in Aceh, much to the resentment of the local Acehnese. The strong local Islamic identity and the resentment against Jakarta contributed to the founding of the Aceh independence movement (Gerakan Aceh Merdeka ('Free Aceh'—better known by its acronym, GAM) in 1976. The movement is led by Hasan di Tiro, who was able to obtain the support of Libya, which provided military training for some 600 Acehnese. The GAM political leadership has been based in Sweden, where GAM has been able to publicize the plight of the Acehnese and its independence agenda for Aceh. At the same time, it has been able to raise funds from sympathizers abroad, many of whom are from the Acehnese diaspora. GAM is left-wing and nationalist in orientation and has opposed the presence of militant religious groups in Aceh, on the grounds that the Aceh struggle is against Indonesia and not a religious war. GAM rebuffed overtures by **al-Qa'ida** when its leaders visited Aceh in 2000. The end of the authoritarian Suharto regime in Indonesia in May 1998 emboldened the advocates of secession and GAM intensified its insurgent activities in early 1999.

Through Swiss mediation, GAM signed a Cessation of Hostilities Framework Agreement on 9 December 2002, which was expected to involve maximum autonomy following a referendum. However, the cease-fire soon broke down and was followed by a declaration of martial law by the government in March 2003. The situation stabilized sufficiently for martial law to be replaced by a state of civil emergency in May 2004. Disaster struck in December 2004 when a major earthquake and tsunami devastated the province. International relief efforts helped to open up a province where access for foreigners had hitherto been restricted. The devastation of the province and the evident need for major reconstruction were the background to a peace agreement in August 2005, in which GAM agreed to end the insurgency and to participate in the political process. In turn, the government agreed to withdraw its 50,000 troops in Aceh. However, given the presence of fundamental political, economic and social grievances in the province, which have never been satisfactorily addressed or rectified, fears have already been expressed over whether the peace agreement will last. (*See* Map 8.)

Grand Mosque attack (1979)

On 20 November 1979 a group of several hundred Sunni Muslim dissidents seized the Grand Mosque in Mecca in Saudi Arabia, taking hundreds of pilgrims hostage. The leader of the group was Juhaiman Ibn Muhammad Ibn Saif al-Utaiba, a radical Sunni cleric from one of the most respected families in Saudi Arabia. The act of rebellion was carefully planned and the rebels were well armed and prepared for a lengthy siege. Juhaiman's justification for the rebellion was that the ruling as-Saud (al-Saud) family had forfeited its legitimacy through corruption, ostentation and its mindless imitation of the West. He hoped that the attack would galvanize the population into a general rebellion that would result in the fall of the as-Saud regime. In the context of the recent Revolution in Iran (1979) that had overthrown the Shah on the same grounds, the rebellion should not have come as a surprise, given the obvious ferment of Islamic revivalism in the 1970s. None the less, the desecration of sacred grounds by such a violent act of rebellion came as a shock to the Saudi leadership, since the Grand Mosque surrounded the most holy and sacred of Muslim symbols, the Kaaba. It also violated an injunction of Islam that no blood should be shed in such a holy place. The Saudi leadership had to obtain religious approval for arms to be used in a military assault to suppress the rebellion. The fighting resulted in the death of many of the dissidents as well as of security personnel. The government then executed 63 of the captured rebels in four cities. After this shock, the Saudi government proceeded to implement strict Islamic laws and empower the religious authorities in an attempt to co-opt the fundamentalists as well as radical Islamists. (*See* Map 10.)

Guevarist Revolutionary Army

The Guevarist Revolutionary Army (Ejército Revolucionario Guevarista—ERG) is a left-wing group in Colombia. It emerged as a result of a split from a larger left-wing insurgent group, the **Ejército de Liberación National (ELN)**. The ELN was founded in 1964 and aimed to overthrow the government in Colombia as the Castro revolution had in Cuba. The ELN's centralized structure gave way to a much more decentralized organization in the 1980s. In 1993 the ERG split from it, and has been active in the areas of Choco, Risralda and Antioquia. It is a small group, with about 100 members, and has been involved in a number of kidnappings. In late 2004 three of its members, including its deputy leader, Alias Asprilla, were killed in a confrontation with security forces.

HAMAS

The name of the well-known Palestinian fundamentalist Muslim group, Hamas, is actually an acronym that stands for Harakat al-Muqawama al-Islamia ('Islamic Resistance Movement'). Hamas emerged out of the first Palestinian uprising or *intifada* against the Israeli occupation in 1987. It is in fact the Palestinian branch of the fundamentalist **Muslim Brotherhood**, and was founded and led by Sheikh Ahmed Yassin. Hamas aims to establish an Islamic state in Palestine. It is opposed to the mainstream **al-Fatah** and to the **Palestine Liberation Organization**, which aims to establish a secular Palestinian state. Unlike al-Fatah, it also rejects Israel's statehood. Hamas has carried out numerous suicide attacks on Israeli civilian and military targets in Gaza, the West Bank and in Israel itself. It has also targeted alleged Palestinian collaborators. Despite its espousal of fundamentalist religion, however, it has not generally targeted Western citizens in its terrorist activities. Hamas activists work openly in mosques and in broader Palestinian society, carrying out social, educational and fund-raising activities. Israel has succeeded in killing a number of its leading operatives through so-called precision attacks and by other means, but each time Hamas has retaliated with suicide attacks. Sheikh Ahmed Yassin was arrested in 1989 by Israeli authorities and subsequently sentenced to life imprisonment, but he was released in a prisoner exchange with Jordan in 1997. In March 2004 he was killed in a targeted attack by an Israeli helicopter missile strike. (*See* Map 7.)

Hammerskin Nation

The Hammerskin Nation is a neo-Nazi racist organization founded in the USA in the late 1980s. It is opposed to multi-racialism and subscribes to white supremacist ideology. It has chapters in other countries, including Canada, the United Kingdom, France, Germany, Australia, New Zealand and the Netherlands. It has engaged in a number of anti-Semitic activities, including attacks on synagogues. A number of its members have been convicted of violent race-hate crimes, including harassing, beating and murdering members of ethnic minority groups, in particular blacks. It has affiliations with some racist rock groups, and, indeed, uses hate rock as well as the internet to spread its message and to recruit members, targeting disillusioned young white men with a penchant for violence. Hammerskin Nation is, however, careful in its choice of recruits, requiring aspiring members to spend two years proving themselves before they can join it. As a consequence, its members are highly motivated. Despite lawsuits in the USA, the arrest and conviction of its members, and internal dissension resulting in splits, Hammerskin Nation remains a threat to ethnic minorities.

Harakat ash-Shuhada'a al-Islamiyah

The Harakat ash-Shuhada'a al-Islamiyah ('Islamic Martyrs Movement') is a radical Islamist group in Libya that is opposed to the Qaddafi government there. It aims to overthrow the Libyan regime and to replace it with an Islamic one. The group consists of ex-Afghan *mujahidin* and has repeatedly clashed with government forces along the Egyptian border, where it is reportedly active in the al-Jabar al-Akhdar region. The group attempted to assassinate Col Qaddafi in 1998, attacking his motorcade near the border with Egypt. Very little is known about this group other than that it was led after 1997 by a man named Khaleefa.

Harakat ul-Jihad-i-Islami (HUJI)

The Harakat ul-Jihad-i-Islami (HUJI) ('Movement of Islamic Holy War') is a radical Islamist terrorist group based in Kashmir, Pakistan. It was founded in 1980 in Afghanistan as part of the Pakistan-led network of volunteer *mujahidin* who opposed the Soviet invasion and occupation of Afghanistan. HUJI administered relief and training camps in Afghanistan, and also developed links with other militant groups there. Led by Amin Rabbani, the group thus consists of battle-hardened Pakistani and foreign *mujahidin* with combat experience in Afghanistan. After the Soviet withdrawal from Afghanistan, HUJI continued to train its members there until US-led military action in late 2001 in response to the **September 11, 2001 terrorist attacks** in the USA ousted the **Taliban** government. However, it has concentrated its activities on Jammu and Kashmir in India, aiming eventually to integrate them into Pakistan. It has targeted Indian security forces and government installations. HUJI enjoys the support of Pakistani Punjabi businesspeople and religious leaders in Pakistan, where it has close links with two militant groups, the **Harakat ul-Mujahidin** and the **Jumiat ul-Mujahidin**. HUJI has established links with **al-Qa'ida**, receiving assistance from it to establish an offshoot in Bangladesh known as **Harakat ul-Jihad-i-Islami-Bangladesh**. (*See* Map 9.)

Harakat ul-Jihad-i-Islami-Bangladesh (HUJI-B)

The Harakat ul-Jihad-i-Islami-Bangladesh (HUJI-B) is an offshoot of Pakistan's **Harakat ul-Jihad-i-Islami (HUJI)**. However, it is located and operates in Bangladesh. It was established in 1992, reportedly with the financial assistance of **al-Qa'ida**. Like HUJI, it has close ties with two militant groups in Pakistan, **Harakat ul-Mujahidin** and **Jumiat ul-Mujahidin**. Led by Shauqat Osman and Imtiaz Quddus, the radical group aims to establish an Islamic state in Bangladesh.

It has engaged in various terrorist activities, such as assassinations that have targeted intellectuals, journalists and government officials. It operates several training camps and, not surprisingly, in view of the deep poverty and other economic and social problems in the country, its strength has increased to more than 3,000. (*See* Map 5.)

Harakat ul-Mujahidin (HUM)

Harakat ul-Mujahidin (HUM) is a radical Islamist group in Pakistan that was formerly known as Harakat ul-Ansar. Operating primarily in Kashmir, it advocates the integration of Jammu and Kashmir into a Muslim Pakistan. Originally founded to assist Afghan refugees and *mujahidin* groups fighting the Soviet invasion and occupation of Afghanistan in the 1980s, HUM was later armed by the government of Pakistan to fight the Soviet forces. After the Soviet withdrawal from Afghanistan, it concentrated its activities on Jammu and Kashmir. It has targeted civilians and security personnel in the two Indian-held states. The group consists of several hundred fighters, including battle-hardened veterans of the war in Afghanistan. HUM has close ties with **al-Qa'ida**, and its leader, Fazlur Rehman Khalil, supported the *fatwa*, or edict, issued by **Osama bin Laden** in 1998 calling for attacks on Jews and US citizens. Fazlur later relinquished the leadership in favour of Farooq Kashmiri. HUM spectacularly hijacked an Indian airliner in 1999 and used it to successfully bargain for the release of jailed militant leader, Masood Azhar. HUM maintained training camps in Afghanistan and fought against US-led forces alongside the **Taliban** and al-Qa'ida in late 2001, following US intervention there in response to the **September 11, 2001 terrorist attacks** in the USA. Many members of the HUM have now joined the **Jaish-e-Mohammed**, which was founded by Masood Azhar in 2000. (*See* Map 9.)

Hezbollah

Hezbollah ('Party of God') is a radical Shi'ite Muslim organization in Lebanon, first formed to oppose Israel's invasion of southern Lebanon in 1982, although the impetus came earlier, from the success of the Iranian Revolution in 1979. Key leaders include Sheikh Sayyid Muhammed Hussein Fadlallah, who is Hezbollah's spiritual mentor, and Imad Fayez Mugniyah, its military commander. Hezbollah united various Shi'ite groups in Lebanon, where its objective is the establishment of a religious Shi'ite Muslim state. It is utterly opposed to the State of Israel, as well as to all who collaborate with or are allies of Israel. It is therefore also strongly anti-US in orientation. In addition, Hezbollah also became opposed to the **Palestine Liberation Organization** after it began to negotiate with Israel. Hezbollah has also fought bitterly for power with another Shi'ite organization in Lebanon, **Amal**, in a civil war, in 1988–89, in which Syria sided with Amal and Iran sided with Hezbollah. Since then Amal has lost ground to Hezbollah. Hezbollah has proven to be an effective terrorist organization, having been responsible for the deadly **Marine barracks bombing** in Beirut in October

1983 that killed 241 US soldiers, and various other attacks around the world, including the **Buenos Aires bombing** of a Jewish cultural centre in Argentina in 1994 that killed 86 people. Hezbollah's Saudi wing has also been implicated in the **Khobar Towers bombing** in 1996 that killed 19 US personnel. Since 1992, however, coincidentally with the withdrawal of Israeli troops from southern Lebanon and the ascension to leadership of Sheikh Hassan Nasrallah, it has also participated in open politics in Lebanon. Hezbollah is more than a political party or an armed militia, operating many social services in competition with the state, while maintaining military control over southern Lebanon. It has reportedly established links and exchanged technology with **al-Qa'ida**, despite the latter's Sunni orientation.

Hizb-i Islami Gulbuddin (HIG)

The Hizb-i Islami Gulbuddin (HIG) was one of several *mujahidin* groups that opposed the Soviet invasion and occupation of Afghanistan in the 1980s. Led by Gulbuddin Hekmatyar, it was supported by Pakistani intelligence, which diverted military supplies to this group because of its effectiveness in fighting the Soviets. After the Soviet withdrawal from Afghanistan, however, Pakistan withdrew support from the HIG, owing to Hekmatyar's open ambition to dominate the political scene in Afghanistan. Twice in the 1990s Hekmatyar became Prime Minister, but bitter feuding led to his ouster and exile in Iran after the **Taliban** came to power in Kabul. The **September 11, 2001 terrorist attacks** in the USA resulted in US-led military intervention in Afghanistan in late 2001 that ousted the Taliban and **al-Qa'ida**. Since then the HIG has fought, together with remnants of the Taliban and al-Qa'ida in Afghanistan, to destabilize the new government of Hamid Karzai. From its bases in eastern Afghanistan and in the tribal areas of northern Pakistan, HIG has been relatively effective and dangerous, attacking US and other allied forces stationed in Afghanistan, as well as UN personnel and Afghan government targets. It is estimated to have several hundred fighters.

Hizb ul-Mujahidin (HM)

The Hizb ul-Mujahidin (HM) is a violent separatist group in the Indian-held state of Jammu and Kashmir, whose integration with Pakistan it advocates. Consisting of native Kashmiris led by Syed Salahuddin, it was founded in 1989 and is considered by some to be a militant wing of the Pakistani fundamentalist party, the Jamaat-i-Islami. The HM has close links with other Kashmiri and Pakistani militant groups, such as the **Hizb-i Islami Gulbuddin (HIG)** and, in particular, the **Lashkar-e-Taiba (LET)**. Like other similar Kashmiri groups, it once had training camps in Afghanistan. It has undertaken attacks on security forces as well as on government officials, sometimes in co-operation with other militant groups. Ghazi Shahabuddin became its military commander in Kashmir in early 2005, replacing Ghulam Rasool Dar who had been killed in a clash with Indian forces. The HM is believed to be the largest, most militant, and best supported of the several militant groups that operate in Jammu and Kashmir. (*See* Map 9.)

Hizb ut-Tahrir

The Hizb ut-Tahrir al-Islami (Islamic Party of Liberation) is a radical Islamist movement based in Central Asia, although many of its supporters can be found in Western Europe today. The movement aims to return Islam to its original state of purity through the establishment of an Islamic caliphate in Central Asia that would be ruled strictly according to Islamic law, the *Shari'a*. The movement was founded in 1953 in Jerusalem and aims to educate Muslims about the desirability of this goal and also to wage a political struggle that would eventually result in the dissolution of secular governments. The subversive, radical Islamist nature of its ideology attracted the attention of Middle Eastern governments as it spread, resulting in periodic crackdowns that led to the death or imprisonment of many of its members. In Central Asia it has attracted a fairly substantial following in Uzbekistan, Tajikistan, Kyrgyzstan, Kazakhstan and in Xinjiang province in the People's Republic of China, not least because of the political and economic instabilities that succeeded the dissolution of the Soviet Union in 1992. Members of the movement have been accused of involvement in separatist and terrorist activities, and of having established links with other radical Islamist groups, such as the violent **Islamic Movement of Uzbekistan**. The movement itself denies any involvement in violence and various experts have pointed out that there has yet been no evidence linking its members to direct violence. However, the subversive nature of its ideology, its ultimate objective of eliminating the existing governments, its secretive nature and its espousal of holy war, or *jihad*, has resulted in the close attention of the security apparatuses of Central Asian governments as well as of Russia. Its dissemination of anti-Semitic propaganda also resulted in its being banned in Germany. The movement operates clandestinely, in small autonomous cells, making it difficult to detect or to allow accurate estimates of its strength. However, it has certainly become a transnational movement that traverses ethnic lines and national boundaries, and it is regarded as the most influential and popular Muslim movement in Central Asia, where it is believed to have thousands of members.

Iparretarrak

Iparretarrak is a Basque group that campaigns for a separate Basque state in the Basque region in France and Spain. It is the French counterpart of the **Euzkadi Ta Askatasuna (ETA)** movement in northern Spain. Iparretarrak emerged from a labour dispute in the Basque region in France in 1973. Its use of terrorist tactics resulted in its being banned in 1978. The group has targeted government installations and the security forces. It is a small group, with an estimated strength of less than 100. Members of ETA have been able to shelter amongst its Basque sympathizers in southern France.

Iran Embassy Siege (1980)

The Iran embassy siege began when six terrorists who were believed to be either members of or affiliated to the Iranian **Mujahedin-e-Khalq (MEK)** occupied the embassy of Iran in Knightsbridge, London, United Kingdom, on 30 April 1980. The MEK was opposed to the Shah of Iran as as well as to clerical rule, and is the main anti-government opposition group in Iran, having taken refuge in Iraq after the Iranian Revolution in 1979. In return for ending the embassy siege, they demanded the release of some 91 anti-government activists arrested by the new Iranian regime of Ayatollah Khomeini. Twenty-six hostages were taken, although five were subsequently released. When the terrorists killed a hostage on the sixth day of the siege, the British authorities ordered Special Air Services (SAS) commandos to rescue the remaining captives. On 5 May the assault team, before a live television audience world-wide, stormed the embassy and killed five of the six terrorists. One hostage died in the SAS assault, apparently shot by one of the terrorists. The remaining terrorist, Fowzi Nejad, was subsequently convicted and sentenced to life imprisonment.

Iran Hostage Crisis (1979)

The Iran hostage crisis began on 4 November 1979 after the US Embassy in Tehran, Iran, was occupied by a group of some 500 Iranian students among a crowd of several thousand that had gathered to protest against US support for the Shah of Iran, Mohammed Reza Pahlavi. The Iranian Revolution of 1979 had resulted in the fall of the Shah's regime and his departure for the USA. The new government led by Ayatollah Khomeini took over at a time of revolutionary fervour and a deep outpouring of anger over the excesses of the Shah's regime. Emotions ran high after Ayatollah Khomeini urged Iranians to demonstrate against the USA and Israel. When the US Embassy was occupied there were 90 people inside, but some hostages, including all of the women, were freed. The remaining 52 US citizens remained captive. Their captors demanded the return of the Shah to Iran to face trial. The US Carter Administration immediately imposed economic sanctions on Iran, ending oil imports, expelling Iranians from the USA, and 'freezing' Iranian assets. In February 1980 the government of Iran issued a set of demands in return for the release of the hostages, including the return of the Shah and an apology for previous US actions in Iran. In response, the USA mounted a commando operation to rescue the hostages. 'Operation Eagle Claw', however, went badly wrong. During a rendezvous with C-130 refuelling aircraft in the Iranian desert, three of the helicopters carrying the assault team broke down and it was decided to cancel the rescue mission. As one of the helicopters took off, however, it collided with a C-130 aircraft and crashed, killing eight US servicemen. It was widely believed that the rescue disaster was responsible for President Carter's defeat in presidential elections held in November 1980. The start of the bitter Iran–Iraq conflict and the death of the Shah in July 1980, however, paved the way for negotiations. The hostages were finally freed in January 1981 after some 444 days in captivity, in exchange for the 'unfreezing' of Iranian assets. In 2003 Iran's leading dissident cleric, Grand Ayatollah Hossein-Ali Montazeri, once designated as Khomeini's successor, described the seizure of the US Embassy in 1979 as wrong.

Irish National Liberation Army (INLA)

The Irish National Liberation Army (INLA) is a splinter group of the **Irish Republican Army (IRA)**. It emerged in 1974 after the IRA decided to join the peace process in the early 1970s, abandoning armed struggle. INLA is Marxist in orientation and aims to establish a communist state that would comprise both Northern Ireland and the Republic of Ireland. Despite a strength of less than 100, the terrorist attacks it has carried out have included the deadly **Omagh bombing** in 1998, which it reportedly carried out in a joint operation with another extremist group, the Real IRA. Since then the INLA has declared a cease-fire but has yet to disarm.

Irish Republican Army (IRA)

The opposition of the Irish Republican Army (IRA) to British rule in Ireland dates from the 1800s. In 1916 the forerunner of the IRA, the Irish Republican Brotherhood, carried out the Easter uprising which led to the execution of a number of its leaders. A state of civil war ensued until the Anglo-Irish Treaty of 1921 created the independent state of Ireland, although Northern Ireland remained within the United Kingdom. The IRA opposed the agreement, as well as the new government of Ireland, leading to a civil war between the IRA and the forces of the Irish Free State with innumerable atrocities committed by both sides. From the 1950s, however, the IRA concentrated its activities on ending British rule in Northern Ireland. Internal dissension amongst the IRA leadership, together with the failure of the IRA to protect Catholics in the Catholic-Protestant civil conflict in 1969, led to a split and to the establishment of the Provisional IRA (PIRA or Provos), which soon eclipsed the Official IRA to become the leading Catholic extremist organization in Northern Ireland. The Official IRA also joined the peace process in the early 1970s, prompting even more defections. In 1974 a further split led to the establishment of the Irish Republican Socialist Party, which set up a paramilitary wing, the **Irish National Liberation Army (INLA)**. From the 1970s onwards the leadership of the IRA passed from mainly southern-based members to those in Northern Ireland led by Gerry Adams and Martin McGuinness. The PIRA carried out a number of successful attacks, including the assassination of Earl Mountbatten in 1979. PIRA targeted both government and military personnel. Adams and McGuinness, however, took over the leadership of PIRA's political wing, Sinn Fein, and negotiated the 1998 Good Friday Agreement under which the PIRA undertook to disarm and participate in the political process, although its goal remained the unification of Northern Ireland with the rest of Ireland. However, the Northern Ireland peace process has been hampered by the emergence of violent splinter groups and by continued paramilitary and criminal activity by the IRA itself. The Real IRA emerged in 1998 to oppose the peace process, and has carried out a number of attacks on Protestants and British security forces, including the **Omagh bombing** in August 1998 that was reportedly a joint operation with the INLA. The Real IRA has an estimated 200 members. Its leader, Michael McKevitt, together with a number of its activists, has been arrested by the authorities. However, it continues to pose a security threat due to the rejection by its members of the peace process. Another extremist group is the Continuing IRA, which continues to oppose both the British and the Irish governments. A small group of fewer than 100, it has also rejected the Good Friday Agreement and continues to carry out terrorist attacks.

Islamic Great Eastern Raiders Front

The Islamic Great Eastern Raiders Front (Islami Buyuk Dogu Akincilar Cephesi) is a radical Islamist group in Turkey. Established in the 1970s by Salih Mirzabeyoglu, it opposes the government of Turkey, advocating its violent overthrow and its replacement by an Islamic state. The basis of its grievances lies with its opposition to the secular nature of the state in Turkey, with the government enforcing strict control over religious fundamentalists. It is also anti-Western and anti-capitalist in orientation, as its own ideology, formulated by Necip Fazil Kisakurek, who died in 1983, is both left-wing as well as based on Islamism. Necip wanted to establish another Turkish caliphate throughout the Muslim World based on pure Islamic values. It has carried out attacks on churches, synagogues, banks and bars. Salih Mirzabeyoglu was arrested in 1998 as have been a number of its activists. However, the group has proved to be resilient, with an autonomous cell-like structure that emphasizes independent action. Despite the close attention of the state security apparatuses, it has continued to carry out terrorist attacks, including its involvement, reportedly together with **al-Qa'ida**, in the deadly **Istanbul bombings** of November 2003. The first bombing, on 15 November, targeted two synagogues, killing 20 people and wounding more than 200. The second bombing, on 20 November, targeted the British consulate and a branch of the HSBC Bank, killing 25 people and wounding over 390.

Islamic International Peace-keeping Brigade

The Islamic International Peace-keeping Brigade is one of the several major Chechen rebel organizations. This group is motivated by radical pan-Islamic ideology, is believed to have close connections with **al-Qa'ida** and receives funding from sources linked to al-Qa'ida in Saudi Arabia. A significant proportion of its estimated 400 fighters consists of Arab and other foreign-born *mujahidin*. The group was reportedly established in 1998 by Shamil Basayev and Ibn al-Khattab, an Arab who served as its *emir*, or spiritual leader. The group apparently contributed personnel for the **Moscow theatre siege** in which

128 theatre-goers died after an attempt to end it by Russian forces. After al-Khattab's death in early 2002, another Arab, Abu al-Walid, took over the leadership of the Brigade. Basayev himself reportedly gave up formal authority over the group, which was reorganized in 2002, in order to concentrate on leading his own organization, **Riyadus-Salikhin Reconnaissance and Sabotage Battalion of Shahids**. Al-Walid was reportedly killed by Russian security forces in April 2004.

Islamic Jihad

Islamic Jihad is a radical Islamist group in Egypt. Founded in the late 1970s by Abbud az-Zumur and Mohammed al-Faraq, it aims to overthrow the government of Egypt and replace it with one that would rule strictly according to Islamic, or *Shari'a*, law. In 1981 Islamic Jihad assassinated President Anwar Sadat in response to his policy of pursuing peace with, and recognizing, Israel. In 1993 it assassinated Egypt's interior minister and Prime Minister. A tough crackdown by the Egyptian authorities from the early 1980s resulted in either the arrest or the death of many of Islamic Jihad's leaders and operatives. This enabled Dr Ayman Muhammad Rabi' az-Zawahiri (al-Zawahiri), a surgeon, and Mohammad Atef to emerge as the leaders of the group. Az-Zawahiri led the group to embrace pan-Islamic radical ideology and established terrorist training camps in Afghanistan, where members of the Islamic Jihad were trained in carrying out suicide attacks in Egypt. In 2001 his organization merged with **al-Qa'ida**, with which it shared a similarly radical outlook as well as a readiness to use violence to realize the agenda of a pan-Islamic order. Islamic Jihad still exists as an entity in its own right, but its identity has to all intents and purposes become indistinguishable from that of al-Qa'ida. Members of Islamic Jihad, however, exert much influence within al-Qa'ida. Indeed, az-Zawahiri became the loyal deputy and strategic adviser to al-Qa'ida's leader, Osama bin Laden, while Atef became the operations commander, masterminding al-Qa'ida's terrorist activities world-wide. After the **September 11, 2001 terrorist attacks** in the USA, Atef was killed in the US-led attack on Afghanistan in search of al-Qa'ida bases.

Islamic Movement of Uzbekistan (IMU)

The Islamic Movement of Uzbekistan (IMU) is an amalgamation of radical Islamists in Central Asia. It was established in 1998 with the objective of overthrowing the secular government in Uzbekistan led by Islam Karimov. This objective soon broadened to include other Central Asian governments, with the aim of replacing them with a pan-Islamic entity that would rule strictly according to Islamic, or *Shari'a*, law. This pan-Islamic entity would cover Greater Turkistan, which would comprise Uzbekistan, Kyrgyzstan, Kazakhstan, Tajikistan, Turkmenistan and Xinjiang province of the People's Republic of China. (*See* Map 3.) Although it has an estimated strength of less than 1,000, it is considered a serious terrorist threat as it espouses violent pan-Islamic radical ideology and has established close ties with **al-Qa'ida**. Led by Tahir Yuldashev and Juma Namangani, its armed opposition to the Uzbekistan government resulted in a harsh crackdown and the flight of many of its operatives to neighbouring Tajikistan and Kyrgyzstan. The IMU also established bases in Afghanistan, launching terrorist attacks against the Uzbekistan government from early 1999. In late 2001 it renamed itself the Islamic Movement of Turkestan in order better to reflect its broader objective of a pan-Islamic caliphate covering Central Asia. However, the group became involved in the aftermath of the **September 11, 2001 terrorist attacks** on the USA. These attacks led to US-led military operations in Afghanistan in late 2001 in order to eradicate al-Qa'ida and **Taliban** bases in Afghanistan. IMU fighters fought alongside the Taliban but were routed. Namangani was killed in the fighting in a US air strike, although Yuldashev escaped. However, the IMU continues to be a grave security threat in the Central Asian republics owing to its trained and motivated cadre and its strong links with al-Qa'ida and other militant groups in Pakistan and Afghanistan.

Islamic Salvation Front

The Islamic Salvation Front (Front islamique du salut—FIS) is a fundamentalist Muslim political organization in Algeria. It was founded in 1989 in response to the democratic ferment there that had led to a new constitution and the promise of democratic elections. Led by Abbasi Madani and Ali Belhadj, the FIS espoused a fundamentalist agenda with the aim of creating an Islamic state ruled by the *Shari'a*, or Islamic law. The FIS participated in local elections held in 1990 and was able to capitalize on the Islamic revival that was sparked, in part, by the country's dire economic situation. It won control of a large number of local government councils, and received more votes than the ruling party. In the approach to general elections in 1991–92, however, it was involved in organizing a general strike and this led to the arrest of Madani and Belhadj. None the less, the FIS won a parliamentary majority in the first round of voting in 1991. The ruling National Liberation Front government then intervened to annul the elections. It also banned the FIS, forcing it to go underground. The FIS then established an armed wing, the Islamic Salvation Army (Armée islamique du salut—AIS), in order to wage terrorist violence with the aim of overthrowing the government. Some more radical members later split to establish a militant faction, the **Armed Islamic Group** (Groupe islamique armé—GIA). While the AIS and the GIA initially co-operated in targeting the government, the GIA soon alienated the AIS/FIS by its unrestrained use of extreme terror tactics, including the massacre of entire villages. The government released Madani in 1997 and he has since led the FIS in a more moderate direction by distancing it from the GIA's extreme violence, declaring that it would not establish a religious state, and attempting to broker a peace deal to end the vicious civil conflict. The fighting, which has cost more than 100,000 lives thus far, has also decimated the FIS. Moreover, a government amnesty in 1999 resulted in the surrender of many FIS fighters. In 2000 the FIS was itself dissolved. However, extremists in the GIA and in a new terrorist group, the **Salafist Group for Call and Combat (Groupe salafiste pour la prédication et le combat—GSPC)**, which has links with **al-Qa'ida**, have continued the fight against the government, although the level of violence has decreased considerably.

Istanbul Bombings (2003) – *see* Islamic Great Eastern Raiders Front

Jaish-e-Mohammed (JEM)

The Jaish-e-Mohammed (JEM) is a radical Islamist group in Pakistan that seeks to unite Indian-held Jammu and Kashmir with Pakistan. Another of its objectives is to fight the USA—not surprising given its adherence to radical pan-Islamic ideology. It was founded in 2000 by Masood Azhar, a former leader of the **Harakat ul-Mujahidin (HUM)** who was captured by Indian security forces in 1994. Azhar was released in 1999 as part of the bargain that HUM negotiated with the Indian authorities after it hijacked an Indian airliner. Many members of HUM have now joined the new organization. The JEM forged close ties with **al-Qa'ida**, as well as with the **Taliban** regime in Afghanistan, maintaining training camps in Afghanistan until US-led military intervention following the **September 11, 2001 terrorist attacks** in the USA. Azhar is believed to have established close ties with Osama bin Laden, who provided funding to JEM. JEM has been implicated in several terrorist attacks, including a suicide attack in Srinagar, Kashmir, anti-Christian attacks in Pakistan, and an attack on the Indian parliament in December 2001. Within Pakistan, JEM's inflammatory public rhetoric alarmed the authorities. In 2002 the organization was banned, its assets were 'frozen' and Azhar was placed under house arrest. The JEM, which had several hundred members, soon splintered into two groups, the Khuddum ul-Islam and the Jamaat ul-Furqan, both of which were also banned by the Pakistan government in 2003. (*See* Map 9.)

Jama'at at-Tawhid wal-Jihad

The Jama'at at-Tawhid wal-Jihad (JTJ—Monotheism and Holy Struggle Movement) is a radical Islamist group in Iraq that has carried out attacks on US and coalition forces currently deployed there. It was founded by Abu Musab az-Zarqawi (al-Zarqawi), a Jordanian. Formerly a petty criminal in Jordan, he became a changed man after his experience as a *mujahidin* fighting the Soviet invasion of Afghanistan in the 1980s. On his return from Afghanistan he plotted to overthrow the monarchy in Jordan and replace the government there with one that would strictly implement *Shari'a*, or Islamic, law. He was arrested and spent seven years in jail for his subversive activities. After his release he plotted to attack US and Israeli tourists, and fled Jordan when the authorities began to search for him. He was subsequently tried *in absentia* and sentenced to death by the Jordanian authorities. Some reports assert that he founded the JTJ in Germany as an anti-Jewish militant cell. He then returned to Afghanistan, where his organization was based in Herat. There are conflicting reports that he is either an **al-Qa'ida** operative or that his organization in fact competed with al-Qa'ida for recruits. After the US-led intervention in Afghanistan in late 2001 in response to the **September 11, 2001 terrorist attacks** in the USA, az-Zarqawi departed for Iraq, where he reportedly established links with the radical **Ansar al-Islam** in Kurdish northern Iraq. Following the US-led attack on and occupation of Iraq in 2003, he developed his organization into a network of local and foreign *mujahidin* fighters resisting US and coalition forces. The JTJ is implacably opposed to the presence of foreign troops as well as to the post-Saddam government in Iraq—on the grounds that it has been imposed by the USA. The JTJ has targeted foreign troops, Iraqi government security personnel and installations, and civilians working for humanitarian organizations through suicide car and truck bombings. The JTJ has been blamed for some of the most deadly attacks in Iraq, such as the **United Nations headquarters bombing** in Baghdad that killed 23 people, including the UN envoy, Sergio Vieira de Mello; the **Karbala and Baghdad bombings** in 2004 that killed many Shi'ites; the assassination of the Shi'ite religious leader, Ayatollah al-Hakim; a suicide boat attack on oil pumping stations on the coast; the assassination of the president of the Iraqi Governing Council; many bomb attacks on Iraqi security personnel and installations; and the beheading of a number of kidnapped foreigners, whose gruesome murders were videotaped for distribution. The JTJ has grown rapidly and has begun to be able to co-ordinate country-wide attacks using both terrorist and guerrilla tactics. It established a strong presence in cities such as Samarra and Fallujah. US-led coalition forces recaptured Samarra in September 2004. Fallujah was attacked by US-led forces in April 2004, and again, more successfully, in November. Almost daily attacks throughout Iraq have continued, however. Although not all of the attacks are carried out by JTJ—there are other insurgent groups, including nationalists and ex-Ba'athists—it is none the less regarded as the greatest threat to the peace and stability of Iraq. The US government has offered a bounty of US $25m.—the same amount as offered for Osama bin Laden—for the capture of az-Zarqawi. In October 2004 az-Zarqawi pledged his allegiance to al-Qa'ida. From its small beginnings the JTJ is, as a consequence of the conflict in Iraq following US-led intervention in 2003, fast developing into a major terrorist and insurgent force, supported by Sunni Muslims in Iraq as well as by foreign volunteer *mujahidin* from all over the Muslim World. Just as Afghanistan in the 1980s precipitated the development of al-Qa'ida, Iraq after the US-led intervention has become the breeding ground for a potentially even more lethal, post al-Qa'ida global terrorist network. The JTJ's successful blend of violent terrorist tactics and guerrilla attacks has seriously impeded the reconstruction of the country and delayed US plans for a return to some semblance of peace and stability. Dealing with the az-Zarqawi network will be a serious test for the USA, its coalition allies and the government in Iraq. It will require a long-term US military commitment to Iraq and the ability to absorb casualties, which amounted to 2,000 US soldiers killed and more than 12,000 wounded by the end of October 2005, not including the death of many civilians and of coalition and Iraqi government security personnel. Given this group's interest in weapons of mass destruction and its radical pan-Islamic ideology, it is also not inconceivable that it could attempt mass casualty attacks against US and Western targets outside of Iraq at some point in the future. (*See* Map 6.)

Japanese Red Army

The Japanese Red Army was a radical left-wing terrorist group that aimed to overthrow the government of Japan and establish communism world-wide. A splinter group of the Japanese Communist League-Red Army Faction, its leader was a woman activist, Fusako Shigenobu. It established close ties with other militant groups, including Palestinian ones. The group became much-feared in the 1970s and 1980s as an international terrorist organization as a result of activities such as hijacking commercial aircraft and attacks such as the **Lod Airport attack** in Tel-Aviv, Israel, in 1972 in which 26 people were killed and 78 wounded. The Japanese Red Army established cells in a number of Asian cities and was able to establish its base of operation in Lebanon, where it sheltered in Syrian-controlled areas. The small group of less than 40 activists was gradually hunted down over the years, and Shigenobu was herself finally arrested in 2000 in Osaka, Japan. The Japanese Red Army is now believed to be inactive.

Jemaah Islamiah (JI)

The Jemaah Islamiah (JI), or al-Jama'ah al-Islamiyyah ('Islamic Group'), is a radical Islamist terrorist network active in south-east Asia and Australia. Its founding has been dated to 1 January 1993 and credited to Abdullah Sungkar. However, the genesis of the JI can be traced back much earlier, to the failed Darul Islam rebellion in Indonesia in the 1950s, and to the establishment of the religious boarding school, the Pondok al-Mukmin (later called Pondok Ngruki), in Solo, Central Java, in 1971 by Abu Bakar Bashir and Sungkar, where many JI leaders received their education. Bashir and Sungkar fled from the repression of the Suharto regime in Indonesia in 1985 to Malaysia, where they built up a following among Malaysians and Indonesian émigrés. With contacts established with the *mujahidin* then fighting Soviet forces in Afghanistan and the return of south-east Asian volunteers enthused with radical religious fervour, the stage was set for the creation of the clandestine regional network in 1993. According to the *Pedoman Umum Perjuangan al-Islamiyyah*, or *General Guide for the Struggle of Jemaah Islamiah*, the founding document of the JI, three principles guide the network: the Daulah Islamiyah, or Islamic state, as a stepping stone to the restoration of the global Islamic caliphate; the process of preparing for the Daulah Islamiyah through a persistent and patient moulding of the individual, the family and the group; and the prominence of military training and armed struggle (Jihad

Musallah). It shares the beliefs and objectives of **al-Qa'ida** so closely that it can in fact be described as having been penetrated and co-opted by it.

The JI is not a centralized organization, but, rather, a loose network of individuals and autonomous cells united by these principles, and it has been able to operate throughout the Malay archipelago and in Australia using ex-*mujahidin* contacts. There are four main operational networks: Mantiqi 1 covering Thailand, Malaysia and Singapore; Mantiqi 2 covering Indonesia; Mantiqi 3 covering the Philippines; and Mantiqi 4 covering Australia. It has an estimated 3,000 members, many now fugitives following the JI's exposure in the wake of the abortive Singapore bomb plots of late 2001, in which it planned, in collaboration with al Qa'ida, a major series of terrorist attacks in Singapore targeting Western embassies, several key US companies, US ships and military personnel, and local military facilities. The JI has been blamed for the **Bali attack** of 12 October 2002 that killed 202 people, the Marriott Hotel bombing of 5 August 2003 that killed 12 people, the attack on the Australian Embassy in Jakarta in September 2004 that killed 11 people, and a second attack in Bali in October 2005 that killed 23 people. Despite the arrest of many of its operatives, including its leading military commander, Hambali, the size of the JI and the spread of radical teachings have meant that the threat of radical violence has persisted.

Jumiat ul-Mujahidin (JUM)

The Jumiat ul-Mujahidin (JUM), a breakaway group from the **Hizb ul-Mujahidin (HM)**, is a violent separatist organization in Pakistan that is dedicated to ending India's rule over Jammu and Kashmir and uniting the two areas with Pakistan. The JUM, which emerged in 1990, is uncompromising in its aims, rejects any negotiations and views the use of force as the only means to resolve the Kashmir issue. The group has lost ground, however, to other separatist Muslim groups in Kashmir owing to competition and to offensives by the Indian government, which have weakened it. Although it originally consisted of Kashmiris, there are now a number of Pakistanis in the group. It has carried out attacks against Indian military targets in Kashmir. (*See* Map 9.)

Karbala and Baghdad Bombings (March 2004)

Among the many insurgent bomb attacks on US-led forces and civilians in Iraq, the co-ordinated suicide attacks against Shi'ite worshippers celebrating the Muslim festival of Ashoura in Karbala and Baghdad on 2 March 2004 stand out as the most deadly and co-ordinated examples since the US-led attack on and occupation of the country in 2003. The toll of the bombings was estimated at 271 dead and 393 injured by the Iraqi Governing Council, while the US military authorities put the number of dead at 181 and that of those injured at 573. Many of the dead were pilgrims from neighbouring Iran. At Karbala tens of thousands of pilgrims had gathered around the Imam Hussein shrine, one of holiest to Shi'ites. A suicide bomber walked into the crowd and detonated a bomb, which was followed by grenade and other bomb explosions in the area around the shrine. At about the same time, a suicide attack at the al-Kadhimiya mosque in Baghdad killed many worshippers there. The US authorities blamed **al-Qa'ida** and its local affiliate, the **Jama'at at-Tawhid wal-Jihad** led by Abu Musab az-Zarqawi (al-Zarqawi), for the attacks, which apparently aimed to sow animosity among Sunnis and Shi'ites in order to provoke civil strife that would complicate US-led plans to return Iraq to normalcy. The Iraqi judge who investigated the attacks concluded that it had been financed from abroad, and probably carried out by al-Qa'ida. Al-Qa'ida itself denied responsibility, blaming instead 'American crusaders'. (*See* Map 6.)

Kach

Kach is a radical Jewish organization founded in 1977 by an American rabbi, Meir Kahane. It advocates the restoration of the biblical state of Israel, an objective that would involve the expulsion of Arabs from Israel and the establishment of a Greater Israel. It also espouses the use of violence to deal with Arabs and others engaged in anti-Semitism. Kahane contested elections held in 1984, winning a seat in the Israeli parliament. In 1988, however, Kach was disqualified from contesting the general election on grounds of being racist and undemocratic. The assassination of the charismatic Kahane in New York in 1990 by a Muslim led to internal dissension and to the emergence of a splinter group, Kahane Chai ('Kahane Lives'). Kach soon became dominated by those from the West Bank Jewish settlement of Kiryat Arba, who organized the Committee for Road Safety to protect Jewish drivers. Kach also became involved in vigilante and other violent actions against Palestinians. It opposed the Oslo peace accords in 1993 that led to the establishment of the Palestinian Authority in the West Bank and Gaza Strip. In 1994 a member of Kach was responsible for the massacre of 29 Muslims in the Tomb of the Patriarchs in Hebron. This led to the banning of the organization, causing its members to go underground. (*See* Map 7.)

Kachin Independence Organization (KIO)

The Kachins are a mountain tribe living in the border region of Myanmar (formerly Burma) that adjoins India and China. Many are Christians and they expected to have their own independent state after the Second World War. After Burma gained independence from Britain in 1948, however, Kachin State was incorporated into the Union of Burma. In the 1960s the Kachins rose in revolt. The Kachin Independence Organization (KIO) built up a force of some 5,000 regular soldiers and funded its armed struggle through the control of jade mines. In 1994, war-weary from its confrontation with superior government forces, it concluded a cease-fire agreement with the central government. However, it lost control of jade mining, which has been taken over by foreign firms granted concessions by the central government. Instead, the KIO has been given timber concessions. The KIO is not the only Kachin militia organization. Others include the New Democratic Army-Kachin (NDA-K) and the Kachin Democratic Army, which have also made peace with the central government. (*See* Map 1.)

Kakurokyo

Kakurokyo is an extreme left-wing group in Japan that has rejected the political process and conducted terrorist attacks against the state. The group is anti-capitalist and anti-government. It is also strongly opposed to the USA. It has targeted facilities and members of the government, including the security forces. In July 1993 it carried out three attacks, two with rockets on US military facilities, and the third with a bomb on the UN Environmental Program building at the Osaka Exposition, in protest at the G-7 Summit in Tokyo. In 1998 mortars were fired into Narita Airport, causing one injury and the closure of the runway. However, no fatalities have occurred as a result of its infrequent and sporadic attacks, which indicate that the purpose of its bombings is symbolic.

Kampulan Mujahidin Malaysia (KMM)

The Kampulan Mujahidin Malaysia (KMM) is a violent, radical Islamist group (later officially referred to as the Kamulan Militan Malaysia) in Malaysia. Founded by Zainon Ismail, an Afghan *mujahidin* veteran, in October 1995, it advocates the use of violence to overthrow the government and set up a Muslim state ruled by *Shari'a*, or Islamic, law. Numbering just under 100, many members of the group were either ex-Afghan *mujahidin* or had trained in **al-Qa'ida** camps in Afghanistan in the 1990s after the Afghan conflict ended. Malaysian authorities began arresting members of the group in December 2001 and placing them under preventive detention. KMM has been accused of possessing weaponry, and of carrying out robberies, bombings (including that of an Indian temple) and the murder of a Christian state assemblyman. Malaysian authorities have also alleged that the group planned attacks on US citizens. KMM is believed to have forged ties with other regional radical groups, such as the **Jemaah Islamiah (JI)**, and also participated in Muslim-Christian religious violence in Maluku, Indonesia.

Karen National Union (KNU)

The Karen National Union (KNU) is a separatist movement in Karen State, Myanmar (formerly Burma). The Karen, many of whom are Christian, felt that their support for the British against the Japanese during the Second World War had fostered assurances of later independence. They thus opposed being incorporated into a Burmese state when it gained independence from Britain in 1948. The Karens launched a separatist rebellion in late 1948, and were joined by defecting units from the state's army, many of whom were Karen. In 1990 the National League for Democracy, led by Aung San Suu Kyi, was victorious in legislative elections, but it subsequently suffered violent repression at the hands of the military regime. Many student activists fled to Karen safe areas and, with

Karen help, established the armed **All Burma Student Democratic Front**. However, this prompted the central government to take steps to crush the Karens once and for all. The government was able to exploit internal Buddhist-Christian divisions within the KNU, leading to the defection of the Buddhists to the government side. In January 1995 the KNU stronghold of Manerplaw fell, and more than 100,000 Karen refugees fled across the border to Thailand. The KNU, its strength now reduced to 4,000–5,000 ill-equipped fighters, resorted to guerrilla tactics. The movement finally opened negotiations with the government in 2003, with long-time KNU leader Bo Mya meeting Prime Minister Khin Nyunt in the capital, Yangon, in 2004. (*See* Map 1.)

Khobar Towers Bombing (1996)

On 25 June 1996 a bomb in a fuel truck that was parked near a perimeter fence destroyed the Khobar Towers complex in Dhahran, Saudi Arabia. Nineteen US servicemen were killed in the attack, in which more than 370 Saudi Arabian and US citizens were also injured. The target of the bombing was clearly US and allied military forces, which had been using the King Abdul Aziz Air Base in Dhahran since the first Gulf War in 1990 to support coalition air operations in Iraq. The Khobar Towers complex itself contained living quarters as well as administrative offices. Although security personnel spotted the truck bomb and raised the alarm, there was insufficient time for an evacuation to be completed before it exploded. None the less, this early warning has been credited with saving several dozen lives. At least six high-rise apartment buildings in the complex were severely damaged or destroyed. No organization claimed responsibility for the attack, but in June 1997 Canada extradited a suspect, a member of the Iranian Revolutionary Guards, to the USA. It is believed that the attack was carried out by the Saudi Arabian chapter of **Hezbollah**, a Shi'ite extremist group backed by Iran. In June 2001 the Saudi Arabian authorities charged 13 Saudi Arabians and a Lebanese with carrying out the terrorist act. Although no Iranian official was named, the USA alleged that the attack had been inspired and supervised by elements of the Iranian government. The National Commission on Terrorist Attacks (or 9-11 Commission) also concluded, in its 2004 report, that **al-Qa'ida** may have assisted the group in obtaining explosives.

Khmer Rouge

The Khmer Rouge is the popular term for the Communist Party of Kampuchea (CPK), which was founded in the early 1950s. The Khmer Rouge was led by French-educated Khmers who wished to expel the French and their allies from Cambodia, and to create a communist state there. Its ideology was Maoist as it emphasized the leading revolutionary role of the peasantry, but, owing to its intolerance and arbitrary cruelty, its methods may be described as Stalinist. At the same time, it pursued a xenophobic, ultra-nationalist agenda. Led by Pol Pot, it recruited in the countryside among poor peasants and built up a reputation for ruthlessness, dedication and guerrilla prowess. In April 1975 the Khmer Rouge seized power after the fall of the corrupt Lon Nol regime in the wake of the communist victories in Indochina at the end of the Viet Nam War. The Khmer Rouge now embarked on a reign of terror, murdering some 1.7m. Cambodians, one-quarter of the population, in an attempt to carry out a pure communist revolution. In order to put an end to persistent border instability, Viet Nam invaded Cambodia in 1978 and installed in power the Heng Samrin regime, comprising former Khmer Rouge cadres who had fled to Viet Nam to escape its deadly internal purges. The Khmer Rouge fled into the jungle to conduct a long guerrilla campaign, in alliance with non-communist nationalists under the umbrella Coalition Government of Democratic Kampuchea (CGDK). The CGDK received the strong support of the People's Republic of China and the Association of South-East Asian Nations (ASEAN). In 1991 the International Conference on Cambodia produced the Paris peace accord which ended the Cambodian conflict. The Khmer Rouge, however, refused to accept the result of elections held in 1993. Defections and losses in combat caused its numbers to decline. Pol Pot himself was tried by the Khmer Rouge and died in 1998. By 1999 the Khmer Rouge had ceased to be an effective force.

Korean Air Flight 858 Bombing

The bombing of Korean Air Lines Flight 858 in November 1987 is one of the most publicized cases of a state's use of terrorism against another state. The civilian passenger airliner, a Boeing 707 carrying 115 passengers and crew, departed from Baghdad, Iraq, for Seoul, South Korea, on a regular flight, with scheduled stopovers at Abu Dhabi, United Arab Emirates, and Bangkok, Thailand. However, while flying over the Andaman Sea, the aircraft was destroyed by explosives that had been left on the aircraft. All passengers and crew were killed. Two North Korean agents, who had left the aircraft in Abu Dhabi, were later arrested in Bahrain as they awaited a delayed flight to Rome, Italy. Both attempted to commit suicide, but one, a female agent named Kim Hyun-Hee, survived. Under interrogation in South Korea, she confessed that the bombing had been ordered by Kim Jong Il, son of the then President of North Korea, Kim Il Sung. The motive appeared to be a response to South Korea's hosting of the Olympic Games in 1988. Kim Hyun-Hee was sentenced to death, but later converted to Christianity, was pardoned and married one of her South Korean interrogators. She also wrote a bestseller, *The Tears of My Soul*. The bombing of Flight 858 was preceded by a North Korean commando attack in Rangoon, Burma, in 1983 that killed 21 South Korean and Burmese officials. Both events reinforced perceptions in the USA and elsewhere that North Korea was a rogue state that supported and carried out terrorism.

Kosovo Liberation Army (KLA)

The Kosovo Liberation Army (KLA) is a separatist organization that emerged in 1992 following the dissolution of the former Yugoslavia, with the objective of uniting Kosovo with Albania and Macedonia to create a Greater Albania. The KLA carried out insurgent attacks on Serbian security services in Kosovo, prompting a harsh Serbian crackdown that alienated Albanians in Kosovo and helped the KLA expand the size of its insurgent force to an estimated 20,000 in the late 1990s. The harsh crackdown in Kosovo and the undisputed human rights violations that took place also resulted in US and NATO intervention, initially in the form of the air bombardment of Serbia. This, and the threat of NATO ground intervention, led to Serbia's capitulation, the withdrawal of its security forces from Kosovo and their replacement by a UN peace-keeping force. With its immediate objective of removing Serbian authority having been achieved, the KLA ceased its insurgent activities. There have since been various allegations of the KLA's involvement in organized crime and illicit drugs activities. The status of Kosovo remains unresolved and this has impeded economic development and led to growing unemployment among the young. These economic circumstances contributed to continued ethnic tension and to anti-Serbian rioting in early 2004. There is little support in Europe, particularly on the part of Russia, which supports Serbia, for an independent Kosovo, which it is feared would encourage other outbreaks of violent separatism. Serbia itself is also opposed to any such outcome, as Kosovo is regarded as the birthplace of Serbian civilization.

Kurdish Democratic Party (KDP)

The Kurdish Democratic Party (KDP) is one of the two major political organizations in Kurdish northern Iraq, the other being the **Patriotic Union of Kurdistan (PUK)**. The KDP was founded in 1946 by Mullah Mustalafa-al-Barzani, and its membership was drawn from Kurdish tribal clans. It commands several tens of thousands of guerrillas, or *peshmergas*, in the north, and fought the Saddam Hussein regime for many years in pursuit of Kurdish autonomy. The Kurds suffered terribly for their opposition to Saddam Hussein's regime: chemical weapons were deployed against Kurdish villages in the 1980s as the central government attempted to suppress the KDP. Since the end of the first Gulf War in 1991 and the establishment of a no-fly zone by the USA and its allies in northern Iraq, the KDP has, together with the PUK, become the *de facto* government in Iraqi Kurdistan. However, it became involved in a bitter civil war with the PUK in a struggle for power that ended only after US mediation brought about an agreement in Washington, DC, in 1998. The KDP is led by Masoud Barzani, son of its founder al-Barzani. Masoud's adroit political manoeuvring since he became leader in 1979 has been credited with ensuring the survival of the KDP. At various times during the 1980s he obtained the support of Iran against Saddam Hussein; obtained Saddam's support against the PUK in the 1990s; and achieved a reconciliation with the PUK before the US-led intervention in Iraq in 2003. The KDP and the PUK established an umbrella group, the Democratic Patriotic Alliance of Kurdistan, to contest elections in Iraq in 2005.

Kurdistan Workers' Party

The Kurdistan People's Party (Partiya Karkeran Kurdistan—PKK) was founded in 1974 as the National Liberation Army, with the objective of establishing an independent Kurdish state, principally for the Kurdish people living in eastern Turkey. Kurdish grievances include the lack of recognition of their linguistic, cultural and political rights by Turkey. The organization changed its name to the Kurdistan Workers' Party in 1978. The PKK is leftist in orientation and received funding and assistance from Syria. It was able to train in Syrian-controlled areas in Lebanon. Establishing itself in Kurdish areas in eastern Turkey, the PKK, through its armed wing, the People's Liberation Army of Kurdistan, began to carry out armed attacks in the 1980s, targeting Turkish security and government personnel, installations and tourists. In the 1990s it also targeted Turkish diplomatic and commercial interests in Western Europe in a series of terrorist attacks. At its peak its fighting strength numbered in the thousands. Its violent terrorist campaign resulted in the death of an estimated 10,000 people. After Syria withdrew its support, however, and Turkey's security forces achieved a number of successes against it, the PKK's long-time leader, Abdullah Öcalan, fled to Kenya, where he was arrested. After extradition from Kenya to Turkey in 1999, Öcalan was sentenced to death, although the sentence has not been carried out. He then offered a cease-fire and peace negotiations. The PKK publicly renounced terrorism in 2002, changing its name to the Kurdistan Freedom and Democracy Congress. In another reorganization, in 2003, an umbrella group, the Kurdish People's Conference, was established with the objective of pursuing Kurdish rights through the political process in Turkey. In late 2003, in another change of name, the group restyled itself as Kongra-Gel. The PKK and its successor organizations have refused to disarm and clashes between Kurdish fighters and Turkish forces have continued. Several thousand Kurdish fighters have also taken refuge in Kurdish-controlled northern Iraq. (*See* Map 6.)

Lashkar-e-Jhangvi (LEJ)

The Lashkar-e-Jhangvi (LEJ) is a radical Islamist group in Pakistan that was formed in 1996 by Akram Lahori and Riaz Basra. The LEJ aims to overthrow the Musharraf government in Pakistan and to replace it with one that would rule strictly according to *Shari'a*, or Islamic, law. It is also strongly anti-Shi'a in orientation. Many of its members are battle-hardened, ex-Afghan *mujahidin* who fought Soviet forces in Afghanistan in the 1980s. A breakaway faction of the Sunni sectarian organization, **Sipah-e-Sahaba Pakistan**, which was involved in anti-Shi'a sectarian violence and was subsequently banned by the government of Pakistan, the LEJ itself was reported to have split into two factions in 2000. It has particularly close links with **al-Qa'ida**, sharing its radical, pan-Islamic ideology as well as co-ordinating terrorist operations with it. It is also believed to have established close ties with other radical Pakistan-based groups, such as **Harakat ul-Mujahidin** and the **Jaish-e-Mohammed (JEM)**, which are also believed to have close ties with al-Qa'ida. The LEJ has been involved in violent activities, including anti-Shi'a and anti-Iranian attacks, the murder of four US oil workers in Karachi, Pakistan, in 1997, the attempted assassination of the then Prime Minister, Nawaf Sharaf, in 1999, the murder of US journalist Daniel Pearl, and the car bomb attacks in Karachi in 2002 that killed 12 French nationals. The LEJ has an estimated strength of some 300.

Lashkar-e-Taiba (LET)

The Lashkar-e-Taiba (LET—'Soldiers of the Pure') is the armed wing of the Islamist missionary organization, the Markaz-ud-Dawa-wal-Irshad (MDI—'Centre for Religious Learning and Social Welfare'), in Pakistan. It was formed in 1990 in Afghanistan and led by Hafiz Mohammed Saeed. Many of its members are drawn from the ranks of ex-*mujahidin* who fought Soviet forces in Afghanistan in the 1980s. Despite its association with Kashmiri secessionism, its members are mostly Pakistanis drawn from religious schools in Pakistan. LET subscribes to radical Islamist ideology of the *salafi* variety, and has an ambitious pan-Islamic agenda of uniting under the banner of Islam not just Pakistan but also parts of surrounding countries and the Indian-held state of Jammu and Kashmir. LET has particularly close links with **al-Qa'ida**, as it did with the **Taliban** regime in Afghanistan, and reportedly received funding from Osama bin Laden. It also fought the US-led intervention in Afghanistan after the **September 11, 2001 terrorist attacks** in the USA. LET's parent organization, the MDI, was in fact co-founded by Abdullah Azzam, Osama bin Laden's mentor, and was reportedly generously funded by bin Laden himself. The LET has been involved in a number of terrorist attacks in Kashmir and India, including that on an Indian army barracks in Delhi in December 2000, the attack on the Indian parliament in December 2001, believed to be a joint operation with **Jaish-e-Mohammed**, and the **Mumbai bombing** in India in August 2003 that killed 52 people and wounded 200. Pakistan banned the LET in 2002, but most of its leaders remain free. LET has continued to exist under the name Jama'at-ud-Dawa, led by Maulana Abdul Wahid Kashmiri. (*See* Map 9.)

Laskar Jihad ('Holy Struggle Warriors')

Before its disbandment in October 2002 the Laskar Jihad had, in its short existence, achieved the distinction of being the most violent radical Islamist group in Indonesia. The Laskar Jihad is the armed wing of the Forum Komunikasi Ahlus Sunnah Wal Jamaáh (FKAWJ—'Sunni Communication Forum'). This group was founded by radical Muslim *pasentren* (Muslim boarding school) leaders and preachers in early 1998 following the demise of the Suharto regime. Led by Ja'far Umar Thalib, the FKAWJ does not believe in Islamic parties and subscribes to radical *salafi* ideals and teachings. In January 2000 the FKAWJ established the Laskar Jihad on the grounds that Muslims were being persecuted by Christians in places such as Maluku, West Papua and North Sulawesi, and that the government was unwilling or unable to protect the Muslim community. The Laskar Jihad deployed some 3,000 armed volunteers to play the role of *mujahidin* in the Maluku islands, where they mounted attacks on Christian villages and were seen co-operating with army units in attacks on Christian neighbourhoods in Ambon. Neutral observers have strongly suspected that the Laskar Jihad had links with sections of the Indonesian armed forces. The group was officially disbanded hours before the **Bali attack** on 12 October 2002. According to its legal adviser, this was due to internal divisions over policy and ideology, in particular Thalib's approach to waging holy war, or *jihad*. However, its parent organization, the FKAWJ, has continued to carry out such activities as administering religious schools and publishing radical tracts. Thalib was placed on trial for inciting violence in the Malukus, but was acquitted in January 2003. (*See* Map 8.)

Laskar Jundullah

The Laskar Jundullah ('Army of God Force') in Indonesia was founded by Agus Dwikarna, who is now serving a 17-year jail sentence in the Philippines for possession of explosives, and Omar al-Faruq, a Kuwaiti of Iraqi parentage believed to be the most senior **al-Qa'ida** operative in south-east Asia until his arrest in Indonesia in June 2002. Agus Dwikarna himself has close links with the al-Qa'ida leadership, having acted as a guide for two of its leaders, az-Zawahiri (al-Zawahiri) and Mohammed Atef, when they visited Indonesia in 2000. Laskar Jundullah is a legally registered organization, provides security guards in South Sulawesi and proclaims as its objective the implementation of Islamic law. It is openly anti-Christian and has been involved in provoking religious tensions in Maluku and Poso. Indeed, Dwikarna established a military training camp near Poso in 2001 and the group co-ordinated the dispatch of volunteers to the southern Philippines for training by Moro rebels. In December 2002 Laskar Jundullah members bombed a McDonald's restaurant in south Sulawesi killing three people. In May 2005, Omar al-Faruq escaped from US custody while under US detention in Bagram, Afghanistan. (*See* Map 8.)

Liberation Army of Preševo Medveđja and Bujanovac

The Liberation Army of Preševo Medveđja and Bujanovac (UCPMB) is an ethnic Albanian insurgent movement formed in 2000 that aims to unite several Albanian-dominated southern Serbian municipalities with the Albanian-dominated region of Kosovo. Following the break-up of Yugoslavia in 1991, Serbia was faced with ethnic strife within its borders between Serbians and the minority Muslim ethnic Albanians. The conflict in Kosovo between the Serbian government and the **Kosovo Liberation Army (KLA)** spread to the southern Serbian provinces, to the towns of Preševo, Medveđja and Bujanovac, with its estimated 80,000 ethnic Albanian population. Indeed, many members of the UCPMB were from the KLA. The group launched attacks on government forces in late 2000, using as a base the demilitarized zone between Kosovo and Serbia that separated North Atlantic Treaty Organization (NATO) forces and Serbia following the conclusion of the conflict in Kosovo. Concerned that the crisis could spark a wider conflict, NATO handed the demilitarized zone back to Serbia and negotiated a cease-fire in 2001. This resulted in the disbandment of the UCPMB and the surrender of its weapons by May 2001. This was facilitated by a generous amnesty, the willingness of NATO to permit the guerrillas to enter Kosovo provided they surrendered their weapons, and a pledge by the government of Serbia to address the inequalities that Albanians faced in the south, although it was clear that the municipalities would remain within Serbia. It has been reported that some members of the UCPMB have become involved in organized criminal activities, such as arms-smuggling and drugs-trafficking. Hardline members of the group who refused to surrender are also reported to have formed a new guerrilla organization. This led to the arrest by NATO forces of UCPMB leader Shefket Musliu, a development much resented by hardline Albanians.

Liberation Front of Quebec

The Liberation Front of Quebec (Front de libération du Québec—FLQ) is a violent separatist group in Canada that was founded in 1963 with the objective of establishing an independent Quebec. It espoused Marxist ideology and the use of terror tactics, such as kidnappings, robberies, bombings and assassinations. The group was organized into cells which carried out a number of attacks, targeting the government as well as prominent members of the English-speaking population, including their businesses. The terrorist campaign culminated in October 1970 in the kidnap and murder of the Quebec Vice-Premier, Pierre Laporte. This prompted the government to authorize special wartime measures to arrest hundreds of FLQ activists. This, combined with a loss of public support for such violence, led to a greatly diminished level of activity, supporters of independence turning to the political process instead. However, sporadic attacks, such as the firebombing of cafés in Montreal in 2001, still occur.

Liberation Tigers of Tamil Eelam (LTTE)

The Liberation Tigers of Tamil Eelam (LTTE) is regarded as one of the most effective separatist-terrorist groups in the world. The LTTE was founded in 1976 with the objective of establishing an independent Tamil state in northern Jaffna, Sri Lanka, in order to free Tamils from what it perceived to be the political and economic domination of Sri Lanka's majority Sinhalese Buddhists. Armed conflict began in the early 1980s, with the Tamil Tigers, as its members are commonly known, engaging the security forces of Sri Lanka with such success that large parts of the northern and eastern coastal areas are today under its *de facto* control. The LTTE, led by Velupillai Prabhakaran, proved to be very resourceful, motivated and effective. It established an international network for spreading political propaganda, procuring weapons, and raising funds from the Tamil diaspora worldwide. It also received sympathetic support from Tamils in Tamil Nadu province in neighbouring India. It is well organized and trained, with its own effective intelligence capabilities, suicide squads and naval attack detachments that have carried out daring raids at harbours or at sea. Indeed, the LTTE demonstrated the devastating effects of the use of suicide bombings on a wide scale. It also perfected techniques for seaborne terror attacks. The scale of violence was such that the Indian government under Rajiv Gandhi intervened to help broker a peace accord in 1985 that was enforced by Indian peace-keepers. This collapsed in 1987, with the LTTE taking on both the Indian and Sri Lankan governments. Indian peacekeepers eventually withdrew in 1990. In 1991 Rajiv Gandhi was assassinated by the LTTE in Madras, India. The LTTE waged guerrilla warfare on a large scale, in tandem with an urban terrorist campaign. The latter included the assassination of President Ranasinghe Premadasa in 1993 as well as assassinations of numerous military, government and political leaders. Bombing attacks have also targeted government installations, infrastructure such as power stations, railway and bus stations, as well as security forces. Urban attacks launched by the LTTE have included the bomb attack in 1987 on a bus station in Colombo that killed or wounded more than 300 people; a train bombing in 1996 that killed 70 people and wounded 600; the bombing of the Central Bank in Colombo in 1996 that killed 91 people; the truck bombing of the World Trade Center in Colombo in 1997 that killed more than 100 and wounded 1,400; the bombing in 1998 of the Temple of the Tooth, Buddhism's holiest shrine; and the audacious attack in 2001 that closed Colombo's international airport. Tired of the continued violence that has claimed tens of thousands of lives, both the LTTE and the government finally agreed to a cease-fire and political negotiations under Norway's mediation in 2002.

Liberians United for Reconciliation and Democracy (LURD)

The Liberians United for Reconciliation and Democracy (LURD) is an umbrella group of anti-government forces in Liberia that emerged in 2000. The LURD was opposed to the government of Charles Taylor, who won the presidential elections held in 1997 following eight years of civil war. However, his government was tainted by allegations of corruption and repression. This has provided the impetus for gathering opposition to his regime. The various rebel groups came together in 2000 to form the LURD in neighbouring Sierra Leone. The LURD obtained support from Guinea and Sierra Leone, where large numbers of Liberian refugees now live as a result of the civil conflict. The LURD has engaged Liberian forces in a number of clashes, capturing a number of towns. Another, new rebel group, the Movement for Democracy in Liberia, has also participated in the conflict. In 2003 fighting engulfed the capital, Monrovia. In July the USA intervened amid increasing international pressure on Taylor to leave the country. Taylor subsequently resigned and accepted an offer of asylum in Nigeria. A UN peace-keeping force has now been deployed to supervise the peace accords and to reintegrate former rebels into their communities. In 2004 a struggle for power within the

LURD escalated into street-fighting in Monrovia that forced UN peace-keepers to intervene. Elections were scheduled to take place in late 2005.

Libyan Islamic Fighting Group

The Libyan Islamic Fighting Group ('Al-Jama'a al-Islamiyyah al-Muqatilah bi-Libya') is a radical Islamist group dedicated to the overthrow of the Qaddafi regime in Libya and its replacement by a government that would rule according to *Shari'a*, or Islamic, law. Founded in around 1995 by ex-*mujahidin* who had fought in Afghanistan in the 1980s, the group has targeted Col Qaddafi in various failed assassination attempts, as well as Libyan security forces. The group adopted radical pan-Islamic ideology and established close links with **al-Qa'ida** as well as with other radical groups in the Middle East. Indeed, some of its leaders are believed to also be members of al-Qa'ida. The group is also believed to have collaborated with the **Moroccan Islamic Combatant Group** in the **Casablanca bombings** in Morocco in May 2003 that killed 45 people. It is a secretive group with an estimated strength of 300. Little else is known about it. The USA has designated it as a terrorist group, and considers it a serious threat to US personnel and interests in Libya.

Lockerbie

'Lockerbie' is a reference to the bombing of a Pan Am Boeing 747 airliner which exploded above Lockerbie, Scotland, on 21 December 1988. All 249 people on board as well as 11 people on the ground were killed. The cause of the explosion was a device packed with plastic explosives that had detonated in the cargo section of the aircraft. After much investigation, it was concluded that two alleged Libyan agents, Abdel Baset Ali al-Megrahi and Lamen Khalifa Fhimah, had been responsible for the attack. Libya was requested by the UK and US governments to extradite both suspects for trial, but refused and was subsequently the object of a UN-led economic sanctions regime. There has been much speculation over the motives for the attack, some of it focused on the fact that several alleged US Central Intelligence Agency operatives were killed in it, and some on an Iranian connection—the attack having possibly been an Iranian-sponsored reprisal for the accidental shooting down of an Iranian airliner by a US warship, the USS *Vincennes*, during the first Gulf War in 1990–91. The UK and US governments have maintained that the two men acted with the sanction of the government of Libya and, possibly, that of Iran. One year after the Lockerbie bombing, a French UTA passenger aircraft exploded over the Sahara, killing 170 people. Again, Libya was held responsible. In 1999 Libya finally agreed to surrender the Lockerbie suspects to a neutral third country, Netherlands, for trial by Scottish judges under Scottish law. Abdel Baset Ali al-Megrahi was found guilty and sentenced to life imprisonment, while Lamen Khalifa Fhimah was found not guilty and released. The Lockerbie bombing raised serious issues regarding the safety of commercial civilian aircraft from terrorist attack. In 2003 the UN lifted the sanctions that had been imposed on Libya after it agreed to pay US $2,700m. in compensation to the victims of the Lockerbie bombing and US $170m. to the victims of the UTA bombing.

Lod Airport Attack

On 30 May 1972 three members of the **Japanese Red Army** arrived in Israel on an Air France flight. On entering Tel-Aviv's international airport, the Lod Airport (later renamed Ben Gurion Airport), they attacked passengers and staff in the ticketing counter area using automatic weapons and grenades. One of the terrorists was shot by security personnel, while another committed suicide. A third was captured. Twenty-six people were killed and 78 wounded in the attack, including a number of Christian pilgrims from Puerto Rico. The sole survivor of the terrorist team, Kozo Okamoto, was sentenced to life imprisonment in Israel. However, he was released in 1983 as part of an exchange of prisoners with Palestinian militant groups. Okamoto converted to Islam and disappeared in Lebanon. Responsibility for the airport attack was later claimed by the **Popular Front for the Liberation of Palestine**, which lauded the three Japanese terrorists for their support of the Palestinian struggle.

London Bombings (2005)

On 7 July 2005 a co-ordinated series of bomb attacks struck London's rail and bus transportation system. Three bombs exploded on packed trains during the morning rush hour, while a fourth destroyed a double-decker public bus. Fifty-two people were killed and more than 700 were injured in the attacks, which were meticulously planned and carried out by four suicide bombers. Exactly two weeks later, on 21 July, similar attacks were attempted by four would-be suicide bombers, but were aborted when the bombs failed to explode. Subsequent investigations revealed that the suicide bombers were either British Muslims or refugees who had come to live in Britain, had subscribed to radical Islamist ideology and joined terrorist cells. Immediately after the attacks, a hitherto unknown group, 'al–Qa'ida in Europe', claimed responsibility and further claimed that they were in response to Britain's participation in US-led interventions in Iraq and Afghanistan. The attacks bore a striking similarity to the **Madrid train bombings** of March 2004 that were carried out by radical Islamists in order to punish Spain for its involvement in Iraq and Afghanistan. The London bombings prompted much apprehension over the number of undetected terrorist cells in Britain that could be planning further attacks. In the confusion and heightened tension following the London bombings, a Brazilian electrician on his way to work was tragically mistaken for a terrorist and killed by anti-terrorist police on the Underground, sparking fears over the danger to civil liberties as a consequence of the attacks. Although the overwhelming majority of British Muslims condemned the bombings, they had also exposed the sense of alienation felt by some over Britain's foreign policies, particularly its involvement in Iraq and Afghanistan. However,

Britain's failure to curb domestic militant activity, its lax asylum laws, lack of effective judicial powers to counter terrorism, and the presence of some 3,000 British Muslims previously trained by **al-Qa'ida** and the **Taliban** in Afghanistan before US-led intervention in 2001, could be cited as possible contributory factors which made terrorist attacks almost a certainty.

Lord's Resistance Army (LRA)

The Lord's Resistance Army (LRA) was founded in the late 1980s and is an insurgent group that seeks to overthrow the government of Uganda. Led by Joseph Kony, it subscribes to a radical, millenarian form of Christianity. The LRA uses violence and intimidation, attacking government forces and civilians. It has also gained notoriety for its use of children, whom it kidnaps and presses into service as fighters. Indeed, it is estimated that the bulk of its fighting strength consists of child-fighters. Another unsavoury practice is its use of female children as sex slaves. The group has been responsible for senseless and brutal attacks against both Ugandans and foreigners. The LRA received support from neighbouring Sudan, which granted it sanctuaries in retaliation for Uganda's alleged support for the rebel **Sudan People's Liberation Army**. This almost led to open conflict between Uganda and Sudan in 1995. However, a reconciliation between Sudan and Uganda, mediated by the USA, resulted in Sudan's co-operation after 2002 and has helped to reduce the threat from the LRA. Through its sheer brutality and random violence, the LRA has also alienated the Acholi people in northern Uganda where it operates. However, the situation remains unstable, as many as 1m. people having been displaced as a result of the conflict. Peace talks have made little progress. Despite its reduced strength, today estimated at 1,500–4,500, the LRA continues to pose a serious threat to Uganda's security.

Loyalist Volunteer Force (LVF)

The Loyalist Volunteer Force (LVF) is a paramilitary Protestant group that has both fought against the **Irish Republican Army (IRA)** as well as engaged in vigilante action against Catholics in Northern Ireland. The LVF claims to represent Protestants in Northern Ireland and aims to defend the continued presence of the territory within the United Kingdom. The LVF is a splinter group of the **Ulster Volunteer Force (UVF)** that emerged in 1996 owing to its disagreement with the UVF's policy of pursuing a cease-fire in tandem with the British government's ongoing peace negotiations with the IRA. Led by Billy Wright, the LVF resumed violent attacks on both Catholics as well as Protestants who supported the peace process. Wright was assassinated by the **Irish National Liberation Army** in 1997. The LVF agreed to abide by the cease-fire that resulted from the Good Friday Agreement in 1998, but it is believed that sections of it have continued to engage in violence as the Red Hand Defenders.

Luxor Massacre

The massacre of tourists at Luxor in Egypt in 1997 was carried out by the radical Islamist group, **al-Gama'a al-Islamiyya**. On 17 November six terrorists disguised as policemen arrived at the ancient Hatshepsut Temple in Luxor, a famous tourist site. Having killed four security personnel at the entrance to the Temple, they proceeded to kill as many foreign tourists as possible using their firearms. Fifty-eight tourists died in the attack, including 35 Swiss. The police finally surrounded the terrorists and killed all six of them. The al-Gama'a al-Islamiyya claimed responsibility for the attack and warned tourists not to visit Egypt. It also issued a number of demands that included the severing of diplomatic relations with Israel, the implementation of Islamic, or *Shari'a*, law in Egypt, and the release of the group's spiritual leader, Sheikh Omar Abdel-Rahman, who had been sentenced to life imprisonment in the USA for his role in the **World Trade Center bombing** in 1993 in New York. However, the attack outraged many Egyptians, and threatened the tourism industry on which millions of Egyptians depended for a living. There was widespread condemnation of the group, enabling the government to take harsh measures to suppress it.

Madrid Train Bombings

On 11 March 2004 a co-ordinated series of bomb attacks on the Madrid subway in Spain during the morning rush hour killed 191 people and injured more than 1,800. Thirteen bombs were used in the attacks, of which 10 exploded on board four commuter trains. The blasts were carried out at three subway stations: Atocha, El Pozo and Santa Eugenia, all in south-east Madrid. It was Spain's worst terrorist attack, and one of the worst in Europe in contemporary times. Initially blamed on the Basque separatist organization, **Euzkadi Ta Askatasuna**, it soon became clear that radical Islamist groups were involved. The Spanish authorities named the **Moroccan Islamic Combatant Group** as the main suspect. The group, which has adopted a radical, pan-Islamic ideology, is believed to have close links with **al-Qa'ida**, and was also responsible for the **Casablanca bombings** in Morocco in May 2003 that killed 45 people. After the Madrid attacks, Spanish police recovered part of a mobile telephone SIM card, which led to the arrest of a telephone shop owner. A number of other suspects, mostly Moroccan, were also arrested, but seven suspects blew themselves up when they were trapped by security forces in their Madrid flat. Among them was the alleged leader of the train attacks, Serhane Abdelmajid Fakhet, who was from Tunisia. The Madrid bombings were apparently an act of revenge for Spain's involvement in the Iraq conflict. Indeed, Osama bin Laden had issued a public warning in October 2003 that included Spain in the list of countries that al-Qa'ida would retaliate against for having participated in the US-led intervention in Iraq in 2003, following the **September 11, 2001 terrorist attacks** in the USA. The new socialist government that took power in Spain after elections held shortly after the Madrid attack announced the withdrawal of Spanish troops from Iraq.

Manuel Rodríguez Patriotic Front

The Manuel Rodríguez Patriotic Front was founded in 1983 and is the armed wing of the Chilean Communist Party. Named after the hero of Chile's war of independence against Spain, the group is dedicated to the overthrow of Chile's government and the establishment of a communist state. It has attacked US businesses, bombing, for instance, McDonald's restaurants. It has not been particularly active, however, and its declining strength is today estimated at less than 100.

Maoist Communist Centre (MCC)

The Maoist Communist Centre (MCC), previously known as the Dakshin Desh, is a Maoist insurgent group in India that first appeared after a peasant rebellion in 1967 in Naxalbari, West Bengal. Ironically, the rebellion was suppressed by the then communist-led state government. This led to defections and to the establishment of the MCC. The MCC consists of extremist elements who have rejected participation in the political process and espouse violence for revolutionary objectives. It bases its support on poor peasants, using the same ideology and tactics as used by Mao Zedong in revolutionary China to surround the cities from the countryside. The MCC's objective is to liberate poor and landless peasants and to establish a communist state, starting with a revolutionary zone in remote areas. It is active in a number of Indian states, such as Bihar. In some of these 'liberated areas', the MCC has administered land reform, class struggle, socialist justice and tax collection. Together with the **People's War Group**, the Maoist rebel movement has been sustained by the deep poverty and socio-economic disparities that exist in rural India. (*See* Map 5.)

Marine Barracks Bombing

On 23 October 1983 a truck driven by a suicide bomber crashed through the entrance of the US Marines headquarters at Beirut International Airport in Lebanon and detonated an estimated 5,400 kg of TNT explosive. The four-storey building was destroyed and many US soldiers inside it were killed—a total of 241 people died in the attack, including 220 US Marines. Another 60 were injured in the bombing. A simultaneous truck bomb attack on a French paratrooper barracks in Beirut killed 58 French troops and injured 15 others. The attack on the US Marines remains the deadliest terrorist attack on US citizens overseas, and one of the most devastating terrorist attacks in contemporary times. The blast was later described as one of the largest non-nuclear explosions ever recorded. The attacks were blamed on the militant Shi'ite organization, **Hezbollah**, which is backed by Syria and Iran. Hezbollah has been implacably opposed to the USA due to its support for the Shah of Iran prior to the Iranian Revolution in 1979. It also opposed the USA and France for their attempts to intervene in Lebanon—where Hezbollah is an influential force—as part of an international peace-keeping operation. The bombing of the US Marines barracks followed a bomb attack on the US Embassy in Beirut in April 1983 that killed 63 people, including 17 US citizens. Despite pledges to the contrary, the USA eventually withdrew from Beirut and Lebanon, having failed to retaliate against Hezbollah. In 2003 a US judge concluded that Iran had been responsible for the bombing.

Mehdi Army

The Mehdi Army is a Shi'ite militia that consists of several thousand fighters who are loyal to the radical cleric Moqtada as-Sadr (al-Sadr) in Iraq. It was established in mid-2003, following the US-led intervention in Iraq, by as-Sadr, who controls a network of Shi'ite charities. These charities were established by his famous father, the respected cleric Ayatollah Mohamad Sadeq as-Sadr, who was murdered by the Saddam Hussain regime in 1999. The Mehdi Army emerged to patrol the streets in poor sections of Baghdad, distributing food in an area renamed Sadr City after the fall of the Saddam regime. While Moqtada as-Sadr is young and is considered to be inexperienced, especially when compared to the much older clerics who dominate the Shi'ite community in Iraq, he has a committed following among young, poor and disaffected Shi'ites. The name 'Mehdi' refers to a revered figure in Shi'ite history. Moqtada lacks a proper religious education and thus claims authority solely on the basis of lineage. This is not viewed favourably by other Shi'ite clerics in Iraq and his relationship with them has been tense. Indeed, it is suspected that he may have been responsible for the assassinations of major Shi'ite religious leaders, such as that of Ayatollah Sayyid Mohamed Baqir al-Hakim in August 2003, although his followers have blamed the attack on Sunni insurgents. Moqtada as-Sadr believes in clerical rule, a position at odds with the dominant Shi'ite religious authority, the moderate Grand Ayatollah Ali as-Sistani. There have in fact been clashes between the Mehdi Army and the **Badr Corps**, which was led by al-Hakim. Moqtada as-Sadr has made inflammatory speeches denouncing the foreign occupation, and led an uprising against US-led forces in Najaf following the closure of his newspaper, *Al-Hawza*, for inciting violence. An Iraqi judge also issued a warrant for his arrest for the murder of a leading Shi'ite cleric, Imam Abdul Majid al-Khoei. The result was much fighting between the Mehdi Army and US-led forces in Najaf, Basra and Sadr City in April 2004. Following the intervention of Grand Ayatollah Ali as-Sistani in August 2004, Moqtada as-Sadr agreed to disband his militia. While he did not participate in the elections in early 2005, his followers constitute a powerful bloc within the United Iraqi Alliance of Shi'ite groups that is loosely led by as-Sistani, and he is perceived as a champion of the Shi'ite poor in Iraq. Following the elections in Iraq in 2005, his followers have used violent intimidation tactics to enforce Islamic, or *Shari'a*, law among Shi'ites in Iraq. (*See* Map 6.)

Mong Tai Army

The Mong Tai Army was the armed organization led by the alleged drugs lord, Khun Sa, in Myanmar (formerly Burma). It had Shan and Wa tribespeople in its ranks, as well as ethnic Chinese from the Kuomintang forces that fled China after the communists took power there in 1949. Myanmar provides the bulk of the world's supply of opium, and the USA has accused Khun Sa of being one of the world's biggest drugs lords. In 1989 the military regime in Myanmar began negotiations with all of the ethnic insurgent groups that had been fighting the central government since independence in 1948, at a time when it was being challenged internally by pro-democracy forces. In January 1996 Khun Sa and his Mong Tai Army formally surrendered. In return for ending the insurgency and surrendering weaponry, Khun Sa was allowed to live under close government supervision in Yangon, the capital city, where he could engage in legitimate businesses though not in drugs-trafficking. He was, moreover, not to be prosecuted or extradited to the USA to face charges for drugs-trafficking. Some of his Shan followers then joined the **Shan State Army** to continue the armed struggle against the central government. While the Mong Tai Army network disintegrated, other groups, such as the Wa (see **United Wa State Army**), have taken over its role and, overall, drugs production in Myanmar has not declined. (*See* Map 1.)

Moro Islamic Liberation Front (MILF)

The Moro Islamic Liberation Front (MILF) is the largest Muslim separatist organization in the southern Philippines. The result of a split between left-wing nationalist and religious factions within the **Moro National Liberation Front (MNLF)** in 1978, the MILF was formally constituted in 1984. It was critical of the leftist orientation of the MNLF and sought to emphasize its Islamic credentials and identity through the pursuit of an independent Muslim Moro state. Led by Hashim Salamat, a religious leader trained at Al-Azhar University in Cairo, Egypt, the MILF had become the main Moro rebel movement by the 1990s. The MILF grew rapidly, eclipsing the MNLF, especially after the latter signed the Davao peace accord in 1986. Many of its members gained combat experience in Afghanistan as volunteers fighting alongside the anti-Soviet *mujahidin* resistance forces. It has a reported strength of about 18,000 and is in *de facto* control of large areas of several provinces in Mindanao. It has its own Consultative Assembly and draws popular support from Muslims throughout Mindanao. The MILF established links with **al-Qa'ida**, which provided it with both funding and training. However, the MILF publicly distanced itself from al-Qa'ida after the **September 11, 2001 terrorist attacks** in the USA. None the less, there is evidence that some MILF factions maintained relations with the al-Qa'ida-linked **Jemaah Islamiah (JI)** which carried out the **Bali attack** on 12 October 2002, by providing refuge and training for JI operatives who were fugitives from regional authorities. Hashim died in August 2003 from natural causes, and was succeeded by the MILF military commander, Murad Ebrahim, considered a more nationalist-oriented leader. The USA, which dispatched military advisers to the Philippines in 2002, has, for its part, acted pragmatically by not including the much larger MILF on its list of terrorist groups, preferring to target the more extremist **Abu Sayyaf Group**. The political nature of the MILF's demands at least leaves open the possibility of a political compromise eventually being reached in ongoing negotiations with the government of the Philippines.

Moro National Liberation Front (MNLF)

The Moro National Liberation Front (MNLF) was a major Muslim separatist insurgent organization in the southern Philippines until the late 1990s. The influx of Catholics into Muslim Moro lands in the south after their forced incorporation into the colonial administration of the Spaniards and then the USA by the end of the 19th century, led to alienation, landlessness and poverty amongst the Moros. In 1968 a massacre of Moro recruits to the Philippine Army was the catalyst that led eventually, in 1972, to the establishment of the MNLF. Led by Nur Misuari, the MNLF had the support of Libya. It began a bitter guerrilla campaign against the Philippine armed forces that ultimately cost more than 100,000 lives. A split in 1978 resulted in the establishment of the **Moro Islamic Liberation Front (MILF)**, which has sought to emphasize its Islamic credentials and identity, in contrast to the more left-wing and secular orientation of the MNLF. In 1996, as a result of mediation by Indonesia and the Organization of the Islamic Conference, the MNLF accepted the Davao peace accord, under which it would administer a Southern Philippines Council for Peace and Development to oversee development projects in Mindanao, and Misuari would become governor of the Muslim autonomous region. However, the agreement was denounced as a capitulation by the MILF, which continued fighting. Misuari's failure to bring about development in the Muslim autonomous region was partly due to the continued fighting. In 2001 he brokered a unification with the MILF, rebelled and fled to Malaysia, which in 2002 handed him back to the Philippines to face trial.

Moroccan Islamic Combatant Group

The Moroccan Islamic Combatant Group (Groupe islamique combattant marocain—GICM) was founded in Morocco in the 1990s following a split within the radical Shabiba Islamiya, which dates back to 1969. The GICM's objective is the overthrow of the government of Morocco and the establishment of an Islamic state. Consisting of ex-*mujahidin* who had fought in Afghanistan in the 1980s and others who had trained there in the 1990s, the group has adopted radical pan-Islamic ideology and established close links with **al-Qa'ida**. Indeed, some of its members are believed also to be members of al-Qa'ida and to work closely with it in pursuit of its global *jihadist* agenda. The GICM has also established links with other North African radical groups, and operates not only in Morocco but also in Western Europe, moving among the Muslim diaspora. The USA designated the group as a terrorist organization in 2002, a prescient move considering the infamy it achieved soon after. The GICM has been held responsible for two recent bomb attacks, namely, the **Casablanca bombings** in May 2003 that killed 45 people, and the **Madrid train bombings** in Spain on 11 March 2004, which killed 191 people and injured some 1,800. After the Casablanca bombings four members of the GICM were executed and 39 sentenced to long terms of imprisonment. The Madrid bombings were believed to be an act of revenge for Spain's involvement in Iraq following US-led intervention in the aftermath of the **September 11, 2001 terrorist attacks** in the USA. Indeed, the impact of the attack was such that the new socialist government that came to power following elections that took place shortly after the train bombings announced the withdrawal of Spanish troops from Iraq. After the Madrid attacks, Spanish police arrested a number of suspects, most of them Moroccan, but several others blew themselves up when they were trapped by security forces in their Madrid flat. The Moroccan authorities believe that the group is led by Taeb Bentizi and Mohamed Guerbouzi. The secretive GICM is believed to have 'sleeper' cells in various western European countries.

Moscow Theatre Siege (2002)

The Moscow theatre siege in late 2002 began when 40 armed male and female Chechen terrorists took more than 700 people hostage in a Moscow theatre on 23 October, during a performance of the musical *Nord-Ost*. The operation was well planned and executed, with the terrorists securing the auditorium with explosive charges and many of the female terrorists wearing belts filled with explosives. Russian security forces soon surrounded the theatre but were warned by the leader of the group, Movsar Barayev, that they would detonate the explosive charges if any rescue attempt were made. Movsar, the nephew of the Chechen warlord, Arbi Barayev, demanded the withdrawal of Russian troops from Chechnya and threatened to execute the hostages if the demand was not met. In view of his credentials as the leader of the terrorist group, the **Special Purpose Islamic Regiment**, the security services took his threat seriously. The terrorists released Muslims in the audience and the Red Cross managed to secure the release of several of the hostages before the siege ended in bloodshed. Two days after the hostage crisis began, an apparent attempt by some hostages to escape resulted in shooting inside the auditorium. This led the authorities to believe that the hostages were being executed, resulting in an immediate assault by commandos of the special forces. A chemical, later identified as a fentanyl derivative, was pumped into the theatre to incapacitate those inside, thus allowing the commandos to enter and kill the Chechen terrorists. However, the amount of gas used was so great and the required medical support so deficient that 128 of the hostages died, leading to much criticism of the mismanaged rescue attempt. The siege was none the less a dramatic affair that was widely covered by the international media, and demonstrated the severity of the security threat from Chechen separatist rebels even in the capital. The leader of another Chechen rebel group, Shamil Basayev of the **Riyadus-Salikhin Reconnaissance and Sabotage Battalion of Shahids (Martyrs)**, claimed responsibility for the siege, leading to the conclusion that this was a joint terrorist operation. The Russian government accused a Chechen envoy, Akhmed Zakayev, of involvement in the siege, but although he was detained in Denmark for one month, he was released for lack of evidence and later found political asylum in Britain. The Moscow theatre siege was followed by other terrorist attacks, such as the suicide attack in December 2002 in Grozny, Chechnya, that killed 72 people, and the **Beslan school siege** in September 2004 that killed 344 people.

Movement for Democracy and Justice in Chad

The Movement for Democracy and Justice in Chad (Mouvement pour la démocratie et la justice au Tchad—MDJT) is a rebel group in Chad that sought to overthrow the regime of Idriss Deby there. Chad's history since its independence from France in 1960 has been marked by violence. Libya played a key role in a civil war that began there in the mid-1970s. In 1990 power was seized by Idriss Deby, a former defence minister, whose ensuing regime was characterized by repression and corruption. A series of rebellions against Deby took place, including one by the MDJT, which was led by Deby's former defence minister, Youssef Togoimi. The MDJT commenced armed opposition in 1998, most of the subsequent fighting taking place in northern Chad after 2000. In January 2002 the MDJT signed a peace accord, but hardline elements continued fighting. However, the withdrawal of support by Libya and the death of Togoimi in September 2002 led to the gradual decline of the insurgency.

Movement for the Liberation of Congo (MLC)

The Movement for the Liberation of Congo (Mouvement de libération congolais—MLC) emerged as a result of civil conflict in the Democratic Republic of the Congo (DRC—formerly Zaire). After independence from Belgium in 1960 the DRC suffered considerable internal instability. After 1996 war between the Hutus and the Tutsis and genocide in Rwanda spread to the DRC, where Hutu militiamen fled after being defeated by the Tutsis. In 1997 Laurent-Désiré Kabila overthrew the regime of Mobuto Sese Seko with the support of Rwanda and Uganda. However, he soon quarrelled with his foreign backers, this dispute resulting in the creation of the Tutsi-dominated **Congolese Rally for Democracy (RCD)**, backed by Rwanda and Uganda, in 1998. The RCD accused the government of mismanagement and nepotism. A fierce internal power struggle within the RCD led it to split into several factions after mid-1999, of which the largest were the RCD-Kisangani (RCD-ML), led by Ernest Wamba dia Wamba and backed by Uganda, and the RCD-Goma, led by Emile Ilunga and backed by Rwanda. In 1999 Uganda also helped to establish another rebel group, the MLC, which is led by Jean-Pierre Bemba, a wealthy businessman with access to gold, diamonds, timber and other significant resources. The MLC is considered to be the best organized of the rebel groups fighting the Kabila government in Kinshasa. The three main rebel groups were able to take control of one-third of the country in the north. For his part, Kabila turned to Angola, Zimbabwe and Namibia for support, which prevented the rebels from advancing further. The tremendous scale of the violence since 1996 is estimated to have cost the lives of more than 200,000 people, and to have led to the displacement of more than 4m. The Lusaka peace accord of August 1999 was finally implemented by Laurent-Désiré Kabila's son, Joseph, after Laurent- Désiré was assassinated in 2001. Under the accord a UN peace-keeping force was deployed and all foreign forces were withdrawn from the DRC. In 2003 a power-sharing agreement was signed in Pretoria, South Africa, and elections were scheduled to take place in 2006. However, violence continued in late 2004, raising fresh doubts over the DRC's future stability. (*See* Map 2.)

Movement of Democratic Forces in the Casamance (MFDC)

The Movement of Democratic Forces in the Casamance (Mouvement des forces démocratiques de Casamance—MFDC) is a separatist movement in Senegal's southern province of Casamance. The antecedents of the group date to 1947, before Senegal gained independence from France in 1960. In 1982 the MFDC emerged and it has fought against the central government in Dakar since then, using neighbouring Guinea-Bissau as a base of operations. Indeed, until his overthrow in 1999, President João Bernardo Vieira of Guinea-Bissau was alleged to have supported the MFDC's activities. The MFDC has not only advocated the separation of Casamance province from Senegal, but also its union with Gambia and Guinea-Bissau. Underlying the revolt has been a sense of injustice at the under-development of Casamance and the adherence to Christianity by the local Diola, in contrast to the Muslim-dominated central government. The MFDC was led by a priest, Abbé Augustine Diamacoune Senghor, and has maintained that Casamance has its own national identity, separate from the rest of Senegal, and that it had in fact been forcibly colonized by the north. The MFDC split into two factions in the early 1990s, Abbé Senghor leading the more moderate of the two, and Salif Sadio leading the more hardline. In 1996 widespread allegations of voting irregularities in elections led to renewed violence against the central government. Both the rebels and government forces are alleged to have committed various abuses. In 2000 the long rule of the Socialist Party came to an end with the ascension to power of Abdoulaye Wade, who stated that the main priority of his government would be to end the violence. In October 2003 the moderate wing of the MFDC announced the end of the rebellion. However, the hardline faction has continued fighting. More than 800 people have died in the generally low-level insurgency since hostilities were renewed in 1998.

Movement of the Revolutionary Left

The Movement of the Revolutionary Left (Movimiento de la Izquierda Revolucionaria—MIR) is a left-wing insurgent group in Chile. It was formed in 1965 by idealistic school dropouts and university students from Concepción and Santiago. The MIR cadres carried out agrarian reform by seizing rural land from absentee landlords and establishing collective or co-operative enterprises on behalf of poor, landless Indians. Until the mid-1990s the MIR received the support of a number of states, such as Cuba, Angola, Mozambique and Nicaragua. The group engaged in terror attacks, rejecting the open political process that the Allende government offered in 1970. Under the military regime of Gen. Pinochet in 1973–78 the MIR was suppressed and many leaders and activists were killed or exiled. From 1978 the MIR's armed struggle was revitalized when its leader, Miguel Enríquez, returned to Chile. However, his death at the hands of security forces in 1983 led to the decline of the MIR and its ability to mount large-scale operations.

Mujahedin-e-Khalq (MEK)

The Mujahedin-e-Khalq (MEK—'People's Holy Warriors') is the main anti-government opposition group in Iran. Formed in 1963 after a failed uprising against the Shah of Iran, the MEK has a philosophy that combines Islam and Marxism, and it is led by intellectuals, not clerics. It engaged in anti-Shah as well as anti-US activities, targeting US civilian and military personnel, until the Iranian Revolution in 1979. The MEK, however, also opposed clerical rule under the regime of Ayatollah Khomeini, which had little tolerance for socialist ideas. Soon, state repression resulted in the arrest and death of many of the MEK's members. After 1979 it was forced to seek refuge in Iraq, where the regime of Saddam Hussain provided it with support. Elements linked to the MEK are believed to have been involved in the **Iran embassy siege** in London in 1980. The MEK claims its legitimacy from the National Coalition of Resistance of Iran (NCRI), which is a coalition of opposition Iranian groups. The MEK carried out terrorist attacks in Iran as well as on Iranian interests in a number of other countries, with the objective of overthrowing the government in Tehran. In 1981 it assassinated a number of high-ranking officials in a series of bomb attacks, including the then President, Prime Minister and Chief Justice. It was also responsible for a series of attacks on Iranian embassies abroad in 1992. From its safe bases in Iraq the MEK launched a series of attacks against Iranian security personnel and installations from early 2000. Following the US-led intervention in Iraq in 2003, the MEK surrendered and its weapons were confiscated, thus ending its terrorist operations against Iran.

Mumbai Bombings (1993)

The Mumbai bombings took place in Mumbai, India, on 12 March 1993. A total of 15 bombs, mostly car bombs packed with plastic explosives, were detonated at various locations throughout the city. The targets included three hotels, banks, government offices, shopping centres, an airline building and also the Mumbai Stock Exchange. A total of 257 people were killed and more than 1,400 injured in the co-ordinated attacks. The attacks took place against the background of the destruction of the Babri mosque at Ayodhya in 1992 by Hindu fundamentalists and subsequent Hindu-Muslim rioting in early 1993 that claimed more than 600 lives. Indian investigators believe that one of the key perpetrators was a Mumbai criminal, Dawood Ibrahim, who had built up a lucrative gold and silver smuggling business, although he also managed legitimate businesses. During the

Hindu-Muslim riots in early 1993 his businesses suffered greatly, and he allowed his underground criminal organization to be used to transport explosives into the city for a series of retaliatory attacks. He fled India after the bombings, apparently seeking refuge in Pakistan. This led the Indian authorities to allege that either Pakistan or some of the fundamentalist Muslim groups involved there in agitation for Kashmir's independence had played a role in the Mumbai bombings. In August 2003 two similar car bomb attacks in Mumbai, in which 52 people were killed, were attributed by India to **Jaish-e-Mohammed** and **Lashkar-e-Taiba**.

Munich Massacre (1972)

The Munich massacre took place during the Summer Olympic Games in Munich, Federal Republic of Germany, in 1972. On 5 September eight terrorists belonging to **Black September** entered the Games 'village' and the two apartments used by the Israeli team. The terrorists were from Palestinian refugee camps in the Middle East and were led by Lutiff Afif. Two Israeli athletes were killed and nine others were taken hostage. The group demanded the release of 234 Palestinians imprisoned in Israel. The German authorities entered into negotiations and agreed to provide the terrorists with safe passage to Egypt. When the terrorists and the hostages arrived at the airport, however, German police snipers opened fire on them. In the ensuing exchange of gunfire, the nine hostages were all killed, as were five of the terrorists and a German policeman. Israel withdrew its team from the Games immediately, as did Egypt, which feared reprisals for its athletes. The Games were suspended for one day, then resumed, a decision that was supported by the government of Israel. The attack exposed serious shortcomings in German counter-terrorism, leading to the establishment of a dedicated unit, the GSG 9. Israeli warplanes bombed **Palestine Liberation Organization** bases in Syria and Lebanon in retaliation. Israeli intelligence agents hunted down Black September and other Palestianian leaders and operatives all over Europe and the Middle East, assassinating a number of them, including all but one of those involved in the planning or execution of the Munich massacre.

Muslim Brotherhood

The Muslim Brotherhood (Jumiat al-Ikhwan al-Muslimin—Society of Brothers) began as a Muslim revivalist movement founded by Hasan al-Banna in Egypt in 1928. In time it became known as the progenitor of radical Islamism and as the forerunner of contemporary Islamist terror groups. Al-Banna argued that Islam was a comprehensive way of life, including politics and social affairs. It is fundamentalist in its orientation and rejects all Western influences and secular practices. The Brotherhood's uncompromising stand on the issue of government according to the *Shari'a*, or Islamic, law, as well as its espousal of violence to achieve its ends soon set it on a collision course with the Egyptian government. After terrorist acts by its members against the state, the Brotherhood was banned and al-Banna himself was killed in 1949. After its failed attempt to assassinate

President Nasser, some of its members were executed, thousands were arrested and others fled to surrounding Arab countries. Over the years, the Brotherhood has established many chapters throughout the Middle East, Central Asia and further afield, and has demonstrated diverse ways of approaching its objectives. Some branches have been involved in founding terrorist organizations, while in some countries, such as Jordan, they have operated within the political system. Various Middle Eastern governments have sought to use its influence, but in many cases it has been outlawed or similarly suppressed. The large Syrian branch of the Brotherhood, for instance, was eliminated by President Assad after an assassination attempt was made on him. In 1980–82, in a military operation, thousands of members of the Brotherhood were massacred and membership of it was made punishable by death. Some prominent Brothers have included the theologians of radical Islamism, such as its founder, al-Banna, and Sayyid Qutb; Ahmed Yassin, the founder of **Hamas**; and Dr Ayman az-Zawahiri (al-Zawahiri), the deputy leader of **al-Qa'ida** and leader of **al-Gama'a al-Islamiyya** of Egypt.

Muslims Against Global Oppression

The Muslims Against Global Oppression (MAGO) is an Islamist organization in South Africa that was led by Moain Achmad until his arrest. The only bomb attack attributed to it to date was on the Planet Hollywood restaurant in Cape Town in August 1998. Two people died in the attack, for which MAGO later denied responsibility. The group is anti-US and has mobilized protests against US and British foreign policy and alleged US and British oppression of Muslims in Afghanistan and Iraq. MAGO is believed to have links with other radical organizations outside of South Africa, as well as with the South African Muslim vigilante group, the **People Against Gangsterism and Drugs**.

Muttahida Qami Movement (MQM)

The Muttahida Qami Movement (MQM), which was previously known as the Mohajir Qami Movement, is a Muslim political organization in Pakistan that represents the Urdu-speaking Mohajirs who came to live in Pakistan after its creation in 1947 as a result of the partition of India. The MQM was formally established in 1984 to represent the interests of the Mohajirs, who have complained that they have been marginalized economically and unfairly discriminated against by the Sindhis. There has since been persistent unrest in the provinces of Sindh, Punjab and in the north-west, including in the key city of Karachi. The MQM has participated in national politics, winning its first electoral seats in 1988. It later participated in an alliance with the Pakistan Muslim League led by Nawaf Sharif that won elections held in 1997, but the allies soon quarrelled and the MQM later withdrew. In 1999 a court sentenced two MQM members to death for the 1997 car ambush and murder in Karachi of four US employees of a US oil company, although the MQM denied that it had been involved. The MQM split into two warring factions, the Muttahida Qami Mahaz or MQM (A), led by founder Altaf Hussain, and the Mohajir Qami Movement Haqiqi or MQM (H). The factional fighting as well as violence between Mohajirs and Sindhis in Karachi led to such violence that a state of emergency was declared in May 1998. The MQM has been blamed by the government for a number of bomb attacks in Karachi. The MQM has been back in favour in recent times, however. President Musharraf of Pakistan has enlisted its help in countering radical religious extremists in Pakistan, and some of its members now occupy senior government positions. (*See* Map 9.)

National Council for Khalistan

The National Council for Khalistan is a Sikh separatist group that has pursued a violent campaign for a separate Sikh state of Khalistan in Punjab, India (*see* Map 9). Jagjit Singh, of the Akali Dal, the main Sikh political party, has been described as being instrumental in promoting the cause of Khalistan, to the point of collaborating with Pakistan during the Indo–Pakistani War in 1971. This resulted in the expulsion of Singh and his followers from the Akali Dal and their establishment of the National Council for Khalistan in 1972. A more militant youth wing, the Dal Khalsa, was formed in 1979. In 1982 Sikhs clashed with Hindus over the issue of the sale of tobacco and alcoholic liquor in the environs of the Golden Temple at Amritsar, the holiest of the Sikh shrines, leading to the banning of the National Council for Khalistan. In 1984 Indian security forces also forcibly evicted militants from the Golden Temple, an action that so outraged Sikhs that it led to Prime Minister Indira Gandhi's assassination in 1984. This in turn resulted in inter-religious strife and the arrest of many Sikh activists. A number of militant Sikh organizations have become active both in India and amongst the Sikh disapora world-wide since the banning of the National Council for Khalistan. These groups include the Dashmesh and Babbar Khalsa, both of which are active in Canada and Germany. Sikh militants have been blamed for the **Air India bombing** in 1985 which killed 329 people.

National Democratic Front of Bodoland (NDFB)

The National Democratic Front of Bodoland (NDFB) is a separatist movement in Assam, north-east India. The NDFB was formed in 1986 as the Bodo Security Force and renamed in 1994. Led by Ranjan Daimary, it is dominated by Christians. Its main grievances have been the under-development of Assam and the influx of settlers from Bengal. Its objective is therefore to detach the state from India and to set up an independent state of Bodoland. The NDFB has carried out bombings, kidnappings and murders. It operates in several districts in Assam, but also uses neighbouring Bhutan as a refuge. Since 2002 the arrest of some of its leaders and Bhutan's co-operation with Indian security forces have led to the decline of the group. However, it still has an estimated 1,500 members and has continued to mount terror attacks. (*See* Map 5.)

National Liberation Army (Bolivia)

The National Liberation Army (Ejército de Liberación Nacional-Bolivia—ELN-B) was formed in Bolivia in 1966 by Che Guevara. In 1967 Guevara was captured by Bolivian security forces and executed, thereby becoming a legendary hero for leftists throughout Latin America. The ELN that he founded fought on until its eventual defeat in the early 1970s. However, a revived ELN that emerged in the early 1990s has attacked domestic targets. Little is known about the revived ELN other than that it is estimated to have fewer than 100 members.

National Liberation Army (Colombia) – *see* Ejército de Liberación Nacional (ELN)

National Liberation Front of Tripura (NLFT)

The National Liberation Front of Tripura (NLFT) is a separatist insurgent group in Tripura, north-east India. It was formed in 1989 by Dhananjoy Reang for the purpose of creating an independent Tripura state. The group suffered splits in 1993, 2000, 2001 and 2003, owing to internal power struggles. These divisions have also resulted in clashes among the various factions. The two main factions are headed by Nayanbashi Jamatiya and Biswamohan Debbarma. The upper ranks of the NLFT leadership are predominantly Christian, and the group maintains camps in Bangladesh. The NLFT has carried out a number of terrorist attacks, including the assassination of politicians and officials. Despite the surrender of hundreds of insurgents since 2000 as a result of infighting and pressure from security forces, and the beginning of peace talks in 2001, the NLFT remains an active and dangerous terrorist organization. It is estimated to have about 1,500 members. (*See* Map 5.)

Nationalist Socialist Council of Nagaland (NSCN)

The Nationalist Socialist Council of Nagaland (NSCN) is a separatist movement in the state of Nagaland, in India, that has been agitating for the establishment of a Greater Nagaland for all ethnic Nagas in the Indian states of Assam, Manipur, Arunachal Pradesh, and even in neighbouring Myanmar (Burma). Considered to be the longest-running insurgency in India, the roots of the Nagaland revolt, which erupted in the 1950s, can be traced to the forced incorporation of the Christian Naga people into the Union of India when the country became independent in 1947. In 1975 moderate Nagas opted to sign a peace agreement with the government, but in 1980 hardline elements established the NSCN to continue the armed struggle. A split in 1988 produced two groups, the NSCN-IM, led by Isaac Muivah, and the NSCN-K, led by Khaplang. The NSCN-IM is Maoist in orientation, and, with a strength of some 6,000 guerrilla fighters, has been the more successful faction,. The NSCN-K, meanwhile, has about 3,500 guerrillas. The groups resort to extortion and other criminal activities to support their operations. Bitter internecine fighting between them has hampered a peace process initiated by the government. It is alleged that the NSCN-IM has established links with the separatist **United Liberation Front of Assam (ULFA)** in neighbouring Assam state. (*See* Map 5.)

New People's Army (NPA)

The New People's Army (NPA) is the military wing of the Communist Party of the Philippines (CPP). The Maoist CPP was established in 1969 and attracted many poor plantation workers and farmers exploited and mistreated by wealthy landowners and their security forces. Under martial law, the administration of President Ferdinand Marcos initially achieved some success in combating the CPP, capturing in 1978, and subsequently exiling to the Netherlands, its leader, José Maria Sisón. However, popular dissatisfaction with deeply entrenched social and economic inequalities, political repression, corruption and landlord abuse under the Marcos regime fuelled the insurgency. By 1985 the CPP had become one of the fastest growing communist insurgencies in the world, with more than 20,000 guerrillas operating in the countryside. However, the success of the People Power revolution in overthrowing Marcos in 1986 marginalized it to a certain extent. In addition, the CPP was weakened by infighting. However, severe entrenched inequalities in the Philippines, and the failure to carry out land reform, has resulted in the continuation of the insurgency. The CPP-NPA thus remains a threat to security, and was discovered in September 1999 to be planning an urban bombing campaign and to assassinate leading government officials, including President Joseph Estrada. The strength of the NPA was estimated at 10,000 guerrillas in 2004. A breakaway faction, the **Alex Boncayao Brigade**, has conducted a campaign of urban terrorism.

New Red Brigades – *see* Red Brigades

Ogaden National Liberation Front (ONLF)

The Ogaden National Liberation Front (ONLF) is a separatist group that emerged in 1984 to fight for the independence of the Somali people in Ethiopia. The Somali people had been forcibly incorporated into Ethiopia in the late 19th century and have since suffered considerable socio-economic discrimination. In addition, the separatist movements were encouraged by the regime of Siad Barre which took power in Somalia in 1969. After the overthrow of Haile Selassie in 1974 in Ethiopia, Barre provided support to the Western Somali Liberation Front, in the hope of eventually creating a greater Somalia drawn from large parts of Ethiopian territory. However, the Front was defeated in the civil conflict in 1977–78 and subsequently declined. The deterioration of Ethiopia's economy caused widespread hardship which resulted in a splinter group emerging as the ONLF in 1984.

Based in the south east of Ethiopia, the ONLF reignited the armed struggle in 1988 through the use of low-level insurgency tactics. The ONLF, like the other major Ethiopian rebel movement, the **Oromo Liberation Front**, has resorted to urban terror attacks in recent years as a result of pressure from Ethiopia's security forces. Since the **September 11, 2001 terrorist attacks** in the USA, the Ethiopian government has alleged that close ties exist between the ONLF and the radical Islamist **al-Ittihaad al-Islami (AIAI)**. The ONLF has, however, distanced itself from the AIAI as well as disavowed any links with international terrorism. (*See* Map 4.)

Oklahoma City Bombing (1995)

In April 1995 a huge truck bomb demolished part of a federal building housing the Federal Bureau of Alcohol, Tobacco and Firearms (ATF) in Oklahoma City, USA, killing 168 people, including 19 children in a day-care centre located in the building. Until the **September 11, 2001 terrorist attacks** in the USA, this was the worst terrorist attack the USA had ever suffered. Although radical Islamist terrorists were initially suspected of having carried out the attack, subsequent investigations led to the arrest of two US citizens, Timothy McVeigh and Terry Nichols, who were supporters of extreme right-wing anti-government militia groups. McVeigh was a military veteran of the first Gulf War (in 1991), but had been attracted to the right-wing movement and impressed by the white supremacist novel, *The Turner Diaries*, in which a truck bomb is detonated at the headquarters of the Federal Bureau of Investigation (FBI). The Oklahoma bomb attack, which involved the use of ammonium nitrate, was timed to take place on the second anniversary of the raid led by the ATF on the Branch Davidian sect at Waco, Texas, in 1993, which concluded in a violent confrontation and the death of 80 sect members. Timothy McVeigh was sentenced to death and executed, while Terry Nichols was sentenced to life imprisonment. The Oklahoma bombing was a huge shock to the USA due to the fact that it was perpetrated by US citizens on civilians. It demonstrated the vulnerability of civilians in urban centres and prompted fears that a new form of mass casualty terrorism was emerging in the USA.

Omagh Bombing (1998)

The Omagh bombing, which took place on 15 August 1998 in Omagh, Northern Ireland, United Kingdom, was a massive car bomb attack carried out by the Real IRA, a splinter group of the **Irish Republican Army (IRA)**. The Real IRA emerged in 1998 to oppose the Good Friday Agreement which sought to resolve the Catholic-Protestant sectarian conflict in Northern Ireland. Twenty-nine people were killed in the attack—and some 220 injured—the highest death toll from an act of terrorism in some 30 years of civil conflict in Northern Ireland. The attack was unusually (for Northern Ireland) indiscriminate: among the dead were both Catholics and Protestants, Spanish tourists and a pregnant woman. Although the warnings of an impending attack that are customary were received, they failed to give ample time for evacuation and, moreover, proved false with regard to its location. The Omagh bombing attack provoked widespread condemnation from all sectors, including Catholics and Protestants, in Northern Ireland. The Real IRA claimed responsibility, but apologized for the high toll of deaths and injuries. In January 2002 Colm Murphy was convicted for his part in the bombing and sentenced to 14 years' imprisonment. Although a BBC documentary in 2000 named all of the prime suspects for the attack, there have been no further convictions owing to lack of evidence.

Oodua People's Congress (OPC)

The Oodua People's Congress (OPC) is a militant Yoruba separatist movement in Nigeria. Formed in 1997, it opposed the authoritarian rule of Sani Abacha, and joined with other political groups in fighting for the restoration of democracy. Extrajudicial killings in 1998 radicalized some of the OPC's supporters, who established a more militant splinter group, the Oodua Liberation Movement (OLM). The OPC's base of support lies in south-western Nigeria with the Yoruba, who dominate the key port of Lagos and number as many as 30m. The Yoruba, many of whom are Christian, have been involved in sectarian conflict with the Muslim Hausa and Fulani from northern Nigeria. The latter are represented by the Muslim-dominated Arewa People's Congress. Despite the transition to democracy in 1999, the subsequent introduction of Islamic law in Nigeria has precipitated violent ethno-religious clashes in major cities between southern Christian and northern Muslim tribal groups. The OPC has been blamed for precipitating clashes with Muslim Hausas in Lagos that have led to retaliatory attacks on Yorubas living in the north. The objective of the OPC/OLM is secession and the creation of a separate Yoruba homeland. Given the size of its support base, it is an important key to Nigeria's stability.

Orange Volunteers

The Orange Volunteers is a paramilitary organization in Northern Ireland that supports the maintenance of the *status quo* there, that is, rule by Britain. The group, purporting to represent Protestant interests, is opposed to making concessions to the **Irish Republican Army (IRA)**, and to any form of union with the Republic of Ireland. The organization was formed in the early 1970s and has engaged in violent activities directed primarily against Catholics, including bombings and assassinations. After the Good Friday Agreement had been concluded in 1998, extremists from both sides emerged to continue with campaigns of violence. These included, on the Catholic side, the Continuing IRA and the Real IRA, while on the Protestant side, extremists from the **Loyalist Volunteer Force** joined the Orange Volunteers to carry out vigilante attacks on members and supporters of the IRA.

Organisasi Papua Merdeka (OPM)

West New Guinea (Irian Jaya), previously under Dutch rule, came under the control of Indonesia in 1962. In 1965 the Organisasi Papua Merdeka (OPM—Free Papua Movement) was formed. Guerrilla warfare subsequently ensued. The OPM has continued to attract local support due to the sense of exploitation and domination by the dominant Muslim Javanese, in a resource-rich province populated by Christian Irianese. The long list of unresolved grievances includes decades of abuse by the military, dispossession from ancient tribal lands, destruction of indigenous cultures, high levels of alcoholism and a massive influx of some 1m. Indonesian settlers in recent years. The porous border between Irian Jaya and Papua New Guinea, and the presence of Melanesian sympathizers of the OPM in Papua New Guinea and the Pacific islands, have also sustained the conflict. Indeed, the current military leader of the OPM, John Nek Nek, is a founding member of an influential political movement called Melanesian Solidarity, which counts among its members prominent figures in Papua New Guinea, Vanuatu and Solomon Islands. The OPM was split by factionalism, but Nek Nek's emergence, as the leader of the 'progressive' faction in the Movement, has united the north and south factions. It has also led to a change in strategy. Nek Nek has steered the OPM away from its traditional reliance on church groups and non-governmental organizations towards greater self-reliance, better training and a focus on attacking economic targets. (*See* Map 8.)

Oromo Liberation Front (OLF)

The Oromo Liberation Front (OLF) is a separatist movement in Ethiopia that aims to create a separate state of Oromia. The Oromo people in Ethiopia have suffered many years of economic hardship and socio-economic disparities in a country dominated by the Amhara and Tigre ethnic groups. The deterioration of Ethiopia's economy provided the impetus to separatist rebellion in the early 1970s, and in 1973 the OLF was formed, initially to fight for greater autonomy. The overthrow of the regime of Haile Selassie in 1974 and its replacement by a Marxist system resulted in the formation of a national front of opposition groups, the Ethiopian People's Revolutionary Democratic Front (EPRDF), which the OLF also joined. The EPRDF overthrew the Mengistu regime in Ethiopia in 1991, but the OLF soon defected amid widespread famine and tensions with the dominant force in the EPRDF, the Tigrayan People's Liberation Front led by Meles Zenawi. Civil war soon resumed, in which the OLF resorted to urban terror tactics in the face of superior government forces. Since the **September 11, 2001 terrorist attacks** in the USA, the Ethiopian government has claimed that close ties exist between the OLF and the other major separatist group, the **Ogaden National Liberation Front** on the one hand, and the radical Islamist **al-Ittihaad al-Islami (AIAI)** on the other. The OLF has, however, distanced itself from the AIAI as well as disavowed any links with international terrorism. (*See* Map 8.)

Osama bin Laden – *see* al-Qa'ida

PKK – *see* Kurdistan Worker's Party

Palestine Liberation Front (PLF)

The Palestine Liberation Front (PLF) is a breakaway faction of the **Popular Front for the Liberation of Palestine–General Command (PFLP-GC)**. The PFLP-GC itself was established by Ahmed Jibril after a major split occurred in the **Popular Front for the Liberation of Palestine (PFLP)** in 1968. The PFLP-GC has always maintained an uncompromising stance with regard to Israel, and opposed the Oslo peace accords of 1993. Jibril's pro-Syrian sympathies divided the group during its involvement in the Lebanese civil war in the 1970s. This led to the establishment of the PLF in 1977, under Jibril's long-time lieutenant, 'Abu Abbas'. Conflict between the two groups then erupted, resulting in hundreds of deaths. The PLF itself split into three factions in 1982, of which that led by Abbas is the largest. The PLF carried out a number of terror attacks, the best known of which is the *Achille Lauro* **hijack** in 1985. This led, however, to the eviction from Tunisia of the Abbas faction, which was forced to relocate to Iraq under the protection of Saddam Hussain. The PLF's Abbas faction allied itself with Yasser Arafat, joined the **Palestine Liberation Organization** and also accepted the Oslo peace accords. Abbas was arrested in 2003 in Iraq after US-led forces occupied the country, as he was still wanted in connection with the murder of a US citizen in the *Achille Lauro* hijack. He died in controversial circumstances in US custody in March 2004. The PLF has several hundred members, based mostly in Lebanon and Tunisia, but has little support within the Palestinian territories.

Palestine Liberation Organization (PLO)

The Palestine Liberation Organization (PLO) is an umbrella organization of various Palestinian groups which aim to create an independent state of Palestine. Established in 1964, it was first headquartered in Cairo, Egypt. In 1968 Yasser Arafat became its leader. His **al-Fatah** group soon became dominant within the PLO, although its very fractiousness made it difficult for him to exert full control. The PLO carried out a number of terrorist attacks against Israel, but suffered major set-backs when Jordan expelled it in 1970, and when Israeli forces forced its evacuation from southern Lebanon in 1982. Despite its use of violence, the UN formally recognized the PLO as the representative of the Palestinian people as early as 1974. The PLO's acceptance of the Oslo peace accords in 1993 led to its transformation from erstwhile terrorist/guerrilla movement into governing authority, in the form of the Palestinian Authority (PA). The PLO's renunciation of terrorism and its recognition of the right of Israel to exist led to serious internal dissension. Some al-Fatah members joined the **al-Aqsa Martyrs' Brigades**,

Hamas or **Palestinian Islamic Jihad** to carry out suicide terrorist attacks on Israel. Within the PLO, groups such as the **Popular Front for the Liberation of Palestine (PFLP)** and the **Popular Front for the Liberation of Palestine-General Command (PFLP-GC)** have opposed the Oslo peace accords and continued to carry out terrorist attacks. Arafat died in 2004, and was succeeded by Mahmud Abbas. (*See* Map 7.)

Palestinian Islamic Jihad (PIJ)

Palestianian Islamic Jihad (PIJ—'Harakat al-Jihad al-Islami al-Filastini') is a radical Palestinian Islamist organization dedicated to pan-Islamic ideology as well as the destruction of the State of Israel. A violent offshoot of the **Muslim Brotherhood**, it was founded by Palestinian students in Egypt in the late 1970s and was led, until his assassination in 1995 in Malta, by the charismatic Fathi Shkaki. Shkaki and his colleagues were inspired by the Iranian Revolution in 1979 and admired Ayatollah Khomeini for his achievements, even though this was a Shi'ite revolution. The leadership of the PIJ was exiled to Lebanon after the first Palestinian uprising, or *intifada*, in 1987, where it built links with Syria, Iran and with the Iranian-backed **Hezbollah**. The group has carried out terrorist attacks against Israeli civilian and military targets in the Israeli-occupied territories, particularly in the Gaza Strip. It was responsible for a suicide bomb attack that killed 13 people in March 1996 in Tel-Aviv. Since Shkaki's death, allegedly at the hands of the Israeli intelligence service, the group has lost ground to **Hamas**. It currently has less than 1,000 members. (*See* Map 7.)

Patriotic Union of Kurdistan (PUK)

The Patriotic Union of Kurdistan (PUK) was founded in 1975 to represent the aspirations of the Kurdish minority in northern Iraq for an autonomous Kurdish homeland. Led by Jalal Talabani, it opposed the Iraqi regime of Saddam Hussain for many years, and also clashed with the other major Kurdish opposition group, the **Kurdish Democratic Party (KDP)**. The PUK officially subscribes to social democracy and helped to co-ordinate the unsuccessful uprising against Saddam Hussain's regime after the first Gulf War in 1991. Both the PUK and the KDP controlled the no-fly zone that was introduced by the USA and its allies after the end of the first Gulf War. The PUK and the KDP then fought each other in a bitter war for control of Iraqi Kurdistan, with the PUK supported by Iran, and the KDP receiving assistance from Saddam Hussain's regime. In 1998 both sides were brought together by the USA under an agreement signed in Washington, DC. Since the US-led military intervention in and occupation of Iraq in 2003, senior PUK figures, including Talabani, have served on the Iraqi Governing Council. The PUK joined forces with its rival, the KDP, as well as smaller Kurdish parties, to form an umbrella organization, the Democratic Patriotic Alliance of Kurdistan, to contest the elections that were held in Iraq in 2005. The PUK today claims to have 150,000 members, drawn from all sectors of Kurdish society, in particular the urban intelligentsia. (*See* Map 6.)

Pattani Mujahideen Movement

The Pattani Mujahideen Movement ('Gerakan Mujahideen Islam Pattani'—GMIP) is a small Muslim separatist group in southern Thailand founded by ex-Afghan *mujahidin* in 1995, adding to the confused fragmentation of Muslim rebel groups there. Its operational chief is Nasae Saning, who formerly resided in Malaysia before fleeing that country to avoid arrest. Another leader, Wae Ka Rae, was trained in Afghanistan, and is believed to maintain ties with **al-Qa'ida**. Little else is known about this group, except that it is believed to share the pan-Islamic radical ideology of al-Qa'ida and maintained links with the **Kampulan Mujahidin Malaysia**.

Pattani United Liberation Organization (PULO)

The Pattani United Liberation Organization (PULO) is a major Muslim separatist movement in southern Thailand. Formed in 1968 to oppose the assimilation policies of Thailand's government at that time, it is led by intellectuals educated in the Middle East and Pakistan. It has been involved in a number of violent attacks, including, in 1993, a bombing campaign that targeted Buddhist temples, schools, railway trains and army patrols. In 1998 it launched another wave of bomb attacks. The government's more enlightened approach to counter-insurgency and greater sensitivity to Muslims after 1975 resulted, however, in a gradual decline in the strength of PULO, from a peak of 1,000 fighters in the 1970s to fewer than 100 by the late 1990s. The Pattani separatists also became increasingly fragmented. PULO itself split in 1995, New PULO emerging from the division. Then, in late 2001, a campaign of co-ordinated violence began, signalling a revival of the insurgency. It is believed that an umbrella organization, Bersatu, has been formed to reconcile PULO and New PULO. There is, as yet, no credible evidence to link these groups with **al-Qa'ida** or its radical pan-Islamic agenda, and neither so far has targeted Westerners in its attacks. However, the tough counter-terrorism policy of the government of Thaksin Shinawatra could transform these separatist movements. The nature of this policy was epitomized by the killing of 108 Muslim rebels by government forces in a single day, 28 April 2004, including a number who had sought refuge in an historic mosque, and by the death of 84 Muslim demonstrators at the hands of the security forces in October 2004. Apart from PULO, other active rebel groups include the **Barisan Revolusi Nasional**, its splinter group, Barisan Nasional Pembebasan Patani (BNPP), and the radical Gerakan Mujahideen Islam Pattani (GMIP—**Pattani Mujahideen Movement**).

People Against Gangsterism and Drugs (PAGAD)

People Against Gangsterism and Drugs (PAGAD) is a violent Muslim vigilante organization in South Africa. Founded in 1996 in Cape Town, it has been responsible for violent attacks on drug dealers and organized criminals, in actions initially much applauded by local communities and even the government owing to the failure of the local police to deal with their activities. PAGAD has, however, also begun to target anti-PAGAD clerics, academics who have criticized it and officials who have investigated its activities. It has also become anti-Western and anti-government in its orientation, posing a potentially serious security threat, as it has targeted tourist attractions, gay nightclubs, synagogues and moderate Muslims. Between 1996 and 2000 it was responsible for hundreds of bomb attacks. PAGAD is led by Abdus Salaam Ebrahim, is organized into small cells and is believed to have links with radical Islamist groups elsewhere. Designated as a terrorist organization, the group remains active although it has in recent years been weakened by security and judicial action. PAGAD is believed to have close connections with another radical group, **Muslims Against Global Oppression**, and may in fact share a common identity.

People's Fighters Group

The People's Fighters Group (Grupos de Combatientes Populares—GCP) is an opposition group in Ecuador. It is Marxist in orientation, having originally been formed as the military wing of the Communist Party in Ecuador. The group has professed admiration for Che Guevara and espouses anti-imperialist and anti-capitalist views. It opposed the government of Ecuador and has been critical of various aspects of government policies. The group has concentrated on economic disruption, with the aim of undermining the government. It has also carried out pamphlet bomb attacks in various locations, including in Cuenca, on the occasion of a 'Miss Universe' contest in May 2004. Pamphlet bombs were also detonated in June 2004 in three cities in protest at the meeting of the Organization of American States in Quito, Ecuador, to discuss a regional free-trade agreement. The GCP claimed that this was an 'expansion of imperialism'.

People's War Group (PWG)

The People's War Group (PWG) is a communist insurgent group in Andhra Pradesh state in India. Designated by the USA as a terrorist organization, the PWG is Maoist in orientation and has used guerrilla tactics in its attempts to overthrow the current political and economic system and replace it with a communist one. The Group was founded in 1980, and has found support not only among peasants, but also among trade unions and student groups. The PWG is believed to have also established close ties with the **Liberation Tigers of Tamil Eelam (LTTE)** as well as with the **Communist Party of Nepal**. The links with the latter have given rise to concern, as both groups allegedly aim to extend the communist insurgency in the Indian sub-continent through closer co-operation. The PWG has targeted government forces and officials, and anyone else it classifies as a class enemy. It has disrupted elections through violence and intimidation, as well as targeted transport infrastructure. More than 6,000 people have died since the insurgency began in 1980. Negotiations between the government and the PWG have made no progress as yet.

Polisario Front

The Polisario Front (Frente Popular para la Liberación de Saguia el-Hamra y Río de Oro—Frente Polisario) is a Saharawi separatist movement in southern Morocco. The Front operates in the area that was formerly the Spanish colony of Western Sahara, jurisdiction over which was transferred to Morocco and Mauritania in 1975 when Morocco became independent. The Front was established in 1973, initially to combat Spanish colonialism. After 1975 it directed its struggle against Morocco and Mauritania from its bases in neighbouring Algeria, and with the support of the governments of Algeria and Libya. The Front established a Saharawi Arab Democratic Republic in exile, now recognized by some 70 countries as well as the African Union. Within Morocco Polisario waged a guerrilla war, targeting government installations and economic targets. However, the subsequent loss of support by its state sponsors resulted in a UN-brokered peace treaty between the Front and Morocco in 1991. However, the impasse over the role and future of Moroccan settlers in Western Sahara has prevented a referendum on the territory's future from being held, although, surprisingly, the cease-fire has lasted for more than a decade. The Front remains in control of refugee camps along the Algerian border and in parts of Western Sahara. The conflict is thus currently dormant, but, as the underlying issues remain unresolved, it could potentially re-emerge.

Popular Front for the Liberation of Palestine (PFLP)

The Popular Front for the Liberation of Palestine (PFLP) is a militant Palestinian organization that aims to establish a democratic socialist state in Palestine. Founded in 1967 by George Habash, it is Marxist-Leninist in orientation. The PFLP gained international notoriety in 1977 when it hijacked a Lufthansa civilian jetliner to Mogadishu, Somalia, where the hijackers demanded the release of imprisoned members of the extreme left-wing **Red Army Faction** in Germany, among other demands. The hostage crisis ended when German commandos from the GSG9 counter-terrorism unit stormed the aircraft and killed three of the four hijackers. The PFLP was subsequently affected by internal dissension, which led to the formation of a major splinter group, the **Popular Front for the Liberation of Palestine–General Command**. The PFLP recovered and launched a number of international terrorist attacks, in particular airline hijackings in joint operations with other left-wing terrorist groups, such as the **Japanese Red Army**, to publicize the Palestinian cause. The PFLP was an integral part of the **Palestine Liberation Organization (PLO)** and was expelled from Jordan amid much violence in 1970, in the events now known as Black September. However, the PFLP opposed the Oslo peace accords in 1993 and joined the rejectionist front of extremist groups based in Damascus, Syria. Habash resigned in 2000 and was replaced by Abu Ali Mustafa, a firm advocate of terrorist operations against civilian and military targets in Israel. He was assassinated by Israel in 2001 in a missile strike, and was succeeded by Ahmed Sadat. The PFLP has been largely marginalized by more overtly religious groups, such as **Hamas** and **Palestinian Islamic Jihad**.

Popular Front for the Liberation of Palestine–General Command (PFLP-GC)

The Popular Front for the Liberation of Palestine–General Command (PFLP-GC) was established by Ahmed Jibril after a major split occurred in the **Popular Front for the Liberation of Palestine (PFLP)** in 1968. The PFLP-GC proved to be extremist in its orientation, rejecting all negotiation with the State of Israel, which it sought to destroy. It is a leading member of the rejectionist front that opposes the Oslo peace accords of 1993, and therefore also opposes the **Palestine Liberation Organization**. With the support of Syria, the group has launched many terrorist attacks on Israel since the 1970s. The pro-Syrian orientation, however, divided the group during its involvement in the Lebanese civil war in the 1970s, with a number of activists defecting with Ahmed Jibril's long-time deputy, 'Abu Abbas', to establish the **Palestine Liberation Front** in 1977. The two groups then waged a vicious internecine war, resulting in hundreds of deaths. Since the late 1980s Syria has gradually withdrawn its support from the PFLP-GC. Like the PFLP, the PFLP-GC has been overtaken by more overtly religious groups, such as **Hamas** and **Palestinian Islamic Jihad**.

Popular Resistance

Popular Resistance (Laiki Antistasi) is an extreme left-wing Greek group that has carried out several bomb attacks since June 2002. It is anti-government and anti-capitalist in orientation. In October 2002 it carried out a grenade attack in protest at the death of 82 passengers in a ferry accident at Paros, which was partly the result of lax safety regulations. The group blamed the Greek government and capitalism for the tragedy. Its choice of targets, particularly tax offices, reflects its anger at the government and what it regards as its collusion with capitalism in exploiting the people. The shadowy group, which has an estimated membership of less than 100, is believed to be well organized and capable of mounting more attacks.

Popular Revolutionary Army (Ejército Popular Revolucionario—EPR)

The Popular Revolutionary Army (Ejército Popular Revolucionario—EPR) is an anti-government terrorist organization in Mexico. An amalgamation of some 14 left-wing terrorist and guerrilla groups, it first emerged in 1996 in response to the death of 18 villagers in Coyuca de Benítez at the hands of the police. Its objective is the overthrow of the government of Mexico and its replacement by a socialist state. The group has carried out a number of attacks since 1996, targeting the security forces. The EPR has financed itself through criminal activities such as bank robberies, kidnappings and, reportedly, the illegal drugs trade. Run as a tight, secretive organization, it maintains cells in a number of states in Mexico. The reported dogmatism and élitism of the EPR has led several groups, notably the **Revolutionary Armed Forces of the People (FARP)**, to split from it.

Posse Comitatus

The Posse Comitatus is a loose movement of extreme right-wing activists in the USA that adhere to a particular pseudo-religious ideology based on Christian Identity. The movement is virulently anti-Semitic and xenophobic, and regards the federal US government in Washington, DC, and all national institutions as illegal, as a violation of citizens' rights and as under Jewish control. The movement holds racist beliefs, holding those of Northern European stock to be the chosen people of the Bible, and all others, such as blacks, Jews and other non-whites, as inferior or even sub-human. The movement believes in vigilantism, and sees the (US) county as the highest legitimate authority, not the state or federal government. Within the county, the sheriff, as the highest legitimate authority; the sheriff can form a 'posse' of citizens to enforce the law, and, in turn, citizens can depose him. Members of the movement have been very hostile towards federal authority, and refuse, for instance, to pay taxes. Members have been involved in numerous criminal activities, such as tax evasion, murder, death threats, possession of weapons and counterfeiting. The movement, which had as many as 15,000 members in the 1970s, subsequently began to decline dramatically, especially after the death of posse leader Gordon Kahl in a shoot-out with police in 1983.

Rahanawein Resistance Army (RRA)

The Rahanawein Resistance Army (RRA) is a clan-based militia group in southern Somalia. Following the ouster of the Siad Barre regime in 1991, Somali state institutions collapsed and the country suffered from famine and violent clashes between clans that were led by various regional warlords. The north has declared the independent state of Somaliland under the **Somali National Movement**, which, however, has become heavily factionalized and fallen into violent clan-based civil war. In central Somalia the **United Somali Congress** has faced internal violence that resulted in the killing of Gen. Mohammed Aideed in 1996. The withdrawal of UN peace-keepers left his son, Hussein Aideed, in control of central Somalia. Hussein wished to extend control over the south, but has been opposed by the RRA, another clan-based group that is supported by Ethiopia. The RRA has taken control of the Bay and Bakol regions in southern Somalia, but since 2000 has itself split into three warring factions, led, respectively, by Hassan Mohamed Nur Hatigudud and his two former allies, Sheikh Aden Mohamed Odobe and Mohamed Ibrahim Habsade.

Red Army Faction (RAF)

The Red Army Faction (Rote Armee Fraktion—RAF), also known in the 1970s as the Baader-Meinhof Group after its two founders, is a violent left-wing terrorist organization in Germany. Founded in 1970, members of the group carried out bank robberies and attacked US personnel and installations in West Germany, as well as West German government targets. In 1972 both of its founders, Andreas Baader and Ulrike Meinhof, were arrested. In 1975 an attack by members of the group on the West German Embassy in Sweden resulted in the death of two German officials and two members of the group. In 1976 Meinhof committed suicide and Baader and other RAF leaders were sentenced to life imprisonment. In 1977 the **Popular Front for the Liberation of Palestine** hijacked a Lufthansa civilian jetliner to Mogadishu, Somalia, where, among other things, the hijackers demanded the release of imprisoned members of the RAF. The hostage crisis was ended when German commandos from the GSG9 counter-terrorism unit stormed the aircraft and killed three of the four hijackers. This event was followed by the suicide in prison of Baader and other RAF members. The RAF continued its operations under new leadership, targeting key German officials and businessmen for kidnap or assassination, and carrying out bomb attacks on US and NATO personnel and installations. However, by the late 1990s such activities seemed meaningless as the group's former sanctuary in East Germany had disappeared after reunification, and the group was no nearer to achieving communism in Germany. In 1998 the RAF issued a communiqué in which it declared an end to its armed struggle.

Red Brigades

The Red Brigades (Brigate Rosse) was founded by Renato Curcio in Italy in 1969. A product of left-wing student protest movements, it became the leading communist terrorist organization in Italy in the 1970s and 1980s. The Red Brigades carried out assassinations of members of the state establishment—businesspeople, trade unionists, politicians and government officials—whom they regarded as class enemies. The Red Brigades were responsible for the kidnapping of US Army Brig.-Gen. James Dozier, the senior US official at NATO's headquarters in Verona, Italy, in 1981. They were also responsible for the **Aldo Moro murder** in 1978. Aldo Moro was a leader of the Christian Democrats political party in Italy, had twice been Italy's Prime Minister, and was responsible for arranging an historic compromise that brought the Italian Communist Party into the government. The murder of the popular Moro led to concerted police action against the group amid widespread public anger and condemnation. Facing arrests and decline, in 1984 the group split into two factions, the Communist Combatant Party and the Union of Combatant Communists. Subsequent terror attacks included the murder of the US chief of the Sinai Multinational Force and Observer Group in 1984, that of Italian Gen. Licio Giorgieri in 1987 and that of the Italian senator Roberto Ruffilli in 1988. Thereafter, mass arrests appeared to have halted the group's activities. However, the remaining members of the Communist Combatant Party have regrouped and are today known as the New Red Brigades. They have resumed assassinations, beginning with the murder in 1999 of a senior adviser of the then Prime Minister. In 2002 Marco Biagi, a professor of economics who advised President Silvio Berlusconi, was killed. In 2003 nine suspected members of the New Red Brigades were arrested. The New Red Brigades' strength is estimated at about 50.

Revolutionary Armed Forces of the People (Fuerzas Armadas Revolucionarias del Pueblo—FARP)

The Revolutionary Armed Forces of the People (FARP—Fuerzas Armadas Revolucionarias del Pueblo) is a splinter group of the larger terrorist organization, the **Popular Revolutionary Army (Ejército Popular Revolucionario—EPR)** in Mexico. FARP has an agenda that is anti-globalization and anti-USA, and first announced its presence in a pipe bomb attack outside a government building in Pueblo, Mexico, in early 2000. FARP subsequently carried out a number of attacks on US companies or affiliated enterprises, including a McDonald's restaurant, a General Motors dealership and the Mexican bank, Banamex, reportedly in protest at its merger with the US Citigroup. So far nobody has been killed in any of the group's attacks. FARP is reportedly funded through criminal activities, such as kidnapping and extortion

Revolutionary Armed Forces of Colombia (Fuerzas Armadas Revolucionarias de Colombia—FARC)

The Revolutionary Armed Forces of Colombia (Fuerzas Armadas Revolucionarias de Colombia—FARC) is the largest left-wing insurgent group in Colombia—and all Latin America. It originated in 1949 as a small militia led by Manuel Marulanda Vélez, who established a base area in Marquetalia which was subsequently overrun by government forces. He subsequently established links with the Colombian Communist Party and formally founded the FARC in 1966. The FARC declared war on the government of Colombia, with the aim of establishing a communist state. From an ill-equipped force of several hundred fighters, FARC has grown into a disciplined and well-armed guerrilla force of some 18,000 combatants, controlling large swathes of the Colombian countryside and maintaining a presence in an estimated 60% of Colombia's municipalities. It has been able to attract to its cause large numbers of peasants, the poor and other dispossessed in an unequal society. The FARC has engaged the Colombian army, and has also attacked governmental and military installations. It derives substantial profit from kidnapping-for-ransom activities, as well as the taxation of, and participation in, Colombia's lucrative drugs trade. It has taken hostage US nationals and Colombian politicians and governors, including a presidential candidate. It attempted to participate in the political process in 1984–87 as the Patriotic Union, but thousands of its politicians and officials were killed by right-wing paramilitary groups and the military. Attempts at political negotiations in the late 1990s also foundered due to the opposition of right-wing groups. Indeed, the Uribe government that took power in Colombia in 2002 has pledged to wipe out the FARC. Owing to the FARC's involvement in the drugs trade, the US government has taken an active interest in its insurgency, providing much-needed financial and material aid to the Colombian armed forces to support their campaign against the FARC. The FARC has also fought the right-wing paramilitary organization, **Autodefensas Unidas de Colombia (AUC)**. FARC continues to be led by the veteran Manuel Marulanda Vélez.

Revolutionary Front for Communism (Fronte Rivoluzionario del Comunismo—FRC)

The Revolutionary Front for Communism (Fronte Rivoluzionario del Comunismo—FRC) is a left-wing terrorist group in Italy. It is a 'new' organization in the sense that it has taken up the mantle of revolution from the **Red Brigades** which were active in the 1970s and 1980s. Like the Red Brigades, the group is anti-US, anti-capitalist, opposes globalization and uses violence. It has carried out bomb attacks on big businesses (such as the Italian car-maker Fiat), diplomatic missions, government installations and labour union offices, as well as on government officials. Some of the attacks have been made in protest at the death of activist Carlo Giuliani, who was shot and killed by police during an anti-globalization riot at the G8 summit in Genoa, Italy, in 2001. Very little, however, is known about this group.

Revolutionary Nuclei

The Revolutionary Nuclei is a left-wing terrorist group in Greece that espouses strong anti-US, anti-NATO and anti-capitalist views. Believed to consist of former members of the **Revolutionary People's Struggle**, this group has attacked US companies and government installations and vehicles in a series of bomb and arson attacks, most of which took place in 1999–2000. Most of these attacks, like those of similar left-wing groups in Greece, have not targeted civilians, although one, on the Intercontinental Hotel, did kill a Greek woman The group is believed to be small, with less than 100 members. It remains active despite the lack of action in recent times as it has not formally disbanded.

Revolutionary People's Struggle

The Revolutionary People's Struggle (Epanastatikos Laikos Agonas—ELA) is a Greek left-wing group that emerged in the late 1970s in opposition to the military regime then in control of Greece. The ELA continued to oppose the Greek government even when democracy became established. It is strongly anti-US and has demanded the removal of US military bases in Greece. The ELA has carried out many bomb attacks on economic, government and US targets since the mid-1970s. However, it is a small group of less than 100 and has never sought to kill large numbers of people. The ELA appeared to have become largely inactive by the late 1990s, but its members have established smaller violent cells and groups that have continued to challenge the government.

Revolutionary Proletarian Initiative Nuclei

The Revolutionary Proletarian Initiative Nuclei is a small but violent communist terrorist group in Italy. It is an offshoot of the now-defunct **Red Brigades**, whose logo and Marxist-Leninist rhetoric it employs. This obscure group of less than 20 people is believed to have established ties with the **New Red Brigades** and is considered dangerous because of its espousal of violence. So far, however, its attacks—such as that in April 2001 on the Institute of International Affairs in Rome, Italy—have focused on property.

Revolutionary Organization 17 November

The Revolutionary Organization 17 November was a radical Greek left-wing terrorist organization that emerged after the brutal police suppression of students demonstrating against the then military junta in Greece at Athens Polytechnic Institute on 17 November 1973. It demanded the withdrawal of US bases from Greece, Greece's withdrawal from both the European Union and NATO, and the withdrawal of Turkish forces from Cyprus. It was virulently anti-government, anti-US and anti-capitalist, as well as ultra-nationalist. Although the strength of the group was believed to be less than 30, it was able to carry out 23 assassinations—targeting US and Greek officials and businessmen, including the station chief of the US Central Intelligence Agency in Athens in 1975 and the British defence attaché in 2000—until it was uncovered in 2002. The *modus operandi* was motorcycle drive-by shootings, car bombings and rocket attacks. The length of time it took the Greek government to track down the group led to charges of incompetence and allegations of the security services' collusion with it. The Greek government's efforts to eradicate this group became more urgent as the 2004 Athens Olympic Games approached. In 2002 the group was uncovered by chance. Savas Xiros, a painter of religious icons, was badly wounded when a bomb he was carrying at the Greek port of Piraeus exploded. Two of his brothers were subsequently arrested, as was Alexandros Giotopoulos, a former university professor of economics, who was the group's chief ideologue, and Dimitris

Koufodinas, the group's director of operations. In all, 19 of its members were tried in 2003, and 15 of the defendants were convicted. Both Giotopoulous and Koufodinas were sentenced to life imprisonment. Some uncertainty remains as to whether the group has become inactive. In September 2003 responsibility for a bomb attack carried out on the Greek courthouse where the group's members had been tried was claimed by a hitherto unknown group calling itself **Revolutionary Struggle**. This group subsequently carried out a bombing campaign against government targets, and also threatened foreigners intending to travel to Greece for the 2004 Olympic Games. There has been speculation that this new group consists of 17 November members and sympathizers who escaped arrest.

Revolutionary Struggle

Revolutionary Struggle is a new left-wing terrorist group in Greece that began a series of bomb attacks from September 2003. There has been speculation that this new group consists of members of **Revolutionary Organization 17 November** members and sympathizers who escaped arrest in 2002. It threatened foreigners intending to travel to Greece for the 2004 Olympic Games, but the Games none the less concluded without incident. Very little is known of Revolutionary Struggle, but it appears similar to the many other anti-US, anti-capitalist left-wing terrorist groups that have characterized Greek politics in contemporary times.

Revolutionary United Front (RUF)

The Revolutionary United Front (RUF) is a rebel group in Sierra Leone. The background to the civil conflict there lies in the political instability and economic collapse that occurred in the early 1990s, the result of years of mismanagement under the governments of Siaka Stevens and Saidu Mornoh. The RUF was founded in the 1980s with the objective of overthrowing the government, re-establishing multi-party democracy and ending corruption. However, an unstated objective has been the control of lucrative diamond-mining concessions. The group received the active support of President Charles Taylor of neighbouring Liberia, and began its violent insurrection in 1991. After a long and tortuous process, free democratic elections were finally held in 1996, in which Tejan Kabbah was victorious. The response, however, was a military coup and the replacement of the Kabbah Government by a military junta. The junta then invited the RUF to join the government. In 1998, following the intervention of the Economic Community of West African States' Monitoring Group, the junta was overthrown and the Kabbah government restored. This led to heavy fighting, with the RUF taking the capital, Freetown, in 1999 amidst much violence that resulted in the deaths of over 5,000 people. The arrival of UN peace-keepers after a peace agreement was signed did not stop the fighting, the scale of which has so far displaced half of the population, and caused some 500,000 to flee to neighbouring countries as refugees. The UN contingent itself came under attack and some 500

UN soldiers were briefly held hostage in 2000. The RUF's fortunes, however, began to wane after its leader, Foday Sankoh, was imprisoned in 2001. Despite having its numbers reduced to several hundred compared to the thousands at its peak, the RUF remains a serious threat to security in Sierra Leone due to its access to arms from Liberia and other countries.

Riyadus-Salikhin Reconnaissance and Sabotage Battalion of Shahids

The Riyadus-Salikhin Reconnaissance and Sabotage Battalion of Shahids (Martyrs) is a radical Chechen Islamist group led by Shamil Basayev, an ex-Afghan *mujahidin* fighter. The aim of the group is the secession of Chechnya from Russia and the establishment of a pan-Islamic Muslim state covering Chechnya as well as other neighbouring Muslim areas, such as Dagestan. In 1991, after the collapse of the USSR, Chechnya declared its independence, provoking thereby a Russian invasion. In 1994–96 Aslan Maskhadov and Dzhokar Dudayev waged a war against Russia that eventually spread to nearby Ingushetia, Dagestan and north Ossetia. Mashkadov became President of Chechnya in 1997, one year after signing a peace agreement with Russia. In 1999, however, Shamil Basayev and foreign-born *mujahidin* fighters, such as Ibn al-Khattab, invaded neighbouring Muslim Dagestan. This, together with a series of attacks that were attributed to Dagestan militants on apartments in Russia, in which 293 people were killed, led Russia to wage a second war on Chechnya. In October 2002 Basayev claimed responsibility for the **Moscow theatre siege**, in which 128 theatre-goers were killed, although other Chechen groups also contributed to the operation, as it was led by Movsar Barayev, the leader of the **Special Purpose Islamic Regiment**. Basayev then resigned from Maskhadov's group, taking with him his Battalion of Shahids. The split was inevitable, given Maskhadov's more nationalist and moderate approach. In contrast, Basayev's group embraces a radical, pan-Islamic ideology and has strong links with **al-Qa'ida**. Indeed, many Chechens fought in Afghanistan in the 1980s, including Basayev himself, who forged a close relationship with al-Qa'ida. Basayev's group has since carried out suicide attacks, such as that in December 2002 which destroyed the headquarters of the Russian-installed Chechen government in Grozny and killed 72 people. In 2004 the group claimed responsibility for a number of attacks, such as the assassination of the Russian-appointed Chechen President, Akhmad Kadyrov, the **Beslan school siege**, a Moscow subway bombing in which 10 people died, and the destruction of two civilian airliners in which 89 people were killed.

Rohingya Solidarity Organization (RSO)

The Rohingyas are a minority group in the state of Arakan in Myanmar (formerly Burma). They are distinguished by their adherence to Islam, in contrast to the overwhelming majority of Burmans who are Buddhist. The Rohingyas have never regarded themselves to be part of the Burmese state, and have been in rebellion since Burma gained independence from Britain in 1948. The Rohingyas, who numbered about 1.3m. in 1998, have been subject to discrimination, abuse and violence that led many of them to flee to Bangladesh in 1978 and, again, in 1991. In response to political marginalization, economic under-development and perceived religious discrimination, the Rohingyas have formed several separatist rebel organizations, including the Rohingya Solidarity Organization (RSO). The RSO was founded in the early 1980s by Muhammad Yunus, a medical doctor, having split from the more moderate Rohingya Patriotic Front. The RSO has developed links with like-minded radical Muslim organizations, such as the **Harakat ul-Jihad-e-Islami** in Bangladesh, the **Hizb-i-Islami** led by Gulbuddin Hekmatyar in Afghanistan, the **Hizb ul-Mujahideen** in Kashmir, and, reportedly, with **al-Qa'ida**. The RSO aims to establish an independent state in Arakan and has been able to draw support from battle-hardened ex-*mujahidin* who fought against Soviet forces in Afghanistan in the 1980s, as well as from the many refugees that frequent offensives by the Myanmar armed forces have created. (*See* Map 1.)

Russian National Unity

The Russian National Unity (RNE—Russkow Natsionalnoe) is an ultra-nationalist paramilitary organization that has also participated in the political process in Russia. It was founded in 1990 and led by Aleksandr Barkashov. The RNE gained a high public profile through its participation in the siege of the Russian parliament in 1993. It was able to profit from the frustrations felt by many ordinary Russians at the political instability and economic collapse that accompanied the disintegration of the USSR, emerging as a champion of the poor and of those in the provinces *vis-à-vis* the Moscow-based élites. Economic hardship provided a perfect rationale for an outburst of anti-Semitism, in which Jews were blamed for the problems that confronted Russia. The RNE strongly advocated the deportation of Jews and Caucasus minorities, and espoused a xenophobic ultra-nationalism based on military discipline and the defence of the motherland, thus inviting strong comparisons with fascism and Nazism. RNE members train with weapons and explosives, which the organization has stockpiled. RNE chapters have spread throughout the former USSR, especially where there are sizeable Russian communities. Within Russia it has carried out attacks on Jews and synagogues and desecrations of Jewish cemeteries, has disseminated anti-Semitic literature and been responsible for attacks on foreigners. Growing unease at its militancy resulted in Barkashov's expulsion from Russia in 2000. The RNE is also effectively banned from the capital, Moscow. While it had as many as 100,000 members at its peak in the late 1990s, membership of and public support for the RNE has declined as the political and economic situation in Russia has become more stable under the Putin government. None the less, the RNE retains a following in the provinces.

Salafist Group for Call and Combat (GSPC—Groupe salafiste pour la prédication et le combat—GSPC)

The Salafist Group for Call and Combat (Groupe salafiste pour la prédication et le combat—GSPC) is a radical Islamist organization in Algeria. The GSPC is an offshoot of the extremist **Armed Islamic Group (GIA—Groupe islamique armé)**, which itself split from the fundamentalist **Islamic Salvation Front (FIS—Front islamique du salut)**. Both the GIA and the FIS waged a bitter civil war against the Algerian government after it had annulled the result of elections held in 1992, which would have brought the FIS to power. The GSPC broke away from the GIA in 1996 and is led by an ex-Afghan *mujahidin* fighter, Mokhtar Belmokhtar. As its name implies, it subscribes to puritanical *Salafist* ideology. Its objective is the establishment of an Islamic state ruled strictly by the *Shari'a*, or Islamic law. The GSPC has attempted to distance itself from the unrestrained terror tactics of the GIA, which has included attacks on the civilian populace at large, and has instead directed its attacks exclusively against military and government personnel. Government offensives and the general alienation of the public on account of the GIA's indiscriminate tactics have opened the way for the GSPC's ascendancy within the radical Islamist opposition to the secular, military-dominated government of Algeria. The GSPC has established close links with **al-Qa'ida**, and some reports have attributed its establishment to efforts by Osama bin Laden to distance the radical cause from the excesses of the GIA. The operations of the GSPC extend beyond Algeria, as it has links with European Islamists and some support among Algerian migrants in France. The GSPC has been blamed for several abortive attacks in Europe, but the French authorities have reduced its capacity to act there. In 2003 the GSPC came into international prominence after it kidnapped 32 Europeans and held them hostage in the Sahara desert. The hostages were released after the reported payment of a ransom by the German government.

Saudi Bombings (2003)

On 12 May 2003, 35 people were killed in four suicide bombings in Riyadh, Saudi Arabia, including the 12 attackers themselves. The dead consisted of Saudi Arabian citizens together with foreigners from eight countries, including nine US citizens. Three of the attacks were on housing complexes where foreigners, particularly European and US citizens, lived. More than 600 people were arrested in the aftermath of the attacks, and scores of militants were committed to stand trial. The attacks were followed by another at an oil installation in May 2004, in which 22 people, mainly foreigners, were killed. There has also been a series of violent confrontations between security forces and militants that have almost always resulted in deaths. The terrorist actions were carried out by **al-Qa'ida** as part of its attempt to destabilize the Saudi Arabian government and punish the USA for its actions in Iraq and elsewhere. (*See* Map 10.)

Save Kashmir Movement

The Save Kashmir Movement is a terrorist organization that is opposed to Indian rule over Kashmir. It first emerged in 2002 and is believed to be a relatively small group of less than 50 members. However, it has carried out a series of violent terrorist attacks and high-profile assassinations. In December 2002 it killed Abdul Aziz Mir, a member of the People's Democratic Party and of the Jammu and Kashmir legislative assembly. In March 2003 Abdul Majid Dar, a former commander of the **Hizb ul-Mujahidin (HM)**, was assassinated by the group. Dar led the HM in Kashmir itself, but had declared a cease-fire in July 2000 as well as opened negotiations with the Indian authorities. In 2001 the HM expelled him for his increasingly moderate views and for signs that he was preparing to participate in the political process. The Save Kashmir Movement has been involved in other assassinations, targeting moderate Muslim leaders who might be inclined to work with the Indian government. In April 2004 the group claimed responsibility for a grenade and small arms attack on an election rally that resulted in nine deaths and in injuries to two state ministers. (*See* Map 9.)

September 11, 2001 Terrorist Attacks

The terrorist attacks in the USA on 11 September 2001 were carried out by 19 members of **al-Qa'ida**. Four commercial airliners on domestic flights in the USA were hijacked by the 19, who were divided into four teams. Two of the aircraft, American Airlines Flight 11 and United Airlines Flight 175, were deliberately crashed into the World Trade Center in New York, causing both of its towers to collapse. This, in turn, severely damaged other buildings and train subway stations in the vicinity. The World Trade Center had been the subject of a major attack in 1993 (see **World Trade Center Bombing**). A third aircraft, American Airlines Flight 77, was crashed into the Pentagon in Washington, DC, the location of the headquarters of the US Department of Defense. A fourth aircraft, United Airlines Flight 93, which was *en route* to another target, crashed in a field in Pennsylvania after passengers attempted to regain control of it from the hijackers. It is believed that this fourth target may have been the US Congress on Capitol Hill, or the White House in Washington. In all, 2,986 people of some 80 nationalities were killed, including those on the four aircraft. This was much higher than the most lethal single act of contemporary terrorism until that time, the **Abadan theatre attack** in which more than 400 people were killed in Iran in 1978. The high number of casualties and the huge political, economic and social impact of this single terrorist event on 11 September 2001 distinguished it from previous contemporary terrorist attacks. It appeared to mark the emergence of a new form of lethal, mass-casualty terrorism that would alter the nature of terrorism. The attacks were a huge shock to the USA, as this was the first major foreign attack on its territory since the surprise attack by Japanese forces on Pearl Harbor in 1941, in which some 2,400 people were killed. Initially, there was confusion and panic prompting the introduction of security measures that halted aviation traffic for several days. The immediate economic impact was also severe. Major stock markets in New York remained closed until 17 September 2001, and US stocks lost as much as US $1,200,000m. of their value during the week.

On 12 September 2001 the United Nations condemned the terrorist attacks and affirmed the right of self-defence of states, should they be attacked. US President George W. Bush declared a 'war on terror' after the attack. The USA also swiftly mobilized international support against terrorist groups, including the perpetrator of the 11 September attack, al-Qa'ida. (Although al-Qa'ida initially denied involvement in the attack, Osama bin Laden claimed responsibility for it in a videotaped speech in October 2004.) Numerous arrests were made world-wide as governments hunted down radical Islamists linked to al-Qa'ida. In late 2001 US-led forces joined with the opposition Northern Alliance in Afghanistan in 'Operation Enduring Freedom' to overthrow the **Taliban** regime that had supported al-Qa'ida training camps and the presence of its operatives in Afghanistan. However, al-Qa'ida's leader, Osama bin Laden, as well as the Taliban leader, Mohammed Omar, escaped capture and are believed to be sheltering in sympathetic tribal areas along the Afghan-Pakistan border. Operation Enduring Freedom was followed by the US-led intervention in and occupation of Iraq in 2003. Although US forces achieved a swift victory, it dissipated much of the international goodwill and sympathy that the USA had gained in the immediate aftermath of the September 11 terrorist attacks, especially when it became obvious that Iraq had neither weapons of mass destruction nor any links with al-Qa'ida, as the Bush administration had earlier claimed.

In the USA the attacks on 11 September 2001 exposed fundamental weaknesses in counter-terrorism, intelligence, immigration control and airport security. It spurred action dramatically to improve domestic security, leading to the creation of the Department of Homeland Security. The Patriot Act was also passed, giving law enforcement agencies extraordinary powers of surveillance, search and arrest in order to eradicate terrorism, and giving rise to concerns over the possible abuse of these powers and the erosion of civil liberties. After lengthy deliberations the National Commission on Terrorist Attacks (or 9-11 Commission), an independent commission created by congressional legislation, concluded, in a report released on 22 July 2004, that the emergence of al-Qa'ida in the late 1990s 'presented challenges to US governmental institutions that they were not well-designed to meet', specifically citing the failure of imagination that prevented the government from understanding the nature of the terrorist threat posed by al-Qa'ida before the 11 September 2001 attacks. The Commission also concluded that the attacks had been carried out by al-Qa'ida operatives, and affirmed that while there had been contacts between al-Qa'ida and the Iraqi regime of Saddam Hussain, no collaborative relationship between them existed. The Commission also called for the appointment of a head of national intelligence and the establishment of a counter-terrorism centre.

Shan State Army

The Shan State Army (SSA) is an ethnic insurgent group in Myanmar (formerly Burma) that has been in continuous revolt against the central government since 1948. In the largest of the seven ethnic states in Myanmar the Shans number some 8m. people. Military offensives by the government, particularly in the 1990s, have had a disastrous impact on the livelihood of the Shans. Since 1996, 500,000 people have been displaced and more than 100,000 have fled to Thailand. Within Shan state the rebel Shan State Army in the north (SSA-North) and the Shan State National Army (SSNA) in the central areas agreed to a cease-fire with the government in 1989. The Shan State Army-South (SSA-South), formerly known as the Shan United Revolutionary Army, however, has refused to abandon its struggle. It is led by Yord Serk, whose followers were part of the **Mong Tai Army** led by Khun Sa, but who rejected its surrender to the Myanmar government in 1996. It has an estimated strength of 2,000–6,000 guerrillas. Despite its prior links to the Mong Tai Army, which was heavily involved in the drugs trade, the SSA-South today insists that it has an anti-drugs policy. (*See* Map 1.)

Sharm esh-Sheikh Bombings (2005)

On 23 July 2005 a co-ordinated series of suicide bomb attacks took place in the resort town of Sharm esh-Sheikh in Egypt. Located on the southern tip of the Sinai peninsula, the resort is popular with local, Arab and Western tourists. Three bombs were detonated, one at a crowded market, and two at hotels. A suicide car bomber rammed the Ghazala Gardens Hotel, destroying much of its front and causing many casualties. At least 88 people were killed and more than 100 injured, the majority of them local Egyptians, although several European tourists were also killed. The attack followed a bomb attack on Red Sea resorts in October 2004 in which 34 people were killed. Two hitherto unknown groups, the Abdullah Azzam Brigades-al Qa'ida in Syria and Egypt and Mujahidin Egypt, claimed responsibility. Whatever the veracity of their claims, authorities believe that radical Islamists, possibly from Pakistan, were responsible. The attack raised serious fears for the future of the tourism industry in Egypt, a major source of income.

Shining Path

The Shining Path (Sendero Luminoso) is a radical Maoist communist insurgent movement in Peru. Founded by a former university professor, Abimael Guzmán, in the late 1960s, the Shining Path espouses radical and uncompromising Maoist ideals. Its political agenda is the overthrow of the Peruvian government and all existing institutions, followed by the remoulding of society in accordance with communist ideals and principles. The group claims to represent poor peasants and is thus strongly opposed to capitalism. From 1980 the Shining Path waged a campaign of violence that resulted in the death of some 30,000 people, including government officials, businessmen and landlords. It also carried out massacres of peasants who were accused of supporting the government. In rural areas the Shining Path gained support among poor peasants and students. It has also carried out attacks in the capital. At its peak the Shining Path had as many as 10,000 fighters. In 1992, however, Guzmán was captured in Lima. He subsequently issued a call for a cease-fire as the government succeeded in arresting or killing insurgent leaders and defections occurred as a result of President Fujimori's amnesty programme. Guzmán's successor, Oscar Ramírez Durand, was also captured in 1999. The Shining Path thus entered a phase marked by decline and reverses in the 1990s. Its remaining activists, estimated to number in the hundreds, are believed to have been responsible for recent kidnappings and narcotics-trafficking pursued to help fund the movement. The fall of the Fujimori government in 2000 resulted in the resurgence of the movement. Attacks on post-Fujimori government targets have included a car bomb attack in March 2002 outside the US Embassy in Lima, in which 10 people were killed, and the taking of 71 hostages near a gas pipeline under construction in 2003, although they were subsequently released.

Silent Brotherhood – *see* The Order

Sipah-e-Sahaba

The Sipah-e-Sahaba/Pakistan (SSP—Guardians of the Prophet) is an extremist Sunni Muslim religious organization in Pakistan that advocates sectarian violence against Shi'ite Muslims. The Sipah-e-Sahaba broke from the main Deobandi Sunni organization, the Jumiatul Ulema-e-Islam in 1985, and was originally known as the Anjuman Sipah-e-Sahaba. The group claims to be a response to the militancy of Shi'as in Punjab state after the Iranian Revolution in 1979. However, it may also have received some encouragement from the government of Zia ul-Haq in Pakistan to counter demands for greater democracy. Its political objectives are the reduction of the power and influence of Shi'as in Pakistan and the administration of the country strictly as a Sunni state, on the grounds that Sunnis constitute the majority of the population. The SSP has been able to attract some Sunni support in areas where Shi'a landlords have maintained a feudal-like hold on economic and social power. Led by Maulana Azam Tariq until his assassination in October 2003, the SSP has participated in the political process and runs many religious schools, or *madrassahs*, in Pakistan. It has been linked to the deaths of many prominent Shi'ites and to attacks on Shi'ite mosques. It, in turn, has been targeted by Shi'ite extremists, and several of its leaders have been assassinated. The SSP is believed to have close links with the **Jaish-e-Mohammed**, a terrorist group active in Kashmir. The SSP, however, has denied that it has been involved in terrorism and has maintained a low profile since the military coup in Pakistan in 1999. However, it has opposed Pakistan's alliance with the USA after the **September 11, 2001 terrorist attacks** in New York and Washington, DC, claiming that the USA was involved in a war against Islam. It

Somali National Movement (SNM)

The Somali National Movement (SNM) is one of a number of insurgent groups active in Somalia since the fall of the Siad Barre regime and the disintegration of the state in 1991. It was founded in 1981 by ethnic Isaaq émigrés living in London, United Kingdom, with the objective of ousting the repressive Barre regime. It subsequently transferred to Ethiopia, which provided it with support in the form of arms. The SNM began its anti-government insurgency in 1992, achieving some successes, including the kidnapping and subsequent release of 11 (mostly French) medical aid workers in 1987. However, a peace agreement between Ethiopia and Somalia in 1988 led to the withdrawal of Ethiopia's support. This, in turn, led the SNM to launch a major offensive in northern Somalia in order to establish bases within the country. It was successful in capturing territory and a large number of government troops defected to it. It also established an alliance with the **United Somali Congress (USC)** which fought the Barre regime in central Somalia. In 1991 the USC captured the Somali capital, Mogadishu, and overthrew the Barre regime, causing the complete collapse of the state machinery as Somalia descended into clan-based civil war. In the north, the SNM declared the independent state of Somaliland, which has failed to gain international recognition. The SNM is led by Mohamed Ibrahim Egal, whose leadership has been challenged by other clans, resulting in instability and fighting in Somaliland.

Special Purpose Islamic Regiment

The Special Purpose Islamic Regiment began as a criminal gang following the break-up of the USSR in the early 1990s and the declaration of Chechen independence in 1991. In 1999, however, with the outbreak of the second Chechnya conflict with Russia, the group, led by Arbi Barayev, established links with radical Islamists, resulting in its transformation into a radical pan-Islamic rebel organization espousing the objective of a pan-Islamic state in Chechnya and beyond. Arbi Barayev died in 2001 and was succeeded by his nephew, Movsar Barayev, who commanded the team drawn from several Chechen groups that carried out the **Moscow theatre siege** in October 2002, an operation that led to the death of 128 theatre-goers. He and his comrades died in the operation. Khamzat Tazabayev then took over the group, but he was in turn reportedly killed in early 2004. The group is small, with about 100 members, but has none the less carried out many attacks in the Caucasus and in Russia.

Sudan People's Liberation Army (SPLA)

The Sudan People's Liberation Army (SPLA) was founded in 1983 by a Sudanese military officer, John Garang. The impetus to the SPLA's rebellion lay with the central government's attempts to implement *Shari'a*, or Islamic, law throughout the country. The people of southern Sudan, who are mainly Christians and animists, were opposed to this policy. The rebellion also had its roots in the failure of nation-building since Sudan became independent in 1956. The country has remained riven by racial, ethnic and religious conflict between the Muslim north and the non-Muslim south. Southerners have also perceived themselves to be unfairly discriminated against, as well as marginalized, and have struggled for many years for some form of autonomy or even independence. The SPLA aimed to re-establish a democratic and secular Sudan, forming an alliance with other opposition groups under the umbrella of the National Democratic Alliance. It has been opposed by government forces and various Muslim militias. The Sudanese civil war cost the lives of some 1.5m. people. The SPLA attacked not only government troops and installations, but also targeted the oil industry in the south in order to check the flow of revenues to the central government. In early 2002 the SPLA merged with the Sudan People's Democratic Force to create the Sudanese People's Liberation Army/Sudan People's Liberation Movement. The greater cohesion of the opposition, as well as mediation by the USA, Libya, Egypt and the Intergovernmental Authority on Development (IGAD), and sanctions declared by the USA, resulted in peace negotiations that culminated in the signing of a power-sharing agreement in Kenya in July 2002. In 2004 another agreement led to Garang's appointment as Vice-President of Sudan. However, the crisis in Darfur has continued unabated, with the Front for the Liberation of Darfur (later called the Sudan Liberation Army/Movement), and the Justice and Equality Movement, two separate rebel groups that are not part of the peace process, battling with the government-backed Muslim militia organization, the *Janjaweed*, for control of the province. The fighting in Darfur, which began in early 2003, has claimed more than 180,000 lives. It also led to a huge humanitarian crisis, with some 2m. made homeless.

Superferry Bombing (2004)

On 27 February 2004 a bomb placed on a ferry in Manila Bay in the Philippines exploded, killing 118 people on board the vessel in the worst terrorist attack in south-east Asia since the **Bali attack** in October 2002, and the single most deadly terrorist incident in the Philippines. Investigations later revealed that an **Abu Sayyaf Group** operative had placed a television set containing 3.6 kg of explosive on board Superferry 14, which was detonated with a timing device once the ship had sailed. Responsibility for the attack was immediately claimed by the Abu Sayyaf Group.

State Defence Council-Majlis ul-Shura

The State Defence Council-Majlis ul-Shura is the main resistance co-ordinating body of the breakaway Chechen republic led by Aslan Maskhadov that declared independence from Russia in 1991. Chechnya has rebelled against Moscow's authority on a number of occasions. In 1944 the Chechens were exiled to Central Asia by Stalin for alleged collaboration with Nazi Germany. The autonomous republic was reinstated in 1957 and the population returned. In 1991, after the collapse of the USSR, Chechnya declared its independence, prompting a Russian invasion. In 1994–96 Aslan Maskhadov and Dzhokar Dudayev waged a war against Russia that eventually spread to nearby Ingushetia, Dagestan and north Ossetia. Dudayev was killed in 1996. Maskhadov signed a peace agreement with Russia in the same year, and was elected as President of Chechnya in 1997. In 1999, however, Chechen military commander Shamil Basayev and foreign-born *mujahidin* fighters, such as Ibn al-Khattab, invaded neighbouring Muslim Dagestan. This invasion, together with attacks attributed to Dagestan militants on apartments in Russia which killed 293 people, provoked Russia into a second war on Chechnya in 1999. The capital, Grozny, was occupied by Russian forces, whereupon Aslan Maskhadov left for the mountains to continue the fight against Russia. The State Defence Council established a military committee in 2002 to better co-ordinate the confusing array of armed groups and militias operating in Chechnya and beyond. It is regarded as nationalist and moderate, in contrast to other Chechen groups, such as the **Riyadus-Salikhin Reconnaissance and Sabotage Battalion of Shahids**, led by Shamil Basayev, which broke away from Maskhadov's command in 2001, the **Special Purpose Islamic Regiment** and the **Islamic International Peace-keeping Brigade**, which are motivated by radical pan-Islamic ideology. Maskhadov was killed by Russian forces in March 2005.

Taliban

The Taliban (also transliterated as Taleban) ruled Afghanistan from 1996 until its overthrow in the US-led intervention of late 2001. The Taliban was founded by Mullah Mohammed Omar in 1994 in Kandahar and consisted of religious students and graduates of religious schools, or *madrassahs*. Many of these were also combat-experienced veterans of the resistance against Soviet forces in the 1980s. The Taliban espoused a vision of a unitary Afghanistan ruled strictly according to Islamic, or *Shari'a*, law. It received support from the government of Pakistan, which was concerned by the continuing civil strife in Afghanistan, and also from many Pashtun Afghans who were revulsed by the internecine violence and warlordism that plagued Afghanistan after the Soviet withdrawal. Pakistani volunteers from religious schools also joined the Taliban. Its offensives against various warlords, such as Rashid Dostum, Ismail Khan and Gulbiddin Hekmatyar, in 1994–96 resulted in the capture of key cities, including Kandahar and the capital, Kabul. Once in power, the Taliban proceeded to remould Afghanistan into the kind of society that conformed to its fundamentalist interpretation of Islamic law. It banned music, dancing, art and television. Women were not allowed to be educated in schools or to work, and had to be completely covered when appearing in public. Men were required to wear beards and turbans, and to pray at the required times. Criminals and those who failed to comply with this interpretation were subject to harsh penalties, including execution and amputation. These policies, as well as the Taliban's destruction of two historic Buddhist statues at Bamiyan, provoked international criticism. Indeed, the Taliban regime was recognized by very few countries, with the notable exceptions of Pakistan and Saudi Arabia. Nevertheless, it is recognized that the Taliban did establish a semblance of peace and order after years of warfare and violence. Its policies *vis-à-vis* corruption and crime, as well as its uncompromising refusal to deal with existing warlords, earned it much domestic respect. The Taliban entered into an alliance with **al-Qa'ida** owing to the strong personal bonds between Mullah Mohammed Omar and Osama bin Laden. Al-Qa'ida and the Taliban established *mujahidin* camps where thousands of militants from around the world were trained. Al-Qa'ida fighters were also integrated into the Taliban's armed forces. In 1998 the USA attacked several of these camps near Khost with cruise missiles, charging that they were being used to train terrorists. The Taliban was opposed by various groups, mainly consisting of Uzbeks and Tajiks gathered around the Northern Alliance and led by the same warlords that the Taliban had earlier deposed. After the **September 11, 2001 terrorist attacks** in the USA, the USA and its allies intervened in Afghanistan on the side of the embattled Northern Alliance. This led to the capture of Kabul, the defeat of the Taliban regime and the destruction of *mujahidin* training camps. Mohammed Omar and Osama bin Laden both escaped in the ensuing chaos and are believed to be hiding among tribal supporters in northern Pakistan. The Taliban has regrouped in the border areas and remains a source of instability to the elected government of Hamid Zarzai. (*See* Map 9.)

The Order

The Order (also known as the Bruders Schweigen, or Silent Brotherhood) is an offshoot of the extreme right-wing **Aryan Nations** in the USA. It was founded in 1983 by Robert J. Matthews and espoused neo-Nazi white supremacist views based on William Pierce's novel, *The Turner Diaries*. Members of The Order began to accumulate funds—for the purpose of overthrowing the federal government—through robberies and counterfeiting operations. They also carried out bomb attacks on synagogues. A Jewish talk show host, who had unwisely goaded white supremacists, was murdered in Denver in June 1984. Proceeds from criminal activities were used to set up paramilitary training camps and to purchase weapons. The death of Matthews in a confrontation with police in 1984, together with the arrest, conviction and imprisonment of a number of the organization's members, effectively terminated the activities of The Order.

Tokyo Subway Attack

On 20 March 1995, during the morning rush hour, members of the religious cult **Aum Shinrikyo** carried out an attack on the Tokyo subway, using sarin nerve gas, in which 12 people were killed and more than 5,000 were injured. The cult had hoped that the chaos ensuing from a successful mass casualty terrorist attack—the first in contemporary times—would allow it to take power in Japan. Members of the sect were tried in April 1996 and 13, including its leader, Shoko Asahara, were eventually sentenced to death, although none of the death sentences have yet been executed. Aum Shinrikyo was not outlawed, and is now known as Aleph. It has apologized for the attack and established a compensation fund. None the less, it remains on the US Department of State's list of terrorist groups.

Tunisian Combatant Group

The Tunisian Combatant Group (Jama'a Combattante Tunisienne), also known as the Tunisian Islamic Fighting Group, is a radical Islamist terrorist group formed in Tunisia in around 2000. It is led by Tarek Maaroufi and Saifallah Ben Hassine. Its objective is the overthrow of the government in Tunisia and the establishment of an Islamic state ruled according to *Shari'a*, or Islamic, law. It is a secretive movement comprised of small, autonomous cells that operate in Western Europe as well as in Tunisia. It is profoundly anti-Western and anti-US. The Group is believed to have established close links with **al-Qa'ida**, as well as with other radical Islamist groups, such as the **Salafist Group for Call and Combat** in Algeria. It has been implicated in a number of terrorist conspiracies. Its leader, Tarek Maaroufi, was arrested by Belgian authorities in December 2001, charged, in October 2004, with terrorism-related activities and sentenced to five years' imprisonment. In 2003 an Italian court sentenced members of the group to prison terms for terrorism-related activities.

Tupac Amaru Revolutionary Movement

The Tupac Amaru Revolutionary Movement (Movimiento Revolucionario Tupac Amaru—MRTA) is the second largest communist guerrilla organization in Peru, after the **Shining Path**. The MRTA is Marxist-Leninist in orientation and was founded by Víctor Polay Campos in 1984 with the objective of overthrowing the government in Peru, ending the presence and influence there of US capitalism, and transforming the country into a communist Marxist state. It has sought a populist base among poor peasants, the intelligentsia, students and trade union members. Indeed, the group is named after Tupac Amaru, who is revered by native Peruvians for his rebellion against Spanish rule in the 18th century. The MRTA achieved some initial successes, including, in 1987, the capture of territory, but the subsequent success of military operations launched against it, that led to the capture of Campos, resulted in its gradual decline. In 1996 the MRTA occupied the Japanese Embassy while a major reception was being held there, taking some 450 hostages, although most were later released. The hostage crisis lasted for five months, until April 1997, when a commando operation resulted in the death of all 14 hostage-takers and the release of the remaining 72 hostages. Other leaders of the MRTA have been arrested and imprisoned in

Bolivia. The MRTA has failed to carry out any major attack since then and is no longer considered to be a serious security threat.

Tupamaro Revolutionary Movement

The Tupamaro Revolutionary Movement (Movimiento Tupamaro de Venezuela) is an extreme left-wing group in Venezuela. It emerged in 1998 as a neighbourhood vigilante group in a working-class district of Caracas that targeted criminal gangs. Like the now defunct Tupamaros in Uruguay and the **Tupac Amaru Revolutionary Movement** in Peru, the group named itself after the 18th-century Peruvian revolutionary hero, Tupac Amaru, who had fought the colonial Spanish and for Indian rights. The group, led by José Pinto, professes left-wing and anti-capitalist views and has expressed its admiration for Che Guevara, although it has denied any involvement in attacks against oil companies in Venezuela. Its support base is among the urban poor. Unusually, it has also professed public support for the socialist government of President Hugo Chávez Frías, which has come under pressure from right-wing forces in the country, notably in an attempted military coup in 2002.

Turkish Hezbollah

The Turkish Hezbollah was founded in the early 1980s with the objective of overthrowing the current secular government of Turkey and establishing an Islamic state ruled strictly in accordance with Islamic law. The group is not related to **Hezbollah** in Lebanon. The Turkish Hezbollah originally trained with the **Kurdistan Workers' Party (PKK)**, but soon quarrelled and fought with it on account of its secular approach and its alleged anti-Muslim focus. Turkish Hezbollah also targeted academics, journalists, religious leaders and others who it felt supported the secular Turkish state. The government's offensive against the group since 2000 has resulted in the arrest or death of hundreds of its members, including its leader, Huseyin Velioglu. Turksih Hezbollah was suspected of involvement in the **Istanbul bombings** in November 2003 that targeted synagogues and British interests.

Ulster Defence Association (UDA)

The Ulster Defence Association (UDA) is a Loyalist Protestant paramilitary organization in Northern Ireland. It was formed with the purpose of maintaining the *status quo* and ensuring that the province remains within the United Kingdom instead of being detached to become part of the (Catholic) Republic of Ireland. The UDA was formed in the early 1970s as an amalgamation of local Protestant vigilante groups that had been organized in response to the threat posed by the **Irish Republican Army (IRA)**. The UDA, which has about 4,000 members, has been accused of vigilantism and revenge killings, often in response to IRA attacks. However, up to 1992, when it was banned, it was able to participate in the political process as a legal party, as the acts of violence in which it was alleged to have been involved were carried out by the Ulster Freedom Fighters, widely regarded as an arm of the UDA. The Ulster Freedom Fighters attempted to assassinate IRA leader Gerry Adams on a number of accasions, coming close in 1984 when he survived despite being hit by four bullets. It also co-operated with the **Ulster Volunteer Force**. The UDA was weakened, however, by internal rifts, with Billy Wright leaving it in 1996 to establish the rival **Loyalist Volunteer Force**. The UDA signed the Good Friday Agreement in 1998, as did the IRA. The British government charged in October 2001 that the UDA, through the continued violent activities of splinter groups such as the **Orange Volunteers** and the Red Hand Defenders, had violated its cease-fire. Within the group, severe internal dissension and competition for power resulted in open violence between the UDA's political leadership and its *de facto* armed wing, the Ulster Freedom Fighters, after the latter's leader was expelled from the UDA. A cease-fire between the two factions was declared in February 2003.

Ulster Volunteer Force (UVF)

The Ulster Volunteer Force (UVF) is a Loyalist Protestant paramilitary organization in Northern Ireland. It was formed as a response to the increasing militancy of Catholics who had been agitating for a united Ireland outside of the United Kingdom. The UVF is also considered to be the oldest Loyalist organization as its antecedent was established as early as 1912. The UVF was resurrected in the mid-1960s as a means to defend the interests of Protestants in Northern Ireland and to maintain the *status quo*, that is, for the province to remain part of the United Kingdom. The UVF was banned in 1966 for its role in the revenge killings of Catholics. This did not stop its use of violence against Catholics. In retailiation for IRA attacks on Protestants, it often carried out terrorist attacks on innocent civilians in Ireland. For instance, car bombings in Ireland in 1974 claimed the lives of 32 people and wounded more than 200. The UVF's resort to violence soon alienated many Protestants who were tired of the internecine fighting in the province. The UVF thus progressively moderated its use of violence in the 1990s, declared a cease-fire in 1994 and formed a Protestant Unity Party to contest elections to the Northern Ireland Assembly. The UVF also participated in the Northern Ireland peace process and supported the Good Friday Agreement in 1998. However, it has since become the target of extremist elements who have not only defected to splinter groups but also targeted the UVF.

UNITA

UNITA (União Nacional para a Independência Total de Angola, or National Union for the Total Independence of Angola) is a political organization in Angola that has been an active participant in the country's civil war. UNITA was formed as a result of a split within the independence movement. In 1966 Jonas Savimbi broke with the National Liberation Front of Angola (Frente Nacional para a Libertacão de Angola—FNLA) to form UNITA, which is dominated by ethnic

Ovimbundus and subscibes to Maoist communist ideology. After independence in 1975, Angola descended into civil war. While the Soviet-backed socialist Popular Movement for the Liberation of Angola (Movimento Popular para a Libertacão de Angola—MPLA) took power with the assistance of Cuban troops and forced the FNLA into exile, UNITA received support from the USA and South Africa and thus managed to survive in the highland areas of the interior and the south-eastern part of Angola. Throughout the 1980s the civil war was waged as a proxy war between a Soviet-backed regime and a US-supported opposition (albeit Maoist in orientation). In 1989, following the end of the Cold War, Cuban troops were withdrawn and a cease-fire was negotiated. The MPLA also renounced Marxism and declared its commitment to democracy. A subsequent election under UN auspices, however, resulted in a resumption in armed conflict after UNITA failed to win an overall majority. In 1995, after another peace agreement had been concluded, UN peace-keepers were deployed in Angola, but UNITA once again rebelled. The death of Savimbi in February 2002 led to UNITA's military demise. In 2002 the UN was able to broker a peace agreement in which UNITA finally agreed to disarm and demobilize its armed wing. Despite turmoil over the post-Savimbi leadership, UNITA still exists as a political party and is today led by Isaias Samakuva.

United Liberation Front of Assam (ULFA)

The United Liberation Front of Assam (ULFA) is a major insurgent group in India's Assam state. The roots of its rebellion lie in the increasing political, economic and cultural marginalization of the Assamese people as a result of the migration of Muslims from East Bengal and other ethnic groups from elsewhere in India. In 1979 the ULFA was founded with the objective of gaining independence for Assam. The ULFA established ties with neighbouring separatist groups, such as the **Nationalist Socialist Council of Nagaland (NSCN)**, and is alleged to have engaged in arms-smuggling and drugs-trafficking in order to raise funds and acquire weapons. Military offensives by the Indian government have led ULFA guerrillas to seek sanctuary in nearby Bhutan. This, in turn, led Bhutan's army to mount military operations against the insurgents, with the support of Indian security forces. The group remains a threat to security, however, given the persistence of fundamental grievances in Assam. (*See* Map 5.)

United National Liberation Front (UNLF)

The United National Liberation Front (UNLF) is an insurgent group in the state of Manipur in India. It is the oldest of at least 24 rebel groups in the fractured separatist movement in that state. The roots of conflict in Manipur state lie in ethnic rivalry there between the Hindu Meiteis, and non-Meiteis, such as Nagas, Kukis and migrants from outside, such as Muslim Pangals, as well as perceived discrimination and lack of development. The rebellions in neighbouring Assam and Nagaland (see **United Liberation Front of Assam** and **Nationalist Socialist Council of Nagaland**) have also affected Manipur, with Naga separatists in nearby Nagaland claiming half the territory in Manipur as part of Greater Nagaland. The UNLF was formed in 1964 and is Maoist in orientation. Indeed, its cadres received training in China, and it was UNLF cadres who then established other revolutionary groups in the 1970s, such as the People's Liberation Army (PLA) and the People's Revolutionary Party of Kangleipak (PREPAK), to fight for independence. The Kukis also established their own Kuki National Army. In 1999 the UNLF, the PLA and PREPAK established an umbrella organization called the Manipur People's Liberation Front, with the aim of uniting all ethnic groups in the struggle for independence from India. The UNLF has an estimated strength of 2,500, while the PLA has some 3,000 guerrillas and PREPAK some 1,500. The targeting of Muslims by the Meiteis resulted in the establishment of militant Muslim groups, adding to the confusing array of armed insurgent groups in Manipur. In all, the various insurgent groups are said to number some 20,000. In order to survive in such an isolated and under-developed state, most of the insurgent groups have engaged in criminal activities such as kidnapping, extortion and smuggling. They have also disrupted elections, and attacked security personnel and government officials. (*See* Map 5.)

United Nations Headquarters Bombing, Baghdad (2003)

On 19 August 2003 a truck bomb destroyed part of the building housing the UN headquarters in Baghdad, Iraq. Twenty-three people were killed, including the head of the mission, veteran UN diplomat, Sérgio Vieira de Mello. The truck bomb was placed close to his office, suggesting that he was the intended target. Following this attack, all but a small contingent of about 50 foreign UN workers were evacuated from Baghdad. Responsibility for the attack was claimed by **al-Qa'ida** several days after it took place, but it is believed to have been carried out by **Jama'at at-Tawhid wal-Jihad**, the radical Islamist group led by Abu Musab az-Zarqawi (al-Zarqawi).

United Somali Congress (USC)

The United Somali Congress (USC) is one of the several insurgent groups that emerged in the 1980s with the objective of ousting the regime of Siad Barre in Somalia. In 1991 it succeeded in capturing the Somali capital, Mogadishu, and overthrew Barre's regime. Subsequently, however, Somalia descended into anarchy as a result of violent clan-based warfare. The USC was led by Ali Mahdi, its financial backer, but he was opposed by other clans as well as by his own military commander, Gen. Mohammed Aideed. The complete collapse of the Somali state resulted in famine in 1992. This led, in turn, to UN intervention in the form of the United Nations Operation in Somalia (UNSCOM). Led by the USA, the multinational force deployed numbered some 37,000, but failed to establish order or stability owing to the extent of the clan-based fighting. In 1993 an ill-advised attempt to arrest Aideed led to the deaths of 18 US Special Forces soldiers and some 500 Somalis. A unilateral US withdrawal was effected within months of the incident. Aideed himself was opposed by other clans and was killed in 1996. He was succeeded by his son, Hussein Mohamed Aideed. Hussein wished to extend his control to the south, but was opposed by the **Rahanawein Resistance Army** and the Digil Salvation Army, both of which were supported by Ethiopia. In August 2001 a national reconciliation conference in Djibouti resulted in the establishment of a 245-member National Assembly, but this was immediately challenged by insurgent groups. In 2004 another national reconciliation conference resulted in the formation of a Transitional Parliament and the election of a President, but fresh fighting among various clan-based warlords continued throughout the year. Somalia remains a 'failed state'.

United Tajik Opposition (UTO)

The United Tajik Opposition (UTO) was a party to the civil war in Tajikistan that erupted with the dissolution of the USSR in 1992 and Tajikistan's subsequent independence. The roots of the conflict between the pro-Russian Kouliabis and the ethnic Muslim groups within the UTO coalition lie in the artificial creation of the state of Tajikistan within the USSR from an assortment of rival ethnic and clan groups. Resource competition against a background of severe economic difficulties before and immediately after the disintegration of the USSR, together with increasing nationalism among Tajiks, resulted in open warfare in 1992. The UTO's dominant party is the Islamic Rennaissance Party, led by Said Abdullo Nuri, which has its own armed militia. The government, however, was supported by Russia and the opposition was soon forced to flee to Afghanistan. The fighting resulted in the internal displacement of some 500,000 people and many thousands of deaths. The Islamic Renaissance Party (IRP) was banned in 1993. A peace-keeping force deployed by the Commonwealth of Independent States sealed Tajikistan's borders against radical Islamist infiltration from Afghanistan. In 1997 a peace agreement was signed whereby the opposition was to be permitted to participate in the political process. This has led to the participation of the IRP in government. However, the more pressing security threat to the government stems from the activities of other radical Islamist groups, such as the **Islamic Movement of Uzbekistan** and the **Hizb ut-Tahrir**. (*See* Map 3.)

United Wa State Army (UWSA)

The United Wa State Army (UWSA), an armed ethnic group in Myanmar (formerly Burma), is considered by the US Department of State to be one of the world's most heavily armed narcotics-trafficking organizations. The UWSA has a strength of more than 20,000 well-equipped soldiers. The Wa are an ethnic group living along the periphery of Myanmar, one of the many ethnic groups that refused to accept the authority of the central government after Burma became independent in 1948. The Wa joined the Burma Communist Party (BCP), providing the bulk of its fighters in its armed insurrection against the central government. However, the pro-Chinese orientation of the BCP led to a Wa mutiny in 1989 and to the disintegration of the BCP. The Wa, led by Bao Youxiang and others, then formed the UWSA, but concluded a peace agreement with the central government in 1989. In return for peace, the Wa received full autonomy over their territory, named Special Region Two. The Wa were able to profit from the narcotics trade, producing amphetamines and heroin for the Thai and international drugs markets, although the UWSA itself claims to have an anti-drugs policy. The surrender of the high-profile drugs lord, Khun Sa, and the disbandment of his **Mong Tai Army** in 1996, allowed other drugs lords to take control of the lucrative trade, in alliance with the Wa. The Myanmar government has not taken effective action against the drugs problem, and has treated the UWSA as a useful border force as well as an ally against elements of the **Shan State Army** that are still fighting the central government. (*See* Map 1.)

USS *Cole* Bombing (2000)

On 12 October 2000 a US warship, the USS *Cole*, was attacked by suicide bombers using a small, fast craft packed with explosives, as it lay anchored in the port of Aden in Yemen. Seventeen sailors were killed and 39 others were injured in the attack, which damaged but did not sink the ship. The Yemeni radical Islamist group, the **Aden Abyan Islamic Army (AAIA)**, claimed responsibility for the attack. Investigations later indicated that the attack had been directed by leading **al-Qa'ida** operatives. Six militants, comprising five Yemenis and one Saudi Arabian, were subsequently arrested. In September 2004 two al-Qa'ida members, Abd ar-Rahim an-Nashiri, the Saudi mastermind of the attack, and Jamal al-Badawi, were sentenced to death for their roles in the bombing. Jamal's sentence was later commuted to 15 years' imprisonment. The other four were sentenced to terms of imprisonment ranging from five to 10 years. Abd ar-Rahim an-Nashiri was tried *in absentia* as he was being detained by US authorities in an undisclosed location. (*See* Map 10.)

World Trade Center Bombing (1993)

On 26 February 1993 a truck bomb exploded in the underground car park of the World Trade Center in New York, USA, killing six people and injuring more than 1,000. The key figure involved in the attack was Ramzi Yousef, who was trained and financed by **al-Qa'ida**. Ramzi, a Kuwaiti citizen, entered the USA on a false passport in 1992. In preparation for the attack, he constructed a 600-kg bomb using commercially available chemicals. His plan was to cause one of the World Trade Center's twin towers to collapse onto the other but this did not happen as the bomb was not powerful enough. The World Trade Center was chosen by radical Islamists because of its iconic status as a symbol of the USA's financial and economic power: a successful terrorist attack on it would have a major political and economic impact. A further aim was to punish the USA for its support of repressive Middle Eastern regimes that have been opposed by radical Islamists. In May 1994 four militants, Mohammed Salameh, Nidal Ayyad, Mahmud Abouhalima and Ahmad Ajaj, were convicted and sentenced to life imprisonment for the attack. In October 1995 Sheikh Omar Abdel Rahman, a blind cleric who preached in Brooklyn, New York, and who is the spiritual leader of the Egyptian militant group, **al-Gama'a al-Islamiyya**, was sentenced to life imprisonment for masterminding the bombing. Ramzi Yousef fled the USA and was involved in other terrorist plots, including the abortive 'Operation Bojinka', which aimed to destroy 11 US-bound airliners over the Pacific in January 1995. He was arrested in Pakistan in 1995 and surrendered to the US authorities. Yousef was convicted in 1998 and sentenced to life imprisonment. The World Trade Center was attacked once again, and destroyed, in the **September 11, 2001 terrorist attacks**.

Yemen Islamic Jihad

Yemen Islamic Jihad is a radical Islamist group in Yemen. It was formed after the withdrawal of Soviet forces from Afghanistan in the early 1990s, from returning Yemeni *mujahidin* volunteers under Tariq al-Fadhli to pursue their aim of establishing an Islamic state in Yemen ruled strictly according to Islamic, or *Shari'a*, law. It subscribes to radical *Salafi* teachings, is anti-Western and wishes to remove Western presence and influence in the region. The group established close ties with **al-Qa'ida**, operating openly and freely until implicated in terrorist attacks, such as the attempted assassination of Egyptian President Hosni Mubarak in 1995. In 2000 the group was believed to have been involved, together with its splinter group, the **Aden Abyan Islamic Army (AAIA)**, and with al-Qa'ida, in the **USS *Cole* bombing**. The group has several hundred members and enjoys some support among sections of the Yemeni élite. It has a presence in southern Yemen, where remote desert mountain ranges have proven to be useful hide-outs. Since the **September 11, 2001 terrorist attacks** in the USA, Yemen has come under intense US pressure to take action against the militants. As a result, its security forces have clashed violently with members of the group. (*See* Map 10.)

Zapatista National Liberation Army

The Zapatista National Liberation Army (Ejército Zapatista de Liberación Nacional—EZLN) was the result of a revolt by native Indians in the Mexican state of Chiapas in 1994. The Chiapas Indians cited the erosion of their culture, corruption and socio-economic inequalities as reasons for their rebellion. Led by 'Marcos', the movement was named after Emiliano Zapata, a hero of the Mexican Revolution in 1910 who is revered for seeking a fair distribution of land and an end to repression. The Chiapas Indians captured a number of towns, temporarily occupying San Cristóbal de las Casas, aided by indigenous Indian security personnel who had defected to the EZLN. A cease-fire was soon agreed and the government subsequently entered into negotiations with the EZLN, signing the San Andrés Accord, which met some of the demands of the Chiapas Indians. However, the failure of the government to ratify the accord led to continuing tension, with right-wing paramilitary groups targeting the EZLN and its alleged sympathizers. A state of tension and low-level war has existed since then between the armed forces and right-wing paramilitaries on the one hand, and the Zapatistas on the other. In July 2003 'Marcos' issued a communiqué reaffirming that armed struggle would remain the *modus operandi* of the EZLN.

Maps and Statistics

Maps

MAP 1: BURMA/MYANMAR

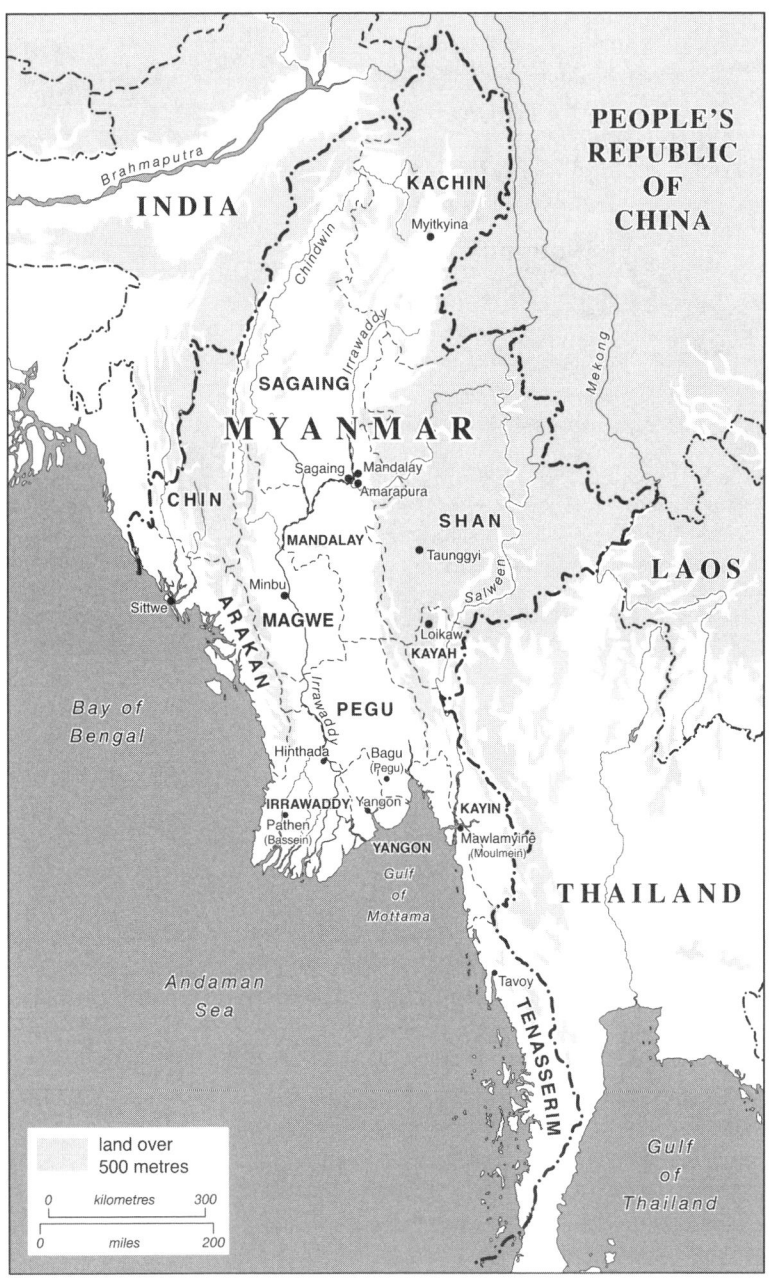

MAP 2: CENTRAL AFRICA

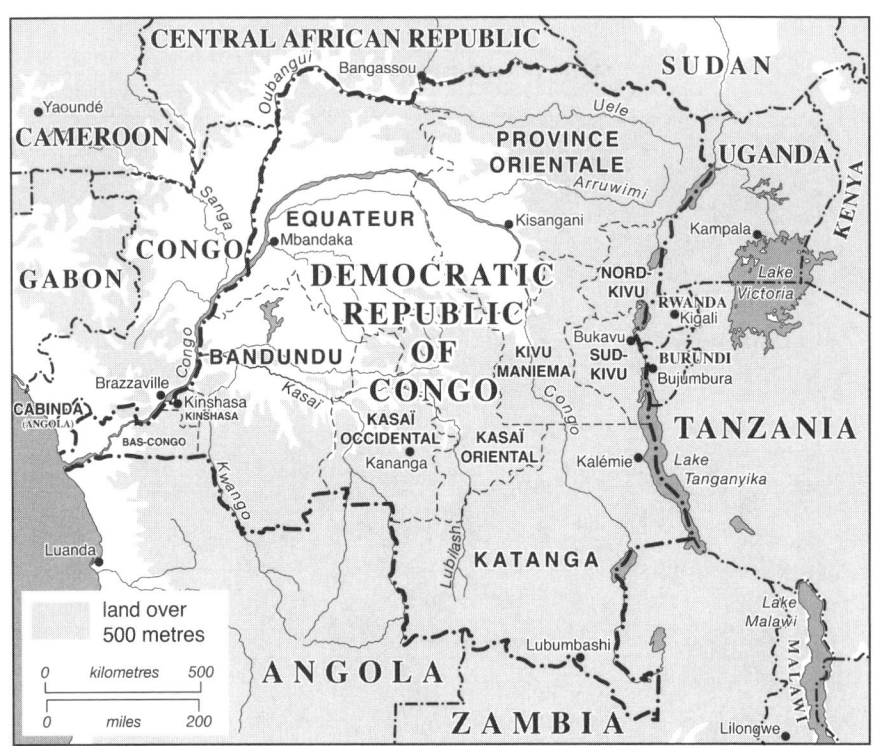

MAP 3: CENTRAL ASIA

MAP 4: ETHIOPIA

MAP 5: INDIA

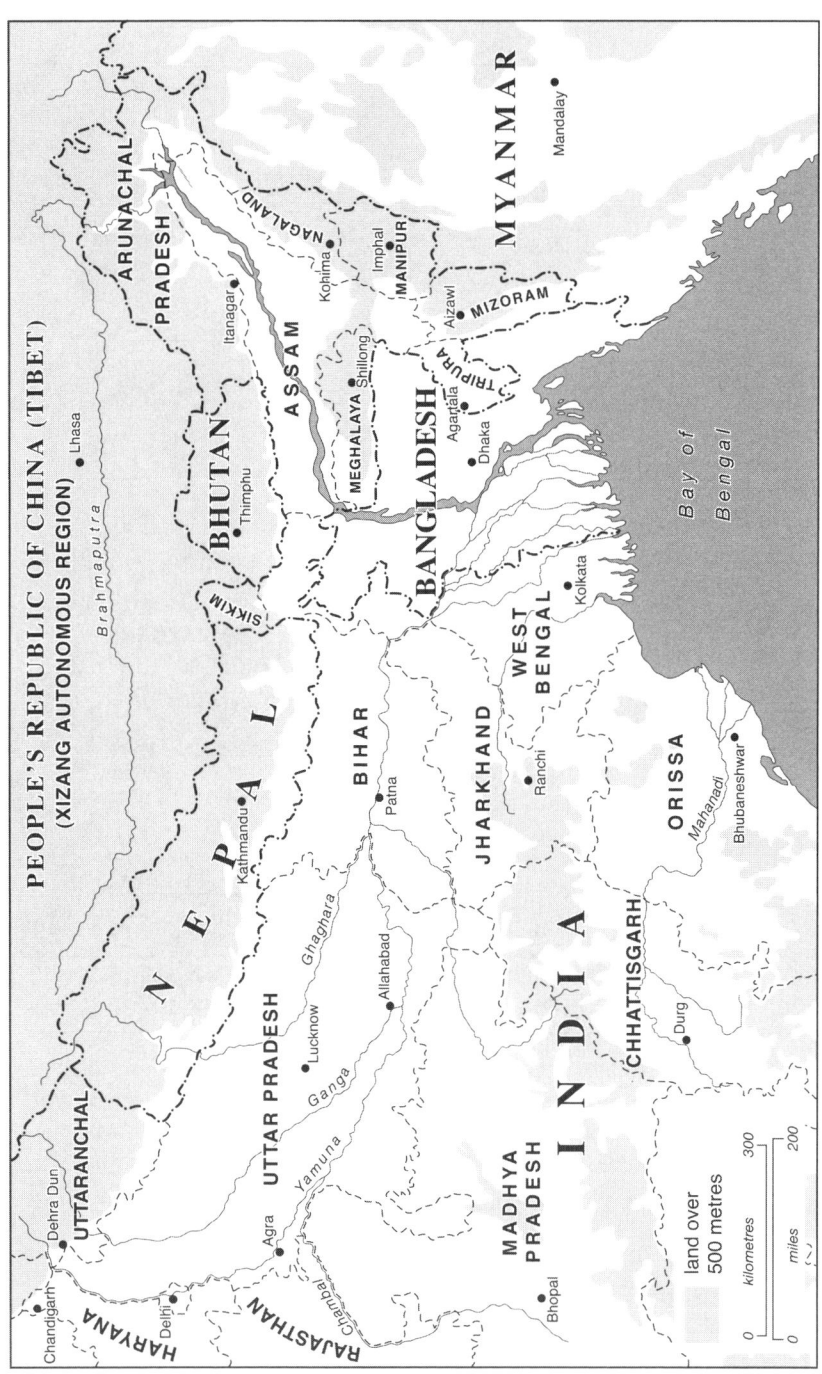

MAPS AND STATISTICS

MAP 6: IRAQ

MAP 7: ISRAEL/PALESTINE

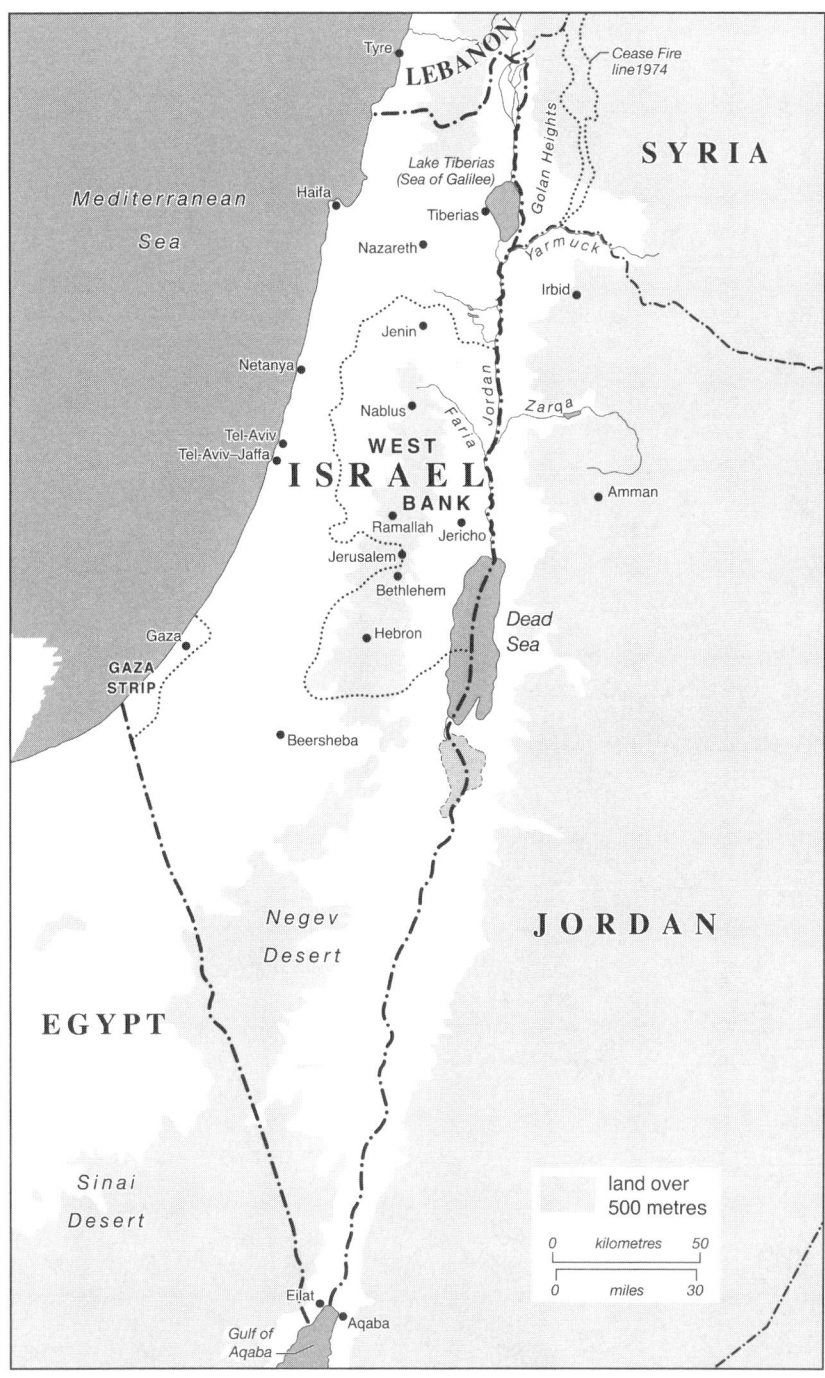

MAP 8: THE MALAY ARCHIPELAGO

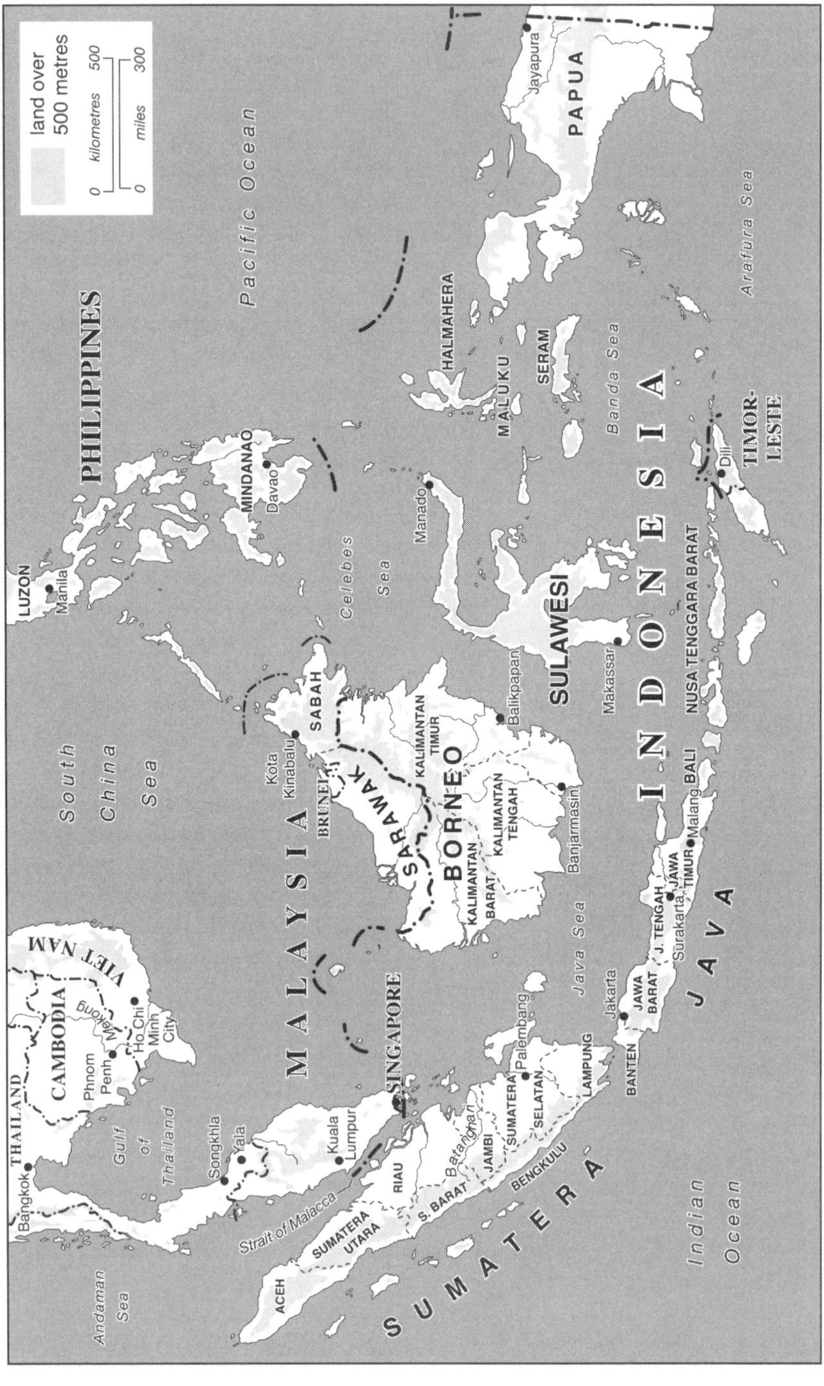

MAP 9: NORTH-WEST INDIAN SUB-CONTINENT

MAPS AND STATISTICS

MAP 10: SAUDI ARABIA

Charts and Statistics

TERRORIST INCIDENTS BY REGION, 1 JANUARY 1968 TO 31 AUGUST 2005

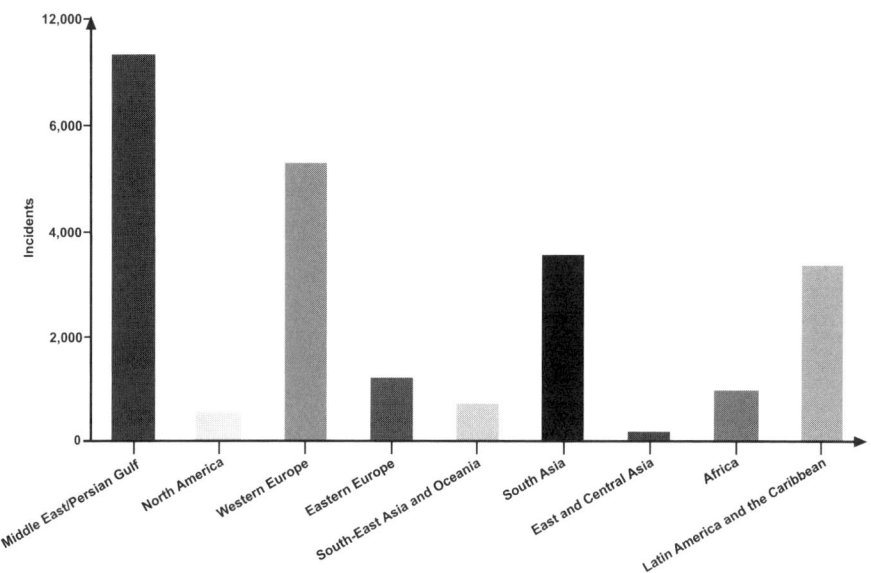

Data for 1968–97 cover only international incidents.
Data for 1998–present cover both domestic and international incidents.
Source: MIPT Terrorism Knowledge Base. Incident Analysis Wizard. Website, accessed 21 September 2005. Available from http://www.tkb.org/ChartModule.jsp. Incident data are drawn from the RAND Terrorism Chronology and RAND-MIPT Terrorism Incident Database as available through the Terrorism Knowledge Base (www.tkb.org).

TERRORIST INJURIES BY REGION, 1 JANUARY 1968 TO 31 AUGUST 2005

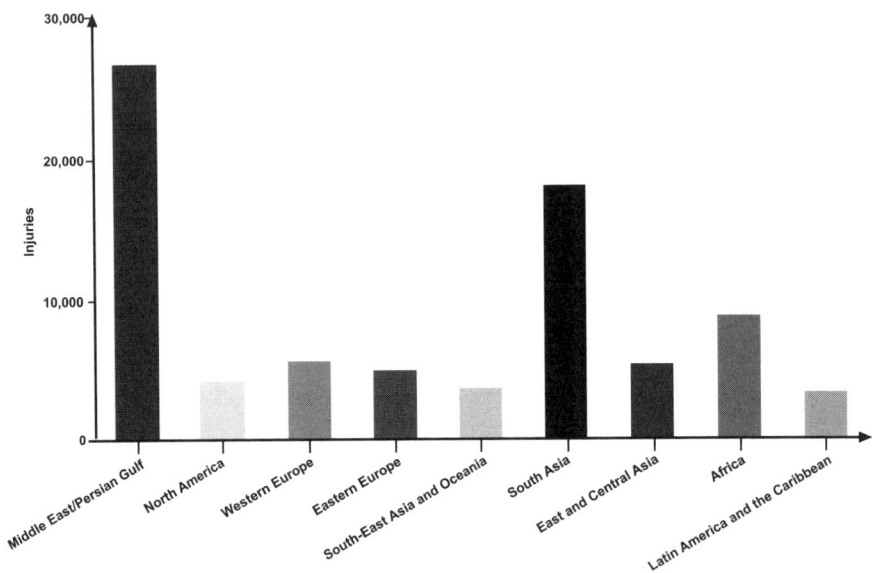

Data for 1968–97 cover only international incidents.
Data for 1998–present cover both domestic and international incidents.
Source: MIPT Terrorism Knowledge Base. Incident Analysis Wizard. Website, accessed 21 September 2005. Available from http://www.tkb.org/ChartModule.jsp. Incident data are drawn from the RAND Terrorism Chronology and RAND-MIPT Terrorism Incident Database as available through the Terrorism Knowledge Base (www.tkb.org).

TERRORIST DEATHS BY REGION, 1 JANUARY 1968 TO 31 AUGUST 2005

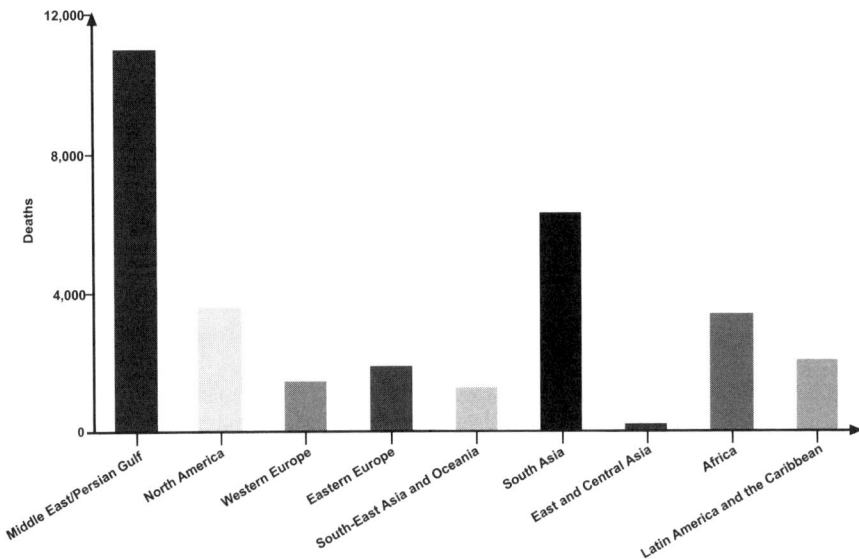

Data for 1968–97 cover only international incidents.
Data for 1998–present cover both domestic and international incidents.
Source: MIPT Terrorism Knowledge Base. Incident Analysis Wizard. Website, accessed 21 September 2005. Available from http://www.tkb.org/ChartModule.jsp. Incident data are drawn from the RAND Terrorism Chronology and RAND-MIPT Terrorism Incident Database as available through the Terrorism Knowledge Base (www.tkb.org).

MAPS AND STATISTICS

Terrorist Incidents by Region, 1 January 1968 to 31 August 2005

Region	Incidents	Injuries	Fatalities
Africa	989	8,755	3,357
East and Central Asia	202	5,352	227
Eastern Europe	1,229	4,931	1,875
Latin America and the Caribbean	3,407	3,550	2,078
Middle East / Persian Gulf	7,360	26,776	10,983
North America	581	4,217	3,574
South Asia	3,555	17,965	6,282
South-East Asia and Oceania	735	3,685	1,248
Western Europe	53,01	5,603	1,447

Data for 1968–97 cover only international incidents.
Data for 1998–present cover both domestic and international incidents.
Source: MIPT Terrorism Knowledge Base. Terrorism incident reports. Website, accessed 21 September 2005. Available from http://www.tkb.org/IncidentRegionModule.jsp. Incident data are drawn from the RAND Terrorism Chronology and RAND-MIPT Terrorism Incident Database as available through the Terrorism Knowledge Base (www.tkb.org).

Terrorist Incidents by Target, 1 January 1968 to 31 August 2005

Target	Incidents	Injuries	Fatalities
Abortion Related	5	2	2
Airports and Airlines	805	2,377	2,258
Business	3,314	12,235	5,055
Diplomatic	2,634	8,325	1,252
Educational Institutions	435	1,351	487
Food or Water Supply	10	5	0
Government	3,481	7,751	3,651
Journalists and Media	497	235	188
Maritime	134	263	130
Military	802	4,437	1,479
Non-Governmental Organization	287	257	268
Other	1,501	2,293	1,592
Police	1,689	6,124	3,398
Private Citizens and Property	4,056	14,281	5,841
Religious Figures/Institutions	804	5,530	1,897
Telecommunication	125	73	42
Terrorists	222	518	407
Tourists	242	1,513	584
Transportation	924	12,002	2,017
Unknown	668	925	324
Utilities	727	337	199
TOTAL	23,362	80,834	31,071

Data for 1968–97 cover only international incidents.
Data for 1998–present cover both domestic and international incidents.
Source: MIPT Terrorism Knowledge Base. Terrorism incident reports. Website, accessed 21 September 2005. Available from http://www.tkb.org/IncidentTargetModule.jsp. Incident data are drawn from the RAND Terrorism Chronology and RAND-MIPT Terrorism Incident Database as available through the Terrorism Knowledge Base (www.tkb.org).

MAPS AND STATISTICS

Terrorist Incidents by Tactic, 1 January 1968 to 31 August 2005

Tactic	Incidents	Injuries	Fatalities
Armed Attack	3,950	10,865	6,118
Arson	882	299	369
Assassination	2,193	955	2,774
Barricade/Hostage	203	2,201	896
Bombing	13,728	62,957	16,098
Hijacking	233	376	482
Kidnapping	1,702	114	796
Other	155	425	233
Unconventional Attack	55	2,440	3,004
Unknown	261	202	301
TOTAL	23,362	80,834	31,071

Data for 1968–97 cover only international incidents.
Data for 1998–present cover both domestic and international incidents.
Source: MIPT Terrorism Knowledge Base. Terrorism incident reports. Website, accessed 21 September 2005. Available from http://www.tkb.org/IncidentTacticModule.jsp. Incident data are drawn from the RAND Terrorism Chronology and RAND-MIPT Terrorism Incident Database as available through the Terrorism Knowledge Base (www.tkb.org).

Select Bibliography

Select Bibliography

General

Adams, James. *Financing of Terror: The PLO, IRA, Red Brigades, and M-19 and Their Money Supply.* New York, Simon and Schuster, 1986.

Addison, Michael. *Violent Politics: Strategies of Internal Conflict.* Basingstoke, Palgrave, 2002.

Alagappa, Muthiah. *The National Security of Developing States.* Dover, Auburn House, 1987.

Alexander, Yonah. *State Sponsored Terrorism.* Washington, DC, Center for Contemporary Studies, 1986.

Alexander, Yonah, and Leventhal, Paul (Eds). *Preventing Nuclear Terrorism: The Report and Papers of the International Task Force on Prevention of Nuclear Terrorism.* Lexington, Lexington Books, 1987.

Alibek, Ken. *Biohazard.* New York, Random House, 1999.

Anderson, Sean Kendall, and Sloan, Stephen. *Terrorism: Assassins to Zealots.* Lanham MD, The Scarecrow Press Inc., 2002).

Arquilla, John, and Ronfeldt, David. *Networks and Netwars: The Future of Terror, Crime, and Militancy.* Santa Monica, RAND, 2001.

Atkins, Stephen. *Encyclopedia of Modern Worldwide Extremists and Extremist Groups.* New York, Greenwood Press, 2004.

Barber, Benjamin. *Jihad vs McWorld: How Globalism and Tribalism are Reshaping the World.* New York, Ballantine, 1996.

Barnaby, Frank. *Instruments of Terror.* London, Satin Books, 1996.

Barnhart, Stephen R. *International Terrorism and Political Violence.* Victoria, B.C., Canada, Trafford, 2002.

Baumann, Bommi. *Terror or Love.* New York, Grove Press, 1977.

Beckatt, Ian F. W. *Encyclopedia of Guerilla Warfare.* New York, Checkmark, 2001.

Benjamin, David, and Simon, Steven. *The Age of Sacred Terror.* New York, Random House, 2002.

SELECT BIBLIOGRAPHY

Best, Steven. *Terrorists or Freedom Fighters: Reflections on the Liberation of Animals*. New York, Lantern, 2004.

Booth, Ken. *Worlds in Collision: Terror and the Future of Global Order*. New York, Palgrave, 2002.

Bray, Michael. *A Time to Kill*. Maryland, Advocates for Life Publishers, 1994.

Brynjar, Lia, and Hansen, Annika. *An Analytical Framework for the Study of Terrorism and Asymmetric Warfare*. Kjeller, Norwegian Defence Research Establishment, 1999.

Byman, Daniel, Chalk, Peter, and Hoffman, Bruce. *Trends in Outside Support for Insurgent Movements*. Santa Monica, RAND Corporation, 2001.

Cameron, Gavin. *Nuclear Terrorism: A Threat Assessment for the 21st Century*. Basingstoke, Macmillan Press, 1999.

Celmar, Marc. *Terrorism, U.S. Strategy and Reagan Policies*. New York, Greenwood Press, 1987.

Chalk, Peter. *Non-Military Security and Global Order. The Impact of Extremism, Violence and Chaos on National and International Security*. London, Macmillan, 2000.

Charters, David (Ed.). *The Deadly Sin of Terrorism*. Westport, Greenwood Press, 1994.

Clarke, Richard. *Against All Enemies: Inside America's War on Terror*. New York, Free Press, 2004.

Cline, Ray. *Terrorism as State-Sponsored Covert Warfare*. Fairfax, VA: Hero Books, 1986.

Corbin, Jane. *Al Qaeda: The Terror Network That Threatens the World*. New York, Nation Books, 2003.

Cragin, Kim, and Chalk, Peter. *Terrorism and Development: Using Social and Economic Development to Inhibit a Resurgence of Terrorism*. Santa Monica, Rand, 2003.

Crenshaw, Martha (Ed.). *Terrorism in Context*. University Park, Pennsylvania State University Press, 1995.

Davis, Paul K., and Jenkins, Michael. *Deterrence and Influence in Counterterrorism: A Component in the War on Al-Qaeda*. Santa Monica, Rand, 2002.

Gareau, Frederick H. *State Terrorism and the United States: From Counterinsurgency to the War on Terrorism*. Atlanta, GA, Clarity Press, 2004.

George, Alexander (Ed.). *Western State Terrorism*. New York, Routledge, 1991.

Guelke, Adrian. *The Age of Terrorism and the International Political System.* London, I. B. Tauris, 1995.

Gunaratna, Rohan. *Inside Al-Qaeda: Global Network of Terror.* New York, Columbia University Press, 2002.

Gunaratna, Rohan, and Chalk, Peter. *Jane's Counter Terrorism.* Surrey, United Kingdom, Jane's, 2002.

Gunsson, Phil, and Chamberlain, Greg. *The Dictionary of Contemporary Politics of Central America and the Caribbean.* New York, Simon and Schuster, 1991.

Gurr, Nadine, and Cole, Benjamin. *The New Face of Terrorism: Threats From Weapons of Mass Destruction.* London, I. B. Tauris, 2002.

Gutteridge, William (Ed.). *Contemporary Terrorism.* New York, Facts on File Publications, 1986.

Herman, Edward, and O'Sullivan, Gerry. *The Terrorism Industry.* New York, Pantheon, 1990.

Hoffman, Bruce. *Inside Terrorism.* New York, Columbia University Press, 1998.

Holy Terror: The Implications of Terrorism Motivated by a Religious Imperative. RAND, 1993.

Howard, Russell D. *Defeating Terrorism: Shaping the New Security Environment.* Guilford, CT, McGraw-Hill, 2004.

Howard, Russell D., and Sawyer, Reid L. *Terrorism and Counter Terrorism.* Guildford, CT, McGraw-Hill, 2004.

Huband, Mark. *Warriors of the Prophet: The Struggle for Islam.* Boulder, Westview, 1998.

Huntingdon, Samuel. *The Clash of Civilizations and the Remaking of World Order.* New York, Touchstone, 1996.

Jackson, Brian. *Technology Acquisition by Terrorist Groups.* Santa Monica, RAND, 2000.

Jenkins, Brian M. 'International Terrorism: A New Mode of Conflict', in Carlton, David, and Schaerf, Carlo (Eds), *International Terrorism and World Security.* London, Croom Helm, 1975.

Jones, David Martin (Ed.). *Globalisation and the New Terror: The Asia-Pacific Dimension.* Cheltenham, Edward Elgar, 2004.

Juergensmeyer, Mark. *The New Cold War: Religious Nationalism Confronts the Secular State.* Berkeley, University of California Press, 1993.

Terror in the Mind of God: The Global Rise of Religious Violence. Berkeley, University of California Press, 2000.

SELECT BIBLIOGRAPHY

Kaldor, Mary. *New and Old Wars: Organized Violence in a Global Era*. Stanford, Stanford University Press, 1999.

Kaplan, Jeffrey, and Weinberg, Leonard. *The Emergence of A Euro-American Radical Right*. New Brunswick, NJ, Rutgers University Press, 1998.

Kegley, Jr, Charles, and Wittkopf, Eugene. *World Politics: Trend and Transformation*. New York, Worth, 1999.

Kepel, Giles. *The War for Muslim Minds*. Cambridge, Mass., Harvard University Press, 2004.

Khalilzad, Zalmay. *Sources of Conflict in the 21st Century: Regional Futures and U.S. Strategy*. Santa Monica, Rand, 1998.

Laqueur, Walter. *The Age of Terrorism*. London, Weinfield and Nicolson, 1987.

The New Terrorism: Fanaticism and the Arms of Mass Destruction. Oxford, Oxford University Press, 1999.

No End to War: Terrorism in the Twenty-First Century. New York, Continuum, 2003.

Lelyveld, Joseph. 'Interrogating Ourselves', in *New York Times Magazine*, 12 June 2005.

Lesser, Ian, Hoffinan, Bruce, Arquilla, John, Jenkins, Brian, Ronfeldt, David, and Zanini, Michele (Eds). *Countering the New Terrorism*. Santa Monica, Rand, 1999.

Lutz, James, and Lutz, Brenda. *Global Terrorism*. London, Routledge, 2004.

Martin, D., and Walcott, J. *Best Laid Plans*. New York, Harper and Row, 1988.

McLellan, David. *The Thought of Karl Marx*. London, Macmillan Press, 1980.

Mickolus, Edward F., Todd, Sandler, and Murdock, Jean M. *International Terrorism in the 1980s*. Ames, Iowa State University Press, 1989.

Mockaitis, Thomas R., and Rich, Paul B. (Eds). *Grand Strategy in the War Against Terrorism*. London, Frank Cass, 2003.

Nacos, Brigitte. *Terrorism and the Media: From the Iran Hostage Crisis to the Oklahoma City Bombing*. New York, Columbia University Press, 1994.

Nechaev, Sergei. 'The Revolutionary Catechism', reprinted in Rapoport, David C., *Assassination and Terrorism*. Toronto, CBC, 1971.

O'Neill, Bard. *Insurgency and Terrorism, Inside Modern Revolutionary Warfare*. Washington, Brassey's Inc., 1990.

Palti, Leslie. 'Combating Terrorism While Protecting Human Rights', in *UN Chronicle* Vol. XLI (4 November 2004), online edition: http://www.un.org/Pubs/chronicle/2004/issue4/0404p27.html.

Ranstorp, Magnus. 'Terrorism in the Name of Religion', in *Journal of International Affairs*. Summer 1996, Vol. 50, No. 1.

Rapoport, David C. 'Fear and Trembling, Terrorism in Three Religious Traditions', in *American Political Science Review*. Vol. 78, No. 3, 1984.

'Terrorism and Weapons of the Apocalypse', in *National Security Studies Quarterly*. Vol. 5, No. 1, 1999.

'The Fourth Wave: September 11 in the History of Terrorism', in *Current History*. December 2001.

'The Politics of Atrocity', in Alexander, Yonah, and Finger, Seymore M., *Terrorism: Interdisciplinary Perspectives*. New York, John Jay Press, 1977.

Record, Jeffrey. *Bounding the Global War on Terrorism*. Carlisle Barracks, PA, Strategic Studies Institute, December 2003.

Roberts, Brad (Ed.). *Hype or Reality: The 'New Terrorism' and Mass Casualty Attacks*. Alexandria, VA, The Chemical and Biological Arms Control Institute, 2000.

Rubenstein, Alvin. *Alchemists of Revolution: Terrorism in the Modern World*. New York, Basic Books, 1987.

Sageman, Marc. *Understanding Terror Networks*. Philadelphia, University of Pennsylvannia Press, 2004.

Schmid, A. P., and Jongman, A. J. 'Violent Conflicts and Human Rights Violations in the Mid-1990s', in *Terrorism and Political Violence*. Vol. 9, No. 4, 1997.

Schweitzer, Yoram. *The Globalization of Terror: The Challenge of Al-Qaida and the Response of the International Community*. New Brunswick, Transaction Publishers, 2003.

Simon, Jeffrey. *Terrorism and Potential Use of Biological Weapons*. Santa Monica, Rand Corp, 1989.

Sterling, Clair. *The Terror Network*. New York, Holt, Rinehart and Winston, 1981.

Stern, Jessica. *The Ultimate Terrorists*. Cambridge, MA, Harvard University Press, 1999.

Terror in the Name of God: Why Religious Militants Kill. New York, Harper and Collins, 2003.

Tan, Andrew T H, and Ramakrishna, K. (Eds). *The New Terrorism: Anatomy, Trends and Counter-Strategies*. Singapore, Eastern Universities Press, 2002.

Tanter, Raymond. *Rogue Regimes: Terrorism and Proliferation*. New York, St Martin's Griffin, 1999.

Thompson, Leroy. *Rescuers*. New York, Dell, 1988.

Tucker, Jonathan (Ed.). *Toxic Terror: Assessing Terrorist Use of Chemical and Biological Weapons*. Cambridge, MIT Press, 2000.

Volkan, Vamik. *Blood Lines: From Ethnic Pride to Ethnic Terrorism*. New York, Farrar, Straus and Giroux, 1997.

Wardlaw, Grant. *Political Terrorism: Theory, Tactics, and Counter-measures*. New York, Cambridge University Press, 1989.

Weimann, Gabriel. 'WWW.Terror.Net—How *Modern Terrorism Uses the Internet*, in U.S. Institute for Peace, Special Report #116, March 2004.

Whittaker, David J. *Terrorism: Understanding the Global Threat*. London, Longman, 2002.

Wilkinson, Paul. *Terrorism Versus Democracy: The Liberal State Response*. London, Frank Cass, 2001.

Yassin, El-Ayouty. *Perspectives on 9–11*. Westport, CT, Praeger, 2004.

Middle East

Abdo, Geneive. *No God But God: Egypt and the Triumph of Islam*. New York, Oxford University Press, 2002.

Abdo, Geneive, and Lyons, Jonathan. *Answering Only to God: Faith and Freedom in Twenty-First Century Iran*. New York, Henry Holt, 2003.

Ajami, Fouad. *The Arab Predicament: Arab Thought and Practice Since 1967*. New York, Cambridge University Press, 1992.

Alexander, Yonah. *Palestinian Religious Terrorism: Hamas and Islamic Jihad*. New York, Transnational, 2002.

Algar, Hamid. *Roots of the Islamic Revolution in Iran*. Oneonta, Islamic Publications International, 2001.

Ali, Tariq. *The Clash of Fundamentalisms: Crusades, Jihads and Modernity*. New York, Verso, 2002.

Anonymous. *Through Our Enemies' Eyes: Osama bin Ladin, Radical Islam and the Future of America*. Dulles, Brassey's, 2002.

Begin, Menachem. *The Revolt: Story of the Irgun*. Jerusalem, Steinmatzky's Agency, 1967.

Bell, J. Bowyer. *Murders on the Nile, The World Trade Center and Global Terror*. San Francisco, Encounter Books, 2002.

Bergen, Peter. *Holy War Inc. Inside the Secret World of Osama bin Laden.* London, Weidenfeld and Nicolson, 2001.

Bill, James A. *Eagle and the Lion: The Tragedy of American Iranian Relations.* New Haven, Yale University Press, 1989.

Black, Ian. *Israel's Secret Wars: A History of Israel's Intelligence Services.* New York, Grove, 1992.

Bodansky, Yossef. *Bin Laden: The Man Who Declared War on America.* Roseville, Forum, 2001.

Byers, Ann. *Lebanon's Hezbollah.* New York, Rosen, 2002.

Davis, Brian Leigh. *Qaddafi, Terrorism and the Origins of the U.S. Attack on Libya.* Santa Monica, Rand, 1990.

Esposito, John. *The Islamic Threat: Myth or Reality?* Oxford, Oxford University Press, 1992.

Unholy War: Terror in the Name of Islam. New York, Oxford University Press, 2002.

Friedman, Thomas. *From Beirut to Jerusalem.* New York, Anchor, 1990.

Halliday, Fred. *Islam and the Myth of Confrontation.* New York, I. B. Tauris, 1996.

Revolution and Foreign Policy: The Case of South Yemen, 1967–1987. New York, Cambridge University Press, 2002.

Hamdi, Mohamed. *The Politicisation of Islam: A Case Study of Tunisia.* Boulder, Perseus, 2000.

Hatina, Meir. *Islam and Salvation in Palestine: The Islamic Jihad Movement.* Tel-Aviv, Tel-Aviv University, 2001.

Hiro, Dilip. *Islamic Fundamentalism.* London, Paladin, 1989.

Hoveyda, Fereydoun. *The Broken Crescent: The Threat of Militant Islamic Fundamentalism.* Westport, CT, Praeger, 1998.

Hroub, Khaled. *Hamas: Political Thought and Practice.* Beirut, Institute for Palestine Studies, 2000.

Jaber, Hala. *Hezbollah: Born with a Vengeance.* New York, Cambridge University Press, 1997.

Karsh, Efraim, and Kumaraswamy, P. R. (Eds). *Israel, the Hashemites and the Palestinians: The Fateful Triangle.* New York, Cass, 2003.

Kepel, Giles. *Muslim Extremism in Egypt: The Prophet and Pharoah.* Berkeley, University of California Press, 1993.

SELECT BIBLIOGRAPHY

Jihad: The Trial of Political Islam. Cambridge, MA, Harvard University Press, 2002.

Khalaf, Samir. *Civil and Uncivil Violence: The Internationalization of Communal Conflict in Lebanon*. New York, Columbia University Press, 2002.

Laizer, Sheri J. *Martyrs, Traitors and Patriots: Kurdistan after the Gulf War*. London, Palgrave Macmillan, 1996.

Lewis, Bernard. *Islam and the West*. New York, Oxford University Press, 1994.

What Went Wrong: Western Impact and Middle Eastern Response. New York, Oxford University Press, 2001.

The Crisis of Islam: Holy War and Unholy Terror. New York, Random House, 2001.

Lia, Brynjar, and Al-Banna, Jamal. *The Society of the Muslim Brothers in Egypt: The Rise of an Islamic Mass Movement 1928–1942*. New York, Ithica Press, 1998.

Makiya, Kanan. *Cruelty and Silence: War, Tyranny, Uprising and the Arab World*. New York, W. W. Norton and Company, 1994.

McDowall, David. *A Modern History of the Kurds*. London, I. B. Tauris, 1996.

Miller, William H. 'Insurgency Theory and the Conflict in Algeria: A Theoretical Analysis', in *Terrorism and Political Violence*, Vol. 12, No. 1, 2000.

Mishal, Shaul, and Sela, Avraham. *The Palestinian Hamas: Vision, Violence and Coexistence*. New York, Columbia University Press, 2000.

Murphy, John F. *Sword of Islam: Muslim Extremism From the Arab Conquests to the Attack on America*. New York, Prometheus Books, 2002.

Nusse, Andrea. *Muslim Palestine: The Ideology of Hamas*. Amsterdam, Harwood, 1998.

O'Ballance, Edgar. *Islamic Fundamentalist Terrorism, 1979–95: The Iranian Connection*. New York, New York University Press, 1997.

Ojeda, Auriana. *Islamic Fundamentalism*. San Diego, Greenhaven Press, 2003.

Ranstorp, Magnus. *Hizb'allah in Lebanon*. New York, St Martin's Press, 1996.

Reeve, Simon. *One Day in September: The Full Story of the 1972 Munich Olympics Massacre and the Israeli Revenge Operation 'Wrath of God'*. New York, Arcane, 2001.

Reeve, Simon. *The New Jackals: Ramzi Yousef, Osama bin Laden and the Future of Terrorism*. London, André Deutsch, 1999.

Roy, Olivier. *The Failure of Political Islam*. Cambridge, MA, Harvard University Press, 1996.

Saad-Ghorayeb, Amal. *Hizbullah: Politics and Religion*. London, Pluto, 2002.

Satloff, Robert B. *War Against Terror: The Middle East Dimension*. Washington, DC, Washington Institute for Near East Policy, 2002.

Sayigh, Yezid. *Armed Struggle and the Search for State: The Palestinian National Movement, 1949–1993*. Oxford, Clarendon, 1997.

Schwartz, Stephen. *The Two Faces of Islam: The House of Sa'ud from Tradition to Terror*. New York, Doubleday, 2002.

Teitelbaum, Joshua. *Holier Than Thou: Saudi Arabia's Islamic Opposition*. Washington, Washington Institute for Near East Policy, 2000.

Tibi, Bassam. *The Challenge of Fundamentalism: Political Islam and the New World Disorder*. Los Angeles, University of California Press, 2002.

Volpi, Frederic. *Islam and Democracy: The Failure of Dialogue in Algeria, 1988–2001*. New York, Verso, 2002.

Weaver, Mary Anne. *A Portrait of Egypt: A Journey Through the World of Militant Islam*. New York, Farrar, Straus and Giroux, 2000.

White, Paul J. *Primitive Rebels or Revolutionary Modernizers? The Kurdish National Movement in Turkey*. London, Zed Books, 1997.

Willis, Michael. *The Islamist Challenge in Algeria: A Political History*. New York, New York University Press, 1999.

Wright, Robin. *Sacred Rage: The Wrath of Militant Islam*. New York, Touchstone, 2001.

Ziad, Abu-Amr. *Islamic Fundamentalism in the West Bank and Gaza: Muslim Brotherhood and Islamic Jihad*. Bloomington, Indiana University Press, 1994.

Africa

Abdel Salam, A. H., and De Waal, Alexander (Eds). *The Phoenix State: Civil Society and the Future of Sudan*. New Jersey, Red Sea Press, 2001.

Adebajo, Adekeye. *Building Peace in West Africa: Liberia, Sierra Leone, and Guinea-Bissau*. Colorado, Lynne Rienner, 2002.

Adelman, Howard, and Suhrke, Astri (Eds). *The Path of a Genocide: The Rwanda Crisis from Uganda to Zaire*. New Jersey, Transaction Publishers, 2000.

Akhahenda, Elijah. *When Blood and Tears United a Country: The Bombing of the American Embassy in Kenya*. Washington, University Press of America, 2002.

Algeria, Time for Reckoning: Enforced Disappearances and Abductions in Algeria. New York, Human Rights Watch, 2003.

SELECT BIBLIOGRAPHY

Allard, Kenneth. *Somalia Operations: Lessons Learned*. Oregon, University Press of the Pacific, 2002.

Barnett, Michael. *Eyewitness to Genocide: The United Nations and Rwanda*. Ithaca, Cornell University Press, 2002.

Bassett, Thomas J. *The Peasant Cotton Revolution in West Africa: Côte d'Ivoire, 1880–1995*. New York, Cambridge University Press, 2001.

Beckett, Paul, and Crawford, Young (Eds). *Dilemmas of Democracy in Nigeria*. Rochester, University of Rochester Press, 1997.

Berkeley, Bill. *The Graves Are Not Yet Full: Race, Tribe, and Power in the Heart of Africa*. New York, Basic Books, 2002.

Blood Trail: Repression and Resistance in Niger Delta. Lagos, Nigeria, Civil Liberties Organisation, 2002.

Bundu, Abass. *Democracy by Force?: A Study of International Military Intervention in the Conflict in Sierra Leone from 1991–2000*. London, Universal Publishers, 2001.

Cilliers, Jakkie. *Africa and Terrorism: Joining the Global Campaign*. Pretoria, South Africa, Institute for Security Studies, 2002.

Clapham, Christopher (Ed.). *African Guerrillas*. Bloomington, Indiana University Press, 1998.

Clark, John F. (Ed.). *The African Stakes of the Congo War*. Boston, Palgrave Macmillan, 2002.

Clarke, Walter, and Herbst, Jeffrey (Eds). *Learning from Somalia: The Lessons of Armed Humanitarian Intervention*. Boulder, Westview Press, 1997.

Crenshaw, Martha. *Terrorism in Africa*. New York, G. K. Hall and Co., 1997.

Ellis, Stephen. *The Mask of Anarchy: The Destruction of Liberia and the Religious Dimension of an African Civil War*. New York, New York University Press, 2001.

Falola, Toyin. *Violence in Nigeria: The Crisis of Religious Politics and Secular Ideologies*. Rochester, University of Rochester Press, 2001.

Hodges, Tony. *Angola from Afro-Stalinism to Petro-Diamond Capitalism*. Oxford, Indiana University Press, 2001.

Kasozi, A. B. K. *The Social Origins of Violence in Uganda, 1964–1985*. Montreal, McGill-Queen's University Press, 1994.

Maier, Karl. *This House Has Fallen: Nigeria in Crisis*. New York, Allen Lane, 2003.

Mentan, Tatah. *Dilemmas of Weak States: Africa and Transnational Terrorism in the Twenty-First Century*. Burlington, VT, Ashgate, 2004.

Mumdani, Mahmood. *When Victims Become Killers: Colonialism, Nativism and the Genocide in Rwanda*. Princeton, NJ, Princeton University Press, 2001.

Niblock, Tim. *'Pariah States' and Sanctions in the Middle East: Iraq, Libya, Sudan*. Boulder, Lynne Rienner, 2002.

Nzongola-Ntalaja, Georges. *The Congo*. London, Zed Books, 2002.

O'Ballance, Edgar. *The Congo-Zaire Experience, 1960–98*. New York, Palgrave Macmillan, 2000.

Petterson, Donald. *Inside Sudan: Political Islam, Conflict, and Catastrophe*. Boulder, Westview Press, 1999.

Rone, Jemera. *Behind the Red Line: Political Repression in Sudan*. New York, Human Rights Watch, 1996.

Sahnoun, Mohamed. *Somalia: The Missed Opportunities*. Washington, DC, U.S. Institute of Peace Press, 1997.

Saro-Wiwa, Ken. *On a Darkling Plain: An Account of the Nigerian Civil War*. London, Saros International Publishers, 1989.

Suberu, Rotimi T. *Federalism and Ethnic Conflict in Nigeria*. Washington, U.S. Institute of Peace Press, 2001.

Sundiata, Ibrahim K. *Equatorial Guinea: Colonialism, State Terror, and The Search For Stability*. Boulder, Westview Press, 1990.

Tayler, Jeffrey. *Facing the Congo: A Modern-Day Journey into the Heart of Darkness*. St Paul, Ruminator Books, 2001.

Warburg, Gabriel. *Islam, Sectarianism, and Politics in the Sudan since the Mahdiyya*. Madison, University of Wisconsin Press, 2002.

William, Minter. *Apartheid's Contras: An Inquiry into the Roots of War in Angola and Mozambique*. London, Zed Books, 1994.

Williams, Gabriel I. H. *Liberia: The Heart of Darkness*. Victoria, Trafford Publishing, 2002.

Americas

Abane, Richard. *American Militias: Rebellion, Racism & Religion*. Downers Grove, IL, Inter-Varsity Press, 1996.

Anderson, John Lee. *Che Guevara: A Revolutionary Life*. New York, Grove Press, 1997.

Atkins, Stephen E. *Encyclopedia of Modern American Extremists and Extremist Groups*. Westport, CT, Greenwood Press, 2002.

SELECT BIBLIOGRAPHY

Balkin, Karen F. *War on Terrorism*. San Diego, Greenhaven, 2005.

Ball, Patrick, Kobrak, Paul, and Spirer, Herbert F. *State Violence in Guatemala, 1960–1996: A Quantitative Reflection*. Washington, DC, American Association for the Advancement of Science, 1999.

Brill, Steven. *After: How America Confronted the September 12 Era*. New York, Simon and Schuster, 2003.

Chomsky, Noam. *9–11*. New York, Seven Stories Press, 2001.

Dees, Morris. *Gathering Storm: America's Militia Threat*. New York, Harper Collins Publishers, 1996.

Dillon, Sam. *Commandos: The CIA and Nicaragua's Contra Rebels*. New York, Henry Holt, 1991.

Dudley, Steven S. *Walking Ghosts: Murder and Guerilla Politics in Colombia*. New York, Routledge, 2004.

Falkenrath, Richard, Newman, Robert, and Thayer, Bradley. *America's Achilles Heel: Nuclear, Biological and Chemical Terrorism and Covert Attack*. Cambridge, MIT Press, 1998.

Flynn, Kevin, and Gerhardt, Gary. *The Silent Brotherhood*. New York, Signet, 1990.

George, John. *Nazis, Communists, Klansmen, and Others on the Fringe: Political Extremism in America*. New York, Prometheus Books, 1992.

Gorriti, Gustavo. *The Shining Path: A History of the Millenarian War in Peru*. Lima, Editorial Apoyo, 1990.

Hayden, Patrick. *America's War on Terror*. England, Ashgate, 2003.

Hodge, Jr, James F., and Rose, Gideon (Eds). *How Did This Happen? Terrorism and the New War*. New York, Public Affairs/Council on Foreign Relations, 2001.

Hoffman, Bruce. *Terrorism in the United States and the Potential Threat to Nuclear Facilities*. Santa Monica, RAND, 1986.

Holden, Robert H. *Armies Without Nations: Public Violence and State Formation in Central America, 1821–1960*. New York, Oxford University Press, 2003.

Hollander, Nancy Caro. *Love in a Time of Hate: Liberation Psychology in Latin America*. New Brunswick, NJ, Rutgers University Press, 1997.

Koonings, Kees, and Kruijt, Dirk (Eds). *Societies of Fear: The Legacy of Civil War, Violence and Terror in Latin America*. London, Zed Books, 1999.

Landau, Saul. *The Guerrilla Wars of Central America: Nicaragua, El Salvador, and Guatemala*. New York, St Martin's Press, 1993.

Levitas, Daniel. *The Terrorist Next Door: The Militia Movement and the Radical Right*. New York, St Martin's Press, 2002.

Macdonald, Andrew. *The Turner Diaries*. Hillsboro, WV, National Vanguard Books, 1980.

Maharidge, Dale. *Homeland*. New York, Seven Stories Press, 2004.

Marcella, Gabriel, and Schulz, Donald E. *Colombia's Three Wars: U.S. Strategy at the Crossroads*. PA, US Army War College, 1999.

Marighella, Carlos. *For the Liberation of Brazil*. Harmondsworth, Penguin, 1971.

Michael, George. *Confronting Right-Wing Extremism and Terrorism in the USA*. New York, Routledge, 2003.

Palmer, David Scott (Ed.). *The Shining Path of Peru*. New York, St Martin's Press, 1994.

Pillar, Paul R. *Terrorism and U.S. Foreign Policy*. Washington, Brookings Institution, 2001.

Pizarro, Fernando. *New Reflections on Terrorism and Terrorism in America: International Connections*. Chicago, Office of International Criminal Justice, University of Illinois at Chicago, 1988.

Poole, Deborah, and Renique, Gerardo. *Peru: Time of Fear*. London, Latin American Bureau, 1992.

Ronfedt, David, Arquilla, John, Fuller, Graham E., and Fuller, Melissa. *The Zapatista Social Netwar in Mexico*. Santa Monica, Rand, 1998.

Rossi, Ernest E., and Plano, Jack C. *Latin America: A Political Dictionary*. Santa Barbara, CA, ABC-CLIO, 1992.

Sherman, John W. *Latin America in Crisis*. Boulder, Westview Press, 2000.

Snow, Robert. *Terrorists Among Us: The Militia Threat*. Cambridge, MA, Perseus Publishing, 2002.

Sonder, Ben. *Militia Movement: Fighters of the Far Right*. New York, F. Watts, 2000.

Tourish, Dennis. *On the Edge: Political Cults Right and Left*. Armonk, NY, M. E. Sharpe, 2000.

Weaver, Randy, and Weaver, Sara. *The Federal Siege at Ruby Ridge*. Marion, MT, Ruby Ridge Inc., 1998.

Wickham-Crowley, Timothy P. *Guerillas and Revolution in Latin America: A Comparative Study of Insurgents and Regimes Since 1956*. Princeton, Princeton University Press, 1992.

Wilkinson, Daniel. *Silence on the Mountain: Stories of Terror, Betrayal, and Forgetting in Guatemala*. Boston, Houghton Mifflin, 2002.

Woodward, Bob. *Bush at War*. New York, Simon and Schuster, 2002.

Europe

Adams, Gerry. *Free Ireland: Towards a Lasting Peace*. Dingle, Brandon Books, 1995.

Alexander, Yonah. *Europe's Red Terrorists: The Fighting Communist Organizations*. Portland, Frank Cass, 1992.

Terrorism in Europe. New York, St Martin's Press, 1982.

European Terrorism Today & Tomorrow. Washington, Brassey's, 1992.

ETA: Profile of a Terrorist Group. New York, Transnational Publishers, 2001.

Archick, Kristin. *Europe and Counterterrorism*. New York, Nova Science Publishers, 2003.

Aust, Stephan. *The Baader-Meinhof Group: The Inside Story of a Phenomenon*. Anthea Bell, Trans. London, Bodley Head, 1987.

Bell, J. Bowyer. *The Irish Troubles: A Generation of Violence, 1969–1992*. Dublin, Gill and Macmillan, 1993.

The IRA, 1968–2000: Analysis Of A Secret Army. London, Frank Cass, 2000.

Bensahel, Nora. *The Counterterror Coalitions: Cooperation with Europe, NATO, and the European Union*. Santa Monica, Rand, 2003.

Bew, P., Patterson, H., and Teague, Paul. *Northern Ireland: Between War and Peace; The Political Future of Northern Ireland*. London, Scarecrow, 2000.

Bohn, Michael K. *The Achille Lauro Hijacking: Lessons in the Politics and Prejudice of Terrorism*. Washington, Brassey's, 2004.

Bourguereau, Jean M. *German Guerrilla: Terror, Rebel Reaction and Resistance*. Sanday, Orkney, United Kingdom, Cienfuegos Press, 1981.

Chalk, Peter. *West European Terrorism and Counter-Terrorism: The Evolving Dynamic*. New York, St Martin's, 1996.

Clark, Robert P. *Basque Insurgents: ETA, 1952–1980*. Madison, University of Wisconsin Press, 1984.

Collins, Eamon. *Killing Rage*. London, Granta Books, 1997.

Coogan, Tim Pat. *The IRA*. London, Harper Collins, 2000.

Corsun, Andrew. *Armenian Terrorism: 1975–1989*. US Department of State, Office of Security, Threat Analysis Group, August 1981.

Armenian Terrorism: 1984–1987. US Department of State, Office of Secruity, Threat Analysis Group, September 1988.

Drake, Richard. *The Revolutionary Mystique and Terrorism in Contemporary Italy*. Bloomington, Indiana, Indiana University Press, 1989.

Emerson, Steven. *Fall of Pan Am 103: Inside the Lockerbie Investigation*. New York, Putnam, 1990.

Engene, Jan Oskar. *Terrorism in Western Europe: Explaining the Trends Since 1950*. University of Bergen, Edward Elgar, 2004.

English, Richard. *Armed Struggle: The History of the IRA*. New York, Oxford University Press, 2003.

Feraracuti, Franco. 'Ideology and Repentence: Terrorism in Italy', in Reich, Walter, *The Origins of Terrorism*. Cambridge, United Kingdom, 1990.

Fraser, Nicholas. *Voice of Modern Hatred: Tracing the Rise of Neo-Fascism in Europe*. New York, Overlook Press, 2001.

Gall, Carlotta, and de Waal, Thomas. *Chechnya: Calamity in the Caucasus*. New York, New York University Press, 1998.

Hoffman, Bruce. *Right-wing Terrorism in Europe Since 1980*. Santa Monica, RAND, 1984.

Hyland, Francis P. *Armenian Terrorism: The Past, the Present, the Prospects*. Boulder, Westview Press, 1991.

Judah, Tim. *Kosovo: War and Revenge*. New Haven, Yale University Press, 2000.

Kaplan, Jeffrey. *Emergence of a Euro-American Radical Right*. New Brunswick, NJ, Rutgers University Press, 1998.

Kassimeris, George. *Europe's Last Red Terrorists: The Revolutionary Organisation 17 November*. New York, New York University Press, 2001.

Leeuwen, Marianne van. *Confronting Terrorism: European Experiences, Threat Perceptions and Policies*. New York, Kluwer Law International, 2003.

Murphy, Paul J. *Wolves of Islam: Russia and the Faces of Chechen Terror*. Washington, DC, Brassey, 2004.

O'Doherty, Malachi. *The Trouble with Guns: Republican Strategy and the Provisional IRA*. Belfast, Blackstaff Press, 1998.

Pluchinsky, Dennis, 'Middle Eastern Terrorist Activity in Western Europe in the 1980s: A Decade of Violence', in Pluchinsky, Dennis, and Alexander, Yonah (Eds), *European Terrorism: Today and Tomorrow*. McClean, VA, Brasseys, 1992.

'Middle Eastern Terrorism in Europe: Trends and Prospects', in *Terrorism: An International Journal*. Vol. 14, 1997.

Reinares, Fernando. *European Democracies Against Terrorism: Governmental Policies and Intergovernmental Cooperation*. Aldershot, Ashgate, 2000.

Ryder, Chris. *The RUC 1922–1997: A Force Under Fire*. London, Mandarin, 1997.

Sargeant, Jack. *Guns, Death, Terror: 1960's & 1970's Revolutionaries, Urban Guerrillas and Terrorists*. London, Creation, 2003.

Schmid, Alex P. *Western Responses to Terrorism*. Portland, Frank Cass, 1995.

Smith, Michael L. R. *Fighting for Ireland: The Military Strategy of the Irish Republican Movement*. New York, Routledge, 1995.

Stepniak, Sergei. *Underground Russia: Revolutionary Profiles and Sketches from Life*. New York, 1982.

Weine, Steven. *When History is a Nightmare: Lives and Memories of Ethnic Cleansing in Bosnia-Herzegovina*. New Brunswick, Rutgers University Press, 1999.

Woodworth, Paddy. *Dirty War, Clean Hands: ETA, the GAL and Spanish Democracy*. Crosses Green, Cork, Ireland, Cork University Press, 2001.

Wright, Joanne. *Terrorist Propaganda: The Red Army Faction and the Provisional IRA, 1968–86*. New York, St Martin's Press, 1991.

Asia

Abuza, Zachary. *Militant Islam in Southeast Asia: Crucible of Terror*. Boulder, Lynne Rienner, 2003.

Akbar, M. K. *Kargil: Cross Border Terrorism*. New Delhi, Mittal, 1999.

Bajpai, Kanti P. *Roots of Terrorism*. New Delhi, Penguin, 2002.

Barreveld, Dirk J. *Terrorism in the Philippines: The Bloody Trial of Abu Sayyaf, Bin Laden's East Asian Connection*. San Jose, Writers Club Press, 2001.

Bertrand, Jacques. *Nationalism and Ethnic Conflict in Indonesia*. New York, Cambridge University Press, 2004.

Bose, Samantra. *Kashmir: Roots of Conflict, Paths to Peace*. New Delhi, Vistaar, 2003.

Brackett, David. *Holy Terror: Armageddon in Tokyo*. New York, Weatherhill, 1996.

Carey, Peter (Ed.). *Burma: The Struggle for Change in a Divided Society.* New York, St Martin's Press, 1997.

Chandler, David. *A History of Cambodia.* New Haven, Yale University Press, 2000.

Cooley, John. *Unholy Wars. Afghanistan, America and International Terrorism.* London, Pluto Press, 2002.

Dillon, Michael. *Xinjiang: China's Muslim Far Northwest.* London, Routledge, 2003.

Farrell, William. *Blood and Rage: The Story of the Japanese Red Army.* Lexington, Lexington Books, 1990.

Fredholm, Michael. *Burma: Ethnicity and Insurgency.* Westport, CT, Praeger, 1993.

Gunaratna, Rohan. *Sri Lanka's Ethnic Crisis and National Security.* Colombo, South Asian Network on Conflict Research, 2000.

Terrorism in the Asia Pacific: Threat and Response. Singapore, Eastern Universities Press, 2003.

Ganguly, Sumit. *The Crisis in Kashmir: Portents of War, Hopes of Peace.* New York, Cambridge University Press, 1997.

George, T. J. S. *Revolt in Mindanao: The Rise of Islam in Philippine Politics.* Singapore, Oxford University Press, 1980.

Gutoc, Samira Ali. *Causes of Terrorism: The Philippines Amid Southeast Asia.* Oxford, Oxford University, Centre for Islamic Studies, 2003.

Hamilton-Merritt, Jane. *Tragic Mountains: The Hmong, the Americans and the Secret War for Laos, 1942–1992.* Bloomington, Indiana University Press, 1999.

Hellman-Rajanayagam, Dagmar. *The Tamil Tigers: Armed Struggle for Identity.* Stuttgart, Steiner, 1994.

Isaacson, Jason, and Rubenstein, Colin (Eds). *Islam in Asia: Changing Political Realities.* New Brunswick, Transaction, 2001.

Jain, Sharda. *The Politics of Terrorism in India: The Case of Punjab.* New Delhi, Deep and Deep, 1995.

Jones, Owen Bennett. *Pakistan: Eye of the Storm.* New Haven, Yale University Press, 2002.

Kaplan, David, and Marshall, Andrew. *The Cult at the End of the World: The Terrifying Story of the Aum Doomsday Cult, from the Subways of Tokyo to the Nuclear Arsenals of Russia.* London, Crown, 1996.

SELECT BIBLIOGRAPHY

Karim, Afsir. *Counter Terrorism: The Pakistan Factor.* New Delhi, Lancer International, 1991.

Kell, Tim. *The Roots of Acehnese Rebellion, 1989–1992.* Ithaca, Cornell University Press, 1995.

Kessler, R. J. *Rebellion and Repression in the Philippines.* New Haven, Yale University Press, 1989.

Kiernan, Ben. *The Pol Pot Regime: Race, Power and Genocide in Cambodia Under the Khmer Rouge, 1975–79.* New Haven, Yale University Press, 2002.

Kim Hyun Hee. *The Tears of My Soul.* New York, Morrow, 1994.

Kirkbridge, Wayne. *North Korea's Undeclared War.* New Jersey, Hollym, 1995.

Larrabee, F. Stephen. *The Middle East in the Shadow of Afghanistan and Iraq.* New York, Rand, 1995.

Lifton, Robert Jay. *Destroying the World to Save It: Aum Shinrikyo, Apocalyptic Violence, and the New Global Terrorism.* New York, Henry Holt, 2000.

Mahmood, Cynthia K. *Fighting for Faith and Nation: Dialogues with Sikh Militants.* Philadelphia, University of Philadelphia Press, 1997.

Man, W. K. Che. *Muslim Separatism: The Moros of Southern Philippines and the Malays of Southern Thailand.* Singapore, Oxford University Press, 1990.

Marwah, Ved. *Uncivil Wars: Pathology of Terrorism in India.* New Delhi, Indus, 1995.

Millard, Mike, and Hall, Ivan. *Jihad in Paradise: Islam and Politics in Southeast Asia.* New York, M. E. Sharpe, 2004.

O'Balance, Edgar. *The Cyanide War: Tamil Insurrection in Sri Lanka, 1973–88.* London, Brassey's, 1989.

Osborne, Robin. *Indonesia's Secret War: The Guerilla Struggle in Irian Jaya.* Sydney, Allen and Unwin, 1985.

Pettigrew, Joyce M. *Sikhs of the Punjab: Unheard Voices of the State and Guerilla Violence.* New Jersey, Zed Books, 1995.

Power, Samantha. *A Problem from Hell: America and the Age of Genocide.* New York, Perennial, 2003.

Raju, Subramaniam (Ed.). *Terrorism in South Asia: Views from India.* New Delhi, India Research Press, 2005.

Rashid, Ahmed. *Taliban: Militant Islam, Oil and Fundamentalism in Central Asia.* New Haven, Yale University Press, 2000.

Reader, Ian. *Poisonous Cocktail? Aum Shinrikyo's Path to Violence.* Copenhagen, Nordic Institute of Asian Studies Books, 1996.

Reader, Ian. *Religious Violence in Contemporary Japan: The Case of Aum Shinrikyo*. Honolulu, University of Hawaii Press, 2000.

Reese, Maria A. *Seeds of Terror: An Eyewitness Account of Al-Qaeda's Newest Center of Operations in Southeast Asia*. London, Simon and Schuster, 2003.

Rubin, Barnett R. *The Search for Peace in Afghanistan: From Buffer State to Failed State*. New Haven, Yale University Press, 1995.

Fragmentation of Afghanistan. New Haven, Yale University Press, 2002.

Sagdeev, Ronald, and Eisenhower, Susan (Eds). *Islam and Central Asia: An Enduring Legacy or An Evolving Threat?* Washington, Center for Political and Strategic Studies Press, 2000.

Senaratne, Jagath P. *Political Violence in Sri Lanka: 1977–1990*. Amsterdam, VU University Press, 1997.

Singh, Chandrika. *North-East India: Politics and Terrorism*. New Delhi, Manas, 2003.

Smith, Martin. *Burma: Insurgency and the Politics of Ethnicity*. Dhaka, University Press, 1999.

Smith, Paul J. *Terrorism and Violence in Southeast Asia: Transnational Challenges to States and Regional Stability*. New York, Greenwood, 2004.

Sonal, Ashish. *Terrorism & Insurgency in India: A Study of the Human Element*. New Delhi, Lancer, 1994.

Starr, S. Frederick (Ed.). *Xinjiang: China's Muslim Borderland*. New York, M. E. Sharpe, 2004.

Swamy, R. Narayan. *Tigers of Lanka: From Boys to Guerillas*. New Delhi, South Asia, 1995.

Tan, Andrew T H. *Security Perspectives of the Malay Archipelago: Security Linkages in the Second Front in the War on Terror*. Cheltenham, Edward Elgar, 2004.

(Ed.). *A Handbook of Terrorism and Insurgency in Southeast Asia*. Cheltenham, Edward Elgar, 2006.

Thomas, Raju G. C. (Ed.). *Perspectives on Kashmir: The Roots of Conflict in South Asia*. Boulder, Westview, 1992.

Thompson, W. Scott. *The Philippines in Crisis: Development and Security in the Aquino Era, 1986–1992*. New York, St Martin's Press, 1992.

Tiwari, S. C. *Terrorism in India*. New Delhi, South Asian Publishers, 1990.

Tyler, Christian. *Wild West China: The Taming of Xinjian*. London, John Murray, 2003.

Varshney, Ashutosh. *Ethnic Conflict and Civic Life: Hindus and Muslims in India*. New Haven, Yale University Press, 2002.

Zahab, Mariam Abou, and Roy, Olivier. *Islamist Networks: The Afghan-Pakistan Connection*. New York, Columbia University Press, 2004.